AI Deployment and Adoption in Public Administration and Organizations

Gamze Sart
Istanbul University-Cerrahpasa, Turkey

Funda Hatice Sezgin
Istanbul University-Cerrahpasa, Turkey

IGI Global
Scientific Publishing
Publishing Tomorrow's Research Today

Published in the United States of America by
IGI Global Scientific Publishing
701 East Chocolate Avenue
Hershey, PA, 17033, USA
Tel: 717-533-8845
Fax: 717-533-8661
Website: https://www.igi-global.com E-mail: cust@igi-global.com

Library of Congress Cataloging-in-Publication Data

Names: Sart, Gamze, 1967- editor | Sezgin, Funda H. editor
Title: AI deployment and adoption in public administration and organizations / Edited by Gamze Sart, Funda Sezgin.
Description: Hershey, PA : IGI Global Scientific Publishing, [2025] | Includes bibliographical references and index. | Summary: "This book explores the adoption and diffusion of AI in public administration. It examines the opportunities, challenges, and ethical considerations of AI adoption, offering insights into its practical implementation and future impact"-- Provided by publisher.
Identifiers: LCCN 2025001352 (print) | LCCN 2025001353 (ebook) | ISBN 9798337322728 hardcover | ISBN 9798337322735 paperback | ISBN 9798337322742 ebook
Subjects: LCSH: Public administration--Technological innovations | Artificial intelligence | Internet in public administration
Classification: LCC JF1525.A8 A394 2025 (print) | LCC JF1525.A8 (ebook) | DDC 354.750285/63--dc23/eng/20250401
LC record available at https://lccn.loc.gov/2025001352
LC ebook record available at https://lccn.loc.gov/2025001353

British Cataloguing in Publication Data
A Cataloguing in Publication record for this book is available from the British Library.

Table of Contents

Detailed Table of Contents

This study examines the drivers and barriers impacting the adoption and diffusion of artificial intelligence (AI) in public administration. Key drivers, categorized by technological, organizational, environmental, and human factors, are explored as facilitators for effective AI integration. Conversely, significant barriers such as cybersecurity, data privacy, budget constraints, and infrastructural limitations are identified, posing challenges to AI implementation. The study employs an integrated ISM-MICMAC framework to map these drivers and barriers, offering insights into their interdependencies and influence within the public sector. The findings identify key drivers and barriers that must be addressed by strategic initiatives to fully leverage the potential of AI in enhancing public service delivery and administrative efficiency.

Iterative educational and public administration transformation projects (ETP) are important for the enhancements of their sustainability, performances, and longevity. ETPs are complex, due to the inter-linking AI, lack of the adoption of a polymathic and holistic approaches, and the integration of other domains that are needed to finalize such ETPs. In the domains of education and public administration, the main objective is to try to achieve long-term intangible goals and not only to achieve extreme gains dictated by leaders and/or stakeholders. A polymathic and holistic approach privileges interdisciplinary concepts for the implementations of various ETP's phases, sub-domains, and artificial intelligence (AI)-based components. This chapter uses the author's applied holistic and poly-mathematical model (AHMM) for AI (AHMM4AI), which is a variant of the author's generic and polymathic AHMM, which also includes enhancements and findings from his previous research articles and works, which are added to the PWRC4AI, where the PWRC4AI inherits the basic PRWC's characteristics.

This chapter examines how AI might alter public administration by improving efficiency, accessibility, and decision-making. AI automates ordinary jobs, freeing up public servants for high-impact work. Predictive analytics improve government operations by offering data-driven insights for resource allocation and preemptive actions in healthcare, urban planning, and public safety. Chatbots and virtual assistants make government services more accessible to different populations, especially those with linguistic or physical obstacles. The chapter also highlights the ethical and operational issues of AI in public administration. Due to data privacy, security, and algorithmic bias, AI deployment must be transparent, accountable, and fair. Public entities can ethically use AI by following ethical and governance guidelines and gaining public trust. This chapter emphasizes balanced AI deployment to establish an inclusive, efficient, citizen-centered, and adaptable public sector.

Advanced educational and public administration transformation projects (EPTP) are crucial for academic, public sector (PS), and business institutions. Unfortunately, such EPTPs are complex and have high failure rates, because of the various issues like the lack of experienced personal which should have polymathics and artificial intelligence (AI) capabilities and skills and should avoid the simplistic accountants' instant profits approach, which has long-term negative effects. The RPBAI needs to propose a holistic academic, educational, coaching, and research concept (and curriculum/roadmap), which starts in the primary and secondary schools or cycles (PSC), then is monitored in the university cycles (UC) (Bachelor, Master, and Doctorate) and continues in the professional career's upskilling activities. Such a concept and roadmap can be also applied to the PS (especially in the education/academic and industrial ministries) and business enterprises, which makes a synergy of these three majors and hard-linked sectors and domains.

The advent of social networks has undoubtedly changed the way we disseminate information, communicate, and interact with one another. The ways in which AI and social networking are beneficial for higher education have come under much scrutiny. This chapter examines multifaceted roles that AI and social networks play. The chapter starts with the historical context of the social learning theories, reflects the birth and rise of digital networking and differentiates between social networks as used in teaching practices. It also elaborates on possible advantages of the integration of social networks and AI in the context of education as well as the risks it could bring. It also provides a series of case studies in which social networks have been used in successful ways and across different educational contexts. This examination offers insights and strategies for educators, administrators, and policymakers to more successfully implement social networks within education creating richer, more engaging, collaborative, digitally fluent learning contexts.

This study investigates the influence of artificial intelligence (AI) on student enrollment in higher educational institutions in Kerala, with a particular emphasis on the mediating role of customer relationship management (CRM) systems. Employing a descriptive research design, a self-prepared questionnaire was administered to a purposive sample of 200 students, encompassing various educational stages. The findings reveal a significant positive correlation between AI usage and student enrollment, with AI usage accounting for 37.3% of the variance in enrollment outcomes. Furthermore, the analysis indicates that CRM systems partially mediate the relationship between AI and student enrollment, enhancing the effectiveness of AI-driven strategies in the recruitment process. With high reliability demonstrated in the research instrument (Cronbach alpha = 0.827), the study underscores the necessity of integrating AI and CRM technologies to optimize enrollment strategies in the evolving educational landscape.

Many businesses have to operate within the framework of national and international standards to meet customers' expectations, security requirements, and environmental regulations. Compared to other industries, the aviation industry has high-security requirements. However, the continuous publication of documents has resulted in document inflation over time, document-process structure that deviates from a simple philosophy. Given the problem at hand, this study aims to develop a streamlined document processing system that aligns with the lean philosophy in the aviation company under investigation. Documents with a similarity rate exceeding 50% were examined, and a proposal was made to either combine these documents or establish relationships between them. Various machine-learning algorithms are used in this chapter. The accuracy rate of a hybrid model that included the support vector machine (SVM) and logistic regression techniques increased by 6% to 76%. Python was utilised during the research.

As a result of the transition of many systems to the digital age with the developing technology, it has been observed that fraud reports have increased, and this increase requires banks to develop strong systems against these threats. The inadequacy and slowness of the manual method currently used for the solution has led us to address this problem. As a solution to the fraud problem, this chapter presents an innovative method for periodic data analysis and automatic classification of fraud reports using text mining methods using machine learning algorithms. In this study, the authors aim to automate the labeling of incoming fraud reports as “social engineering” and “phishing” with the developed model. By comparing the performance of different algorithms, the random forest algorithm is selected as the most effective model. These results are valuable in terms of practical applicability.

Yeşim Altay, Istanbul University-Cerrahpaşa, Turkey
Ömer Algorabi, Istanbul University-Cerrahpaşa, Turkey
Ayşe Paksoy, Istanbul University-Cerrahpaşa, Turkey

This study uses machine learning-based causal analysis to analyze the relationship between government health spending and socioeconomic characteristics. The research aims to enhance public health and promote economic stability by allocating significant resources to healthcare. Conventional forecasting techniques may struggle to identify complex causal relationships within health data. Machine learning models like causal forest offer a robust analytical tool for understanding health spending dynamics. Data from developed countries between 1970 and 2021 is used, focusing on factors such as cigarette and alcohol use, net savings, average life expectancy, and rates of drug, alcohol, and suicide deaths. The results show that healthcare spending is significantly influenced by life expectancy and income level, while other factors vary based on regional and demographic variations. The study provides valuable insights for policymakers to develop data-driven, equitable health interventions that address specific needs across diverse populations.

Mustafa Güler, Istanbul University, Turkey

Istanbul, hosting millions of tourists annually, faces significant air pollution challenges, impacting both health and climate. The air quality index (AQI) is vital for assessing pollution and its health effects. This study predicts AQI levels in Istanbul using machine learning models (XGBoost and ANN), focusing on pollutants like PM10, NO2, CO, SO2, and O3, with data from 2021-2023. Ensemble methods incorporating meteorological data (temperature, pressure, wind) improved accuracy. Forecasted AQI levels range from "good" to "hazardous," offering actionable insights. The models achieved low error rates, underscoring their effectiveness in supporting air quality management and sustainable health policies through reliable AQI predictions.

Preface

The emergence and spread of Artificial Intelligence (AI) have led significant transformations across many domains. In this context, AI is also expected to have a profound effect on public administration and organizations. Recognizing this, we present *AI Deployment and Adoption in Public Administration and Organizations*.

As editors of this volume, we have curated a collection of contributions from leading researchers, practitioners, and thought leaders, each offering a unique perspective on the adoption and diffusion of AI. This book explores the deployment and adoption of AU in public administration and organizations.

The book addresses a broad spectrum of readers—professional researchers, educators, managers, government officials, and policymakers. By doing so, it underscores the ubiquity of AI and its potential to drive efficiency, enhance decision-making, and foster innovation in public administration and organizations.

The chapters within this book delve into key topics such as AI's influence on public administration, including its application in public services and strategies for successful adoption and diffusion within governmental frameworks.

We hope this volume will not only serve as a guide for understanding AI's transformative potential but also inspire actionable strategies to maximize its benefits. As AI continues to evolve, its role in shaping the future of public administration becomes ever more critical.

We extend our gratitude to the contributing authors for their insightful work and to the readers who will engage with this volume. It is our belief that this book will provide valuable insights, fostering informed dialogue and action in the dynamic intersection of AI and public administration.

ORGANIZATION OF THE BOOK

Chapter 1: Drivers and Barriers to Adoption and Diffusion of AI Applications in Public Administration

Focusing on AI adoption in public administration, this chapter identifies drivers like technological innovation and barriers such as cybersecurity and budget constraints. Using an ISM-MICMAC framework, it maps interdependencies among these factors, offering actionable insights for strategic AI integration in public services.

Chapter 2: Educational and Public Administration: The Polymathic Ratings and Weightings Concept-Based Artificial Intelligence Processes (PRWC4AI)

This chapter introduces the Polymathic Ratings and Weightings Concept (PRWC4AI), a holistic approach integrating interdisciplinary AI methods for educational and public administration transformation. It discusses the Applied Holistic and Poly-Mathematical Model (AHMM4AI) and its role in achieving sustainable, performance-driven, long-term goals in these domains.

Chapter 3: AI Integration in Public Administration: Enhancing Efficiency and Accessibility

The chapter explores how AI can improve public administration through automation, predictive analytics, and virtual assistants. It highlights ethical concerns like privacy and algorithmic bias, advocating for transparent and citizen-centric AI deployment to enhance government service efficiency and accessibility.

Chapter 4: Educational and Public Administration Transformation Projects: The Role of Polymathics-Based Artificial Intelligence (RPBAI)

This chapter proposes a roadmap for embedding polymathic and AI capabilities into educational and public administration projects. It emphasizes starting at the primary education level and extending through professional upskilling to reduce failure rates in transformative projects and foster synergy across academic, public, and business sectors.

Chapter 5: AI and Social Networks: A Transformative Partnership for Education

This chapter delves into the symbiotic relationship between AI and social networks in higher education. It begins with an exploration of social learning theories and the evolution of digital networking, distinguishing between various applications of social networks in educational contexts. By integrating AI, social networks can enhance collaboration, foster engagement, and create digitally rich learning environments. However, these advancements also come with risks, including privacy concerns and potential misuse. Through diverse case studies, the chapter offers practical strategies for educators and policymakers to effectively implement AI-enhanced social networking tools, thereby enriching educational experiences.

Chapter 6: Customer Relationship Management (CRM) Systems: Impact of AI on Post-COVID Student Enrollment in Kerala's Higher Education Institutions

This chapter explores the role of AI and CRM systems in enhancing student enrollment in Kerala's higher education institutions post-COVID. Employing a descriptive design and surveying 200 students, the study demonstrates a 37.3% variance in enrollment outcomes attributed to AI. It identifies CRM systems as partial mediators, emphasizing the need for AI-CRM integration to optimize enrollment strategies.

Chapter 7: Improving Documentation Processes With Data Mining and Machine Learning Methods: A Case Study in the Aviation Industry

This case study addresses document inflation in the aviation industry by applying machine learning to streamline processes. Using hybrid models like SVM and Logistic Regression, it achieves a 76% accuracy rate, illustrating how data-driven methods enhance operational efficiency within strict regulatory frameworks.

Chapter 8: Classification of Fraud Detection in Call Centers Using Machine Learning Techniques

This chapter examines automated fraud detection in call centers using machine learning. Comparing models, it identifies Random Forest as the most effective for categorizing social engineering and phishing fraud reports, offering a scalable solution to address increasing digital-age threats.

Chapter 9: Assessing the Effects on General Government Health Expenditures With Machine Learning-Based Causality Analysis

Employing machine learning models like Causal Forest, this chapter analyzes how socioeconomic factors influence government health expenditures. Using data from 1970–2021, it highlights life expectancy and income as key determinants, providing policy insights for equitable health interventions.

Chapter 10: Air Quality Index Prediction in Istanbul Based on Machine Learning Methods

This study predicts Istanbul's AQI using machine learning models such as XGBoost and ANN, incorporating pollutant and meteorological data. The chapter underscores the effectiveness of ensemble methods for accurate predictions, aiding sustainable air quality management and public health policies.

Chapter 11: Assessing the Causal Impact of Trade Balance, Interest Rates, and Exchange Rates on Unemployment in the Euro Area: A Double Machine Learning Approach

Using Dual Machine Learning methodologies, this chapter examines macroeconomic factors' causal impact on unemployment in the Eurozone. It identifies exchange and interest rates as pivotal variables, offering insights for policymakers to stabilize employment and foster economic growth.

CONCLUSION

In an era characterized by rapid technological advancements and unprecedented global challenges, the chapters in this edited volume offer a comprehensive examination of the transformative potential of artificial intelligence, machine learning, and advanced computational methods across diverse domains.

The authors have masterfully explored critical areas such as the enhancement of public administration efficiency, and the application of machine learning in fraud detection, health expenditure analysis, and air quality forecasting. Together, these studies underscore a shared vision: leveraging technology responsibly and strategically to create sustainable, inclusive, and adaptable systems that respond to the evolving needs of our societies.

As editors, we believe that this collection provides a valuable contribution to the growing body of knowledge on the interplay between technology and human-centered systems. It is our hope that readers—whether scholars, practitioners, or policymakers—will find inspiration and practical guidance within these pages, fostering further exploration and innovation in their respective fields.

This book serves not only as a reflection of current advancements but also as a call to action for interdisciplinary collaboration, ethical considerations, and a balanced approach to technological adoption. By embracing the principles of transparency, inclusivity, and sustainability, we can collectively navigate the complexities of this digital age to achieve a better, more equitable future.

Chapter 1
Drivers and Barriers to Adoption and Diffusion of AI Applications in Public Administration

Sinem Buyuksaatci Kiris
https://orcid.org/0000-0001-7697-3018
Istanbul University-Cerrahpaşa, Turkey

Binnur Gurul
https://orcid.org/0000-0001-8708-702X
Gelisim University, Turkey

ABSTRACT

This study examines the drivers and barriers impacting the adoption and diffusion of artificial intelligence (AI) in public administration. Key drivers, categorized by technological, organizational, environmental, and human factors, are explored as facilitators for effective AI integration. Conversely, significant barriers such as cybersecurity, data privacy, budget constraints, and infrastructural limitations are identified, posing challenges to AI implementation. The study employs an integrated ISM-MICMAC framework to map these drivers and barriers, offering insights into their interdependencies and influence within the public sector. The findings identify key drivers and barriers that must be addressed by strategic initiatives to fully leverage the potential of AI in enhancing public service delivery and administrative efficiency.

DOI: 10.4018/979-8-3373-2272-8.ch001

INTRODUCTION

Modern technologies such as cloud computing, the internet of things, block chain, big data and augmented reality (virtual reality) have become an inevitable part of modern life nowadays. Since change is constant and rapid in modern life due to these technologies, it has become necessary to adopt and diffuse persistent artificial intelligence (AI) in many areas of public administration. This is also why the adoption and diffusion of AI continues to attract great attention of practitioners and researchers in recent years.

Although technological advances in the field of AI, public administrations are still provided with old-fashioned applications. Because of how public budgets are distributed, the majority of resources are allocated to maintaining outdated systems. Compared to private sector services, the situation reduces humans' trust and satisfaction on public services. On the other hand, new and safe adopted AI applications would likely increase the effectiveness and efficiency of public administration while also increasing humans' satisfaction. In addition, innovations provided by new and secure AI applications/services would facilitate public-citizen connection and interaction while reducing the administrative burden of public administration. Mehr (2017) notes that AI can alleviate administrative burdens and streamline complex tasks, which allows government employees to dedicate more time to building meaningful interactions with citizens. By automating routine functions like document search, query responses, and request routing, AI can improve service delivery speed and accuracy, which directly impacts citizen satisfaction and engagement. Moreover, implementing AI in areas like translation, document drafting, and predictive analysis can bridge the gap between government operations and modern citizen expectations, fostering a more responsive and accessible public sector. Therefore, investment in safe and new AI-based technologies has become a critical strategy in public administration in many countries around the world.

The importance and appeal of AI is that it can analyze information faster and at lower cost than humans, potentially leading to new service models. Furthermore, by automating public services and enabling proactive public service delivery, AI has the potential to drastically alter the work that public managers and civil officials perform. For this reason, AI has come to be described as the "new colleague and manager" and the situation has come to humanize AI. Ultimately, AI is used in public administration to find answers to three questions: (i) How can AI be used to improve government functioning and services?; (ii) More generally, how can the risks associated with AI be reduced and how can it be ensured that it is used only for the "public good" in society?; (iii) How can AI augment people's abilities and skills, and how can people and machines work together? (Mellouli et al., 2024; Mergel et al., 2023).

The aim of AI-based public administration is to enable all public services to be in the form of digital services, to provide accessible data to policy makers by bringing together open data at all levels of public administration, and to help them make decisions by providing data that would guide their decision-making processes. Therefore, applications of AI are key to making wise decisions in public administration. For example, data-driven AI applications can predict and measure how tax policy changes would affect a country's macroeconomic indicators. Other instances of how AI applications in public administration can be used are to provide national services for lowering poverty and raising educational standards (e.g., an effective national health insurance or an effectual pension system), to assess potential threats (e.g., terrorist attacks resulting from open access to tourist and immigration data) and to analyze crime data and penalties (e.g., traffic penalties) for strengthening public safety (Di Vaio et al., 2022). Ultimately, AI applications or technologies are well suited for public administration where there are no pre-programmed events or situations and there are constant changes due to environmental factors (Mutawa and Rashid, 2020).

AI offers substantial potential in numerous public sectors, such as education, infrastructure, transportation, telecommunications, data security and management, finance, healthcare, research and development, policymaking, and the legal system (Sharma et al, 2000). Some of the application areas of AI technologies in public administration are climate change and sustainability, politics and Public policy, intelligent transportation and smart cities, disaster management and disaster impact planning, responding to 911 calls, healthcare programs and policies, workforce substitution and employment, crime prediction and public safety, better provision of public services, surveillance and monitoring of military targets, internal efficiency of government agencies and AI based decision-making (Horowitz & Kahn, 2021; Valle-Cruz et al., 2024). Despite the broad spectrum of applications, most studies have concentrated on modifications to the public administration structures that are currently operating in detail, while the creation of completely new structures issue due to new AI technologies has received less attention. Given the particular demands of AI technologies, it is natural that it is more important to consider how current public administration structures might be modified rather than entirely new ones should be put in place. For example, especially the ethical issue of AI in public healthcare brings with it specific requirements, which therefore require further development and more specific implementation of AI applications in healthcare management (Wirtz et al., 2021). The types of AI applications in public administration are personalization (tailored solutions), inspection and enforcement, investigation (e.g., crime), process optimization (resource allocation), maintenance, forecasting, knowledge management and policy analysis (Hoekstra et al., 2021).

The chatbot application can be given as the most basic, common and simplest example of personalized AI application in public administration. The usage of AI-based chatbots in public administration is growing to manage communication processes that span lengthy periods of time and correspond to large volumes for citizens, and to enable faster navigation through complex policies and legislation. Since the chatbots function as a buffer before citizens talk to human operators in the telephone call center. Because of this buffering role, chatbots resolved first-contact questions at a rate of 75-90% at Australian taxation office and reduced the demand for phone calls with human operators by 7% (Henman, 2020). Ease of use and relative advantage, leadership and innovative culture, external shock and individual past experiences are identified as the main factors affecting chatbots adoption decisions and performance success of chatbots (Chen et al., 2024). As a result, chatbots are applications that offer personalized solutions (tailored solutions).

Enhancing the delivery of public services is one of the primary advantages of AI applications in public administration; improving internal management is another. Using chatbots or personalized services based on people's characteristics and prior knowledge, AI-based systems enhance the delivery of public services directly to pertinent persons, residents, or businesses. Because automated decision-makers using AI technology tend to make impartial decisions, they help boost legitimacy and trust in the delivery of public services. This is the best course of action for public administrations looking to decrease and manage corruption, as well as for citizens who don't trust judgments made by bureaucrats. Utilizing AI apps is also a wonderful way to automate and improve the internal management processes of public administration, which raises the efficacy and efficiency of the company and the caliber of services offered to individuals and companies. AI applications are typically used for internal management. They are offered to allocate resources more effectively and efficiently, including financial and human resources management, which improves staff performance and overall management. (Van Noordt and Misuraca, 2022).

In addition to the benefits of AI applications, AI security emerges as an important risk factor. AI security refers to ensuring the performance of AI, which also includes not only information security issues but also security issues in general. Therefore, this risk draws attention to the importance and necessity of AI applications being resilient and secure against negative manipulations by humans. For example, managers' concerns about losing their legal power or their desire to overextend their potential power by obtaining people's data through applications can be considered as possible risks. The risk of misuse of AI can lead to inequality in decision-making processes by introducing bias and can make this situation systematic. Ultimately, AI adoption and diffusion is related to preventing accidents and maintaining the safe operation of AI applications to protect humanity (Wirtz et al., 2019). Even though the potential risks, the adoption and diffusion of AI is inevitable. Therefore, public administration managers need to know the risks in advance and develop strategies and determine policies accordingly.

There are other challenges associated with implementing AI in the public sector. First and foremost, there is an urgent need for capacity building, as the current shortage of qualified field experts hampers the effective delivery of AI-enhanced government services. This gap in expertise complicates the ability of public organizations to leverage AI's full potential. Additionally, the growing demand for AI talent has resulted in significant recruitment hurdles, particularly for the public sector, which often operates under constrained budgets. Consequently, this situation emphasizes the necessity for a more profound and nuanced understanding of AI among both technical specialists and non-technical government personnel. Enhancing this collective knowledge is essential not only for fostering collaboration but also for creating an environment where innovative AI solutions can thrive within government frameworks Alhosani & Alhashmi, 2024).

Public organizations also face moral dilemmas regarding the appropriate contexts for AI usage, which prompt essential discussions about a variety of ethical considerations. One of the most pressing issues is the imperative to avoid discrimination against citizens, ensuring that AI systems do not perpetuate existing biases or create new forms of inequality. This challenge highlights the necessity of scrutinizing the data used to train AI algorithms, as biased datasets can lead to discriminatory outcomes that disproportionately affect marginalized groups.

In order to benefit from AI applications in public services, it is important for managers of public institutions to adopt AI-based systems. It is pointed out in literature that the requirements for the adoption and diffusion of AI applications in the public sector are not understood enough and it is stated that there is still a lack of research on AI applications in public administration (De Sousa et al., 2019; Madan & Ashok, 2023). AI Application in public administration requires a constant exchange between human and technological factors. AI systems are likely to enable the augmentation of existing activities and the development of new businesses, however their characteristics combined with a lack of awareness may hinder their implementation by increasing institutional mistrust (Maragno et al., 2023). It's also unclear where in the public administration hierarchy—micro, meso, or macro—AI technologies should be used, despite the fact that their use is quickly gaining traction due to effective, affordable public service delivery and increased citizen participation (Madan & Ashok, 2023).

Although there are various initiatives on AI applications in public administration in many countries, the drivers and the barriers on processes (including outputs and outcomes) for the adoption and diffusion of AI applications in the public sector need to be identified and systematized. The main objective addressed and investigated in this study is to identify and analyze the drivers and barriers to AI adoption and diffusion on public administration. In this study, leading drivers and barriers affecting AI adoption and diffusion will be identified and classified with detailed literature, and the appropriate relationships between these identified drivers and barriers will be analyzed using integrated ISM (Interpretive Structural Modeling) -MICMAC (Matrice d'Impacts Croisés Multiplication Appliquee a un Classement/ Cross Impact Matrix Multiplication Applied to Classification) approach. MICMAC analysis provides a map of the driving force and dependence strength of the identified variables and then classifies them into four categories. While the ISM method provides a structural hierarchy of relationships between drivers and barriers, the MICMAC analysis allows comments on the system through impact and dependency values.

The structure of this paper is as follows: the next section introduces the conceptual framework, presenting in detail the factors identified as drivers and barriers to the adoption and diffusion of artificial intelligence applications in the public sector. The research methodology section outlines the proposed approach and presents a comprehensive overview of the findings. The final section offers a summary and concluding remarks.

CONCEPTUAL FRAMEWORK

Drivers for The Adoption and Diffusion of AI Applications in The Public Sector

The adoption of Artificial Intelligence (AI) in public institutions is shaped by a range of complex factors. These factors, also referred to as drivers, were determined in this study after a comprehensive and meticulous literature review containing publications from the last five years and categorized into four principal domains: technological, organizational, environmental, and human. Each of these domains encompasses critical factors that serve either to facilitate or to challenge the integration of AI into public sector operations. By addressing each factor comprehensively, public institutions can establish a strong foundation for integrating AI in ways that are efficient, ethical, and aligned with public interests. A thorough understanding of these factors is essential for ensuring effective, ethical, and sustainable AI adoption across public institutions. Furthermore, these factors only support operational improvements but also fosters a resilient, responsive, and accountable public service sector well-equipped to navigate the future of digital governance.

Technological Factors

In the realm of technological factors, the reliability, functionality, and data security and privacy of AI systems stand out as vital considerations. In the public sector, where decision-making directly impacts citizens' lives, the reliability and continuous functionality of AI systems are paramount. Robust and resilient AI applications enhance operational dependability and public trust, which is vital in environments where transparency and accountability are prioritized. AI applications often process large volumes of sensitive data, necessitating rigorous data security measures and privacy protocols. Effective AI adoption requires that public institutions implement strong safeguards to protect against data breaches, unauthorized access, and privacy violations. Trust in AI is significantly influenced by the institution's capacity to manage these risks effectively.

Additionally, the design of AI systems must prioritize usability and interpretability, particularly in public sector settings where complex decision-making processes are involved. User-friendly interfaces and clear, interpretable results empower non-technical users, facilitating AI acceptance and adoption among a broader workforce. The usability and interpretability of models that support decision-making during diagnosis and treatment are crucial, particularly in the healthcare industry (Dorhetso & Quarshie, 2023). Moreover, ensuring transparency in how AI systems produce outputs helps build credibility and user confidence, critical in public service contexts.

Organizational Factors

Organizational factors also play a pivotal role in AI adoption within public sector. Public institutions must possess a robust technological infrastructure to support the demands of AI systems. This infrastructure includes sufficient data storage, processing capabilities, network stability, and cybersecurity measures. Institutions with advanced technological readiness are better positioned to handle the integration of AI tools into their operations seamlessly.

Beyond infrastructure, the employee competence and preparedness of them are equally important for AI adoption and implementation within the public sector, as skilled staff play a pivotal role in ensuring the effective integration of new technologies (Dorhetso & Quarshie, 2023). Public institutions must invest in regular training programs to build employee familiarity with AI systems, foster a data-literate culture, and empower staff to maximize these technologies. Effective training is also a means of reducing resistance to change, as employees who understand AI systems are more likely to engage with them constructively. Competence here refers to employees' capacity to embrace innovative business approaches that enhance organizational performance and provide a competitive edge. Competent employees are invaluable assets, as they actively seek solutions to emerging operational challenges, adapt swiftly to evolving industry standards, and leverage advanced technologies to capitalize on new opportunities. Such employees not only support the adoption of AI but also contribute to an adaptable and forward-thinking organizational culture, which is crucial for sustaining long-term success in public sector innovation.

In addition, Top management support and proactive leadership are crucial for the successful adoption of AI in the public sector. Leaders who actively champion AI initiatives and demonstrate a strong commitment to technological progress set a clear example, fostering an organizational culture that embraces innovation and adaptability. Such leadership not only builds momentum for AI adoption but also establishes a shared vision that motivates employees at all levels. Additionally, an organizational culture that values continuous learning, experimentation, and openness to change supports smoother transitions as new technologies are adopted. This culture of flexibility and growth enables public institutions to navigate the complexities of AI adoption with resilience, making them better equipped to leverage technology for enhanced service delivery and operational efficiency.

When public organizations actively engage with stakeholders—including policy-makers, regulatory bodies, technology providers, and end-users—they gain valuable insights into specific needs, challenges, and ethical considerations. Effective collaboration among these public actors involved in AI initiatives is a crucial driving factor for its adoption and successful implementation (Dorhetso & Quarshie, 2023). Such collaborative efforts foster a shared understanding of objectives, streamline resources, and promote unified approaches, leading to more efficient and innovative solutions. This continuous dialogue helps address any disparities in AI expectations and enhances alignment with public interests, which in turn supports the development of well-integrated and responsible AI applications. Moreover, by leveraging diverse expertise and perspectives, public institutions can optimize their AI systems, making them more adaptable and resilient to emerging demands and complexities.

Organizational inertia specific to public administration can often be characterized by bureaucratic rigidity, centralized decision-making, lack of employee empowerment, status quo bias, and resistance to data sharing within or between institutions. Additionally, this inertia may manifest as a scarcity of resources for innovative projects, high demand for AI experts, and the need for political approval for economic investments. However, despite these challenges, such inertia can also serve as a driving force for AI implementation in the public sector (Madan & Ashok, 2023). As institutions face increasing pressure to modernize and enhance service delivery, the need to overcome internal barriers becomes more pronounced. This creates an impetus for leaders to champion AI initiatives as a means of breaking through bureaucratic constraints. Furthermore, the acknowledgment of resource shortages and expertise gaps can stimulate collaboration with external partners and experts, fostering innovation. By addressing these challenges head-on, public institutions can leverage AI to improve efficiency, enhance public services, and ultimately shift organizational culture toward greater adaptability and responsiveness. In this way, organizational inertia can transform from a hindrance into a catalyst for meaningful change in the public sector.

Environmental Factors

Environmental factors, such as regulatory frameworks, external pressures, and societal expectations, further influence the AI adoption process in public sector. For AI to be effectively integrated into public institutions, it must operate within a well-defined legal and regulatory framework. Clear guidelines on data usage, ethical standards, and accountability ensure that AI deployment aligns with legal and societal norms, safeguarding public interests and rights. Compliance with these standards not only supports the institution's integrity but also builds citizen trust in AI-driven services.

Increasing AI adoption by other public institutions can create competitive pressures and incentives for AI integration (Dorhetso & Quarshie, 2023). Public institutions may adopt AI technologies to maintain their relevance, improve service delivery, and match the operational standards set by their peers. This external pressure can serve as a catalyst for public sector innovation, pushing institutions to pursue AI to enhance efficiency and public service quality. Additionally, vertical pressure is shaped by macro-level frameworks, including regulations, compliance standards, and procurement practices that govern the use of AI technologies (Madan & Ashok, 2023). Policies promoting ethical AI usage or requiring transparency in algorithmic decision-making can significantly influence how public sector entities approach automation. Consequently, the interplay between vertical pressure and competitive dynamics plays a vital role in shaping the landscape of AI adoption in the public sector.

Today's citizens increasingly expect public services that are prompt, accurate, and highly responsive to their needs. AI's capabilities to enhance service speed, precision, and accessibility align seamlessly with these expectations, positioning it as a valuable asset in public service frameworks (Van Noordt & Misuraca, 2020). By streamlining processes, reducing response times, and enabling data-driven decision-making, AI supports the delivery of services that are not only efficient but also accessible and equitable. This alignment with public demand plays a significant role in driving AI adoption within public institutions, as agencies prioritize technologies that meet and exceed modern standards for public service. Ultimately, as societal demand for efficient and fair service delivery grows, public institutions are motivated to embrace AI to keep pace with evolving needs and ensure the consistent delivery of high-quality services.

Human Factors

Human factors, including visionary and innovative leadership, employee engagement, and ethical responsibility and social awareness, are critical to the successful adoption of AI in the public sector. The role of leadership is crucial in fostering an environment conducive to AI innovation. Leaders who are forward-thinking and open to experimentation provide the support and resources necessary for AI initiatives to flourish. They set the tone for organizational adaptation and resilience, which are essential in navigating the uncertainties and challenges associated with new technology integration.

Employee engagement and adaptability is also crucial, as the human response to AI integration is often influenced by perceptions of how technology will impact job roles and responsibilities. Engaging employees in the AI adoption process, providing opportunities for skill enhancement, and addressing potential concerns related to job security contribute to smoother transitions. A supportive work environment that values employee input and adaptability reduces resistance and fosters a sense of ownership in the adoption of new tools.

Ethical responsibility and social awareness further underscores the importance of thoughtful AI integration. Public institutions are entrusted with responsibilities that impact society broadly. As such, ethical considerations, such as fairness, transparency, and accountability, are paramount in AI implementations. Adhering to ethical principles in AI design and deployment is essential for building public trust and ensuring that technology advances the public good. Institutions that prioritize these values in AI applications are more likely to gain social acceptance and foster sustainable, responsible AI practices.

Customer satisfaction is another crucial factor within the human context that significantly influences the adoption and implementation of AI in the public sector (Dorhetso & Quarshie, 2023). When citizens perceive AI applications as enhancing their service experience—through improved efficiency, accuracy, and responsiveness—they are more likely to trust and accept these technologies. High levels of satisfaction can foster a positive feedback loop, encouraging public sector organizations to refine and improve their AI systems based on user input. Ultimately, prioritizing customer satisfaction not only facilitates smoother AI integration but also ensures that these innovations effectively meet the diverse needs of the community, leading to better public services and increased overall acceptance of technological advancements.

Barriers for The Adoption and Diffusion of AI Applications in the Public Sector

Interest in incorporating AI applications into the public sector has been growing consistently over the past decade, driven by the potential to enhance operational efficiency, service quality, and responsiveness to citizens' needs (Wirtz et al, 2019). However, for successful adoption, it is essential to address a range of substantial barriers that currently impede progress. Overcoming these obstacles is critical because AI implementations in the public sector impact broad segments of the population and are often deployed in a generalized manner, not customized to specific community needs. As a result, addressing these barriers is not only necessary for effective deployment but also for ensuring equitable access and minimizing unintended consequences. The primary barriers to successful AI integration are discussed below, focusing on the financial, technological, organizational, and societal challenges that must be resolved to fully realize the benefits of this transformative technology.

Financial Constraints

AI implementation demands substantial investment in both infrastructure and ongoing maintenance. This includes hardware, software, and training costs. The public sector often faces budgetary limitations that make these expenses challenging to justify, particularly given the pressure to maintain other essential services. Furthermore, in many cases, AI projects can fail to deliver immediate returns, making it difficult to secure sustained funding. Therefore, high initial and maintenance costs are crucial barrier that significantly influences the adoption and implementation of AI in the public sector.

Many public sector entities face funding uncertainties and rely on allocations that may fluctuate based on political priorities. As a result, AI projects often receive fragmented or short-term funding, which is insufficient for sustained implementation (Borins, 2001). According to a study by Wirtz et al. (2019), insufficient funding allocations are among the primary reasons for the slow adoption of AI in public services, emphasizing the need for financial stability to realize AI's full potential.

Moreover, the lack of funding for AI initiatives can hinder innovation and continuous development, adversely affecting the efficiency of public services. Public institutions often lack the ability to earmark funds specifically for digital transformation, leading to sporadic advancements rather than continuous improvement. The capacity for long-term planning and investment is crucial not only for the initial stages of AI implementation but also for its sustainable integration into existing systems. Additionally, the absence of collaboration and information sharing among public institutions limits the effective use of resources. To promote the adoption of

AI technologies, it is essential for governments and relevant agencies to develop a more predictable and stable funding model. This approach will allow AI applications to be assessed and improved not only at the outset of projects but also in terms of their long-term impacts.

Human Resource and Knowledge Deficiencies

Many public sector employees lack AI-specific skills, as government agencies often have fewer resources to train staff on new technologies compared to private sector organizations (Mikhaylov et al, 2018; Zuiderwijk et al., 2021). This disparity hinders the ability of public institutions to effectively implement AI solutions. According to Berryhill et al. (2019), building AI literacy among government employees is critical for successful AI integration, as it enables them to understand, trust, and leverage AI systems effectively. Without adequate training, employees may feel overwhelmed by new technologies, leading to resistance or skepticism about AI initiatives. Moreover, the lack of AI expertise can create barriers to collaboration between departments, as employees may not be equipped to engage with data scientists or technology specialists. This situation underscores the importance of investing in training programs that not only focus on technical skills but also on fostering a culture of innovation and adaptability. To facilitate a smoother transition to AI-enhanced operations, government agencies should prioritize continuous learning and development, leveraging partnerships with educational institutions and private sector experts. By equipping public sector employees with the necessary skills and knowledge, organizations can enhance their capacity to utilize AI effectively and ultimately improve service delivery to citizens.

Public sector employees may resist AI due to concerns about job security and a lack of familiarity with digital technologies. Research by Deloitte indicates that a lack of transparency about AI's impact on job roles exacerbates these concerns, as employees are more likely to resist technologies they perceive as threats to their job security. This resistance can stem from fears that AI will automate tasks, rendering their skills obsolete, or from uncertainty about how their roles may evolve in an AI-enhanced environment. In addition, the absence of clear communication regarding the objectives and benefits of AI implementation can foster an atmosphere of distrust and skepticism. When employees are not adequately informed about how AI will support their work and improve service delivery, they may feel marginalized in the decision-making process. This highlights the critical importance of change management and effective communication strategies to ease transitions and foster employee buy-in.

Effective AI implementation in public institutions necessitates a culture that embraces innovation and is receptive to change. This cultural shift often requires strong leadership that is committed to fostering a pro-innovation environment, as leaders play a pivotal role in championing AI projects and securing internal support from various stakeholders. Leaders must not only advocate for the adoption of AI technologies but also actively engage employees in the transformation process. However, the background of many people who manage organizations and the weak culture they create in their work environment are barriers to the adoption of AI applications (Aljneibi, 2020). As Criado et al. (2022) suggest, Chief Information Officers (CIOs) and top managers who demonstrate strong AI advocacy are instrumental in mitigating resistance among employees and increasing the likelihood of successful adoption. Their visible commitment to AI initiatives can inspire confidence and alleviate fears surrounding new technologies. Furthermore, effective leaders must communicate a clear vision for how AI will enhance organizational processes and improve service delivery, thereby aligning the goals of the technology with the values and mission of the institution.

Technological Infrastructure and Integration Challenges

Many government agencies continue to rely on outdated legacy systems that were not designed for integration with modern AI tools. These legacy systems often lack the compatibility necessary for real-time data exchange and analytics, severely limiting the potential of AI applications in critical areas such as predictive analysis and automated decision-making. As a result, agencies may struggle to harness the full capabilities of AI, ultimately affecting their operational efficiency and service delivery to the public. According to Marzouki et al. (2021), the lack of interoperability between these aging systems poses a significant barrier to effective AI integration (Millan-Vargas et al., 2024). Without the ability to seamlessly share data across various platforms, agencies face challenges in consolidating information and generating insights that could enhance decision-making processes. This technological fragmentation not only hampers innovation but also increases the risk of data silos, where vital information remains isolated within departments, making it difficult to leverage comprehensive data for strategic initiatives.

Effective AI models rely on large volumes of high-quality data to function optimally. However, many public agencies struggle with significant data collection and management challenges that hinder their ability to train and implement AI systems effectively (Maragno et al, 2023). One of the primary obstacles is the lack of structured data necessary for AI training, which is often a prerequisite for building robust models capable of delivering accurate insights. In many cases, public sector data is siloed across various departments, creating barriers to accessibility and collaboration (Malomo & Sena, 2017). This fragmentation leads to inconsistencies in data quality and formats, which can severely impact the accuracy and reliability of AI models. For instance, if different departments use varied definitions or methods for collecting similar data, the resulting discrepancies can create confusion and diminish the effectiveness of AI applications designed to analyze this information. The Organization for Economic Cooperation and Development (OECD) emphasizes the critical need for the public sector to develop standardized data management practices (OECD, 2019). By establishing clear guidelines for data collection, storage, and sharing, government agencies can ensure that high-quality data is readily available for AI applications. Standardization not only enhances data quality but also facilitates interoperability between systems, allowing for more comprehensive analysis and more reliable AI outcomes.

Governments handle vast amounts of sensitive data, making cybersecurity a top priority in their operations. However, the public sector often lags behind in implementing robust cybersecurity measures, which are crucial when adopting AI technologies (Henman, 2020). The integration of AI into government systems can amplify vulnerabilities, as data breaches in this context could have far-reaching consequences, potentially compromising citizen privacy, national security, and public trust in government institutions. The reliance of AI on large datasets further complicates the cybersecurity landscape. These datasets often contain personally identifiable information (PII) and other sensitive information, which heightens the risks associated with data breaches. Consequently, government agencies must navigate a complex web of privacy concerns and regulatory requirements. Compliance with data protection regulations, such as the General Data Protection Regulation (GDPR) in Europe, is essential to ensure that personal data is handled responsibly and ethically (Sartor & Lagioia, 2020). Non-compliance can lead to significant legal repercussions and damage the public's confidence in government operations.

Legal and Ethical Issues

The legal frameworks surrounding AI, including those related to accountability, transparency, and data privacy, are still evolving. This dynamic landscape creates uncertainty for public institutions as they attempt to implement AI technologies. The lack of clear regulations can lead to confusion regarding compliance requirements, especially when data is processed across borders, complicating the responsibilities of public agencies in safeguarding sensitive information. Public institutions often face significant challenges in ensuring that their AI initiatives align with existing regulations. For example, the need to balance innovation with privacy concerns can create dilemmas, particularly when dealing with personal data. As highlighted in a study by Pasquale (2020), regulatory clarity is essential for enabling the safe and responsible deployment of AI in public services. Clear guidelines not only help agencies understand their legal obligations but also foster public trust by demonstrating that AI applications are developed and implemented responsibly.

AI systems are inherently prone to biases that may be embedded in their training data, which can lead to unfair outcomes if not carefully managed (Henman, 2020). In the public sector, where AI-driven decisions have direct impacts on citizens—such as in areas like law enforcement, healthcare, and social services—these biases raise significant ethical concerns regarding fairness and transparency. The consequences of biased AI can be particularly severe, potentially exacerbating existing inequalities and leading to discriminatory practices that adversely affect marginalized communities.

Structural and Organizational Barriers

Traditional public sector hierarchies often pose significant challenges to the agility required for successful AI projects. Bureaucratic processes and rigid decision-making structures can create bottlenecks that hinder rapid innovation and impede the effective implementation of AI solutions. These hierarchical frameworks may prioritize adherence to established protocols over flexibility, making it difficult for organizations to adapt to the fast-paced developments in AI technology.

Algorithmic Barriers

AI algorithms, particularly complex models like deep learning, often suffer from a lack of transparency in their decision-making processes, a challenge commonly referred to as the "black box" problem. This opacity poses significant issues in the public sector, where decisions made by AI systems must be transparent, justifiable, and accountable to the public. When citizens are affected by algorithmic decisions—such as those related to resource allocation, law enforcement, or public health—there is an inherent expectation that the processes leading to those decisions are clear and understandable. The difficulty in interpreting how AI models arrive at their conclusions can lead to mistrust among stakeholders and raise ethical concerns about fairness and accountability. If individuals cannot comprehend the rationale behind critical decisions, it undermines their ability to challenge or appeal those decisions, thereby eroding public confidence in government institutions. Research from Ishengoma et al. (2022) suggests that governments should prioritize the development of "explainable AI" frameworks. These frameworks aim to enhance the interpretability of algorithms, making the decision-making processes more understandable to both policymakers and the public.

The inherent opacity of AI systems can significantly erode trust among both employees and the public. When AI technologies operate as "black boxes," their lack of transparency can lead to skepticism about their fairness and reliability (Millan-Vargas et al., 2024). For AI to be accepted and effectively integrated into government services, it is essential that these systems provide clear explanations for their decisions. This transparency enables public officials to justify AI-driven outcomes and respond meaningfully to inquiries from the public, fostering a sense of accountability and legitimacy in government operations (Keller & Drake, 2021).

RESEARCH METHODOLOGY

This study aims to thoroughly examine the factors that drive and hinder the adoption and diffusion of AI within public administration, with a focus on identifying and analyzing the complex relationships between these drivers and barriers. To achieve this objective, an integrated ISM-MICMAC analysis approach was employed as the methodology. The Interpretive Structural Modeling (ISM) technique was utilized to establish the relationships among the identified barriers, while the MICMAC (Matrice d'Impacts Croisés Multiplication Appliquée à un Classement) method was adopted for categorizing these barriers into distinct groups.

The ISM component within this approach primarily serves to unravel the structural relationships among various drivers and barriers, presenting them in a hierarchical model. It simplifies the web of influences by decomposing complex interactions into more manageable layers, allowing users to identify and visualize the most foundational and influential elements. This hierarchical structure effectively categorizes factors by level, showing how upper-level factors, such as strategic goals and regulatory pressures, influence mid-level components (e.g., organizational readiness) and foundational factors like technological infrastructure and resource availability. This structural hierarchy is particularly useful in the public sector context, where long-standing, institutionalized practices and policies often dictate the flow and impact of newer technological initiatives.

MICMAC analysis, on the other hand, categorizes these factors based on their driving and dependence power, enhancing the depth of understanding about how individual elements within the system behave. Through MICMAC, each driver or barrier is mapped according to its influence (driving power) and sensitivity (dependence power), resulting in four distinct categories: autonomous factors (low drive, low dependence), dependent factors (low drive, high dependence), linkage factors (high drive, high dependence), and independent or driving factors (high drive, low dependence). For instance, factors with high driving power but low dependence—often foundational technological and organizational capabilities—are highlighted as strategic priorities, given their ability to impact the entire system. Conversely, highly dependent factors, such as stakeholder buy-in and employee skill levels, are more sensitive to changes in driving factors, indicating areas where targeted intervention can yield substantial results.

Application of Interpretive Structural Modeling (ISM)

ISM, employed in this study to analyze data (i.e., drivers and barriers) obtained from the literature review and expert opinions, is a methodology designed to evaluate the perspectives of a group of subject matter experts, typically comprising 5 to 25 participants. The use of expert groups is advantageous, as it yields more contextually valid data compared to traditional statistical approaches. As a qualitative, inductive method, ISM emphasizes depth of insight over breadth and is effective with as few as 5–7 experts. Ideally, heterogeneous expert groups are composed of 8–12 experts, while homogeneous groups typically range from 13–20 experts. Accordingly, the expert group conducting the ISM analysis should ideally consist of fifteen to twenty-five individuals, each possessing a minimum of ten years of theoretical and practical experience in relevant fields, to ensure the reliability and depth of findings (Abbass et al., 2022; Kumar et al., 2022; Abbass et al., 2023). Given that qualitative ISM studies generally recommend an expert group of this size, this study engaged a homogeneous group of 17 experts to provide credible responses and robust support for the research. Furthermore, to enrich the perspectives within the study, the expert group was diversified into two segments— practitioners (indicated with the abbreviation P) and academicians (indicated with the abbreviation A)—thereby offering a balanced view across both theoretical and applied dimensions. The profiles and characteristics of the expert participants are presented in Table 1.

Table 1. Profile of expert group

#	*Expert Position*	*Experience (Years)*
1	P1	24
2	P2	23
3	P3	26
4	P4	10
5	P5	18
6	P6	13

continued on following page

Table 1. Continued

#	Expert Position	Experience (Years)
7	P7	26
8	P8	10
9	P9	10
10	P10	11
11	P11	28
12	P12	10
13	P13	20
14	A1	10
15	A2	11
16	A3	12
17	A4	12

Warfield (1974) developed a methodology executed in a sequential manner for ISM that systematically applies foundational concepts from graph theory and Boolean algebra. This approach offers two key advantages over similar methods: it is simple, as it does not demand advanced mathematical expertise, and it is efficient, minimizing computational time and resources. The various steps involved in Interpretive Structural Modeling are as follows:

1. **Identification of Barriers:** The first step involves identifying the relevant drivers and barriers associated with the concerned approach. In this study, 17 drivers and 15 barriers to adoption and diffusion of artificial intelligence applications in public administration identified from comprehensive literature survey and through expert opinions. Table 2 and Table 3 show the details for identified drivers and barriers.
2. **Creation of a Structural Self-Interaction Matrix (SSIM):** The SSIM serves as a visual representation of experts' insights regarding the relationships among the identified drivers/barriers. Experts were provided with sufficient information about these drivers/barriers to indicate the direction of their relationships. Then all the experts were asked to evaluate the drivers/barriers based on their knowledge in the public sector and experience. In the SSIM, the symbols used are as follows:
    - V: Indicates that barrier A influences barrier B in a direct way.
    - A: Suggests that barrier B influences barrier A directly.
    - X: Implies a bidirectional influence, meaning both barriers affect each other.
    - O: Denotes that there is no direct relationship between the two barriers.

Table 2. Drivers and barriers explanations used in the study

Driver Code	Driver	References
D1	AI Applications Becoming More Functional	Alhosani & Alhashmi (2024), Dorhetso & Quarshie (2023)
D2	AI Applications Becoming Fast	Zuiderwijk et al. (2020)
D3	AI Applications Facilitating Big Data Analysis	Zuiderwijk et al. (2020), Elezaj et al. (2018), Al-Sai & Abualigah (2017), Malomo & Sena (2017), Yusifov (2016)
D4	AI Applications Being Able to Communicate Interactively	Chen et al. (2024), Henman (2020), Mehr (2017)
D5	Natural Language Processing Feature of AI Applications (Interlingual Agreement)	Mellouli et al. (2024), Mehr (2017)
D6	Support from Management	Dorhetso & Quarshie (2023), Nurski (2023)
D7	Collaboration with Stakeholders	Alhosani & Alhashmi (2024), Dorhetso & Quarshie (2023), Berryhill et al. (2019)
D8	Goal of Providing Authority and Skills to Employee (Staff Empowerment)	Aljneibi (2020)
D9	Knowledge Continuity Independent from the Key Employee	Maragno et al. (2023)
D10	Regulation and Legal Framework	Dorhetso & Quarshie (2023), Madan & Ashok (2023), Maragno et al. (2023), Henman (2020)
D11	External Pressures and Competition	Alhosani & Alhashmi (2024), Dorhetso & Quarshie (2023), Nurski (2023), Madan & Ashok (2023)
D12	Social Expectations	Medaglia & Tangi (2022)
D13	Increasing Respect in Society	Maragno et al. (2023), Van Noordt & Misuraca (2020), Van Noordt & Misuraca (2020)
D14	Customer Satisfaction	Dorhetso & Quarshie (2023), Kuziemski & Misuraca (2020), Zuiderwijk et al. (2020)
D15	Social Awareness	Criado & de Zarate-Alcarazo (2022)
D16	Data and Evidence-Based Decision Making	Dorhetso & Quarshie (2023), Zuiderwijk et al. (2020), Henman (2020)
D17	Reducing Labor Costs with AI Applications	Madan & Ashok (2023), Zuiderwijk et al. (2020), Henman (2020), Mutawa & Rashid (2020)

Table 3. Barriers explanations used in the study

Barrier Code	Barrier	References
B1	High Installation and Maintenance Costs	Millan-Vargas et al. (2024), Alhosani & Alhashmi (2024)
B2	Inadequate Financing and Resource Allocation	Millan-Vargas et al. (2024), Merugu & Hemachandran (2023), Berryhill et al. (2019), Wirtz et al. (2019)
B3	Lack of Long-Term Planning for AI Applications	Aljneibi (2020)
B4	Lack of Skills and Knowledge of Employee in the Field of AI	Millan-Vargas et al (2024), Alhosani & Alhashmi (2024), Nurski (2023), Aljneibi (2020), Van Noordt & Misuraca (2020), Wirtz et al. (2019), De Sousa et al. (2019),
B5	Resistance of Personnel to Change	Millan-Vargas et al (2024),
B6	Lack of an Effective Leader	Millan-Vargas et al (2024), Aljneibi (2020)
B7	Insufficient Infrastructure and Legacy Systems	Millan-Vargas et al (2024), Alhosani & Alhashmi (2024), Dorhetso & Quarshie (2023), Nurski (2023), Maragno et al. (2023), Van Noordt & Misuraca (2020), Berryhill et al. (2019)
B8	Problem of Data Quality, Collection and Management	Millan-Vargas et al (2024), Alhosani & Alhashmi (2024), Madan & Ashok (2023), Maragno et al. (2023), Merugu & Hemachandran (2023), Aljneibi (2020), Berryhill et al. (2019), Wirtz et al. (2019), Mehr (2017)
B9	Problem of Cyber Security and Data Protection	Alhosani & Alhashmi (2024), Wirtz et al (2019)
B10	Legal Uncertainties	Maragno et al. (2023), Ishengoma et al. (2022)
B11	Concerns About Bias and Accountability	Millan-Vargas et al (2024), Alhosani & Alhashmi (2024), Merugu & Hemachandran (2023), Wirtz et al. (2019)
B12	Violation of the Right to Personal Data Protection	Dixit & Kumar (2023), Kumar et al. (2022)
B13	Excess of Bureaucratic Processes	Neumann et al. (2024), Madan & Ashok (2023)
B14	Lack of Integration Between Institutions	Berryhill et al. (2019)
B15	Uncertainty of Operation of AI Algorithms	Alhosani & Alhashmi (2024)

Table 4 and Table 5 present SSIMs prepared for the drivers and barriers to the adoption and diffusion of AI applications in public administration, respectively.

Table 4. Structural self-interaction matrix (SSIM) for drivers

	D17	*D16*	*D15*	*D14*	*D13*	*D12*	*D11*	*D10*	*D9*	*D8*	*D7*	*D6*	*D5*	*D4*	*D3*	*D2*	*D1*
D1	V	V	A	V	O	A	X	A	V	V	V	A	X	X	V	X	X
D2	V	V	V	V	O	A	A	X	V	X	A	A	A	X	V	X	
D3	V	V	O	V	O	V	X	X	V	A	V	A	X	X	X		

continued on following page

Table 4. Continued

	D17	D16	D15	D14	D13	D12	D11	D10	D9	D8	D7	D6	D5	D4	D3	D2	D1
D4	V	V	V	V	V	X	O	O	V	V	V	A	X	X			
D5	V	V	V	V	O	X	X	O	V	V	X	A	X				
D6	V	V	X	V	X	A	X	X	O	X	X	X					
D7	A	X	X	X	X	A	A	X	X	X	X						
D8	V	X	V	V	V	X	X	O	X	X							
D9	V	V	V	V	V	X	A	X	X								
D10	O	X	A	V	V	V	X	X									
D11	O	X	A	V	A	X	X										
D12	O	X	X	X	X	X											
D13	O	A	X	X	X												
D14	O	A	X	X													
D15	X	X	X														
D16	X	X															
D17	X																

Table 5. Structural self-interaction matrix (SSIM) for barriers

	B15	B14	B13	B12	B11	B10	B9	B8	B7	B6	B5	B4	B3	B2	B1
B1	A	V	X	O	O	O	A	X	X	O	O	O	X	X	X
B2	X	V	A	O	O	O	V	X	V	A	O	O	V	X	
B3	X	X	X	X	A	A	X	X	X	A	A	X	X		
B4	X	X	X	V	X	O	V	V	X	A	X	X			
B5	X	X	A	X	X	X	O	V	X	X	X				
B6	V	V	V	O	V	O	O	V	X	X					
B7	V	V	X	V	V	O	V	V	X						
B8	V	X	X	X	X	X	X	X							
B9	X	X	A	X	X	X	X								
B10	X	V	X	V	X	X									
B11	X	A	X	A	X										
B12	A	X	X	X											
B13	O	V	X												
B14	X	X													
B15	X														

3. **Development of the Initial Reachability Matrix:** The initial reachability matrix derived from the SSIM is a binary matrix where the values of 1 and 0 are assigned according to the following guidelines:
    - Cell (i,j) contains V: Assign a value of 1 to the cell (i,j) and 0 to the cell (j,i).
    - Cell (i,j) contains A: Assign a value of 0 to the cell (i,j) and 1 to the cell (j,i).
    - Cells (i,j) and (j,i) both contain X: Assign a value of 1 to both cells (i,j) and (j,i), indicating a bidirectional relationship.
    - Cells (i,j) and (j,i) both contain O: Assign a value of 0 to both cells (i,j) and (j,i), indicating no influence between the barriers.

This matrix is then checked for transitivity to ensure that the relationships are logically consistent.

Table 6 and Table 7 present initial reachability matrices prepared for the drivers and barriers to the adoption and diffusion of AI applications in public administration, respectively.

Table 6. Initial reachability matrix for drivers

	D1	*D2*	*D3*	*D4*	*D5*	*D6*	*D7*	*D8*	*D9*	*D10*	*D11*	*D12*	*D13*	*D14*	*D15*	*D16*	*D17*
D1	1	1	1	1	1	0	1	1	1	0	1	0	0	1	0	1	1
D2	1	1	1	1	0	0	0	1	1	1	0	0	0	1	1	1	1
D3	0	0	1	1	1	0	1	0	1	1	1	1	0	1	0	1	1
D4	1	1	1	1	1	0	1	1	1	0	0	1	1	1	1	1	1
D5	1	1	1	1	1	0	1	1	1	0	1	1	0	1	1	1	1
D6	1	1	1	1	1	1	1	1	0	1	1	0	1	1	1	1	1
D7	0	1	0	0	1	1	1	1	1	1	0	0	1	1	1	1	0
D8	0	1	1	0	0	1	1	1	1	0	1	1	1	1	1	1	1
D9	0	0	0	0	0	0	1	1	1	1	0	1	1	1	1	1	1
D10	1	1	1	0	0	1	1	0	1	1	1	1	1	1	0	1	0
D11	1	1	1	0	1	1	0	1	1	1	1	1	0	1	0	1	0
D12	1	1	0	1	1	1	0	1	1	0	1	1	1	1	1	1	0
D13	0	0	0	0	0	1	1	0	0	0	1	1	1	1	1	0	0
D14	0	0	0	0	0	0	1	0	0	0	0	1	1	1	1	0	0
D15	1	0	0	0	0	1	1	0	0	1	1	1	1	1	1	1	1
D16	0	0	0	0	0	0	1	1	0	1	1	1	1	1	1	1	1
D17	0	0	0	0	0	0	0	0	0	0	0	0	0	0	1	1	1

Table 7. Initial reachability matrix for barriers

	B1	*B2*	*B3*	*B4*	*B5*	*B6*	*B7*	*B8*	*B9*	*B10*	*B11*	*B12*	*B13*	*B14*	*B15*
B1	1	1	1	0	0	0	1	1	0	0	0	0	1	1	0
B2	1	1	1	0	0	0	1	1	1	0	0	0	0	1	1
B3	1	0	1	1	0	0	1	1	1	0	0	1	1	1	1
B4	0	0	1	1	1	0	1	1	1	0	1	1	1	1	1
B5	0	0	1	1	1	1	1	1	0	1	1	1	0	1	1
B6	0	1	1	1	1	1	1	1	0	0	1	0	1	1	1
B7	1	0	1	1	1	1	1	1	1	0	1	1	1	1	1
B8	1	1	1	0	0	0	0	1	1	1	1	1	1	1	1
B9	0	0	1	0	0	0	0	1	1	1	1	1	0	1	1
B10	0	0	1	0	1	0	0	1	1	1	1	1	1	1	1
B11	0	0	1	1	1	0	0	1	1	1	1	0	1	0	1
B12	0	0	1	0	1	0	0	1	1	0	1	1	1	1	0
B13	1	1	1	1	1	0	1	1	1	1	1	1	1	1	0
B14	0	0	1	1	1	0	0	1	1	0	1	1	0	1	1
B15	1	1	1	1	1	0	0	0	1	1	1	1	0	1	1

4. **Partitioning the Final Reachability Matrix:** After deriving the initial reachability matrix, the next step is to verify the matrix's transitivity based on the following rule: if determinant A leads to determinant B, and determinant B leads to determinant C, then determinant A must lead to determinant C. This step is essential because such indirect linkages are not accounted for during the initial construction of the reachability matrix. Ultimately, this process establishes a relationship between A and C, and the entry A-C in initial reachability matrix changes from 0 to 1. After completing the transitivity, the final reachability matrix is achieved Novillo-Villegas et al., 2022; Ullah et al, 2024) . The final reachability matrix is partitioned to classify the barriers into different levels based on their influence and dependency.

Table 8 and Table 9 present final reachability matrices prepared for the drivers and barriers to the adoption and diffusion of AI applications in public administration, respectively.

Table 8. Final reachability matrix for drivers

	D1	*D2*	*D3*	*D4*	*D5*	*D6*	*D7*	*D8*	*D9*	*D10*	*D11*	*D12*	*D13*	*D14*	*D15*	*D16*	*D17*
D1	1	1	1	1	1	0	1	1	1	0	1	0	1	1	0	1	1
D2	1	1	1	1	0	0	0	1	1	1	0	0	1	1	1	1	1
D3	0	0	1	1	1	0	1	0	1	1	1	1	1	1	1	1	1
D4	1	1	1	1	1	0	1	1	1	1	1	1	1	1	1	1	1
D5	1	1	1	1	1	0	1	1	1	1	1	1	1	1	1	1	1
D6	1	1	1	1	1	1	1	1	1	1	1	0	1	1	1	1	1
D7	0	1	0	0	1	1	1	1	1	1	0	0	1	1	1	1	0
D8	0	1	1	0	0	1	1	1	1	1	1	1	1	1	1	1	1
D9	0	0	0	0	0	0	1	1	1	1	0	1	1	1	1	1	1
D10	1	1	1	0	0	1	1	0	1	1	1	1	1	1	0	1	1
D11	1	1	1	0	1	1	0	1	1	1	1	1	0	1	0	1	1
D12	1	1	0	1	1	1	0	1	1	0	1	1	1	1	1	1	1
D13	0	0	0	0	0	1	1	0	0	0	1	1	1	1	1	0	1
D14	0	0	0	0	0	0	1	0	0	0	0	1	1	1	1	0	1
D15	1	0	0	0	0	1	1	0	0	1	1	1	1	1	1	1	1
D16	0	0	0	0	0	0	1	1	0	1	1	1	1	1	1	1	1
D17	0	0	0	0	0	0	0	0	0	0	0	0	0	0	1	1	1

The sum of the 1 values in the rows of the final reachability matrices was used to calculate the driving power, and the sum of the 1 values in the columns was used to calculate the dependence power. These values for drivers and barriers are given in Table 10 and Table 11, respectively.

Table 9. Final reachability matrix for barriers

	B1	*B2*	*B3*	*B4*	*B5*	*B6*	*B7*	*B8*	*B9*	*B10*	*B11*	*B12*	*B13*	*B14*	*B15*
B1	1	1	1	1	1	1	1	1	0	1	1	1	1	1	0
B2	1	1	1	1	1	0	1	1	1	1	1	1	0	1	1
B3	1	0	1	1	0	0	1	1	1	0	0	1	1	1	1
B4	0	0	1	1	1	0	1	1	1	1	1	1	1	1	1
B5	0	0	1	1	1	1	1	1	1	1	1	1	0	1	1
B6	0	1	1	1	1	1	1	1	1	1	1	1	1	1	1
B7	1	0	1	1	1	1	1	1	1	1	1	1	1	1	1
B8	1	1	1	0	0	0	0	1	1	1	1	1	1	1	1
B9	0	0	1	0	0	0	0	1	1	1	1	1	0	1	1

continued on following page

Table 9. Continued

	B1	*B2*	*B3*	*B4*	*B5*	*B6*	*B7*	*B8*	*B9*	*B10*	*B11*	*B12*	*B13*	*B14*	*B15*
B10	0	0	1	0	1	0	0	1	1	1	1	1	1	1	1
B11	0	0	1	1	1	0	0	1	1	1	1	0	1	0	1
B12	0	0	1	0	1	0	0	1	1	0	1	1	1	1	0
B13	1	1	1	1	1	0	1	1	1	1	1	1	1	1	1
B14	0	0	1	1	1	0	0	1	1	0	1	1	0	1	1
B15	1	1	1	1	1	0	0	0	1	1	1	1	0	1	1

Table 10. Dependence power and driving power for drivers

	Dependence Power	*Driving Power*
D1	9	13
D2	10	12
D3	9	13
D4	7	16
D5	8	16
D6	8	16
D7	13	11
D8	11	14
D9	12	10
D10	12	13
D11	12	13
D12	12	14
D13	15	8
D14	16	6
D15	14	11
D16	15	10
D17	16	3

Table 11. Dependence power and driving power for barriers

	Dependence Power	*Driving Power*
B1	7	13
B2	6	13
B3	15	10
B4	11	12
B5	12	12
B6	4	14
B7	8	14
B8	14	11
B9	14	8
B10	12	10
B11	14	9
B12	14	8
B13	10	14
B14	14	9
B15	13	11

Classification of Drivers and Barriers Using MICMAC

MICMAC (Matrice d'Impacts Croisés Multiplication Appliquée à un Classement) analysis is a method used to categorize variables in a graph based on their driving power and dependence power. In this graph, the *x*-axis represents dependence power, while the *y*-axis denotes driving power (Dixit and Kumar, 2023). Through MICMAC analysis, clusters of variables are effectively organized according to these two dimensions, revealing insights into their interdependencies and influence levels (Singh et al., 2019). MICMAC divides variables into four groups, based on their influence and dependence. Key variables with particularly high driving power, for example, are classified as independent variables, indicating their potential to significantly impact other variables within the system (Kumar and Sharma, 2018).

Figure 1. Diagram for dependence power and driving power of drivers

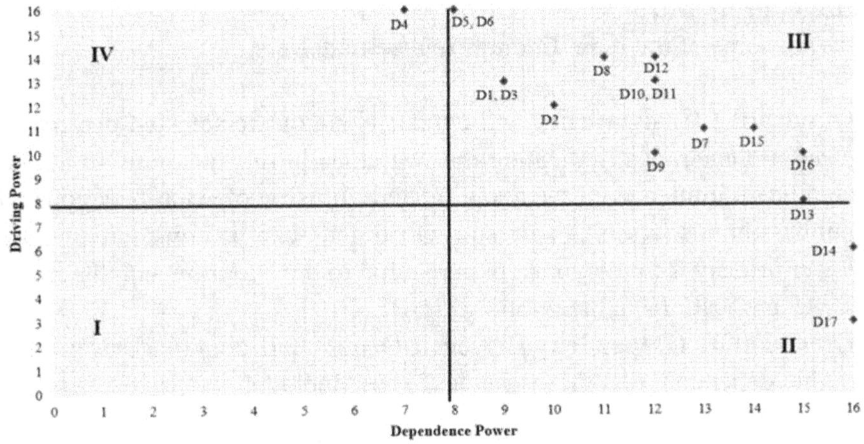

Figure 2. Diagram for dependence power and driving power of barriers

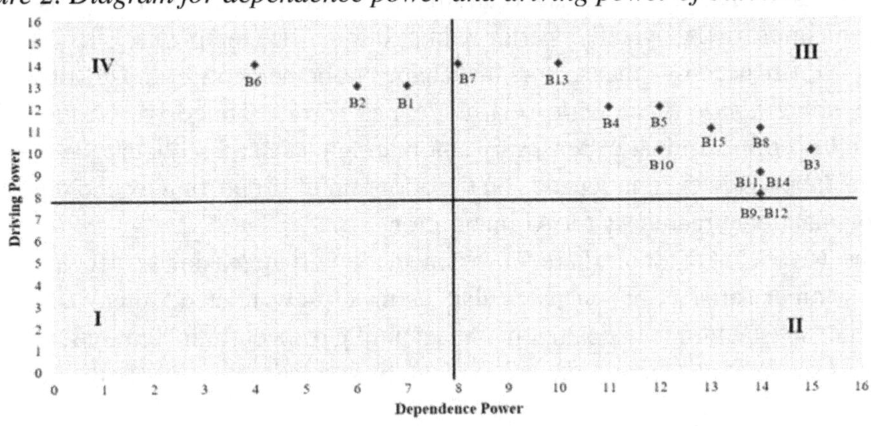

RESULTS

The study identifies several key drivers for the adoption and diffusion of artificial intelligence (AI) applications in public administration, categorized into different quadrants. Each quadrant reflects the nature of these drivers in terms of their influence and dependency, providing insights into which factors policymakers might prioritize or deprioritize.

Here are some of the main findings related to drivers:

- **Quadrant I (Insignificant Influence):** None of the selected drivers are located in Quadrant I, indicating that variables in this quadrant do not have a significant influence on the adoption and diffusion of AI applications within public administration. As a result, Quadrant I can be considered an area of lower priority for policymakers in relation to the adoption and dissemination of AI applications in the public sector.
- **Quadrant II (Dependent Drivers):** Quadrant II contains drivers that are highly dependent on other variables. These include:

Increasing Respect in Society (D13): This driver reflects the perception that AI adoption in public administration could enhance the institution's reputation and public respect. However, it heavily relies on other factors.

Customer Satisfaction (D14): Improved customer satisfaction is identified as a key motivator for adopting AI, as AI can streamline services, increase response accuracy, and improve the overall experience of public service recipients. Like D13, this driver is influenced by other factors that shape public perception and effectiveness.

Reducing Labor Costs with AI Applications (D17): This driver suggests that AI can lower operational expenses by automating tasks and reducing the need for manual labor. However, it depends on the adoption of supporting technologies and on organizational readiness for AI integration.

The drivers in Quadrant II are interconnected, with increasing respect in society and customer satisfaction, in particular, being closely related. Improvements in customer satisfaction may positively impact public respect for institutions, and vice versa, as successful AI implementation in public services reinforces both outcomes.

- **Quadrant III (Autonomous or Influencing Drivers):** Key drivers identified as autonomous or influential are located in Quadrant III. These are typically foundational factors that can independently drive the adoption and diffusion of AI in public administration. Examples include:

AI Applications Becoming More Functional (D1): As AI technology matures, its functional capabilities expand, making it more applicable across various domains within public administration. This enhancement in functionality acts as a direct motivator for adoption, as it increases the technology's practical value.

AI Applications Becoming Faster (D2): Speed improvements in AI applications, particularly in processing and delivering results, significantly appeal to public sector entities aiming to enhance operational efficiency.

AI Applications Facilitating Big Data Analysis (D3): AI's ability to process and analyze large datasets quickly and accurately makes it an essential tool for data-driven decision-making in the public sector.

Natural Language Processing Features (D5): The natural language processing (NLP) capabilities of AI enable effective communication across language barriers, supporting public administration's multilingual needs and improving inclusivity and accessibility of services.

Support from Management (D6): Institutional support is a critical factor, as buy-in from management facilitates resource allocation, strategic alignment, and a conducive environment for AI integration.

Collaboration with Technology Partners (D7): Partnerships with tech providers and developers aid in the smooth integration of AI, offering expertise and resources that public sector entities may lack internally.

Each of these drivers provides an independent push toward AI adoption, making them strategic points for policymakers seeking to accelerate AI diffusion in public administration.

- **Quadrant IV (Strong Influence but Dependent):** Drivers in this quadrant exert a strong influence on the adoption and diffusion of AI applications but are also influenced by other factors. These drivers may amplify AI adoption if complemented by supportive measures. For instance:

Policy and Regulatory Support (D9): Regulatory frameworks and supportive policies can drive AI adoption by creating clear guidelines, ensuring compliance, and promoting safe AI usage in public sectors. However, this driver depends on governmental commitment and alignment with broader digital transformation strategies.

Training and Skill Development (D10): Training public sector employees to effectively use AI applications is essential for successful adoption. Although it strongly influences AI integration, this driver relies on the availability of resources and a culture supportive of continuous learning.

The study also highlights several significant barriers to the adoption and diffusion of AI applications in public administration, organized by their placement within different quadrants based on their influence and dependency.

Here are some of the main findings related to barriers:

- **Quadrant I (Insignificant Influence):** None of the selected barriers fall within Quadrant I, indicating that barriers in this quadrant have minimal impact on the adoption and diffusion of AI in public administration. Consequently, Quadrant I represents a low-priority area for policymakers, as addressing these barriers is unlikely to significantly advance AI adoption.

- **Quadrant II (Dependent Barriers):** Quadrant II includes barriers that are highly dependent on other variables, specifically:

Cybersecurity and Data Protection Issues (B9) and Violation of the Right to Personal Data Protection (B12): These two barriers are highly dependent and significantly influenced by other factors, suggesting they are part of a broader, interconnected set of challenges. The close relationship between these two barriers highlights the critical need to address privacy and security issues comprehensively, as they are foundational to public trust and regulatory compliance in AI applications.

- **Quadrant III (Autonomous or Influencing Drivers):** Several additional barriers play a crucial role in limiting AI adoption within public administration. These include:

Lack of Long-Term Planning for AI Applications (B3): The absence of a strategic, future-oriented approach to AI implementation impedes sustained development and effective resource allocation.

Lack of Skills and Knowledge Among Employees (B4): Many employees in public administration lack sufficient training and expertise in AI, hindering the effective use and integration of AI technologies.

Resistance of Personnel to Change (B5): Resistance from staff toward adopting new technologies, including AI, limits institutional willingness and capacity for innovation.

Insufficient Infrastructure and Legacy Systems (B7): Outdated infrastructure and legacy systems remain significant hurdles, preventing seamless AI integration and creating additional implementation costs.

Data Quality, Collection and Management Challenges (B8): Inadequate data management practices and the absence of standardized data collection processes constrain the effectiveness and scope of AI initiatives. In addition, low-quality or unreliable data provide a significant barrier for companies.

Legal Uncertainties (B10): Ambiguities in legal frameworks regarding AI usage and implications create challenges for public sector entities, limiting risk-taking and innovation.

Concerns About Bias and Accountability (B11): Issues related to algorithmic fairness, bias, and accountability continue to be major obstacles, raising ethical and public trust concerns.

Excessive Bureaucratic Processes (B13): Lengthy bureaucratic processes delay the adoption and implementation of AI, resulting in inefficiencies and diminishing the perceived value of AI investments.

These findings underscore the multifaceted nature of barriers to AI adoption in public administration, highlighting areas where targeted interventions may facilitate more effective AI integration. Addressing these barriers holistically, particularly those with strong interdependencies, will be essential for driving meaningful advancements in AI adoption within the public sector.

- **Quadrant IV (Strong Influence but Dependent):** Three additional barriers that fall within Quadrant IV are characterized by their high driving power but relatively low dependency and impact on the overall adoption and diffusion of AI in public administration. They are fundamental considerations, they are less interconnected with other barriers and present challenges that policymakers alone cannot fully address. These barriers include:

Policy and Regulatory Support High Installation and Maintenance Costs (B1): This barrier represents the substantial financial burden associated with the initial setup and ongoing maintenance of AI systems. While it has a high driving power, it remains relatively independent and has limited influence on the adoption and diffusion of AI as a whole. Policymakers have minimal control over this barrier, as it often depends on external economic and market conditions.

Inadequate Financing and Resource Allocation (B2): A lack of sufficient funding and resources to support AI initiatives serves as a major obstacle. Similar to B1, this barrier is independent and driven by budgetary constraints that are typically outside the direct control of public administrators. Its impact on AI adoption is limited when considered alongside other barriers with higher dependency.

Lack of an Effective Leader (B6): The absence of a strong leadership figure or champion for AI initiatives is another key barrier in Quadrant IV. While an influential factor, it remains relatively independent of other barriers and has a lower direct impact on the widespread adoption of AI. This barrier underscores the importance of organizational culture and leadership commitment but is less actionable for policymakers in isolation.

CONCLUSION

This study has thoroughly examined the drivers and barriers to the adoption and diffusion of AI applications in public administration. Through a comprehensive literature review, we identified and classified the key factors influencing AI implementation. By employing an integrated ISM (Interpretive Structural Modeling) and MICMAC (Cross Impact Matrix Multiplication Applied to Classification) approach, we analyzed the relationships between these drivers and barriers.

This research aims to make both practical and theoretical contributions. The integrated ISM (Interpretive Structural Modeling)-MICMAC (Matrice d'Impacts Croisés Multiplication Appliquée à un Classement) approach offers a comprehensive framework to analyze complex, interconnected factors that influence AI adoption and diffusion in public administration. ISM facilitates the identification of relationships and hierarchies among various drivers and barriers, structuring them into a multi-level model. This hierarchical structure clarifies the influences between factors, highlighting foundational elements that serve as enablers or constraints. MICMAC analysis complements ISM by categorizing these factors based on their driving power and dependence, allowing for a more nuanced understanding of how each element interacts within the broader ecosystem.

By using this integrated ISM-MICMAC approach, public sector leaders can obtain a comprehensive view of the AI adoption landscape, identifying not only the core challenges but also the leverage points for driving sustainable change. This method is particularly beneficial for public administration, where achieving alignment between technological advances and organizational readiness is often a slow, challenging process. In this setting, the ISM-MICMAC approach provides a clear framework to prioritize efforts, allowing decision-makers to address foundational barriers, optimize resource allocation, and foster an environment conducive to successful AI adoption. For example, a public institution might find that while regulatory compliance is a driving factor, organizational readiness and employee skill enhancement are highly dependent and thus require sequential, targeted training programs and infrastructure development.

The structured insights afforded by ISM-MICMAC also facilitate the development of strategies that are resilient to external shifts in political or technological environments. As the approach clearly delineates both influence and reliance among factors, it supports scenario planning, allowing public organizations to anticipate how changes in one area—such as an updated AI regulatory policy—might cascade through dependent factors, affecting technology adoption rates and employee engagement. Moreover, by identifying autonomous factors that may act independently, the framework aids in mitigating risks from external pressures and aligning internal factors toward stable AI integration.

REFERENCES

Abbass, K., Asif, M., Niazi, A. A. K., Qazi, T. F., Basit, A., & Al-Muwaffaq Ahmed, F. A. (2022). Understanding the interaction among enablers of quality enhancement of higher business education in Pakistan. *PLoS One*, 17(5), e0267919. DOI: 10.1371/journal.pone.0267919 PMID: 35617271

Abbass, K., Basit, A., Niazi, A. A. K., Mufti, R., Zahid, N., & Qazi, T. F. (2023). Evaluating the social outcomes of COVID-19 pandemic: Empirical evidence from Pakistan. *Environmental Science and Pollution Research International*, 30(22), 61466–61478. DOI: 10.1007/s11356-022-19628-7 PMID: 35306646

Al-Sai, Z. A., & Abualigah, L. M. (2017, May). Big data and E-government: A review. In *2017 8th international conference on information technology (ICIT)* (pp. 580-587). IEEE.

Alhosani, K., & Alhashmi, S. M. (2024). Opportunities, challenges, and benefits of AI innovation in government services: A review. *Discover Artificial Intelligence*, 4(1), 18. DOI: 10.1007/s44163-024-00111-w

Aljneibi, A. A. (2020). Enablers & Barriers to AI Adopting in Public Services (Master's thesis, The British University in Dubai).

Attri, R., Dev, N., & Sharma, V. (2013). Interpretive structural modelling (ISM) approach: an overview. *Research Journal of Management Sciences*, *2319*(2), 1171.

Berryhill, J., Heang, K. K., Clogher, R., & McBride, K. (2019). Hello, World: Artificial intelligence and its use in the public sector. *OECD Working Papers on Public Governance*, No. 36, OECD Publishing, Paris. DOI: 10.1787/726fd39d-en

Borins, S. (2001). Encouraging innovation in the public sector. *Journal of Intellectual Capital*, 2(3), 310–319. DOI: 10.1108/14691930110400128

Chen, T., Gascó-Hernandez, M., & Esteve, M. (2024). The Adoption and Implementation of Artificial Intelligence Chatbots in Public Organizations: Evidence from US State Governments. *American Review of Public Administration*, 54(3), 255–270. DOI: 10.1177/02750740231200522

Criado, J. I., & de Zarate-Alcarazo, L. O. (2022). Technological frames, CIOs, and Artificial Intelligence in public administration: A socio-cognitive exploratory study in Spanish local governments. *Government Information Quarterly*, 39(3), 101688. DOI: 10.1016/j.giq.2022.101688

De Sousa, W. G., de Melo, E. R. P., Bermejo, P. H. D. S., Farias, R. A. S., & Gomes, A. O. (2019). How and where is artificial intelligence in the public sector going? A literature review and research agenda. *Government Information Quarterly*, 36(4), 101392. DOI: 10.1016/j.giq.2019.07.004

Di Vaio, A., Hassan, R., & Alavoine, C. (2022). Data intelligence and analytics: A bibliometric analysis of human–Artificial intelligence in public sector decision-making effectiveness. *Technological Forecasting and Social Change*, 174, 121201. DOI: 10.1016/j.techfore.2021.121201

Dixit, C., & Kumar, R. (2023). Analyzing Managerial and Technological Barriers to the Adoption of Industry 4.0: An 'ISM' and 'MICMAC' Approach. *IEEE Transactions on Engineering Management*, 71, 3389–3401. DOI: 10.1109/TEM.2023.3343527

Dorhetso, S. N., & Quarshie, B. D. (2023). Ratings of Driving Factors for the Adoption and Implementation of Artificial Intelligence in the Public Sector. *OAlib*, 10(5), 1–20. DOI: 10.4236/oalib.1109982

Elezaj, O., Tole, D., & Baci, N. (2018). Big data in e-government environments: Albania as a case study. *Academic Journal of Interdisciplinary Studies*, 7(2), 117–124. DOI: 10.2478/ajis-2018-0052

Henman, P. (2020). Improving public services using artificial intelligence: Possibilities, pitfalls, governance. *Asia Pacific Journal of Public Administration*, 42(4), 209–221. DOI: 10.1080/23276665.2020.1816188

Hoekstra, M., Van Veenstra, A. F., & Chideock, C. (2021). A Typology for Applications of Public Sector AI. In EGOV-CeDEM-ePart-* (pp. 121-128).

Horowitz, M. C., & Kahn, L. (2021). What influences attitudes about artificial intelligence adoption: Evidence from US local officials. *PLoS One*, 16(10), e0257732. DOI: 10.1371/journal.pone.0257732 PMID: 34669734

Ishengoma, F. R., Shao, D., Alexopoulos, C., Saxena, S., & Nikiforova, A. (2022). Integration of artificial intelligence of things (AIoT) in the public sector: Drivers, barriers and future research agenda. *Digital Policy. Regulation & Governance*, 24(5), 449–462. DOI: 10.1108/DPRG-06-2022-0067

Keller, P., & Drake, A. (2021). Exclusivity and paternalism in the public governance of explainable AI. *Computer Law & Security Review*, 40, 105490. DOI: 10.1016/j.clsr.2020.105490

Kumar, C., Ganguly, A., & Lohan, A. (2022). Understanding the interrelationship of barriers towards business model re-engineering under the evolving privacy laws: An interpretive Structure Modelling approach. *International Review of Law Computers & Technology*, 36(3), 382–403. https://www.tandfonline.com/doi/full/10.1080/13600869.2021.1999302

Kumar, S., & Sharma, R. (2018). Key barriers in the growth of rural health care: An ISM-MICMAC approach. *Benchmarking*, 25(7), 2169–2183. DOI: 10.1108/BIJ-05-2017-0095

Kuziemski, M., & Misuraca, G. (2020). AI governance in the public sector: Three tales from the frontiers of automated decision-making in democratic settings. *Telecommunications Policy*, 44(6), 101976. DOI: 10.1016/j.telpol.2020.101976 PMID: 32313360

Madan, R., & Ashok, M. (2023). AI adoption and diffusion in public administration: A systematic literature review and future research agenda. *Government Information Quarterly*, 40(1), 101774. DOI: 10.1016/j.giq.2022.101774

Malomo, F., & Sena, V. (2017). Data intelligence for local government? Assessing the benefits and barriers to use of big data in the public sector. *Policy and Internet*, 9(1), 7–27. DOI: 10.1002/poi3.141

Maragno, G., Tangi, L., Gastaldi, L., & Benedetti, M. (2023). Exploring the factors, affordances and constraints outlining the implementation of Artificial Intelligence in public sector organizations. *International Journal of Information Management*, 73, 102686. DOI: 10.1016/j.ijinfomgt.2023.102686

Medaglia, R., & Tangi, L. (2022, October). The adoption of Artificial Intelligence in the public sector in Europe: drivers, features, and impacts. In *Proceedings of the 15th International Conference on Theory and Practice of Electronic Governance (ICEGOV)* (pp. 10-18). https://doi.org/DOI: 10.1145/3560107.3560110

Mehr, H. (2017). *Artificial Intelligence for Citizen Services and Government*. Harvard Kennedy School, Ash Center for Democratic Governance and Innovation.

Mellouli, S., Janssen, M., & Ojo, A. (2024). Introduction to the Issue on Artificial Intelligence in the Public Sector: Risks and Benefits of AI for Governments. Digital Government. *Research and Practice*, 5(1), 1–6. DOI: 10.1145/3636550

Mergel, I., Dickinson, H., Stenvall, J., & Gasco, M. (2024). Implementing AI in the public sector. *Public Management Review*, 1–14. DOI: 10.1080/14719037.2023.2231950

Merugu, M., & Hemachandran, K. (2023). AI in Public Sector. *Artificial Intelligence for Business: An Implementation Guide Containing Practical and Industry-Specific Case Studies*, 336-349. DOI: 10.4324/9781003358411-21

Mikhaylov, S. J., Esteve, M., & Campion, A. (2018). Artificial intelligence for the public sector: Opportunities and challenges of cross-sector collaboration. *Philosophical Transactions. Series A, Mathematical, Physical, and Engineering Sciences*, 376(2128), 20170357. DOI: 10.1098/rsta.2017.0357 PMID: 30082303

Millan-Vargas, A. O., Sandoval-Almazan, R., & Valle-Cruz, D. (2024, June). Impact and barriers to AI in the public sector: the case of the State of Mexico. In *Proceedings of the 25th Annual International Conference on Digital Government Research* (pp. 81-89). https://doi.org/DOI: 10.1145/3657054.3657249

Mutawa, M. A., & Rashid, H. (2020, August). Comprehensive review on the challenges that impact artificial intelligence applications in the public sector. In *Proceedings of the 5th NA International Conference on Industrial Engineering and Operations Management* (Vol. 10, pp. 2078-2087).

Neumann, O., Guirguis, K., & Steiner, R. (2024). Exploring artificial intelligence adoption in public organizations: A comparative case study. *Public Management Review*, 26(1), 114–141. DOI: 10.1080/14719037.2022.2048685

Novillo-Villegas, S., Ayala-Andrade, R., Lopez-Cox, J. P., Salazar-Oyaneder, J., & Acosta-Vargas, P. (2022). A roadmap for innovation capacity in developing countries. *Sustainability*, 14(11), 6686. DOI: 10.3390/su14116686

Nurski, L. (2023). Artificial intelligence adoption in the public sector: A case study (No. 03/2023). *Bruegel Working Paper.*

OECD. (2019). *Artificial Intelligence in Society*. OECD Publishing., DOI: 10.1787/eedfee77-

Pasquale, F. (2020). *New Laws of Robotics: Defending Human Expertise in the Age of AI*. Belknap Press., DOI: 10.2307/j.ctv3405w6p

Sartor, G., & Lagioia, F. (2020). The impact of the General Data Protection Regulation (GDPR) on artificial intelligence. *Panel for the Future of Science and Technology*, EPRS | European Parliamentary Research Service. DOI: 10.2861/293

Sharma, G. D., Yadav, A., & Chopra, R. (2020). Artificial intelligence and effective governance: A review, critique and research agenda. *Sustainable Futures : An Applied Journal of Technology, Environment and Society*, 2, 100004. DOI: 10.1016/j.sftr.2019.100004

Singh, M., Kumar, P., & Rathi, R. (2019). Modelling the barriers of Lean Six Sigma for Indian micro-small medium enterprises: An ISM and MICMAC approach. *The TQM Journal*, 31(5), 673–695. DOI: 10.1108/TQM-12-2018-0205

Ullah, S., Jianjun, Z., Hayat, K., Palmucci, D. N., & Durana, P. (2024). Exploring the factors for open innovation in post-COVID-19 conditions by fuzzy Delphi-ISM-MICMAC approach. *European Journal of Innovation Management*, 27(5), 1679–1703. DOI: 10.1108/EJIM-10-2022-0550

Valle-Cruz, D., Gil-Garcia, J. R., & Sandoval-Almazan, R. (2024). Artificial intelligence algorithms and applications in the public sector: a systematic literature review based on the PRISMA approach. *Research Handbook on Public Management and Artificial Intelligence*, 8-26. DOI: 10.4337/9781802207347.00010

Van Noordt, C., & Misuraca, G. (2020, September). Evaluating the impact of artificial intelligence technologies in public services: towards an assessment framework. In *Proceedings of the 13th international conference on theory and practice of electronic governance* (pp. 8-16). https://doi.org/DOI: 10.1145/3428502.3428504

Van Noordt, C., & Misuraca, G. (2022). Artificial intelligence for the public sector: Results of landscaping the use of AI in government across the European Union. *Government Information Quarterly*, 39(3), 101714. DOI: 10.1016/j.giq.2022.101714

Warfield, J. N. (1974). Developing interconnection matrices in structural modeling. *IEEE Transactions on Systems, Man, and Cybernetics*, (1), 81–87. DOI: 10.1109/TSMC.1974.5408524

Wirtz, B. W., Langer, P. F., & Fenner, C. (2021). Artificial intelligence in the public sector-a research agenda. *International Journal of Public Administration*, 44(13), 1103–1128. DOI: 10.1080/01900692.2021.1947319

Wirtz, B. W., Weyerer, J. C., & Geyer, C. (2019). Artificial intelligence and the public sector—Applications and challenges. *International Journal of Public Administration*, 42(7), 596–615. DOI: 10.1080/01900692.2018.1498103

Yusifov, F. (2016, June). Big Data in E-Government: Issues, Opportunities and Prospects. In *Proceedings of 16th European Conference on e-Government (ECEG2016)* (pp. 352-355). ECEG Academic Conferences and Publishing Limited.

Zuiderwijk, A., Chen, Y. C., & Salem, F. (2021). Implications of the use of artificial intelligence in public governance: A systematic literature review and a research agenda. *Government Information Quarterly*, 38(3), 101577. DOI: 10.1016/j.giq.2021.101577

KEY TERMS AND DEFINITIONS

Artificial Intelligence: A branch of computer science that encompasses various techniques and algorithms enabling machines to analyze data, recognize patterns, and make decisions.

Barrier: A "barrier" is an obstacle or hindrance that prevents or restricts progress, movement, or access within a system or process.

Cross-Impact Matrix Multiplication Applied to Classification (MICMAC): A method used to analyze the driving and dependence power of factors within a system, categorizing them into four groups (autonomous, dependent, linkage, and independent) to help identify key elements that influence system behavior and dependencies.

Driver: A "driver" is a factor or element that significantly influences or causes changes in a system or process.

Interpretive Structural Modeling (ISM): A method used to identify and organize relationships among complex factors within a system, creating a hierarchical structure that clarifies dependencies and influences.

Public Administration: The governmental framework responsible for implementing policies, managing public resources, and delivering services to the public.

Chapter 2
Educational and Public Administration:
The Polymathic Ratings and Weightings Concept-Based Artificial Intelligence Processes (PRWC4AI)

Antoine Toni Trad
https://orcid.org/0000-0002-4199-6970
Independent Researcher, France

ABSTRACT

Iterative educational and public administration transformation projects (ETP) are important for the enhancements of their sustainability, performances, and longevity. ETPs are complex, due to the inter-linking AI, lack of the adoption of a polymathic and holistic approaches, and the integration of other domains that are needed to finalize such ETPs. In the domains of education and public administration, the main objective is to try to achieve long-term intangible goals and not only to achieve extreme gains dictated by leaders and/or stakeholders. A polymathic and holistic approach privileges interdisciplinary concepts for the implementations of various ETP's phases, sub-domains, and artificial intelligence (AI)-based components. This chapter uses the author's applied holistic and poly-mathematical model (AHMM) for AI (AHMM4AI), which is a variant of the author's generic and polymathic AHMM, which also includes enhancements and findings from his previous research articles and works, which are added to the PWRC4AI, where the PWRC4AI inherits the basic PRWC's characteristics.

DOI: 10.4018/979-8-3373-2272-8.ch002

INTRODUCTION

This chapter has a multi-dimensional approach to RDPs and ETPs (simply Project) that contains: 1) An innovative and adapted research approach; 2) Presents how to create an In-House Implemented (IHI) Polymathic Transformation Framework (IHIPTF); 3) Uses IHI Methodology, Domain, and Technology Common Artefacts Standard (MDTCAS) that is based Enterprise Architecture (EA) and other existing methodologies; and 4) The Factor' Management System (FMS). The PRWC4AI uses the FMS that includes: Critical Success Areas (CSA), Critical Success Factors (CSF), Key Performance Indicators (KPI), VARiables (VAR) used to interface the Information and Communication Systems (ICS) and Decision-Making System (DMS). The PRWC4AI is based on linking and evaluating of sets of CSAs, CSFs, KPIs, and VARs (simply Factors). The vast majority of Projects have an eXtremly High Failure Rates (XHFR) that is mainly due the lack of a Holistic or Polymathic concepts that are suited for the PWRC and its AI version. This chapter is intended for AI specialists, educators, Project managers and engineers to present how to implement an PRWC4AI for Projects and that be used for DMS and Knowledge Management System (KMS) (simply Intelligence) activities. To avoid confusion to the analysed topics, AI is a specific domain, whereas Intelligence, is the Entity's complete knowledge. The PRWC4AI for enterprises or organizations (simply Entity*)*, needs an agile and collaborative IHIPTF that offers an Action Research (AR) based Learning Process (ARbLP) that can learn and persist experiences from any type of encountered Projects' problems. The PRWC4AI interfaces 1) An common and limited version of EA that has the form of the MDTCAS (Pushpakumara, Jayaweera, & Manjulan, 2021); 2) DMS, Heuristics Decision Tree (HDT), and KMS (simply Intelligence); 3) The AHMM4AI or any other Mathematical Model (MM) (Trad, & Kalpić, 2020a); 4) A pool of ICS services (Trad, 2015a, 2015b); and other IHIPTF modules and phases, as shown in Figure 1.

Figure 1. PRWC4AI's sequence of phases

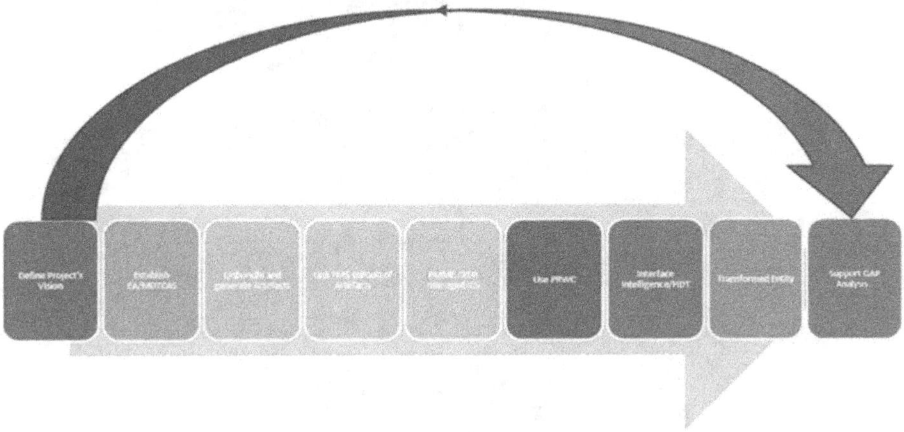

A Project can be defined as set of CSAs to be analysed and this chapter starts with its first CSA which is the RDP.

THE RESEARCH DEVELOPMENT PROJECT

An Innovative Transformational Concept

A Project can have many Viewpoints, that can include:

- "A" for EA and ICS based transformations.
- "C" for complete transformations that combines all Viewpoints.
- "G" for Generic transformations.
- "M" a Meta or Meta-Meta Model / Mathematical; which is this article's focus.
- "F" for Asset, and financial transformations.
- "I" for AI and MM based transformations.
- "O" for Organizational, Enterprise and Business transformations.
- "S" for Security based transformations.

Figure 2. Viewpoint's "I" evolution roadmap

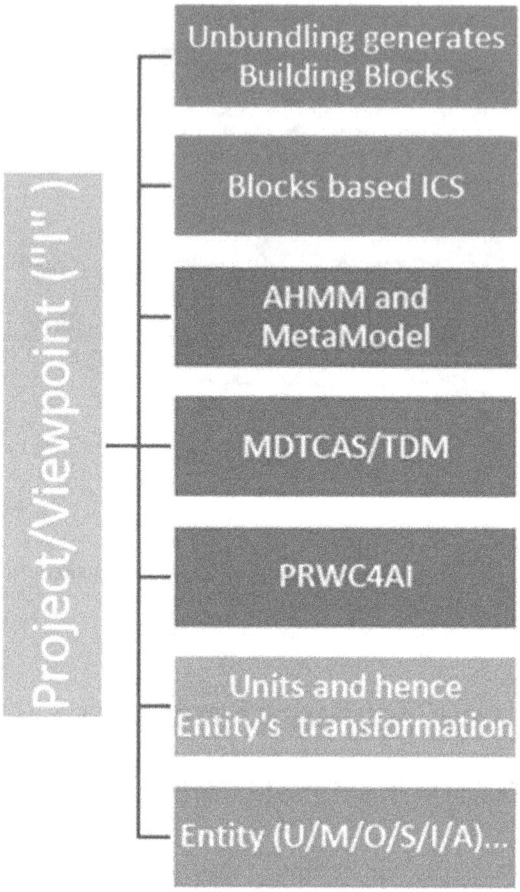

Viewpoint's "I" combines various Viewpoints and has a structured evolution's roadmap for the PRWC4AI, as shown in Figure 2. The presented IHIPTF (or the Transformation Research Architecture Development framework/TRADf) and this RDP follows an evolutive, iterative and recurrent concept, in which each new work (like this one), is just a new brick in its evolutive-wall. The author's concern is that important subjects like Projects and AI/PRWC4AI can be considered as unclear, complex, and unconventional… And that they are not to be aligned with standardized primitive quantitative academic or educational constraints, which is in fact one of the main problems… In fact the rate of 95% of Projects' XHFRs can draw a conclusion that conventional educational and professional standards are a not adapted for Projects (Krigsman, 2008). Therefore, this chapter reuses IHIPTF/ IHIPTF, RDP, and other author's works. This reuse-concept of approaches/resources, and keywords, can be considered by some simplistic automated/robotized tools as duplications or similarities… Which is definitely not the case, because such an approach privileges XHFRs; and the author's approach justifies the search for other approaches… Why shouldn't researchers build their own research innovation, vision, research/methods, IHIPTF, and reuse some parts to deliver a coherent overall AI/ PRWC4AI concept… By just using directed quantitative-standards, there isn't any creative innovation, especially in complex domains which desperately need renewed Polymathic approaches. Otherwise, all academic, business and common domains, will be dictated by monopoles… Therefore, there is a need to identify a Polymathic Researched Literature Review (RLR) and Gap Analysis (GAPA).

Figure 3. The interaction between the Project and the RDP

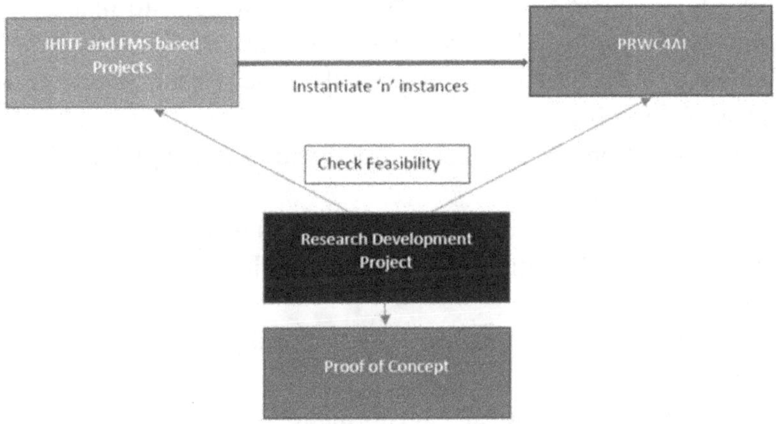

This chapter is related to The Role of Polymathics Based Artificial Intelligence (RPBAI) (Trad, 2024a), RPBAI based Interdisciplinary Core and Concept (RbICC) to ensure educational and Public Sector's (PS) operational excellence and to offer an AI core. The RbICC includes various subjects and application domains like AI, MMs, algorithmics, EA…

The PRLR and the Research/Project GAPA

Project's complexities and their XHFRs s are mainly due to the incapacities in the integration of Polymathic/cross-functional domains and GAFAM's monopolistic attitudes. The PRWC4AI needs the AHMM4AI and ARbLP based HDT, to support Intelligence's operations (Trad, & Kalpić, 2014a). This chapter's Research Question (RQ) is: "Which PRWC4AI characteristics are needed to support Projects?" The PRLR is mainly based on IHIPTF's and author's related works, like:

- Educational and Public Administration Transformation Projects-The Role of Polymathics Based Artificial Intelligence (RPBAI) (Trad, 2024a).
- Trad, A. (2024b). Academic and Educational Transformation Projects-The Role Team-Based Learning in Polymathics For University Cycle (RTBLP4UC). IGI-Global. USA.
- Trad, A. (2024c). Enterprise Transformation Projects- The use of the Polymathic Rating and Weighting Concept (PRWC). IGI-Global. USA.
- Trad, A. (2024d). Academic and Educational Transformation Projects-The Role of Skills in Academic Polymathics Fields (RSAPF). IGI Global. USA.
- The Business Transformation Project's Holistic Agile Management (Trad, & Kalpić, 2022a).
- The Selection, and Training Framework selection and training framework (STF) for Manager's in Business Innovation Transformation Projects–Educational Recommendations (Trad, & Kalpić, 2014b).
- Educational Transformation Project's Remote Group Work (ETPRGW) (Trad, & Kalpić, 2023a).
- The transformation framework-The role security in the global education system (Trad, 2021a).
- The business transformation enterprise architecture framework for innovation: The role of artificial intelligence in the global business education (RAIGBE) (Trad, 2021b).
- Business Transformation Projects: The Role of Psychology-Based Resistance (RPbR) (Trad, 2023b).
- The Societal and Educational Transformation Projects: The Evolution of the Lebanese Diverse Education (ELDES) (Trad, 2023c).
- The selection and training framework for managers in business innovation and transformation projects: The Profile and Education of a Business Transformation Manager - An enterprise architecture approach (Trad, & Kalpić, 2014c).
- Organizational and Digital Transformation Projects-A Mathematical Model for Building Blocks based Organizational Unbundling Process (Trad, 2023d). Where The Unbundling Process (UP) that is followed by a Refinement Process (RP) (simply Disassembling) are Project's critical phase.
- … and many others.

This RDP localized an important research gap that is mainly due to the fact that there isn't: 1) Any identical Polymathic approach to a Project and PRWC4AI; 2) XHFRs; 2) No existing mixed-method; 3) Only Tangible objectives; 4) Concrete FMS and Factors that link to AI-fields; 5) Unifying AI concepts; and 6) CSA Decision Tables (CSA_DT) processing capabilities, as shown in Figure 4.

Figure 4. The FMS based PRWC/PRWC4AI that processes CSA_DTs

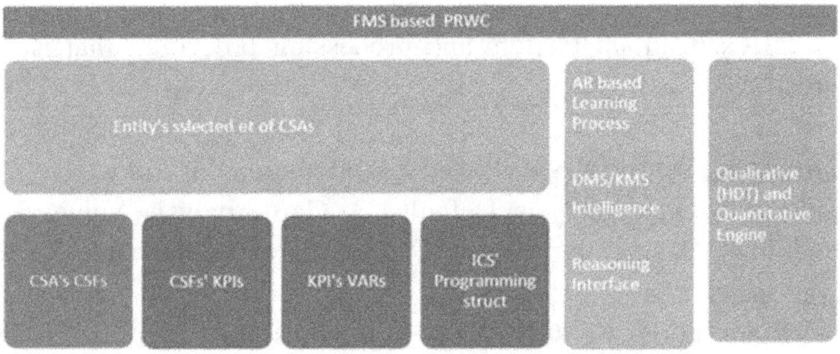

RDP's related Proof of Concept (PoC) uses the following Applied Case Studies (ACS): 1) The insurance domain (Jonkers, Band, & Quartel, 2012a), which is used for ICS, modelling, and EA topics; and 2) PoCs from previous works. An RDP has to setup the PRWC4AI a set(s) of Enumerators (PRWCE), which for this chapter has the following values: 1) Proven (that is equal to 10); 2) Possible (that is equal to 8 or 9); 3) Feasible (that is equal to 7 or 6); 5) Complex (that is equal to 5); 6) Very_Risky (that is equal to 3 or 4); 7) Very_Complex (that is equal to 1 or 2); and 8) Failure (that is equal to 0). Enumerators are to be used in all chapter's CSA/CSA_DT processing and resulting findings.

RDP's Pattern

This chapter like all the author's works use the same pattern which has the following sections (Trad & Kalpić, 2020a):

- An introductory part that explains the overall subject related to the phase's RQ.
- The RDP part that explains the research RQ and concept(s).
- The ACS and PoC related to the final experiment.
- The AI-fields, ICS, ADM, decision making system, represent sections in the work's RQ specific context and integration.
- A specialized part, like in this case is the AI-fields/PRWC4AI.
- Each part (or CSA) contains a table of selected and weighted Factors.
- The conclusion and recommendations that summarizes and concludes the research work.

The RDP CSA/CSA_DT Processing and Resulting Findings

For this CSA's resultant Factors and processing procedure that is shown in Figure 4, are:

- The resultant set of CSA's related CSFs are: 1) Innovative_Concept_Feasibility; 2) Gap_Analysis_Defaults; 3) Gap_Analysis_Value; 5) Mixed_Methodology_Basics; 6) Mixed_Methodology_HDT; and 7) IHIPTF's integration.
- The resultant set of CSF's related KPIs that has the form of an PRWCE.
- The resultant set of KPI's related VARs are: 1) Innovative_Concept_Feasibility_VAR; 2) Gap_Analysis_Defaults_VAR; 3) Gap_Analysis_Value_VAR; 5) Mixed_Methodology_Basics_VAR; 6) Mixed_Methodology_HDT_VAR; and 7) IHIPTF_Integration_VAR. All these VARs are concrete ICS application variables, like for example Mixed_Methodology_Basics_VAR Microsoft's C# language structure as shown in Figure 5 which is a concrete programming structure:

Figure 5. The Mixed_Methodology_Basics_VAR structure

```
    public struct Mixed_Methodology_Basics_VAR
    {
        public Mixed_Methodology_Basics_VAR(
                                            int       MethodologyType,
                                            int       MethodologyStat
                                          )
        {
                ….
        }
        public int cMethodologyType { get; }
        public int cMethodologyStat { get; }
        public string ToString() =>
$"({cMethodologyType},{cMethodologyStat})";
    }
```

The structure will be presented only for this CSA and not for other CSAs.

Table 1. The CSA_DT outcome is 9.20

CSA's CSFs	Related KPIs	Weightings
CSF_RDP_Polymathic_Innovative_Concept	Proven	From 1 to 10. **10 Selected**
CSF_RDP_Gap_Analysis_Defaults	Proven	From 1 to 10. **10 Selected**
CSF_RDP_Gap_Analysis_Values	Complex	From 1 to 10. **08 Selected**
CSF_RDP_Mixed_Methodology_Basics_EERM	Feasible	From 1 to 10. **09 Selected**
CSF_RDP_Mixed_Methodology_Basics_HDT	Feasible	From 1 to 10. **09 Selected**
CSF_RDP_IHIPTF_PRWC4AI	Feasible	From 1 to 10. **09 Selected**

valuation

This CSA_DT uses the defined CSFs and KPIs, as shown in Table 1 that is 9.20 that corresponds to "Mature". The details on how the CSA_DT was processed in the AHMM and PRWC4AI CSAs/sections. A Project is made of many Phases and CSAs, and the first CSA is to establish the Project's BTPAPs (simply Team, that includes other types of specialists).

THE TEAM'S ROLE

Managing Complexities

Project's complexities lie in the transformation of the Legacy AI/ICS heterogenous components to offer an agile, secured, and unbundled AI/ICS. The PRWC4AI is used by the Team to evaluate Project's GAPA (or statuses) and the usage of EA methodologies, and Team's AI-capacities and skills. The author's previous RDP related articles and works, have localized an important research gap related to Projects; that is mainly due to XHFR. And the main reason for such XHFRs is the Polymathic capabilities in management and coordination of Projects, that needs the role and profile of the Architect of Adaptive Business Information System (AofA-BIS). These crucial Project profiles are today represented by business managers profiles (basically financial accountants), which is the main reason for XHFRs (Trad, & Kalpić, 2021a).

Needed AI and Common Skills, and Polymathics

Projects need knowledge related to structure, design, develop and implement effective solutions and to enhance ARbLP based ELPs (Crittenden, 2005). Complex Projects' managers need to coordinate Polymathic Teams who are capable of developing and integration of needed modules (Satterlee, 1996). The Project Team needs cross-functional/Polymathic AI-skills that is based on common (or generic skills) and the capability to quickly getting specialized in needed domains. This characteristic can be found in limited number of Team members and people in general. Polymathic skills can be built on a variant of *Technocrat's* profile; that includes: 1) AI-Fields; 2) Lean architectures and Integrated Development Environments (IDE); 3) AI-Fields integration, 4) Agile Project Management (APM), 5) Coordination of AI/ICS engineers; and 6) PRWC4AI calibration. AI/Intelligence supports the Team and its APM.

APM's Application and a Polymathic Team Profiles

Figure 6. BTPAP's specific skills (The Open Group, 2011d)

IT Architect Roles	Architecture Board Member	Architecture Sponsor	IT Architecture Manager	IT Architecture Technology	IT Architecture Data	IT Architecture Application	IT Architecture Business	Program or Project Manager	IT Designer
Enterprise Architecture Skills									
Business Modeling	2	2	4	3	3	4	4	2	2
Business Process Design	1	1	4	3	3	4	4	2	2
Role Design	2	2	4	3	3	4	4	2	2
Organization Design	2	2	4	3	3	4	4	2	2
Data Design	1	1	3	3	4	3	3	2	3
Application Design	1	1	3	3	3	4	3	2	3
Systems Integration	1	1	4	4	3	3	3	2	2
IT Industry Standards	1	1	4	4	4	4	3	2	3
Services Design	2	2	4	4	3	4	3	2	2
Architecture Principles Design	2	2	4	4	4	4	4	2	2
Architecture Views & Viewpoints Design	2	2	4	4	4	4	4	2	2
Building Block Design	1	1	4	4	4	4	4	2	3
Solutions Modelling	1	1	4	4	4	4	4	2	3
Benefits Analysis	2	2	4	4	4	4	4	4	2
Business Inter-working	3	3	4	3	3	4	4	3	1
Systems Behavior	1	1	4	4	4	4	3	3	2
Project Management	1	1	3	3	3	3	3	4	2

The BTPAP's specific skills (and characteristics) contains also how to integrate the APM in EA's roadmap and Transformation Development Methodology's (TDM) paradigm, and to and Gartner claims that, "the ability to apply versatile and extensive methodological skills in managing business processes is the number one business priority for successful entrepreneurial activities". Project's main difficulties lie in its duration that can be many years… One of the main complexities is how synchronize the APM and the Disassembling of the legacy AI/ICS (Farhoomand, Lynne, Markus, Gable, & Khan, 2004; Trad, & Kalpić, 2021a). APM's integration includes: 1) AI-Fields and Business Processes (BP) and their Models (BPM) implementation; 2) Automated Project's processes (Krigsman, 2008); 3) APM's interfaces to TDM and other; 4) Unification of AI processes; and Intelligence; 5) Separating AI, EA and APM tasks and responsibilities… Therefore, the Project Team needs Polymathic AI and common-skills as shown in Figure (The Open Group, 2011d; Trad, & Kalpić, 2021a).

Managing the Continuum, Repository, and Reference Models

The Team has the responsibility that includes architectural design and documentation at a technical reference model level; and the main types of architects are (The Open Group, 2011d): 1) Leading a Industry Architects groups; 2) System Architect has the responsibility for architectural design and documentation; 3) Industry Architect has the responsibility for EA/TDM design; and 4) Organization Architect has the responsibility for architectural design of a specific Entity.

The TEAM CSA Processing and Findings

This CSA_DT uses the defined Factors, as shown in Table 2, and the result is 8.5 that corresponds to "Risky". The Project starts with UP and RP (simply Disassembling).

Table 2. The CSA_DT outcome is 8.5

Critical Success Factors	AHMM4CBB enhances: KPIs	Weightings
CSF_Team_Managing_Complexities	Complex	From 1 to 10. **08 Selected**
CSF_Team_AI_Common_Polymathics	Feasible	From 1 to 10. **09 Selected**
CSF_Team_APM	Complex	From 1 to 10. **08 Selected**
CSF_Team_IHIPTF_TDM	Feasible	From 1 to 10. **09 Selected**

valuation

DISASSEMBLING PHASE

Disassembling Entity's Legacy

Figure 7. Disassembling based project's approach (Trad, 2023d)

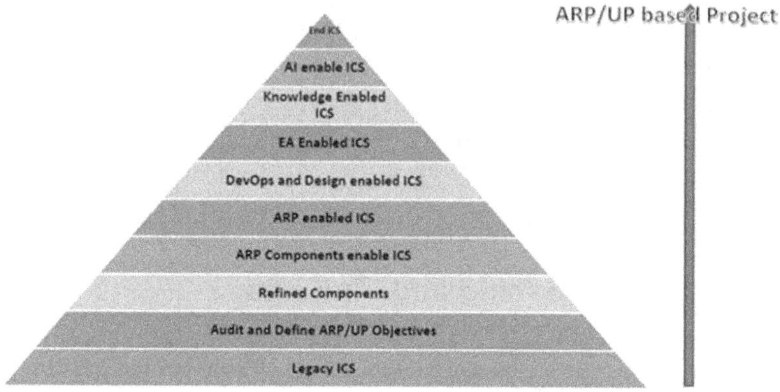

Projects are complex and have XFHRs because they depend on Composite BBs (CBB). CBBs are created by Disassembling process. Where Organizational UP (OUP) is a sequential set of Disassembling processes that transform the Entity's: Legacy AI/ICS structure, ICS' administration, Assets/Resources, Applications/Services, BPMs, and Internal/external collaboration models. Disassembling processes, as shown in Figure 6, deliver a pool of heterogenous CBBs that are (re)used to build Architectural BBs (ABB). Disassembling (that is Automated RPs-ARP) faces difficulties because of the following facts: 1) Entity's heterogenous legacy environments and various types of resistances that are related to: Human profiles/cultures, ICS different viewpoints, financial ambitions, and Project's limited time/budgets; 2) Projects' innovation methods are monopolized for achieving only immediate tangible financial goals, and this the main reason for XHFRs; and 3) Difficulties in interfacing the PRWC4AI. The Disassembling Strategy is the Project's first and major step and if it faces the XHFR then the Disassembling should restart, until it delivers the Entity's pool of refined BBs and a central Entity's Polymathic Dictionary and Glossary (EPDG) (Trad, 2023d).

The EPDG

Figure 8. EPDG's components (Shrivastava, 2023)

Implementing the EPDG in an IHIPTF and Entity offers (Shrivastava, 2023):

- Better chances for success and especially in TDM's activities as shown in Figure 8.
- Improves BPMs coherent developments.
- Optimized common data and terms vocabulary that is needed for business and common definitions.
- A data catalog that enables common vocabulary for development processes.
- Collections of related terms, definitions, and other properties; defined with an IHIPTF and PRWC4AI conventions.

A defines a common Project's language, clears, and defines governance/quality standards.

The Pool of Refined AI and Common CBBs

Projects refined CBBs (and ABBs), use existing AI and common services' architecture frameworks and standards; and they are managed by the TDM which synchronizes Disassembling processes. ABBs are existing templates that are used for instantiating Solution BBs (SBB) that is APplication Domains' (APD) agnostic. The TDM uses The Open Group's (TOG) Architecture Framework (like TOGAF that includes a generic BBs, CBBs, ABBs, and SBBs guidelines that (The Open Group, 1999): 1) Manage packages, functionalities…; 2) Standardizes interfaces that can used for the AI-Fields/PRWC4AI; 3) Supports interoperability; 4) AI/ICS awareness; 5) Uses TDM to manage CBBs and BBs as shown in Figure 9.

Figure 9. TOGAF's BBs are managed (The Open Group, 1999)

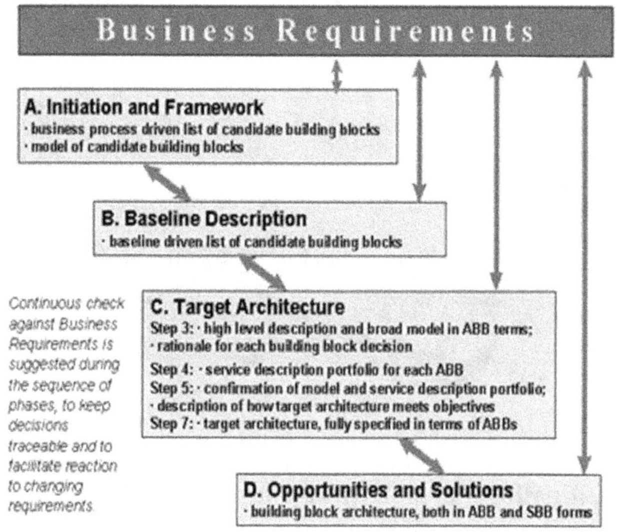

Entity's Reference Models

Figure 10. The TRM's services' categories (The Open Group, 2011c)

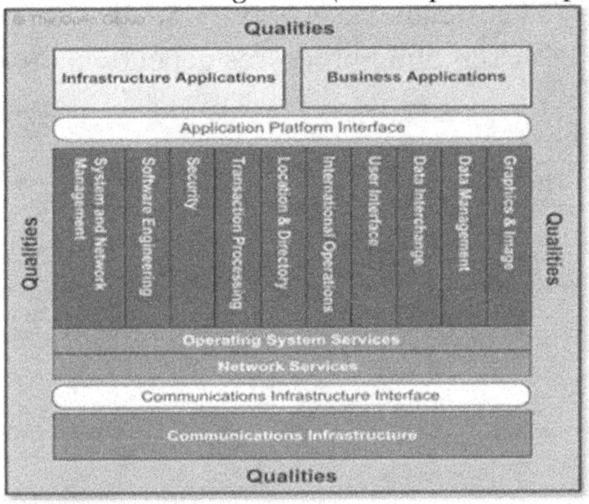

The TDM uses the Technical Reference Model (TRM) that offers a generic concept for CBBs and its services, which makes them interoperable, as shown in Figure 9. CBBs and services' interoperability are ensured by the communications Infrastructure and is leveraged by the transformed ICS. The The MDTCAS offers the common methodological language the "1:1" mapping concept. The TDM depends on requirements, CBBs/BBs, and ABBs that are based on refined services, interfaces, and standards (The Open Group, 2011c). Where Disassembling activities for (Trad, 2023d): 1) Breaking-down legacy components into a set of classified CBBs/BBs; 2) Simplifies the implementation phase and PRWC4AI's interfacing; 3) Aligns CBBs/BBs by using the "1:1" mapping concept; and 4) Enables the development of IHIPTF patterns, templates, and models.

Disassembling Models and Procedures

Disassembling extracts APD and standard/common resources and models that are included in the MDTCAS that can include (Trad, 2023d): 1) Object Management Group's (OMG) Decision Making Notation (DMN) that can be used for modeling operational decisions like in (RedHat, 2022; The Open Group, 2021): 1) Adapting BPMs; 2) CSA_DTs evaluations; and 3) Supporting Disassembling to deliver needed artefacts.

The Disassembling CSA Processing and Findings

This CSA_DT uses the defined Factors, as shown in Table 3 that is 8.25 that corresponds to "Risky". The details on how the CSA_DT was processed in the PR-WC4AI section. The Disassembling processes depend on the established PEMM.

Table 3. The CSA_DT outcome is 8.25

Critical Success Factors	AHMM4CBB: KPIs	Weightings
CSF_Disassembling_Legacy_Transformation	Feasible	From 1 to 10. **09 Selected**
CSF_Disassembling_EPDG	Mature	From 1 to 10. **10 Selected**
CSF_Disassembling_CBB_BB_ABB	VeryComplex	From 1 to 10. **07 Selected**
CSF_Disassembling_Reference_Models	Complex	From 1 to 10. **08 Selected**

valuation

THE PEMM

Basics

There are many ways how to build a PEMM and that depends on the Entity's ICS structure. A PEMM is the an Entity (and Projects') point of reference and that establishes a method on how to avoid commercial-only ICS/AI products, promotes XHFRs detection, and the synchronization of activities. To build a PEMM there is the need to (Trad, & Kalpić, 2020a, 2020b; Trad, 2023e): 1) Implement an EPDG, IHIPTF, PRWC4AI, TDM, and MDTCAS; 2) Implementing AHMM4AI; 3) Use Entity's (and external) data-sources like Relational Data Bases (RDB) and Entity RDBs (ERDB) as shown in Figure 12; 3) An Asset Management System (AMS); and other.

Figure 11. The ERDB based PEMM (Trad, 2023e)

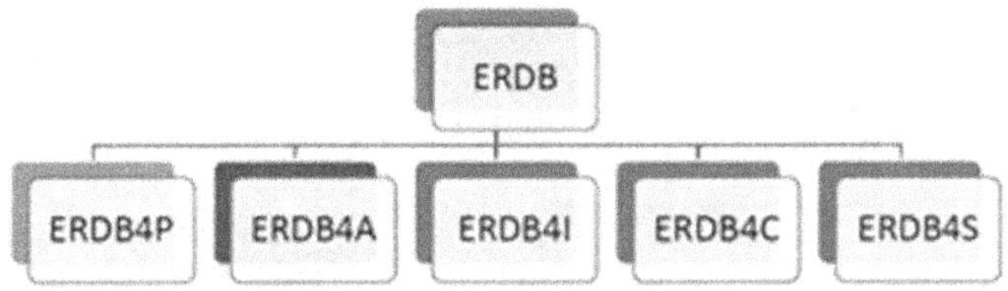

Where the ERDB is the basis of Intelligence that needs Entity Meta-Base (EMB) for storage purposes.

The EMB

Figure 12. The EDM (Google 2022a)

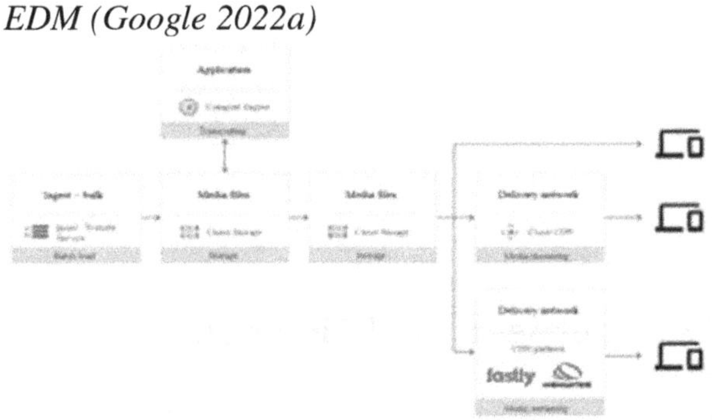

The IHIPTF (like IHIPTF) and uses an EMB that can use the ERDB or any other support to support persistence and cross-Entity checking activities (Codd, Codd, and Salley 1993; IBM, 2022), as shown in Figures 11 and 12. Besides the popular ERDB the EMB can use: 1) An AMS that integrates various types of subsystems like the: Information Technology AM (ITAM), Hardware AM (HAM), and Software AM (SAM); 2) External/Commercial environments like the Enterprise Data Management (EDM) as shown in Figure 12. The EMB is supported by the PEMM.

The PEMM Construct

The PEMM which is the Entity's and Projects' ultimate reference model, supports all IHIPTF modules and its development follows the Dissembling phase; but this is a circular process where the CBBs, AHMM, and PEMM evolve together. Complex models like HDT related modules use the PEMM to link the PRWC4AI (Schmelzer, 2021; Della Croce, T'kindt 2002).

Figure 13. The PEMM

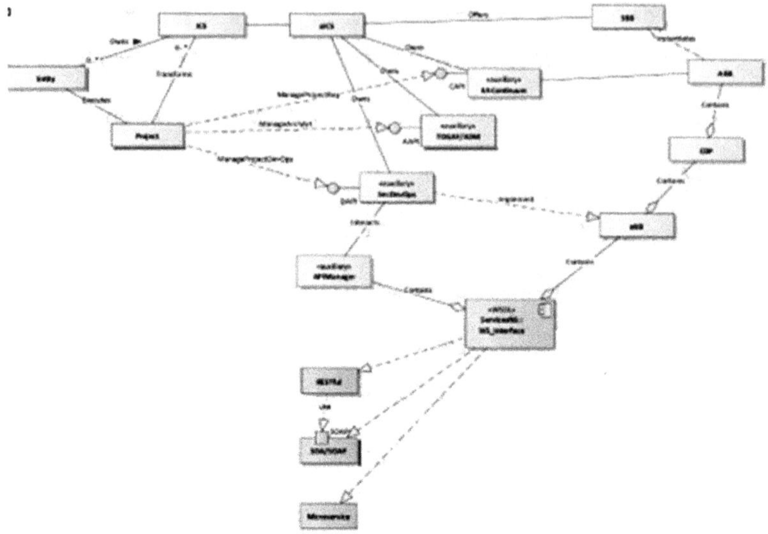

The PEMM CSA Processing and Findings

This CSA_DT uses the defined Factors, as shown in Table 4 that is 8.25 that corresponds to “Risky”. The PEMM depend on the FMS’ integration.

Table 4. The CSA_DT outcome is 8.25

Critical Success Factors	KPIs	Weightings
CSF_PEMM_Basics	Complex	From 1 to 10. **08 Selected**
CSF_PEMM_EMB	Possible	From 1 to 10. **09 Selected**
CSF_PEMM_Relate_Disassembling	VeryComplex	From 1 to 10. **07 Selected**
CSF_PEMM_Construct	Possible	From 1 to 10. **09 Selected**

valuation

THE SET OF FACTORS AND THE FMS' INTEGRATION

Integrating Factors

The FMS can integrate various levels of Projects' risks and the FMS is based on CSAs, where (Myers, Pane, & Ko, 2004; Neumann, 2002; Trad, & Kalpić, 2018a): 1) Each CSA corresponds to an Entity APD or common domain, like for example, logistics; 2) Each CSF maps to a set of requirements and problems, like for example, accounting activities; and 3) Each KPI corresponds to a unique Entity's ICS item that is linked a VAR. Entity's FMS and ICS' libraries and resources are synchronized by the TDM (Lankhorst, 2009). A Factor is evaluated and mapped to the PRWC4AI that is initially estimated in the first TDM iteration and then tuned through all the TDM's iterations (Morrison, 2016). Once the initial set of CSFs has been identified, then the *Project* can use the FMS to tune the next iterations' CSFs. The FMS cyclically links to Project's: Requirements, Architecture blueprints, Intelligence items, ICS components, and aligns CBBs (Syynimaa, 2015). This work is based on empirical engineering models. The proposed FMS delivers a set of Factors that are aligned with IHIPTF's objectives and main constructs like the CSA (Trad & Kalpić, 2018a).

The CSAs

Figure 14. Intelligence subsystem that contains CSAs' information

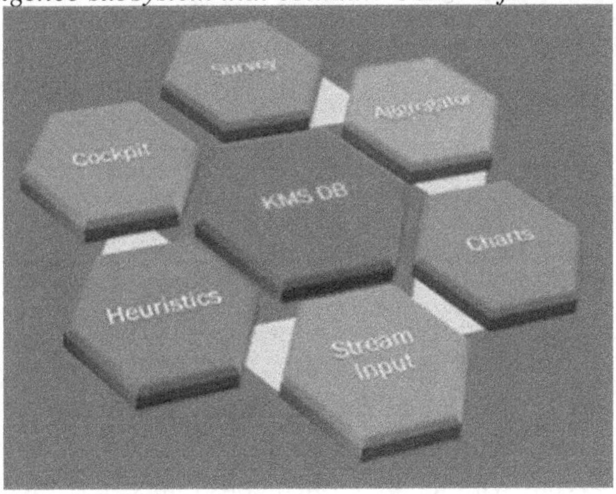

IHIPTF's repository contains and maps to Project's selected CSAs (which in turn map to CSFs, and other types of Project's Intelligence resources, like services, architecture models, requirements) as shown in Figure 14. The CSA maps to CSFs and other Project's resources is supported by the TDM (The Open Group, 2011a; Trad, & Kalpić, 2018a). A Project contains sets of Factors that are selected in the Project's initial/vision phase, where CSAs have: 1) A static view has a similar static structure like the relational model's structure that relates sets of CSAs and CSFs; knowing that integrity checks can applied on them (Lockwood, 1999).

The CSFs

A CSF is a set of integrated KPIs, and a KPI related/maps to a unique Project requirement and/or problem type as shown in Figure 16. The Project Team identifies the initial set of Factors to be managed by the FMS (Peterson, 2011).

Figure 15. The architecture method's interaction

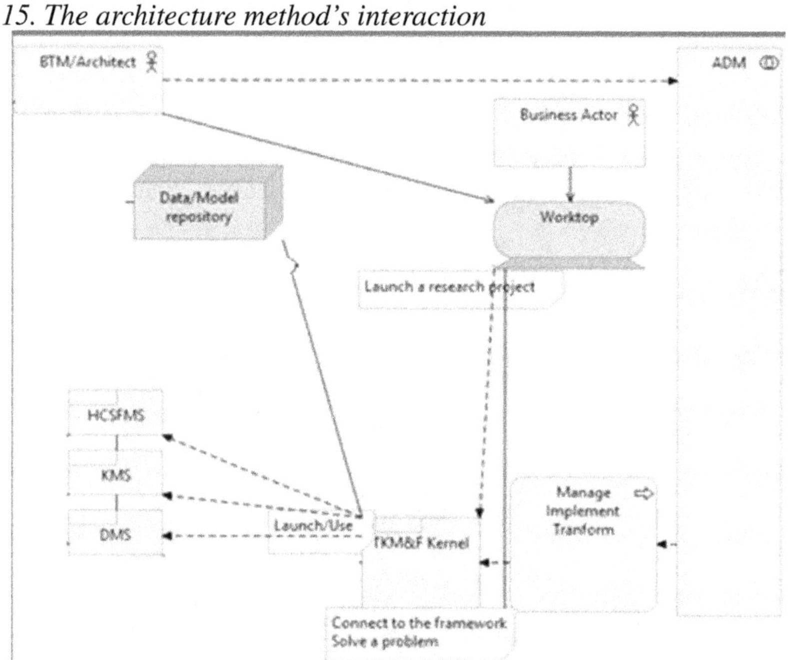

Therefore, CSFs are important for the mapping between the problem types, Intelligence constructs, and other Entity's items and resources. A CSFs reflects a Project problem types with its predefined constraints. The PRWC4AI evaluates performances of CSAs, where CSFs (their corresponding KPIs and VARs) can be internal or external to the frameworks, like (Trad & Kalpić, 2018a, 2020a; Visual Paradigm, 2019): 1) A Project problem type or GAPA is an internal CSF; 2) Intelligence is a real-time engine that uses Factors that correspond to problem type solution(s). The TDM manages the Project's iterations and FMS' interactions; 3)

TDM's preliminary phase selects Factors and sets up the PRWC4AI; 4) The TDM vision and business architecture phases calibrates PRWC4AI's constraints and Objective Functions (OF); 5) ICS' (technology) architecture phase selects technology's sets of Factors; and 6) TDM's requirements management (and test) phase use the PRWC4AI for the evaluation of Factors like KPIs.

The KPIs and VARs

A CSF is a set of KPIs, and a KPI related/maps to a unique Project requirement and/or problem type(s). FMS's default CSFs/KPIs need a detailed PRWC4AI interaction, where a KPI is used for the mapping between Project's objectives, business requirements, VARs, organisational structure (Putri & Yusof, 2009).

Figure 16. The relations between ADM's phases and FMS/factors

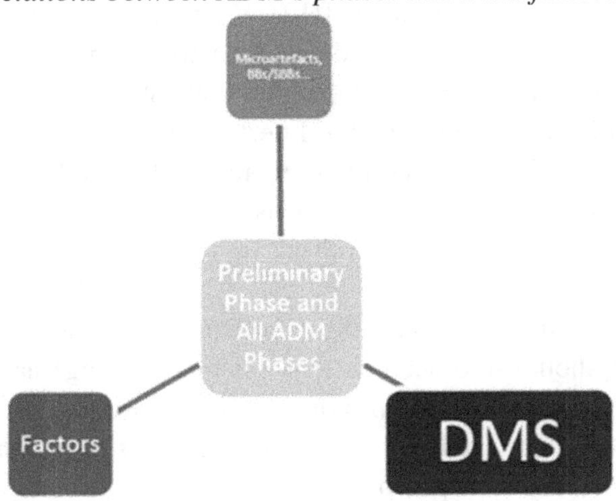

A Project establishes and links initial sets of Factors that is a complex process and that is based on:

Analysis = $\sum$ Factors, abstracts the risk and GAPA on the level of a Project.

Factors = $\sum$ CSAs, abstracts the risk and GAPA on the level of a subsystem or a sub-Project or APD.

CSA = $\sum$ CSFs, abstracts the risk and GAPA on the level of a APD component or topic.

CSF = $\sum$ KPIs, abstracts the risk and GAPA on the level of an CBBs/BBs based SBB or a bundle of services.

KPI = $\sum$ Variables (VAR), abstracts, and attributes of a ICS service(s).

The symbol $\sum$ relates to processing of a series of Project of transformational equations, and not to the definition of ***sumof***.. Decisions based on GAPA(s) for formulating a Project's strategy and status, are based on the analysis of the external and internal CSAs and hence CSFs and KPIs (and VARs). CSFs and KPIs are key elements in Projects and their planning. A CSA is a category (or set) of CSFs where in turn a CSF is a set of KPIs, where a KPI maps (or corresponds) to a single requirement and/or software artefact or a service, where a service can be Service Oriented Architecture (SOA) or Micro Services Architecture (MSA) based. For a Project requirement, feature, or problem type, the Team selects Factors that can interface high-level environments/methods like the Strengths, Weaknesses, Opportunities, Threats (SWOT) as shown in Figure 17 (Trad, & Kalpić, 2018a).

Factors Patterns and Rules

Factors pattern(s) are persisted in IHIPTF's repository and are used by the PRWC4AI because they offer: 1) Predefined Factors to be used by Intelligence; 2) Defined responsibilities, relationships, and content; 3) Relationships between CBBs; 4) Default Factors' values; and 5) Interfaces to PRWC4AI and FMS' rules. A Project starts with TDM's initial phase which is also the feasibility's checking phase. This phase checks if the Project is feasible and the possibilities of XHDRs. The FMS offers the following rules to check Factors (Trad, & Kalpić, 2018a):

- R1:' checking which evaluates their credibility and that can be done by the Team. That should into account that existing rankings are less important. References refer to various types of literature and other resources which are linked to CSFs. The credibility of these references is estimated by KPI that are related to Project requirements. References are empirically weighted as follows (Azadfallah, 2018): 1) The Team's or researcher's experiences that add up to 20% of the estimation's value; 2) Existing statistical checkers like Gartner, Forester and others make 20% of the estimation's value; 3) Various company's and specialists surveying that is 20% of the estimation's value; 4) Factors resultant from application-sources' prototyping that is 20% of the estimation's value; and 5) Using a PoC and Project's statuses build the final 20% of the estimation's value.
- R2: Projects result in organisational changes and these changes' success is measured by Factors by using GAPA or similar concepts.
- R3: Applied modelling language which change in the diagrams and artefacts can help the estimation.
- R4: The Meta-Model which change in the diagrams and artefacts can help the estimation.

- R5: The TDM which is mature and the diffs between phases can help the estimation.
- R6: If the aggregations of all Project's CSA_DTs are positive and exceed the defined minimum, the Project continues to its PoC (or phase 2) where can try to solve problems.

Where there are many Factors dedicated to AI-Fields and PRWC4AI (Merhi, 2023).

The Factors and FMS CSA Processing and Findings

This CSA_DT uses the defined Factors, as shown in Table 5 that is 8.5 that corresponds to "Risky".

Table 5. The CSA_DT outcome is 8.50

Critical Success Factors	KPIs	Weightings
CSF_FMS_Integration	Mature	From 1 to 10. **10 Selected**
CSF_FMS_Factors	Possible	From 1 to 10. **09 Selected**
CSF_FMS_ICS_VARs	Complex	From 1 to 10. **08 Selected**
CSF_FMS_Patterns_Rules	Complex	From 1 to 10. **08 Selected**

valuation

THE AHMM

The Model's Basics

The model has a composite structure and content that can be viewed as follows:

- The statical view, which shows definitions, artefacts, and relationships.
- The behavioral view, which is an instance of the statical view.
- Is the skeleton of the IHIPTF and its modules like the PRWC4AI.
- Defines the interface to external frameworks.
- Defines a Quantitative-Qualitative Research Mixed Model (QQRMM).

The QQRMM

The initial set of Project problem types and their selected/related Factors are initialized in TDM's preliminary phase (or initial iteration). Then, IHIPTF's HDT inputs various sets like: Constraints, Rules, Data-sets, Configurations, and other, which are stored in IHIPTF's repository. The use of simplistic quantitative analysis, is very limited and there is the need for a qualitative method that enriches the Entity's Learning Process (ELP). The QQRMM based HDT evaluates Projects' problem types and to proactively detects violations to the defined constraints and applied rules. The ARbLP based ELP is suitable for complex Projects, because AR is helpful in education and can be defined as the process of learning and improves the quality of transformational and implementation processes. AR provides the Team with valuable experiences and knowledge improve the ELP and supports the resolving Project problems and PRWC4AI tuning processes. AR uses a systematic process and offers solutions for the problems types, where solutions can include bridging/interfacing the gap between PRWC4AI related theory, recommendations, and practices (Hine, 2013). The QQRMM based HDT and related ARbLP based ELP enhance the transformational model and structure.

The Transformational Model and Structure

The adoption of a holistic, cross-functional, and Polymathic modelling approach, is supported by the AHMM and its AHMM4AI variant, which uses a multi-level Disassembling process. The PRWC4AI identifies and assesses strategic and critical Factors and hence risks in order to support and guaranty Entity's operations' and business coherencies, by using the AHMM4AI, which constitutes its structure. For a given Project and PRWC4AI requirement (or problem type), the AHMM4AI based Intelligence identifies the initial sets of Factors and related sets of actions, to be used by the ARbLP based HDT/ELP. There is an immense lack of a Polymathic-holistic approach to Projects and the PRLR used the following resources: 1) Articles and resources related to Projects, FMS, Factors' evaluations, ICS (re)engineering, AI/HDT, …; 2) The author's RDP/PRLR works, and IHIPTF; 3) Project's and PRWC4AI's feasibility concept; 4) Initial sets of Factors; and 5) RDP's use of the Empirical Engineering Research Model (EERM) (Easterbrook, Singer, Storey, & Damian, 2008). A Polymathic-Mathematical Model (PMM) is a subset of real-world system's behaviours, capabilities, and possibilities, where the PMM is a description of a limited and precisely defined reality, which can be abstracted to support a Project and PRWC4AI (Polderman & Willems, 1998). The AHMM is a PMM variant because:

- A PMM provides abstractions of a real-world of a physical system or module (Hinkelmann, 2016).
- Modelling is a descriptive EA/design process, which validates PMM principles (Sankaralingam, Ferris, Nowatzki, Estan, Wood, & Vaish, 2013).
- The usage of EA, AI, and HDT can be used by an PMM.
- The gap between the PMM based Project's adoption and its usage is still very important today (Syynimaa, 2015).
- An PMM that optimizes Projects by using FMS, Factors, and PRWC4AI (Dogan, Çalgici, Arditi, & Gunaydin, 2015).
- A generic variant of the PMM, is the proposed AHMM4AI (Giachetti, 2012; Kim & Kim, 1999).
- An applied PMM is the description of an Entity, Project, and PRWC4AI, using MMs, and languages (Sankaralingam, Ferris, Nowatzki, Estan, Wood, & Vaish, 2013).
- Multi-criteria or a multi-Factors model for Intelligence needs a QQRMM and ARbLP based ELP (Zandia, & Tavana, 2011).
- An PMM is optimal for an EERM based RDPs (Easterbrook, Singer, Storey, & Damian, 2008).
- The PMM is the base of a Project's Meta-Model (Morawski, 2013).
- The PMM is the base structure for Project's and Entity's Viewpoints.
- AI uses PMM to implement Intelligence (National Academies, 1991).

PMM based Viewpoints and Evaluations

The Requirements Viewpoint "R":

mcREQ = m KPI (R1)
mcMapping mcArtefact/mcREQ = mcArtefact + m mcREQ (R2)
FTR = mcREQ (R3)
PRB = m PRB (R4)
REQ = m CSF = U mcREQ (R5)
REQ = U FTR + U RUL + U CNT + U DIA + U REL (R6)
The Viewpoint "I"":
sMA = $\sum$ aBB + $\sum$ sBB + $\sum$ aMVC (I1)
sBB = $\sum$ UP+ $\sum$ sMA + $\sum$ sOPM (I2)
sCBB = $\sum$ sBB + $\sum$ sABB + $\sum$ SBB (I3)
sIBB = $\sum$ sCBB (I4)
Unit = $\sum$ sIBB (I5)
...
sUnit = $\sum$ sSUPL (I10)

....

WGT € {1 … 10} (B1)
mcENT = U mcArtefact (B2)
OU or Sector = APD[n] (B3)
ENT = U OUs (or Sectors (B4)
CSA(OU or APD) = ∑ CSF (B5)
OU_Element = OU[n or element], € {1 … k} (B6)
CSF(OU_Element) = ∑KPI (B7)
KPI = ∑VAR (B8)
TVR = FUN(VAR/ARG) (B9)
FUN(ARG) = WGTxQNT(ARG) v/& WGTxQLT(ARG) (B10)
CSA(i) = CSF(i)*WGT(i)+ CSF(i+1)*WGT(i+1)+… (B11)
CSF(i) = KPI(i)*WGT(i)+KPI(i+1)*WGT(i+1)+… (B12)
KPI(i) = VAR(i)*WGT(i)+VAR(i+1)*WGT(i+1)+… (B13)
VAR(i) = Call to ICS struct… (B14)
∑ WGT = 1 (or 100% max) (B15)
∑ CSF = 1 (or 100% max) (B16)
∑ KPI = 1 (or 100% max) (B17)
∑ VAR = 1 (or 100% max) (B18)

Basic AHMM's Elements and Artefacts

Figure 17. AHMM's nomenclature (Trad, & Kalpić, 2020a)

Basic Mathematical Model's (BMM) Nomenclature

Iteration	= An integer variable "*i*" that denotes a *Project/ADM iteration*	
microRequirement	= (maps to) KPI	(N1)
CSF	= Σ KPI	(N2)
Requirement	= (maps to) CSF = $\underline{U}$ microRequirement	(N3)
CSA	= Σ CSF	(N4)
microMapping microArtefact/Req	= microArtefact + (maps to) microRequirement	(N5)
microKnowledgeArtefact	= $\underline{U}$ knowledgeItem(s)	(N6)
neuron	= action->data + microKnowledgeArtefact	(N7)
microArtefact / neural network	= $\underline{U}$ neurons	(N8)
microArtefactScenario	= $\underline{U}$ microartefact	(N9)
AI/Decision Making	= $\underline{U}$ microArtefactScenario	(N10)
microEntity	= $\underline{U}$ microArtefact	(N11)
Entity or Enterprise	= $\underline{U}$ microEntity	(N12)
EnityIntelligence	= $\underline{U}$ AI/Decision Making	(N13)
BMM(*Iteration*) as an instance	= EnityIntelligence(*Iteration*)	(N14)

The Generic AHMM's Formulation

AHMM	= $\underline{U}$ ADMs + BMMs	(N15)

AHMM's Application and Instantiation for PRWC

Domain	= PRWC	(N16)
AHMM4(*Domain*)	= $\underline{U}$ ADMs + BMMs(*Domain*)	(N17)

Factors define Project's initial nodes that are defined as vital for its success and targets to be reached. AHMM4AI's basic element are used in PRWC4AI and is IHIPTF's specific model. The AHMM4AI nomenclature is presented in Figure 17:

- The symbol $\sum$ indicates summation of PRWC4AI's actions, denoting the relative importance of the set members selected as relevant. Ratings and weightings as integers ranging in ascending importance from 1 to 10.
- The symbol $\underline{U}$ indicates sets union.
- The AHMM4AI defines the Project and PRWC4AI as models.

The Applied Transformation Mathematical Model

The AHMM4AI is composed of: 1) A static view; 2) A dynamic (or behavioural) view; and 3) A pool of reusable ARbLP based scenarios. The AHMM4AI can be modelled using following formula for Entity Transformation Mathematical Model (ETMM) that abstracts the Project:

AHMM4AI=Weigthing$_1$*AHMM4AI_Qualitative+Weigthing$_2$*AHMM4AI_Quantitative (N18).
AHMM4AI = $\sum$ AHMM4AI for an Project iteration (N19).
ETMM = $\sum$ AHMM4AI instances (N20).

Weigthing$_1$ and Weigthing$_2$ are delivered by the PRWC4AI. ETMM's OF optimization is done by using constraints and extra variables that need to be tuned. These variable (for maximization or minimization) can be, for example: Team's Polymathic capacities, costs, or another Factor. For PRWC4AI's PoC the success will be the main and only constraint and success is quantified as a binary 0 or 1, where the objective function minimizes ETMM's risks and identifies PRWC4AI's efficiency. The ETMM is a combination of used methodologies and AHMM4AI. The AHMM4AI is a part and the skeleton of IHIPTF that used scenarios to support PRWC4AI requests (Kim, & Lennon, 2017). The initialization phase generates PRWC4AI problem types and cross-functional aspects to be analysed by using the PRWC4AI (Agievich, 2014).

The AHMM CSA Processing and Findings

This CSA_DT uses the defined CSFs and KPIs, as shown in Table 6 that is 9.40 that corresponds to "Mature".

Table 6. The CSA_DT outcome is 9.40

Critical Success Factors	KPIs	Weightings
CSF_AHMM4AI_Basics_QQRMM	Proven	From 1 to 10. **10 Selected**
CSF_AHMM4AI_Transformational_Model	Possible	From 1 to 10. **09 Selected**
CSF_AHMM4AI_Elements_Artefacts	Proven	From 1 to 10. **10 Selected**
CSF_AHMM4AI_Viewpoints(I)	Possible	From 1 to 10. **09 Selected**
CSF_AHMM4AI_ETMM	Possible	From 1 to 10. **09 Selected**

valuation

THE PRWC4AI

The Role of the PEMM, AHMM4AI, and PRWC4AI

The MetaModel has the following characteristics:

- Has a static and dynamic form.
- Is AHMM's (and hence AHMM4AI) basic structure and its integrity checker.
- It defines Rules, Constraints, HDT, Intelligence, and other basic structures and their integrity checkers.
- Is FMS' basic structure and its integrity checker. Which ensure that Factors are measurable and mapped to a ratings and weighting.
- It aligns Factors and Project's Unit of Work (UoW) that needs the needed level of granularity and responsibility. There also the need to implement The "1:1" mapping, implementation and classification concept.

The ADM based TDM synchronizes MetaModel's implementation and evolution.

Figure 18. The IHIPTF layers of models

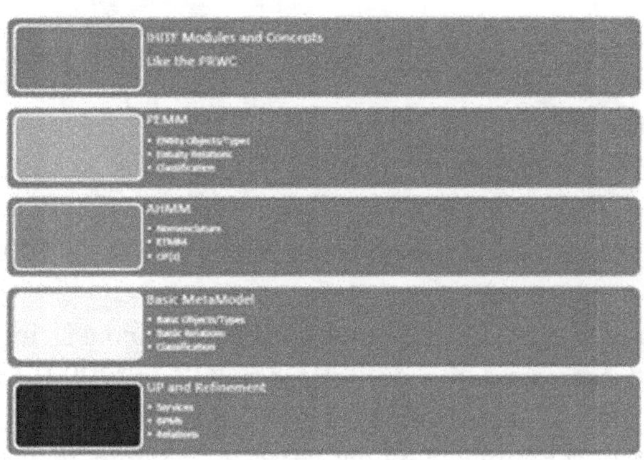

TDM's Role

The TDM manages the Project's implementation phases and PRWC4AI's integration by (Visual Paradigm, 2019):

- The preliminary phase defines the relevant Factors and their weightings.

- The architecture vision and business architecture phases define rules, constraints, and OF(s).
- The information system architecture phase selects the ICS's related Factors.
- The technologies architecture phase selects the technology's related Factors.
- The requirements management and tests phases manage the PRWC4AI based evaluations.

The Project's first phase (or the feasibility phase) uses the PRWC4AI to check the selected Factors (that are stored in CSA_DTs). These checks verify if objectives were reached and proposes a set of next HDT actions.

HDT's Actions

For a Project requirement (or problem type), the IHIPTF identifies the related Factors, to be processes by the HDT based Intelligence. HDT's actions in the form of scenarios are dynamically evaluated (Neumann, 2002). Factors are important for the mapping between the requirements, CBBs, ICS, and Intelligence (Peterson 2011).

A Project can use a standard/commercial PRWC4AI(s) or like in IHIPTF, it builds its own one, which functions as follows:

- The weighting for each CSA is CSA_WGT ϵ { 0.00% … 100.00% } which is a floating point value/percentage values, which are derived from CSA_DT as one CSA_DT and a set of CSFs).
- The selected corresponding weightings to CSF ϵ { 1 … 10 } are fixed integer values.
- The selected corresponding ratings to CSF ϵ { 0.00% … 100.00% } are floating point percentage values.
- A weighting is defined for each PRWC4AI CSF, and a rating for each KPI.
- The selected corresponding ratings for a KPI is KPI_RAT ϵ { 0.00% … 100.00% } and is derived from: 1) An ICS application/module variable(s) (simply VAR); 2) Estimated by the IHIPTF or a domain specialist; or 3) An external concept.
- CSA_WGT = ∑CSF*CSF_WGT.
- CSF_WGT = ∑KPI*KPI_RAT.
- KPI_RAT = ∑VAR*VAR_RAT.

Interfacing the System

It interfaces the system by:

- The AHMM4AI applies the HDT, which uses the PRWC4AI.
- PRWC4AI (Project-iteration i) = ∑CSA*CSA_WGT.
- The AHMM4AI applied a research mixed model, which uses a PRWC4AI.
- Intelligence uses the HDT which is mainly qualitative method and has specific calls to quantitative methods.
- Can use external solutions.

The PRWC4AI can use standard/commercial solutions like:

- The Object Management Group's (OMG) (OMG, 2022): 1) The DMN to support CSA_DTs' evaluations; 2) For implementing business decisions and business rules; and is optimal for Project's status checking; and 3) For HDT's operations.
- The weighted criteria matrix that supports: 1) Intelligence to evaluate Projects; and is based on the evaluation criteria (that has weighted by ratings). By evaluating alternatives based on KPIs with respect to defined criteria; and 2) A decision-making module that evaluates projects based on defined evaluation criteria weighted by ratings.

Interfacing Intelligence and the Evaluation Process

The Intelligence and PRWC4AI use the HDT which is a QQRMM (mainly a qualitative concept that uses targeted quantitative methods). The PRWC4AI needs to be supported by the ARbLP based ELP and Intelligence in order to solve various problem. The PRWC4AI has an objective, to use critical-thinking based concept that combines: 1) ELP; 2) AHMM4AI, and HDT based decision making; 3) FMS; 4) Provides a Polymathic approach; 4) Uses the TDM; and 5) Uses success metrics and rules. The Project's evaluation starts with phase 1 (PHASE_1) called the feasibility phase, which checks if the whole Project is feasible. Then tries to evaluate the success rate using the most important Factors, which are evaluated using the following rules:

- Rule 1: labelled the reference checker, all types of used references, should be credible and are estimated by the author; the notions of official ranking is less important and are ignored.
- PRWC4AI-related references have to be credible and are estimated by the author, Intelligence and have to be conform to IHIPTF's classification concept.
- Rule 2: labelled the change launcher, Projects like GA are the result of *Entity* or organisational changes in regions, the references are evaluated as presented in the previous point (Rule 1).

- Rule 3: labelled the logic checker, an applied modelling language or Natural Language Programming (NLP) for AI (NLP4AI) should be used in a limited manner, in order to make the Project's GA manageable and not too complex.
- Rule 4: labelled the organisational construction, the ADM is considered to be mature, unfortunately that does not mean that Projects' phases are successful and in fact their success rate is very low.
- Rule 5: labelled the Project iteration management, the ADM is appropriate for any *Project's* GA iterative management and interface with IHIPTF's iterations.
- Rule 6: labelled the aggregation phase, if the aggregations of all the Project GA's CSA/CSF tables are positive and exceeds the defined minimum the Project's GA continues to execute the PoC and can be used for a problem solving.
- Project's iterations are the result of evaluated Factors.
- TDM's modelling language capacities and their mappings to KPIs.
- To estimate if the TDM can be used to manage the PRWC4AI and Project, by the use of KPIs.
- The TDM manages IHIPTF's iterations and Factors' tuning.
- If the aggregations of all Project's CSA_DT are positive (the result is stored in the final Table) and exceed the initially defined minimum, then the Project continues to PoC's execution, which uses the selected ACSs.

Evaluating GAPA

GAPA is used to evaluate Project's and its modules performances. Where it can be also used for each Entity's CSA, where CSFs can be: 1) A status for a resource like a requirement; 2) Mapping levels of UP's BBs and PRWC4AI outcomes; 3) GAPAs storage and comparison; 4) TDM phases' synchronization; and 5) HDT based Intelligence requests calls. KPIs relate to VARs from BBs, so HDT's based evaluation processes can automatically estimate the values of CSAs, and CSFs. Therefor, GAPA for:

- For a TDM Iteration (ITR) (G1)
- A Project is done on all CSAs (G2)
- Project(ITR)=CSA(1)*RAT(1)+CSA(2)*RAT(2)+... (G3)
- GAPA(ITR)=Project(ITR)-Project(ITR-1) (G4)
- Risk=$\sum$ GAPA(ITR) (G5)

The PRWC4AI CSA Processing and Findings

Table 7. The CSA_DT outcome is 9.0

Critical Success Factors	KPIs	Weightings
CSF_PRWC4AI_PEMM_AHMM	Complex	From 1 to 10. **08 Selected**
CSF_PRWC4AI_TDM	Possible	From 1 to 10. **09 Selected**
CSF_PRWC4AI_HDT_FMS	Proven	From 1 to 10. **10 Selected**
CSF_PRWC4AI_Intelligence	Possible	From 1 to 10. **09 Selected**
CSF_PRWC4AI_GAPA	Possible	From 1 to 10. **09 Selected**

valuation

This CSA_DT uses the defined Factors, as shown in Table 7 that is 9.0 that corresponds to "Feasible".

THE ADM BASED TDM

Selecting the Viewpoint for the TDM

Projects depend on Entity's structure which needs the application of selected Viewpoint(s) which for this RDP is Viewpoint "M" and "O" is the second one. The TDM synchronizes Project's phases and manages RDP, IHIPTF, PRWC4AI, and the HDT to solve problem types as shown in Figure 19 (Markides, 2011).

Figure 19. ADM's phases (The Open Group, 2011a, 2011b; Holilah, Girsang, & Saragih, 2019)

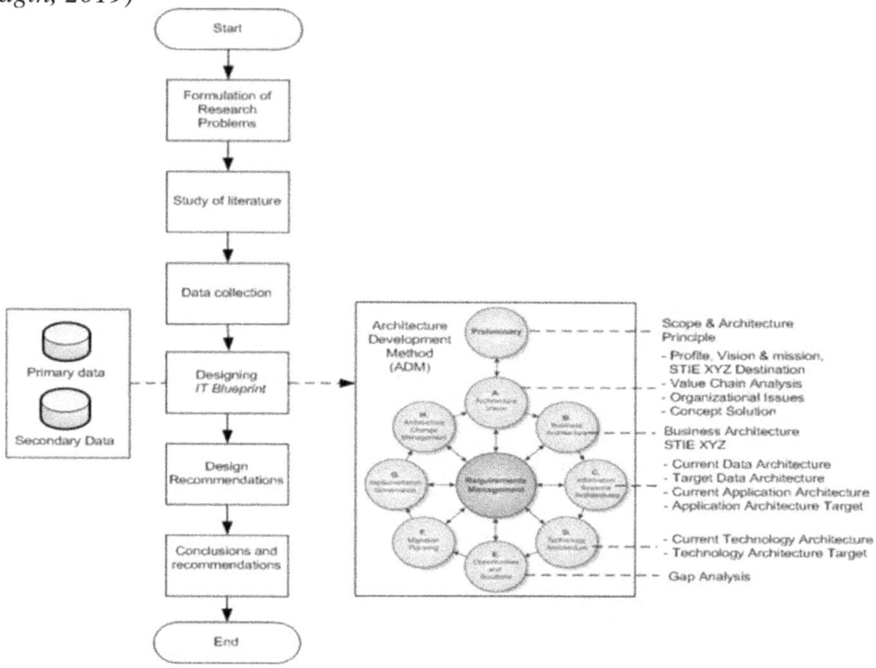

Projects are Polymath which needs cross-functional knowledge and expertise to solve complex APD problems. For modelling the TDM can use existing frameworks like TOGAF/ADM, Unified Modelling Language (UML), or other. Where modelling designs the transformed Entity that includes the PRWC4AI and the TDM manages Project's implementation, and maintenance processes. The TDM supports the PRWC4AI in pointing to the: 1) Right vision(s)/Viewpoint(s); 2) Principles; 3) FMS/Factors; 4) Standards/Frameworks; 5) PEMM and AHMM4AI; 6) Team's skills; 7) GAPA/Intelligence; and 8) MDTCAS and CBBs.

The MDTCAS

The IHIPTF integrates the MDTCAS and TDM to manage CBBs which can be used in APD modelling activities and support a Digital Transformation (DT) (Chaione 2022). The MDTCAS supports UPs to integrate standard methodologies, like TOGAF/ADM. The MDTCAS, as shown in Figure 23, is a mixture of existing methodologies like (Trad, 2023d):

- Legacy methodologies, like the Structure Analysis and Structured Design (SA/SD).
- Object Oriented (OO) Methodology (OOM), UML And ArchiMate.
- The Entity Relationship Diagrams (ERM) for data-modelling.
- DMN that is similar to the PRWC4AI.
- BPM Notation (BPMN).

MDTCAS can use methodologies based on OOM features inherited from three OOM: Rumbaugh, Booch, and Jacobson methodologies (Liu, 2022). The MDTCAS is non-locked-in methodology that supports: 1) The transformation of Mainframe/legacy-code/system to SA/SD models and basic OOM/UML entity-class(es); 2) To transform existing OOM/UML models/diagrams based modules/components to designed/mapped UML/Choreography models, using classes, sequences, communication models, ERM, and BPMN diagrams; 3) Implement the TDM on Spiraled/UML, ADM, DevOps, or other; 4) Use requirements' engineering to specify Use Case (UC), Analysis, Design, Implementation, and Testing diagrams; 5) UCs support the Disassembling process; 6) Assembles refactored CBBs that represent behavior (the functionalities) (Hosiaisluoma, 2022); and 7) Use the PEMM as a reference (Trad, 2023d).

Figure 20. MDTCAS' layers (Trad, 2023d)

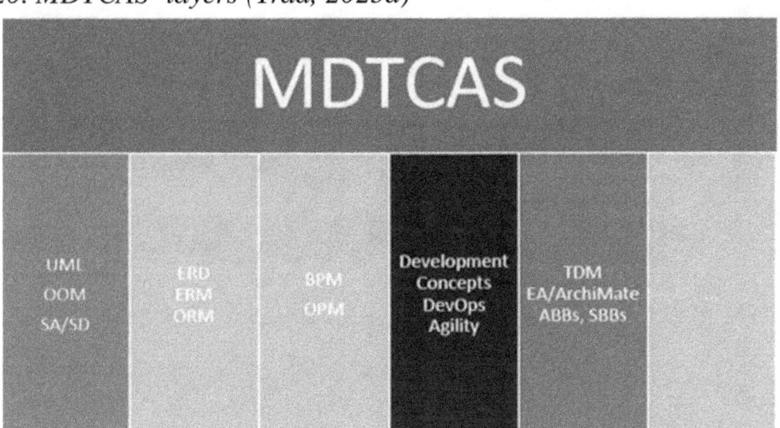

Entity's Cartography and Reference Models

The generation of Entity's EA diagrams, catalogues, and matrixes needs various conditions to be fulfilled first (Trad 2023a):

- The success of the Disassembling process and the establishment of an MDTCAS.
- The establishment of a central a central pool of CBBs.
- Factors to be selected and tuned.
- That the Project is agnostic to any APD and methodology/ICS.
- The EA models and TDM map to Entity's and Project's cartography of applications which are classified.
- Classifications can be done using TOGAF's Application Communication Diagram (ACD).
- The ACD depicts related models and mappings that respect PEMM.
- An ACD represents an existing applications' cartography, or a logical architecture of the transformed ICS.
- A dimension of the applications' cartography should be dedicated to TDM's usage.
- The PEMM supports Entity's application's cartography which part of EA layered concept as shown in Figure 24.
- The EA layered concept includes: Business Architecture; Data Architecture; Application Architecture; and 4) Technology Architecture (Bizzdesign 2022).

Figure 21. EA layered concept

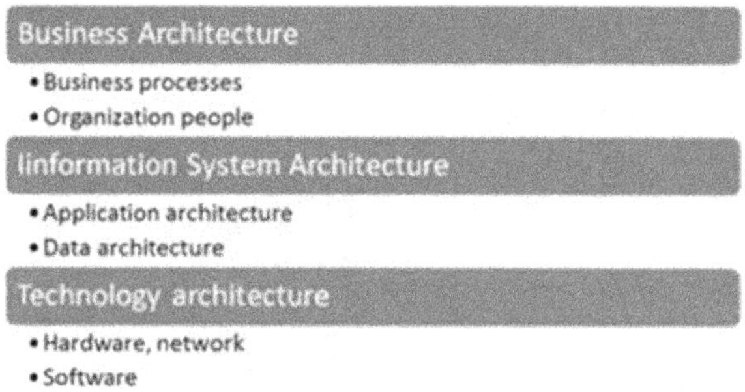

PRWC4AI based Continuous Improvements

The Project can use the PRWC4AI for continuous improvements and ELP enhancements that can include topics like: Evolutive quality, Teams' philosophy, Cross-functional Teams, PEMM as a reference, XHFRs, Governance and renewal, Transformation technics, Linking PRWC4AI to Project's modules, Managers' education ICS' evolutions, Societal changes, Project experiences, … (Satterlee, 1996).

The TDM CSA Processing and Findings

This CSA_DT uses the defined Factors as shown in Table 8 that is 8.75 that corresponds to "Feasible".

Table 8. The CSA_DT outcome is 8.75

Critical Success Factors	KPIs	Weightings
CSF_TDM_Viewpoints	Complex	From 1 to 10. **08 Selected**
CSF_TDM_MDTCAS	Proven	From 1 to 10. **10 Selected**
CSF_TDM_Cartography	Complex	From 1 to 10. **08 Selected**
CSF_TDM_UP_CBBs	Possible	From 1 to 10. **09 Selected**
CSF_TDM_PEMM	Possible	From 1 to 10. **09 Selected**

valuation

INTELLIGENCE

Basics

The FMS and PRWC4AI interface Intelligence which supports complex problem-solving activities. Project's and Intelligence's Polymathic/holistic concepts that is based on the building of complex systems needs a systemic approach (Daellenbach, & McNickle, 2005). The Project and PRWC4AI is supported by Intelligence that is based on various components like the HDT, ELP and other. Intelligence just-in-time solution(s) for pre-defined problem types. Possible solution(s) propose sets of actions, recommendations on changes and their implications. Intelligence integrates the QQRMM, HDT, KMS, and DMS to solve problems and enrich ELPs. PRWC4AI's integration risks' management is an important pre-requisite to finalize a Project (Hussain, Dillon, Chang, & Hussain, 2010).

QQRMM and the Scope

The AHM4PRWC is mainly a qualitative beam-search heuristic tree (Della Croce, & T'kindt, 2002), and in each of its nodes a quantitative call/functions can be executed, with the scopes: 1) Precision or objectivity referring to used data, constraint (or rules); 2) Time (or timestamp) of execution for the tracing system; 3) Space, related to the Entity's space; and 4) Scope of the HDT and hence PRWC4AI.

The HDT uses the IHIPTF NLP4AI that can be used for any APD and in general for hard systems' thinking that integrates scripting subsystem (Moore, 2014). The NLP4AI uses heuristics/rules, EA models QQRMM BBs (Simonin, Bertin, Traon, Jezequel & Crespi, 2010). NLP4AI's are (Clancy, 2019): Efficiency, Simplicity, Less bugs, In-built concurrency constructs, High-level of memory and speed drawbacks, Improves testing…

The HDT

The PRWC4AI is based on the PEMM and AHMM4AI and used FMS to interface the ARbLP/ELP based HDT. The proposed RDP uses the that is indented and is optimal for cautious and evolutive Projects, where AR can be used to improve ELPs (Trad & Kalpić, 2017a; Aksoy, & Ceylan, 2021). The HDT problem-solving process is supported by the ELP based Intelligence. The HDT uses: 1) ANNs that has a set of connected tree-nodes named Artificial Neurons (AN); 2) ELPs based on algorithms; 3) Intelligence is based on a set of AHMM instances based mainly on beam-search based heuristic processing (Della Croce, & T'kindt, 2002); 4) The PRWC4AI support the HDT; 5) AR is as a set of continuous beam-search heuristics processing steps (Järvinen, 2007); 6) Supports fast changes; and 7) The AHMM4AI is responsible for the QQRMM for problem solving and synchronizes a set of AHMM4AI instances that support dynamic tree algorithm, as shown in Figure 22 (Nijboer, Morin, Carmien, Koene, Leon, & Hoffman, 2009) that manages HDT's nodes.

Figure 22. The applied heuristics tree algorithm (Nijboer, Morin, Carmien, Koene, Leon, & Hoffman, 2009)

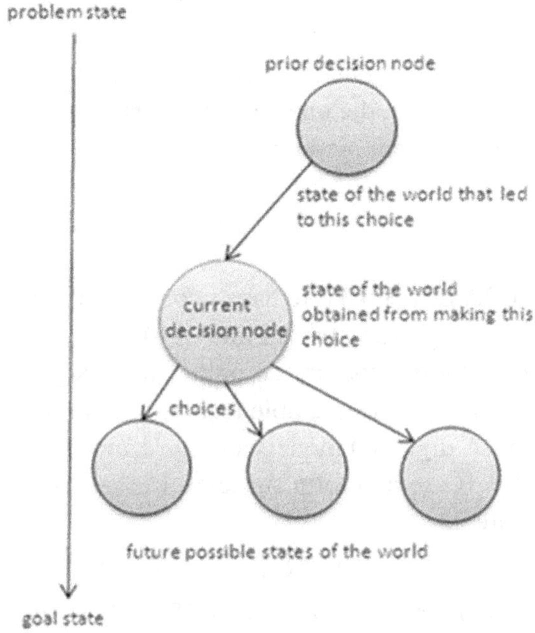

Therefore, ARLP based ELP enables reflective practices that are the basis of a Polymathic/holistic approach to develop Projects and developing an IHI KMS (Leitch, & Day, 2006).

Implementing the IHI KMS and DMS

The ELP manage Entity and Project's Knowledge Items (EPKI) that are related-linked to Entity's/Project's resources and modules like Intelligence. Intelligence supports Entity's KMS which manages EPKIs that are in turn linked to Factors. Intelligence supports Project's enhancements and interfaces the PRWC4AI to evaluate Factors. The KMS identifies the concerned Factors their PRWC4AI evaluation processes. Which also estimates the XHFR (Rockart, 1979). The KMS interfaces the FMS that links a Factor (like a CSF) to one or more EPKI that in turn corresponds to various NLP4AI scenarios. NLP4AI scenarios manage Intelligence's requests and control various IHIPTF activities-actions. The PRWC4AI enables FMS' patterns to enhance-modify the KMS, which delivers information-answers in the form of EPKIs and the needed set of actions. A Project's change request can generate a large set of actions and solutions, which's implementations can generate a new set of problems. A successfully integrated KMS with the FMS can give major advantages in generating automated decision making for dynamic business services' eco-systems (Clark, Fletcher, Hanson, Irani, Waterhouse & Thelin, 2013). Such services are also used by the IHI DMS. The FMS-PRWC4AI based DMS, the Team selects and tunes Factors, which are then orchestrated by the NLP4AI scripts. The DMS is used in all Project's processes which contains sets of Factors that are mapped to CBBs (or sets of actions/services); like the ones that are presented in this chapter's PoC. Intelligence is the most important module for DTs and Projects in general.

DT's Implementation

As shown in Figure 22, DT's goal is to have a common platform of CBBs, BPMs and other artefacts which improve Entity's Time-to-Market (TtM). DTs are strategic objectives but Projects' digitization are complex and have XHFRs (Eira, 2022). The DT uses the PRWC4AI to Disassemble legacy systems and enables the use of TDM, MDTCAS, and EA digitized models and to define DT's scope (Bizzdesign, 2022). A successful DT is the base of a successful Project that needs Polymathic skills as shown in Figure 23.

Figure 23. An APD viewpoint on the rejection of DTs (Eira, 2022)

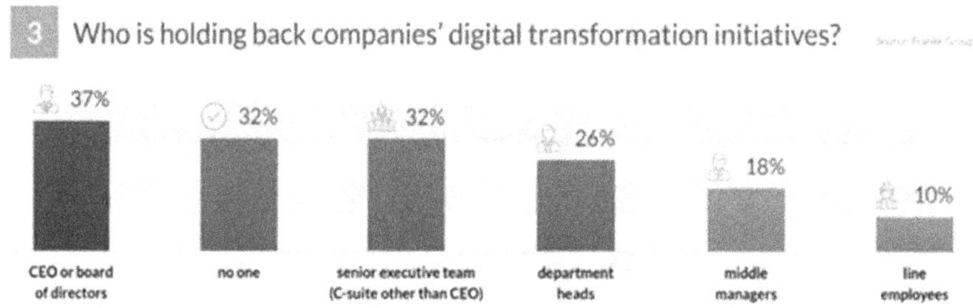

This chapter's section (like this RDP) is an Project CSA, and the PoC is based on PRWC4AI focused ACSs, which are combined with a common EA based ACS that originates from the Open Group (Jonkers, Band, & Quartel, 2012a). The EA based ACS covers Project ICS, EA, modelling, linking KPIs, and basic transformation scenarios.

Figure 24. Four dimensions of cross-functional/polymathic collaboration (Morse, 2020)

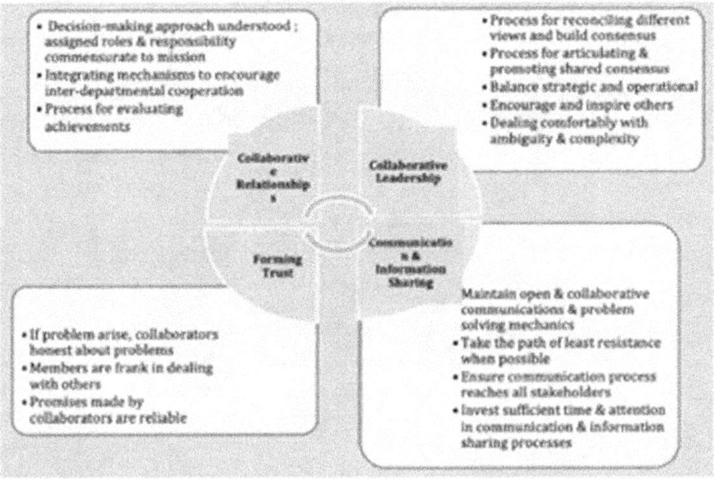

Relevant AI-Fields

The PRWC4AI uses the following AI-Fields and technics:

- An IHI NLP4AI that integrates Factors and their integration with FMS. And the NLP4AI serves as an integration environment for AI-Fields, as shown in Figure 25.
- The IHI ARbLP and HDT which cover Factors heuristics.
- Interfaces Large Language Models (LLM) and Small Language Models (SLM).
- Generative AI (GenAI).

Figure 25. AI-Fields and layers (AIforEducation, 2024)

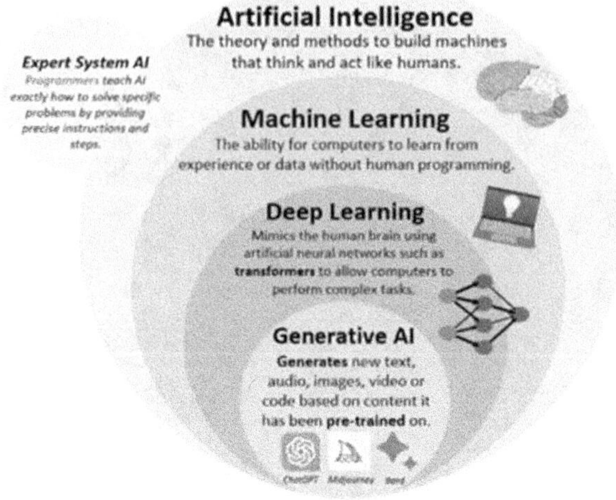

The GAPA

GAPA is done by the DMS which uses the HDT to narrow the Project's gap by using local GAPAs for the: AHMM, FMS-Factors, Pool of CBBs, PEMM-MDTCAS, TDM… The PEMM enables GAPA's execution in various Project's levels, phases, and on various ICS components. GAPA can be done on TDM's phases, to show if there were improvements or regressions.

The Intelligence CSA Processing and Findings

This CSA_DT uses the defined Factors as shown in Table 9 that is 9.25 that corresponds to "Mature".

Table 9. The CSA_DT outcome is 9.25

Critical Success Factors	KPIs	Weightings
CSF_Intelligence_Basics	Proven	From 1 to 10. **10 Selected**
CSF_Intelligence_QQRMM	Proven	From 1 to 10. **10 Selected**
CSF_Intelligence_HDT	Possible	From 1 to 10. **09 Selected**
CSF_Intelligence_DMS_KMS	Possible	From 1 to 10. **09 Selected**
CSF_Intelligence_GAPA	Complex	From 1 to 10. **08 Selected**

valuation

THE PROOF OF CONCEPT

Introduction and ACS

Factors deduced from an ACS, are used in Projects to evaluate success rates and they are managed by a FMS that are used in this PoC, which tries to show how the PRWC4AI estimates Project's success or failure (Lebreton, 1957; Ronald, 1961). The ACS/PoC select and tune Factors with this question in mind: "What are the essential Factors that guaranty success?" (Spencer, 1955). The ACS explains how to manage, register, accept, valuate, and invoice claims related activities (Jonkers, Band, & Quartel, 2012). The ArchiSurance is undergoing a merger where the legacy systems are siloed and use multiple formats and ICS. For this PoC, a holistic approach is tested to structure the sets of Factors and evaluate them with the PRW-C4AI. The transformed ICS has to improve data-quality and Factors evaluations, as shown in Figure 26

Figure 26. Project's transformation goals (Jonkers, Band, & Quartel, 2012)

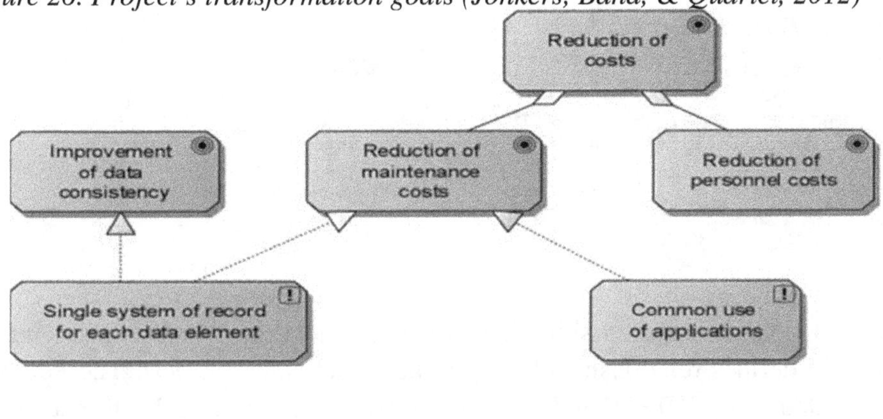

FMS' and TDM's Interactions

The setup of FMS's implementation phases looks as follows:

- phase A or the Architecture Vision phase, establishes an architecture effort and initiates an iteration of the architecture development cycle by setting its objectives/scope, constraints, and goals, which all are translated into sets of Factors for the PoC.

- Phase B or the Business Architecture phase shows how the Project's target architecture implements key requirements and related them to the FMS and PRWC4AI.
- Phase C or the GAPA phase shows and uses the ACD, which shows the modelled target application landscape.
- Phase D or the Target Technology Architecture and GAPA phase shows the final Project's infrastructure.
- Phases E and F, Implementation and Migration Planning; the transition architecture proposes possible intermediate situation and evaluates (with the PRWC4AI) the Project's status using defined Factors.

Evaluating RDP's CSA_DTs

The PRWC4AI interfaces the Intelligence and its Factors which are presented and evaluated in Table 10, and using the CSA_DT's Tables Weighting and Rating Enumerator (CTWRE) that is shown in Figure 27.

Figure 27. The CTWRE's values

CTWRE Label	Limit's Value	Description	Color
Proven, Mature	9.01-10.00	Success	Green
Possible, Feasible	8.51-9.00	Success	Green
Risky	8.01-8.50	Important Risk	Yellow
Complex	7.01-8.00	Unclear	Red
VeryComplex	5.01-7.00	Will probably fail	Red
Impossible	0.00-5.00	Failure	Red

The PRWC4AI-required skills have mappings to Project's resources and the PRWC4AI defines relationships between the Project and Projects. The PoC was implemented using IHIPTF and the initial activity was to setup Factors, then the scripting interface was launched to implement the needed programs to process the Factors/CSAs. After initializing IHIPTF*'s* client, Factors/CSFs were linked to a specific node of the ARbLP/HDT. The programs linked the AHMM4AI instance to the set of HDT/Intelligence actions which uses Intelligence actions. Table 10 presents Phase's 1 results that the PRWC4AI and Projects are "Risky". PRWC4AI is not an independent component and is linked to all IHIPTF's modules. The AHMM4AI's main constraint to implement the PRWC4AI is that CSAs having an average result below 8.0 will be ignored. This work's conclusion with the result of 8.80 implies that PRWC4AI's integration is "Risky" and due to various types of complexities. As Phase 1 is not a "Failure" the PoC continues to IHIPTF's setup.

Table 10. The PRWC4AI RDP's outcome is (rounded) 8.80

CSA Category of CSFs/KPIs	Transformation Capability	Average Result	Table
The RDP's Integration	Mature	From 1 to 10. 9.20	1
Team's Setup	Risky	From 1 to 10. 8.50	2
Disassembling Process	Risky	From 1 to 10. 8.25	[illegible]
PEMM's Implementation	Risky	From 1 to 10. 8.25	[illegible]
FMS' Integration	Risky	From 1 to 10. 8.25	[illegible]
AHMM4AI's Integration	Mature	From 1 to 10. 9.40	6
PRWC4AI's Integration	Feasible	From 1 to 10. 9.0	7
TDM' Integration	Feasible	From 1 to 10. 8.75	8
Inteligence's Integration	Mature	From 1 to 10. 9.25	9
Phase's 1 Outcome	Risky	From 1 to 10. 8.80	10

Evaluate First Phase

IHIPTF's Setup and Configuration

The PoC configures the FMS and Factors then these Factors are mapped to Projects resources and artefacts. The FMS contains the relationships that link Project's requirements, CBBs, NLP4AI scripts, Factors, and Global Unique IDentifiers (GUID). IHIPTF's client's interface that is shown in Figure 28 sets up all the Project's operations like NLP4AI scenarios development and linking scripts to Factors and CBBs.

Figure 28. The IHIPTF's graphical interface

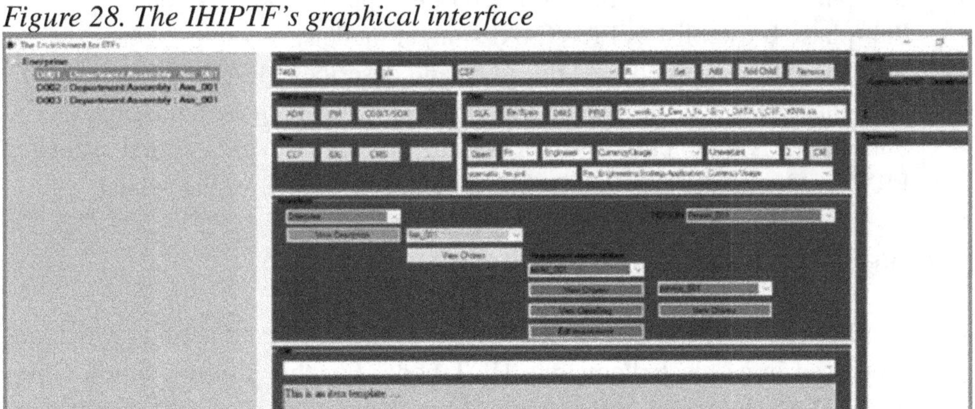

NLP scripts are the backbone of Intelligence and contain the define sets of actions to be processed. The AHMM4AI ensures PRWC4AI's integrity and HDT's tree configuration as shown in Figure 29.

Figure 29. The heuristics tree configuration

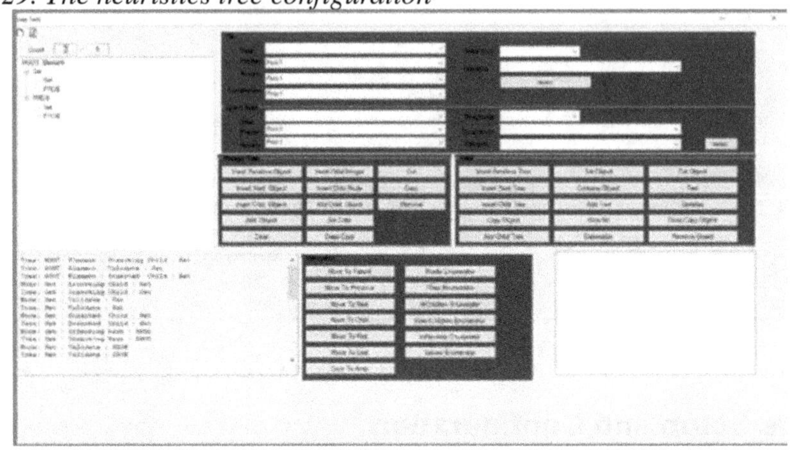

Phase 2-Solving a Concrete Problem

Phase 2 contains the following TDM's steps and operations:

- TDM's setup and its integration with the FMS and PRWC4AI.
- Sub-phase A establishes the Disassembling approach and its goal.
- Sub-phase B establishes PRWC4AI's target models.
- Sub-phase C shows and uses the ACD and describes PRWC4AI's activities.
- Sub-phase D shows the needed PRWC4AI's infrastructural landscape.
- Sub-phases E and F presents intermediate Project's situation(s) and evaluates PRWC4AI; and updates the list of Problem types (PRB) to be solved.

PRBs Solving for a Concrete HDT Node:

- Intelligence solves PRBs, where Factors to defined set of actions which are processed in a selected/concrete HDT node. For this aim the action CSF_KMS_DMS_Integration_Procedure (from the Intelligence CSA) was executed and offers sets of solutions (SOL). Solving PRBs involves the execution of actions and delivering SOLs for multiple Project's activities, where each action can deliver a new PRB and that generates the HDT tree. The HDT uses the QQRMM and contains a dual-OF that contains: 1) In Phase 1 the IHIPTF has implemented NLP4AI scripts to process CSA_DTs, and related PoC's resources to the CSF_KMS_DMS_Integration_Procedure; 2) Intelligence is configured and uses the PRWC4AI support the HDT; 3) Linking HDT's node to data-contents; and 4) The HDT executes the CSF_KMS_DMS_Integration_Procedure and delivers SOL(s).

SOL Nodes activities:

- NLP4AI scripts are called by the PRWC4AI.
- These scripts are processed in the background to deliver PRWC4AI value(s).
- These values are translated into actions, conclusions and recommendations.

CONCLUSION AND RECOMMENDATIONS

This RDP proposes a set of recommendations on how to implement a PRWC4AI for Projects. The PRWC4AI uses Factors to iteratively assert Project's feasibility and because of the low score of 8.80 (Table 10) implies that it is "Risky", and the resultant recommendations are:

- The author uses his IHIPTF to show how and Entity can build an inhouse framework for Projects.
- This RDP uses a QQRM concept.
- The PRLR proved the existence of an important knowledge gap.
- To use an MM (like the AHMM4PAI) and HDT, to support Intelligence's operations.
- The AHMM4AI and ELP based HDT support Intelligence.
- The HDT supports the PRWC4AI.
- Cross-functional/Polymathic skills are needed.
- PRWC4AI, uses existing frameworks.
- The PRWC4AI evaluates Projects' progress.
- The PoC checked PRWC4AI's feasibility.
- The PRWC4AI integration is complex and "Risky".
- Entities and University Cycles (UC) are dominated by single-disciplinary experts.
- UCs must encourage the development of interdisciplinary and Polymathic AI-experts.
- Cross-functional/Polymathic skills building is mainly based on common and AI-Fields.

- The Learning cannot cope with complexity of modern heterogeneous ICS and AI-Fields.
- There is a need for a cross-functional RbICC.
- Students learning concepts that are recurrent in all UCs.
- Educators must have the needed set of AI-skills and experience (academic, and professional).
- The RbICC promotes Polymathism, critical-thinking, and opinion-based concepts.

REFERENCES

Agievich, V. (2014). Mathematical model and multi-criteria analysis of designing large-scale enterprise roadmap. PhD thesis – Mathematical modelling, numerical methods and complexes of programs.

AIforEducation. (2024). Generative AI Explainer. https://www.aiforeducation.io/ai-resources/generative-ai-explainer

Aksoy, M., & Ceylan, T. (2021). An Action Research on Improving Classroom Communication and Interaction in Social Studies Teaching. .DOI: 10.1155/2021/9943194

Azadfallah, M. (2018). *A New Entropy-Based Approach to Determine the Weights of Decision Makers for Each Criterion with Crisp and Interval Data in Group Decision Making Under Multiple Attribute. International Journal of Service Science, Management, Engineering, and Technology (IJSSMET)*. IGI Global. DOI: 10.4018/IJSSMET.2018100103

Bizzdesign. (2022). Digital Transformation. Bizzdesign. https://bizzdesign.com/blog-category/digital-transformation/

Chaione. (2022). Digital Transformation-The 4 Types of Digital Transformation. Chaione.com.

Clancy, L. (2019). Functional programming reaches for stardom in finance. CME Group. https://www.risk.net/risk-management/6395366/functional-programming-reaches-for-stardom-in-finance

Clark, M., Fletcher, P., Hanson, J., Irani, R., Waterhouse, M., & Thelin, J. (2013). *Web Services Business Strategies and Architectures*. Apress.

Codd, E. F., Codd, S. B., & Salley, C. T. (1993). *Providing OLAP (On-line Analytical Processing) to User-Analysts: An IT Mandate*. Codd & Date.

Crittenden, V. (2005). Cross-functional education: The need for case development. February 2005. *Journal of Business Research*, 58(7), 955–959. DOI: 10.1016/j.jbusres.2003.12.004

Daellenbach, H., McNickle, D., & Dye, Sh. (2012). *Management Science - Decision-making through systems thinking* (2nd ed.). Palgrave Macmillian.

Della Croce, F., & T'kindt, V. (2002). A Recovering Beam Search algorithm for the one-machine dynamic total completion time scheduling problem. *The Journal of the Operational Research Society*, 53(11), 1275–1280.

Dogan, S., Çalgici, P., Arditi, D., & Gunaydin, H. (2015). *Critical success factors of partnering in the building design process. METU JFA 2015/2*. Department of Architecture, İzmir Institute of Technology.

Easterbrook, S., Singer, J., Storey, M., & Damian, D. (2008). *Guide to Advanced Empirical Software Engineering-Selecting Empirical Methods for Software Engineering Research* (Shull, F., Eds.). Springer.

Eira, A. (2022). 72 Vital Digital Transformation Statistics: 2023 Spending, Adoption, Analysis & Data. FinancesOnline. https://financesonline.com/digital-transformation-statistics/

Giachetti, R. (2012). A Flexible Approach to Realize an Enterprise Architecture. Department of Systems Engineering, Naval Postgraduate School, Monterey, CA USA. Presented: New Challenges in Systems Engineering and Architecting. Conference on Systems Engineering Research (CSER). St. Louis, MO. Elservier.

Hine, G. S. C. (2013). The importance of action research in teacher education programs. In *Design, develop, evaluate: The core of the learning. environment. Proceedings of the 22nd Annual Teaching Learning Forum, 7-8 February 2013.* Murdoch University. http://ctl.curtin.edu.au/professional_development/conferences/tlf/tlf2013/refereed/hine.html

Hinkelmann, K. (2016). *Modelling in Enterprise Architecture. University of applied sciences northwest Switzerland.* Business School.

Holilah, H., Girsang, A., & Saragih, M. (2019). *Designing IT Blue Print Academic System on Higher Education with Togaf. Journal: Advances in Science*. Technology and Engineering Systems Journal.

Hosiaisluoma. (2022). Holistic Enterprise Development. https://www.hosiaisluoma.fi/blog/archimate-examples

Hussain, O., Dillon, T., Chang, E., & Hussain, F. (2010). Transactional risk-based decision making system in e-business interactions. International Journal of ComputSystSci & Eng, 1, 15-28.

IBM. (2014). *Service Oriented Architecture. "Smart Service Oriented Architecture: Helping businesses restructure. Where are you on the Service Oriented Architecture adoption path?* IBM.

Järvinen, P. (2007). Action Research is Similar to Design Science. Quality & Quantity. Retrieved August 10, 2018, from https://link.springer.com/article/10.1007/s11135-005-5427-1

Jonkers, H., Band, I., & Quartel, D. (2012a). *ArchiSurance Case Study*. The Open Group.

Kim, J., & Lennon, Sh. (2017). *Descriptive Content Analysis on E-Service Research. International Journal of Service Science, Management, Engineering, and Technology (IJSSMET)*. IGI Global., DOI: 10.4018/IJSSMET.2017010102

Krigsman, M. (2008). Business change failures: 9 success tips. Reviewed from https://www.zdnet.com/blog/transformationfailures/business-change-failures-9-success-tips/1080. USA.

Lankhorst, M. (2009). *Enterprise Architecture at Work Modelling, Communication and Analysis*. Springer.

Lebreton, P. (1957). The Case Study Method and the Establishment of Standards of efficiency. Academy of Management Proceedings.

Leitch, R., & Day, Ch. (2000). Action research and reflective practice: towards a holistic view. Taylor & Francis. Queen's University of Belfast, United Kingdom. Retrieved February 10, 2018, from https://www.tandfonline.com/doi/ref/10.1080/09650790000200108?scroll=top

Liu, A. (2022). Rumbaugh, Booch and Jacobson Methodologies. Opengenus. https://iq.opengenus.org/rumbaugh-booch-and-jacobson-methodologies/

Lockwood, R. (2018). Introduction The Relational Data Model. Retrieved January 29, 2019, from http://www.jakobsens.dk/Nekrologer.htm

Markides, C. (2011, March). Crossing the Chasm: How to Convert Relevant Research Into Managerially Useful Research. *The Journal of Applied Behavioral Science*, 47(1), 121–134.

Merhi, M. (2023). An evaluation of the critical success factors impacting artificial intelligence implementation. International Journal of Information Management, 69. DOI: 10.1016/j.ijinfomgt.2022.102545

Moore, J. (2014). Java programming with lambda expressions-A mathematical example demonstrates the power of lambdas in Java 8. Retrieved March 10, 2018, from, https://www.javaworld.com/article/2092260/java-se/java-programming-with-lambda-expressions.html

Morawski, R. (2013, November). An application-oriented mathematical meta-model of measurement. Elsevier. *Journal Measurement*, 46(9), 3753–3765. DOI: 10.1016/j.measurement.2013.04.004

Morrison, M. (2016). Critical Success Factors – Analysis made easy, a step by step guide. rapidBI. Accessed and reviewed in April 2019, https://rapidbi.com/criticalsuccessfactors/

Myers, B., Pane, J., & Ko, A. (2004). Natural programming languages and environments. ACM New York, NY, USA. Accessed and reviewed in April 2019, https://dl.acm.org/citation.cfm?id=1015888

National Academies. (1991). *Artificial Intelligence in Mathematical Modeling. National Academies of Sciences, Engineering, and Medicine. 1991. Research Directions in Computational Mechanics*. The National Academies Press. DOI: 10.17226/1909

Neumann, G. (2002). Programming Languages in Artificial Intelligence. *3rd International Conference on Affective Computing and Intelligent Interaction and Workshops*. IEEE.

OMG. (2022). Decision model and notation (DMN). OMG. https://www.omg.org/dmn/

Peterson, S. (2011). Why it Worked: Critical Success Factors of a Financial Reform Project in Africa. Faculty Research Working Paper Series. Harvard Kennedy School.

Polderman, J., & Willems, J. (1998). *Introduction to Mathematical Systems Theory: A Behavioral Approach. (Texts in Applied Mathematics)* (2nd ed.). Springer Verlag.

Pushpakumara, H., Jayaweera, P., & Manjulan, W. (2021). Using the Open Group Architecture Framework (TOGAF) for Quality Assurance in Higher Education Teaching and Learning. DOI: 10.2139/ssrn.3808691

Putri, N., & Yusof, S. M. (2009). Critical success factors for implementing quality engineering tools and techniques in malaysian's and indonesian's automotive industries: An Exploratory Study. *Journal Proceedings of the International Multi-Conference of Engineers and Computer Scientists.*, 2, 18–20.

RedHat. (2022). Decision Model and Notation (DMN). RedHat. https://access.redhat.com/documentation/en-us/red_hat_process_automation_manager/7.1/html/designing_a_decision_service_using_dmn_models/dmn-elements-example-con

Rockart, J. (1979). Chief Executives Define Their Own Data Needs. Harvard Business Review. Accessed and reviewed in April 2019, https://hbr.org/1979/03/chief-executives-define-their-own-data-needs

Ronald, D. (1961). Management Information Crisis. Harvard Business Review.

Sankaralingam, K., Ferris, M., Nowatzki, T., Estan, C., Wood, D., & Vaish, N. (2013). *Optimization and Mathematical Modeling in Computer Architecture*. Morgan & Claypool Publishers.

Satterlee, B. (1996). Continuous Improvement and Quality: Implications for Higher Education. Warner Southern College.

Schmelzer, R. (2021). Data science vs. machine learning vs. AI: How they work together. TechTarget. https://searchbusinessanalytics.techtarget.com/feature/Data-science-vs-machine-learning-vs-AI-How-they-work-together?track=NL-1816&ad=937375&asrc=EM_NLN_144787081&utm_medium=EM&utm_source=NLN&utm_campaign=20210114_An%20open%20source%20database%20comparison

Shrivastava, R. (2023). Building an enterprise business glossary. Hitachi Vantara. https://community.hitachivantara.com/blogs/rishu-shrivastava/2023/03/23/building-an-enterprise-business-glossary

Simonin, J., Bertin, E., Traon, Y., Jezequel, J.-M., & Crespi, N. (2010). Business and Information System Alignment: A Formal Solution for Telecom Services. *2010 Fifth International Conference on Software Engineering Advances*. IEEE.

Spencer, L. (1955). 10 problems that worry presidents. Harvard Business Review.

Syynimaa, N. (2015). Enterprise Architecture Adoption Method for Higher Education Institutions. Doctoral Thesis. Informatics Research Centre Henley Business School University of Reading. UK.

The Open Group. (1999). *Building Blocks*. Introduction to Building Blocks. The Open Group.

The Open Group. (2011a). Architecture Development Method. The Open Group. USA. The link was reviewed and extracted in February 2018, https://pubs.opengroup.org/architecture/togaf9-doc/arch/chap05.html

The Open Group. (2011b). *TOGAF 9.1. The Open Group*. The Open Group.

The Open Group. (2011c). Foundation Architecture: Technical Reference Model. The Open Group. USA. http://www.opengroup.org/public/arch/p3/trm/trm_dtail.htm

The Open Group. (2011d). Architecture Skills Framework. https://pubs.opengroup.org/architecture/togaf8-doc/arch/chap30.html

The Open Group. (2021). TOGAF Model Patterns. The Open Group._https://sparxsystems.com/enterprise_architect_user_guide/15.2/model_domains/togaf_model_patterns.html

Trad, A. (2015a). *A Transformation Framework Proposal for Managers in Business Innovation and Business Transformation Projects-Intelligent aBB architecture*. Centeris.

Trad, A. (2015b). *A Transformation Framework Proposal for Managers in Business Innovation and Business Transformation Projects-An ICS's atomic architecture vision*. Centeris.

Trad, A. (2021a). The transformation framework-The role security in the global education system. Journal: International Journal of Higher Education Management.

Trad, A. (2021b). The business transformation enterprise architecture framework for innovation: The role of artificial intelligence in the global business education (RAIGBE). Journal: The Business & Management Review.

Trad, A. (2023a). *Academic and Educational Transformation Projects-The Role Team-Based Learning in Polymathics (RTBLP)*. IGI-Global.

Trad, A. (2023b). *Business Transformation Projects: The Role of Psychology-Based Resistance (RPbR). Book: Considerations on Education for Economic, Social, and Environmental Sustainability*. IGI Global.

Trad, A. (2023c). *The Societal and Educational Transformation Projects: The Evolution of the Lebanese Diverse Education (ELDES). Book: Global Perspectives on the Internationalization of Higher Education*. IGI Global.

Trad, A. (2023d). *Organizational and Digital Transformation Projects-A Mathematical Model for Building Blocks based Organizational Unbundling Process*. IGI Global.

Trad, A. (2023e). A Relational DataBase based Enterprise Transformation Projects. Journal *International Journal of Mathematics and Computers in Simulation*, 17, 1–11.

Trad, A. (2024a). *Educational and Public Administration Transformation Projects-The Role of Polymathics Based Artificial Intelligence (RPBAI)*. IGI Global.

Trad, A. (2024b). *Academic and Educational Transformation Projects-The Role Team-Based Learning in Polymathics For University Cycle (RTBLP4UC)*. IGI-Global.

Trad, A. (2024c). *Enterprise Transformation Projects- The use of the Polymathic Rating and Weighting Concept (PRWC)*. IGI-Global.

Trad, A. (2024d). *Academic and Educational Transformation Projects-The Role of Skills in Academic Polymathics Fields (RSAPF)*. IGI Global.

Trad, A., & Kalpić, D. (2014a). The Selection and Training Framework for Managers in Business Innovation and Transformation Projects-An applied mathematics hyper-heuristics model. *Proceedings of the 2014 International Conference on Mathematical Methods, Mathematical Models and Simulation in Science and Engineering (MMSSE 2014).*

Trad, A., & Kalpić, D. (2014b). *The Selection, and Training Framework selection and training framework (STF) for Manager's in Business Innovation Transformation Projects–Educational Recommendations*. Journal EDEN.

Trad, A., & Kalpić, D. (2014c, June). The selection and training framework for managers in business innovation and transformation projects: The Profile and Education of a Business Transformation Manager - An enterprise architecture approach. The Business & Management Review.

Trad, A., & Kalpić, D. (2017a). *An Intelligent Neural Networks Micro Artefact Patterns' Based Enterprise Architecture Model.* IGI-Global.

Trad, A., & Kalpić, D. (2017b). *A Neural Networks Portable and Agnostic Implementation Environment for Business Transformation Projects. The Basic Structure.* IEEE.

Trad, A., & Kalpić, D. (2018a). An applied mathematical model for business transformation-The Holistic Critical Success Factors Management System (HCS-FMS). Journal: Encyclopaedia of E-Commerce Development, Implementation, and Management. DOI: 10.4018/978-1-7998-1009-4.ch003

Trad, A., & Kalpić, D. (2020a). *Using Applied Mathematical Models for Business Transformation. IGI Complete Author Book.* IGI Global.

Trad, A., & Kalpić, D. (2020b). *Business Transformation and Enterprise Architecture: The Holistic Project Asset Management Concept (HPAMC). Book: Handbook of Research on Strategic Fit and Design in Business.* IGI.

Trad, A., & Kalpić, D. (2021a). Business transformation project's architect's profile (BTPAP). *The Business & Management Review.*, 12(2), 137–153.

Trad, A. & Kalpić, D. (2022a). Business Transformation Project's Holistic Agile Management (BTPHAM) CBER 2022.

Trad, A., & Kalpić, D. (2023a). *Educational Transformation Project's Remote Group Work (ETPRGW). Book: Shaping Online Spaces Through Online Humanities Curricula.* IGI Global.

Visual Paradigm. (2019). TOGAF ADM Tutorial. Visual Paradigm. Reviewed from https://cdn.visual-paradigm.com/guide/togaf/togaf-adm-tutorial/02-togaf-adm.png

Zandia, F., & Tavana, M. (2011). *A fuzzy group multi-criteria enterprise architecture framework selection model. Management Information Systems, Lindback Distinguished Chair of Information Systems, La Salle University, Philadelphia, PA 19141*. Elsevier.

Chapter 3
AI Integration in Public Administration:
Enhancing Efficiency and Accessibility

Andi Asrifan
https://orcid.org/0000-0002-9934-6129
Universitas Negeri Makassar, Indonesia

Akbar Akbar
IAIN Palopo, Indonesia

Muhammad Nur
Universitas Muhammadiyah Sidenreng Rappang, Indonesia

Robby Waluyo Amu
Universitas Gorontalo, Indonesia

Hadi Pajarianto
Universitas Muhammadiyah Palopo, Indonesia

ABSTRACT

This chapter examines how AI might alter public administration by improving efficiency, accessibility, and decision-making. AI automates ordinary jobs, freeing up public servants for high-impact work. Predictive analytics improve government operations by offering data-driven insights for resource allocation and preemptive actions in healthcare, urban planning, and public safety. Chatbots and virtual assistants make government services more accessible to different populations, especially those with linguistic or physical obstacles. The chapter also highlights the ethical and

DOI: 10.4018/979-8-3373-2272-8.ch003

operational issues of AI in public administration. Due to data privacy, security, and algorithmic bias, AI deployment must be transparent, accountable, and fair. Public entities can ethically use AI by following ethical and governance guidelines and gaining public trust. This chapter emphasizes balanced AI deployment to establish an inclusive, efficient, citizen-centered, and adaptable public sector.

1. INTRODUCTION

1.1 Overview of AI in Public Administration

AI is transforming public administration by improving government efficiency and citizen service (Kulal et al., 2024) (Pencheva et al., 2020) (Ahn & Chen, 2020). AI could solve public sector issues, including bureaucratic inefficiency and resource allocation, by automating mundane tasks, enabling data-driven decision-making, and enhancing transparency. AI can expedite administrative duties, freeing up resources and allowing civil servants to focus on more difficult and strategic challenges in governments globally. This connection is changing operational frameworks and making governance more responsive, accessible, and citizen-centric.

Service accessibility is one of AI's biggest effects on public administration. Chatbots and virtual assistants improve public involvement by offering 24/7 support, answering citizen questions, and reducing response times (Nirala et al., 2022) (Guo, 2024). This promotes an inclusive service paradigm for various populations like non-native language speakers and disabled people. AI-enabled predictive analytics helps identify public wants and trends, enabling proactive service adjustments to meet changing social needs.

AI is crucial to updating government legacy systems. Many governmental entities have used antiquated, fragmented systems that restrict efficiency and interdepartmental collaboration. AI helps departments share data more smoothly, which is essential for policy execution and resource distribution (Bhumichai et al., 2024) (Han et al., 2024). AI systems can track and analyze choices, making it easier to measure performance and assure alignment with public interests. They can transform internal processes and enable more transparent and responsible governance.

Despite these potential advances, integrating AI into public administration raises data security, privacy, and bias problems. Public trust depends on protecting sensitive personal data held by public entities (Xia et al., 2023). Transparent and fair AI systems must also reduce bias and prevent discrimination. AI implementation must be ethical to provide a balanced and equitable public service model.

1.2 The Growing Role of Technology in Government

Technology has grown from simple instruments to complex digital systems that run modern government (Zhang & Kimathi, 2022) (Mubarik & Khan, 2024). Initially, public administration technology consisted of typewriters and simplistic calculators. Computers, data storage, and telecommunications changed government operations as technology advanced. E-governance began with late 20th-century digitalization, which improved record-keeping, data retrieval, and workflows. These advances led to today's complex, interconnected networks.

Internet and "e-government" services were the next significant revolution. This movement promoted digital portals for public service engagement and information access. Online tax filing, voter registration, and license renewal increased citizen convenience and reduced administrative workloads worldwide (AL-Mashaqbeh, 2023) (Pahlka, 2023). Technology enabled remote and real-time government-citizen contacts, eliminating service delivery bottlenecks and enhancing public satisfaction. E-government introduced real-time data processing in governance, a significant step toward modern AI systems.

AI is the newest step in this process, where technology is no longer only a tool for efficiency but also a driver of proactive, intelligent decision-making. AI has transformed public administration by automating routine operations, improving decision-making, and predicting needs. AI applications are helping governments evaluate massive datasets, find patterns, and respond to health, public safety, and urban planning (Yigitcanlar et al., 2020). In crisis management, resource allocation, and policy planning, AI's predictive analytics assist governments in anticipating problems.

AI's growing usage in public administration shows how technology shapes modern government (Dunleavy & Margetts, 2023) (McDonald et al., 2022). AI-driven solutions improve government services' efficiency, reach, and adaptability, strengthening public administration's responsiveness to society. However, this new technology raises privacy, transparency, and accountability problems. As AI evolves, governments must build ethical frameworks to spread its advantages equitably, creating an inclusive, technologically-empowered public sector that is future-ready.

2. FOUNDATIONS OF AI IN PUBLIC ADMINISTRATION

2.1 Key Concepts of Artificial Intelligence

AI includes a wide range of technologies that allow machines to learn from data, adapt, and make judgments. AI can improve public administration service delivery, decision-making, and operational efficiency (Nirala et al., 2022) (Van Noordt & Misuraca, 2022). Machine learning, automation, and natural language processing are fundamental to AI, and this chapter examines their applications in public sector transformation.

AI's Machine Learning (ML) subset lets systems learn from data and improve without programming. Public administration benefits from ML algorithms' ability to discover patterns in vast datasets and predict and adapt to new data (Sarker, 2021). In predictive analytics, ML helps government agencies identify trends, allocate resources, and solve issues before they become important. ML algorithms help public health officials predict outbreaks and plan responses. Social services use ML for accurate needs assessments, tailored treatments, and resource distribution.

Automation is when technology performs repetitive or time-consuming jobs for humans. Automation is useful in public administration, where bureaucracy slows service delivery (Andersson et al., 2022). Public agencies can eliminate errors, speed response times, and reallocate human resources to strategic duties by automating data entry, form processing, and appointment scheduling. Automatic document processing systems can reduce backlogs and improve service efficiency in government agencies, such as checking social program eligibility or managing tax filings. Automation increases administrative compliance and uniformity, improving public service consistency and reliability.

NLP, another important AI component, helps systems interpret and respond to human language. NLP aids citizen-government contact, improving accessibility and response (Nicolas et al., 2021) (Jiang, 2023). NLP-driven chatbots and virtual assistants let citizens request information, file requests, and follow applications from government services anytime. This technology works well for multilingual services and disabled people. Virtual assistants can help users fill out complicated forms, clarify regulations, and answer common inquiries, relieving frontline staff and improving citizen happiness.

These AI principles make public administration more nimble, responsive, and data-driven. Automation reduces administrative procedures, machine learning increases proactive planning, and NLP engages citizens. These technologies are essential for public sector entities to improve efficiency, serve citizens, and update government processes. This fundamental grasp of AI principles shows how they can alter public administration, creating a more flexible, accessible, and efficient government that can meet society's changing needs.

2.2 The Evolution of AI in Government Operations

AI's integration into government operations has evolved from early automation and data processing systems to powerful AI-powered decision-making tools (Zuiderwijk et al., 2021). This trip shows how governments have used technology to improve public service delivery, complex administrative demands, and resource management efficiency.

Automating administrative activities with computers was the first step toward AI in government. Basic computerization helped governments digitize documents, evaluate statistics, and organize data in the 1960s and 1970s (Paul et al., 2023). These initial automation efforts helped departments switch from paper-based to electronic data management. Though modest, this transition began technology-driven efficiency in public administration and prepared the way for advanced AI applications.

Technology advanced in the 1980s and 1990s, resulting in expert systems (Shao et al., 2022). These rule-based AI systems were among the first to simulate human decision-making by applying specified rules to specific challenges. Government areas like tax administration, healthcare, and resource management used expert systems for fraud detection, medical diagnosis, and sophisticated data processing. Although restricted in adaptability, these early AI systems showed promise for government decision-making automation and stimulated more AI research.

Machine learning (ML) and natural language processing (NLP) helped governments handle greater datasets and automate increasingly complicated operations in the 2000s (Kingsly and Archanaundefined). Machine learning, which learns from data patterns, became valuable for predictive analytics in public health, law enforcement, and environmental monitoring. Law enforcement utilized ML to detect crime hotspots, while public health organizations employed it to anticipate disease outbreaks and optimize response techniques. NLP allows governments to develop chatbots and virtual assistants, giving residents real-time, 24/7 access to information and boosting public involvement and accessibility.

AI now aids government decision-making in resource allocation, policy planning, and citizen service (Kulal et al., 2024). Advanced predictive analytics in modern AI systems help governments anticipate and meet societal requirements. AI models enable urban planners to create efficient infrastructure and optimize traffic flow in real-time, while social services use them to detect and serve vulnerable people. AI-powered sentiment analysis techniques help governmental agencies evaluate public opinion and make more responsive policy decisions.

This evolution from simple automation to advanced AI-driven insights shows how AI has transformed government operations. Governments can now evaluate complicated data, forecast consequences, and make informed decisions to meet changing public requirements (Pencheva et al., 2020). As AI advances, it can improve public sector transparency, efficiency, and accountability, helping governments become more flexible, responsive, and citizen-centric.

2.3 AI and Bureaucratic Efficiency

AI can improve public administration efficiency by streamlining processes, reducing human error, and speeding up jobs (Vogl et al., 2020). Public sector agencies can use AI to restructure inefficient, laborious, and inconsistent operations, creating a more agile and responsive government system that better serves residents. AI reduces bottlenecks, cuts costs, and improves government services.

AI can automate and streamline administrative operations, especially repetitive and time-consuming ones, in bureaucracy. Data entry, document verification, and record management use many government resources. AI-powered automation solutions like RPA can perform these jobs more effectively and accurately (Yendluri et al., 2023). RPA can replace manual entries to transmit data between databases, cross-reference information, and update entries across different systems. Automation lowers human error, ensures correctness, and frees up government workers to handle more difficult tasks.

Data analysis using AI improves decision-making by delivering predictive insights. Machine learning algorithms quickly and accurately find patterns in massive data sets to help make better judgments (Sarker, 2021). Predictive analytics can predict service demand from previous data, helping governments allocate resources. AI can anticipate illness outbreaks and mobilize resources in public health administration. Predicting and preparing for future demands helps government entities be more efficient and resource-conscious.

Another important way AI improves bureaucratic efficiency is error minimization (Wang et al., 2024). Government paperwork and data processing errors can hinder progress and erode public trust. Automation and machine learning let AI analyze data more accurately and with less human intervention, decreasing revisions and redo. Tax administration, healthcare, and social services, where even tiny errors can have serious implications, benefit from this reliability.

NLP and other AI-powered tools streamline government-citizen communication. Chatbots and virtual assistants can answer basic questions in real-time, enhancing accessibility and decreasing customer support workload. This feature improves response times, information accuracy and accessibility, and government-citizen transparency and usability.

3. ENHANCING EFFICIENCY THROUGH AI INTEGRATION

3.1 AI for Automating Routine Government Tasks

AI is transforming ordinary and repetitive operations in public administration that were previously laborious and time-consuming (Johnson et al., 2022). AI automates data entry, document processing, and customer service questions, helping government agencies save money and enhance service delivery. This change from manual to AI-powered automation affects resource allocation, workforce productivity, and service quality.

Data input and document processing are major AI applications in public administration. Government agencies process massive volumes of data daily, including citizen information, tax documents, and licensing applications. Handling this data manually was laborious and error-prone. OCR and machine learning-enabled AI algorithms retrieve, validate, and organize document data automatically (Shahin et al., 2024). OCR technology can digitize handwritten or printed documents, speeding up form and application processing. These automated technologies eliminate human error and paperwork backlogs, allowing government workers to focus on more difficult tasks.

In addition to data entry, AI boosts document processing efficiency. Machine learning algorithms can identify, prioritize, and route documents by content, ensuring requests reach the right department quickly (Al-Hawari & Barham, 2021). This is especially useful in social services and healthcare, as prompt document handling can improve residents' health. AI-based workflow automation can also approve and deny basic requests, simplifying decision-making. By processing paperwork faster, public institutions may serve citizens more efficiently and openly.

AI is also impacting customer service. Government websites increasingly use AI-powered chatbots and virtual assistants to provide 24/7 help (Guo, 2024). These chatbots can answer basic queries, help with applications, and provide instant service updates. This allows residents to seek support at any time and reduces the workload of customer service professionals. By assigning ordinary questions to AI, government officials may focus on more complex matters that require a personal touch, improving service.

Automating repetitive tasks with artificial intelligence is essential to improve government responsiveness and efficiency. AI reduces expenses and administrative delays by automating repetitive tasks, giving citizens faster and more accurate results. AI in public administration involves making government services more accessible, efficient, and responsive to citizens' requirements. AI-driven automation technologies can improve public sector agency operations, making government more effective and citizen-focused (Vogl et al., 2020).

3.2 AI in Decision-Making and Resource Allocation

AI is making public administration more data-driven and efficient in resource allocation, budgeting, and policy formation (Van Noordt & Misuraca, 2022) (Wirtz et al., 2020). AI helps government organizations prioritize, optimize resource use, and improve policy, which results in rising demands and constrained resources. AI can help governments make proactive, accurate decisions that maximize public finances and deliver services quickly.

AI's ability to swiftly and accurately assess vast amounts of data is a major benefit in decision-making (Shrestha et al., 2021). Machine learning algorithms can find patterns, correlations, and trends in large datasets that humans may miss. Healthcare, education, and public safety resource management require accurate forecasting and efficient allocation, making this data-driven method useful. AI-powered predictive analytics can identify disease epidemic hotspots in public health, enabling targeted resource deployment for prevention and treatment. AI can also forecast crime hotspots in law enforcement, optimize resource allocation, and prevent crime.

AI improves budgeting decisions, too. Traditional budgeting uses static, linear estimates that may not account for rapidly changing circumstances or unexpected demands (Steen et al., 2024). However, AI algorithms can dynamically forecast financial scenarios using historical data, economic variables, and real-time inputs. This skill lets governments adapt budgets to changing needs, eliminating resource shortages and overspending. In a public health emergency, AI-driven budgeting models can predict medical supply needs and reallocate cash to ensure availability, minimizing service delays. AI's adaptive approach makes fiscal planning more flexible and responsive to real-world events.

AI aids evidence-based public policymaking, ensuring policies meet needs rather than assumptions. NLP and data analytics can assess public opinion from social media, surveys, and feedback forms to reveal citizen issues and priorities (Khurana et al., 2023). Policymakers can evaluate public emotion and adapt policies to meet citizen expectations. Policymakers can also use AI-driven simulations to estimate the effects of different policies in a risk-free setting. AI models can predict traffic flow, pollution, and public happiness after transportation policy changes.

AI improves decision-making and resource allocation in disaster response and crisis management (Abid et al., 2021). AI-based technologies can process real-time data from weather sensors, social media, and emergency calls to respond quickly to natural disasters and other crises. This ability to foresee requirements, distribute resources, and respond quickly boosts government resilience and supports affected populations.

3.3 Predictive Analytics in Public Administration

Public administration is rapidly using AI-powered predictive analytics to predict trends, improve planning, and optimize resource allocation. AI-based predictive analytics helps government organizations recognize patterns, foresee future demands, and make informed decisions to improve operational efficiency and service delivery by harnessing massive amounts of historical and real-time data (Shawon et al., 2024). By anticipating societal demands and allocating resources accordingly, public administration may quickly and effectively meet them.

Predictive analytics can predict healthcare, transportation, and social service trends (Batko & Ślęzak, 2022). Public health departments use prediction models to track illness trends, locate outbreaks, and allocate preventive resources. Predictive analytics helped governments prepare medical facilities, allocate protective gear, and manage emergency response teams for COVID-19 infection surges. This predictive power helps governmental agencies mitigate health emergencies and allocate healthcare resources to high-need regions.

Predictive analytics is important in transportation and urban development. AI models may predict transportation and infrastructure needs based on population growth, commute patterns, and environmental conditions (Ang et al., 2022). Cities can then plan traffic management, public transit schedules, and road networks to handle commuter traffic surges. Predictive analytics can identify traffic bottlenecks and offer alternative routes or public transportation to decrease congestion. This method increases city mobility, decreases environmental impact, and boosts quality of life.

Predictive analytics improves social service resource allocation for poverty, housing, and education (Edwards et al., 2022). By identifying at-risk communities or populations, social service agencies can build targeted intervention programs to prevent issues from escalating. Predictive models can help local governments distribute housing resources and support services to high-risk locations. A proactive approach promotes equitable resource distribution and public service access for the neediest.

Predictive analytics improves government budget forecasts and financial planning. Many budgeting systems use historical data without considering demand changes or unanticipated events (Steen et al., 2024). AI-based predictive models can use economic indicators and expenditure patterns to make more accurate and adaptive budget forecasts. This optimizes budget allocation, decreasing resource shortages and surpluses and enabling flexible responses to unexpected difficulties.

Predictive analytics helps government agencies with strategic planning and resource allocation. By predicting future difficulties like public opinion shifts or socio-economic changes, predictive models assist policymakers in making data-driven decisions that meet society's changing needs. Public opinion analytics can measure policy sentiment, enabling governments to build policies that meet citizen preferences and anticipate social dynamics that may affect policy approval.

4. IMPROVING ACCESSIBILITY WITH AI

4.1 AI and Digital Inclusion in Public Services

AI is promoting digital inclusion in public services by improving accessibility and service delivery to all citizens (Kulal et al., 2024). Technology may help underserved populations like those with impairments, language problems, or limited access to traditional government services, and governments are realizing this. Public institutions are using AI to make their services more inclusive, responsive, and accessible, promoting equity and leaving no citizen behind.

AI's multilingual services have a major impact on digital inclusion (Mhlanga, 2020). Natural language processing (NLP) and machine translation allow government portals and services to communicate with residents in their native languages. AI-powered translation solutions can immediately translate documents, websites, and chatbot responses for non-native speakers. In varied communities where language barriers prevent access to healthcare, legal aid, and social welfare, this capacity is critical.

By creating adaptive and user-friendly service interfaces, AI is enhancing disability accessibility. AI allows people with visual or hearing impairments to use government services freely using speech-to-text, text-to-speech, and voice recognition (Jnr, 2024). Voice-activated virtual assistants allow people with restricted mobility or eyesight to use digital platforms without visual signals from home or on the go. Real-time transcription services help the deaf and hard-of-hearing participate in online consultations, educational programs, and other public services by translating spoken content into text.

AI-driven digital inclusion technologies connect rural and underserved residents to public services (Marzo2024). Due to infrastructure and isolation, these regions rarely receive government support. AI chatbots and virtual assistants allow remote residents to get 24/7 help with applications, inquiries, and public resources without traveling. AI's real-time processing minimizes wait times and boosts service availability, ensuring marginalized groups receive fast public benefit responses and support.

AI is changing social services by identifying and filling service shortages (James & Whelan, 2022). With data analytics and machine learning, government organizations may discover which populations encounter access restrictions and why. AI can identify underserved demographics or regions for focused outreach and resource allocation. This helps distribute services more evenly by prioritizing high-need locations and supporting accessibility measures.

AI-enhanced digital inclusion boosts public trust and pleasure (Kulal et al., 2024). Governments demonstrate their commitment to fair and equal services regardless of citizens' personal or situational restrictions by committing to accessibility. As society demands universal access to services, this commitment is essential to strengthening government-community partnerships.

4.2 Chatbots and Virtual Assistants in Public Administration

AI-driven chatbots and virtual assistants are enhancing government accessibility and responsiveness by delivering 24/7 citizen support (Nirala et al., 2022). These solutions automate and streamline public service encounters by understanding and responding to a wide range of user requests using NLP and machine learning. Chatbots and virtual assistants make government services more accessible, user-friendly, and flexible to people' requirements 24/7.

Chatbots in public administration can manage many inquiries without human participation. AI-driven chatbots can quickly answer queries about application processes, eligibility requirements, document submission, and service locations (Ittarat et al., 2023). This automation speeds up response times and frees up public service professionals to handle more difficult problems. In tax administration, chatbots can help users file and answer queries about deadlines and forms, enhancing efficiency.

Virtual assistants can help disabled and language-impaired people. Voice-activated virtual assistants make government portals more accessible for people with mobility or vision issues (Vieira et al., 2022). Machine-translation chatbots can interact with citizens in several languages, removing linguistic barriers to critical information in a multilingual society. These methods make public administration more equal by providing consistent, inclusive, and individualized service.

Chatbots and virtual assistants support complicated interactions like organizing appointments, tracking application statuses, and updating data (Nirala et al., 2022) (Ittarat et al., 2023). AI chatbots plan and recall patient appointments, improving attendance and eliminating administrative friction in healthcare. In social services, chatbots can update citizens on benefit applications, minimizing follow-up calls and in-person visits. Support like this enhances user experience and reduces bottlenecks in high-demand services.

The availability and reliability of AI-driven assistants increase citizen trust and engagement with public services (Kulal et al., 2024). With 24/7 help, citizens are more likely to obtain information and complete processes conveniently, improving satisfaction. This accessibility is especially useful during natural catastrophes or public health emergencies when citizens need rapid information or support. Chatbots can provide current safety protocols, resources, and emergency contact information to ensure critical support when needed.

AI-driven chatbots and virtual assistants analyze popular requests, identify high-demand regions, and gather service quality feedback, contributing to data collecting and insights. Public administrators can use this data to improve service design and delivery by identifying citizen wants and pain spots. Chatbots can adapt to shifting citizen expectations and become more integrated into public administration by learning from user interactions.

4.3 AI in E-Government Platforms

Thanks to AI, e-government platforms are becoming more user-friendly, accessible, and tailored (Al-Besher & Kumar, 2022) (Cortés-Cediel et al.,2023). AI-powered e-government systems allow citizens to access a wide range of government information and services through simple, intuitive online portals as public administration moves toward digital services. This shift is boosting operational efficiency and helping governments satisfy citizens' growing demands for fast, tailored, and dependable service.

AI's tailored user experience is a major contribution to e-government platforms. AI systems can personalize content, features, and services by analyzing user behavior with machine learning algorithms. An AI-powered e-government portal may offer suitable services or notify users of forthcoming deadlines based on their history and preferences. For newly registered businesses, the site may include tax information, compliance recommendations, and business permits. Navigation is simpler and more relevant with this tailored approach, improving citizen involvement.

AI-driven e-government systems make digital services more inclusive and accessible (Kulal et al., 2024). E-government websites can support various languages using natural language processing (NLP) methods, allowing residents of different languages to access information and services. Additionally, AI-powered screen readers and voice-activated technologies enable disabled persons navigate digital government portals. Accessibility features make government services available to more people, reducing the digital gap and bringing important services to all.

Besides personalization and accessibility, AI improves e-government efficiency through intelligent automation. Automation can answer routine questions, process applications, and keep records without human intervention, relieving administrative staff. AI-powered technologies can check document authenticity, speeding up processing and assuring consistency. AI reduces human error in data handling and validation, speeding up service delivery and improving accuracy. AI-powered automation frees up government workers to work on more sophisticated and important jobs, enhancing productivity (Yigitcanlar et al., 2024).

E-government platforms also leverage AI-based predictive analytics to predict user demands and allocate resources (Salem et al., 2024). Predictive algorithms can identify popular services and predict demand surges by evaluating previous data and usage trends. This helps government organizations distribute resources to serve high-demand areas and reduce wait times. E-government platforms can prioritize key services and respond to changing conditions during natural disasters and public health emergencies with predictive analytics.

Chatbots in e-government platforms demonstrate how AI improves accessibility and response (Cortés-Cediel et al., 2023). These chatbots answer basic inquiries and help citizens complete forms and submit applications, minimizing confusion and irritation. Chatbots allow citizens to use e-government platforms 24/7. Real-time support answers frequent questions and helps in emergencies, improving customer happiness and government service trust.

5. ETHICAL CONSIDERATIONS AND CHALLENGES IN AI IMPLEMENTATION

5.1 Privacy and Data Security in AI-Driven Public Services

AI integration into public administration raises privacy and data security concerns (Willems et al., 2023) (Kulal, 2024). Effective AI-driven public services require massive volumes of citizen data, from personal to real-time behavioral. Data dependence complicates privacy and security procedures to protect sensitive data. Maintaining public trust in AI-driven government services requires strong data protection policies and privacy protection.

Data privacy is a major issue in AI-driven public services. Training algorithms and improving predicting accuracy in AI systems require large datasets (Jackins et al., 2021). These databases may contain health records, social services history, and biometric data that could compromise privacy. Securely storing and anonymizing predictive healthcare or crime prevention data prevents misuse or illegal access. Avoiding privacy breaches and collecting and analyzing just necessary data requires tight data access rules like data reduction and encryption.

Data security is crucial because public administration organizations handle sensitive data and are major targets for cyberattacks (Mushtaq & Shah, 2024). A cyberattack on AI systems might expose massive amounts of citizen data. AI-driven public services need multi-layered security, including improved encryption, access controls, and real-time anomaly detection. Governments may prevent data breaches by auditing and updating security measures to stay ahead of evolving threats. Data security breaches in AI-processed citizen records or key infrastructure services could have serious ramifications for public safety and trust.

Transparency and accountability are key to privacy and data security. Citizens must comprehend data collection, use, and protection. Data usage regulations and privacy rights should be easily accessible to foster public trust in AI-driven services. Furthermore, accountability mechanisms hold entities using AI systems accountable for privacy violations and misuse. Regulations that require audits, transparency reports, and penalties for data protection violations can increase accountability.

Another difficulty is balancing AI system functionality with ethics. AI-driven analytics and predictive modeling can improve resource allocation and service delivery but using personal data without authorization or anonymization risks overreach. Ethical AI deployment demands minimal unexpected repercussions and data use for its intended goal (Bankins, 2021). This may include privacy impact evaluations before implementing AI systems, data processing that complies with privacy regulations, and ethical principles that preserve citizen rights.

Privacy and data security are essential to ethical AI implementation in public administration. AI-driven public services must respect citizen data and privacy rights to build confidence. Governments may reduce data handling risks and make public sector AI applications safer by following strict security rules, transparent data practices, and accountability mechanisms. As AI technologies grow, privacy and data security must remain a primary priority, demonstrating the commitment to ethical and responsible public administration that respects citizen rights and privacy.

5.2 Bias and Fairness in AI Systems

In public administration, where AI-driven tools make life-changing choices, bias and fairness in AI systems are critical (Osasona et al., 2024). AI algorithms are efficient, but their impartiality depends on their training data and frameworks. Unchecked, these mechanisms can perpetuate or worsen socioeconomic inequities, resulting in biased outcomes that disproportionately affect certain groups. Addressing these challenges is crucial to keeping AI's involvement in public services fair, transparent, and equal for all.

Data used to train AI algorithms is a major source of bias. AI algorithms learn patterns and anticipate based on previous data, which may represent social, economic, and cultural inequities. If an AI system assesses social service eligibility based on historical data with systematic biases, certain groups may be unfairly penalized. Welfare distribution, housing support, and healthcare accessibility may unfairly exclude or deprioritize poor communities. To identify and mitigate these biases, training datasets must be diverse, balanced, and representative of the communities serviced.

Algorithmic design and decision-making criteria also cause AI bias (Ntoutsi et al., 2020) (Belenguer, 2022). Even with balanced data, algorithm structure might cause inadvertent discrimination. An AI model in law enforcement that assigns greater risk scores to individuals based on socio-economic factors may perpetuate preconceptions and increase monitoring or interventions for specific communities. The design phase must include fairness checks and ethical criteria, such as testing AI models for discriminatory outcomes and setting limitations to avoid overemphasizing sensitive factors like race, gender, and socioeconomic status.

AI fairness requires transparency and accountability. Public entities adopting AI-driven technologies must disclose algorithmic decision-making criteria and data sources (Bracci, 2024) (Cheong, 2024). This transparency helps citizens comprehend decisions and voice concerns. Accountability tools, including third-party audits, bias evaluations, and the opportunity to question AI-driven judgments, enable agencies to take responsibility for biased outcomes. Clear routes for recourse boost public trust because citizens can seek redress if AI-driven judgments have unfairly affected them.

Another way to reduce bias is to update and improve AI systems regularly. AI models must adapt to changing social standards and data to remain fair and relevant. Retraining models with new data, including community feedback, or using real-time adversarial debiasing are all options. Governments can increase AI-driven public service fairness and adaptability by upgrading algorithms.

An unbiased AI system in public administration involves data oversight, ethical design, openness, and ongoing monitoring to prevent discrimination (Ntoutsi et al., 2020). AI should promote equality rather than hinder it to provide fair and unbiased service access for all. AI can help create a more egalitarian public sector by lowering gaps when managed properly. AI fairness meshes with public service values, creating a more just and inclusive society.

5.3 Accountability in AI Decision-Making

AI accountability is a major ethical issue, especially when public administration uses AI to make decisions that directly affect citizens or public policy (Busuioc, 2021) (Nordström, 2022). As AI-driven systems get more involved in resource allocation, eligibility assessments, and law enforcement, accountability for these judgments becomes more complicated. AI decision-making must be accountable and transparent to sustain public trust, ethical norms, and citizen rights.

Many AI models, especially complicated machine learning algorithms, are "black box" (Busuioc, 2021). This makes AI accountability difficult. These systems' opaque decision-making procedures make it hard for administrators and citizens to grasp results. Explaining why an AI system rejects welfare payments or assigns a high-risk score in law enforcement is vital. Governments should use interpretable AI models and require explanations for crucial choices. By establishing "explainability," public institutions can build confidence and transparency by explaining their judgments.

Developers who create algorithms, data scientists who train them, and public officials who oversee their deployment are usually responsible for AI-driven public administration choices. Establishing accountability requires clearly defining these positions. Public entities should establish policies that outline obligations at each AI implementation step to hold each partner accountable (Buhmann & Fieseler, 2021). Developer ethical rules, data scientist audits, and public administrator supervision methods could avoid AI system misuse or bias.

Accountability requires clear guidelines and oversight. Establishing independent review boards or third-party audits to analyze AI models periodically can discover biases, flaws, and unforeseen consequences. These audits determine whether AI systems are working properly and following ethical and regulatory guidelines. Additionally, mechanisms should be in place to review and fix AI-based errors and unfair choices, as well as ways for citizens to raise complaints and seek restitution.

Public agencies should adopt human-in-the-loop (HITL) intervention rules for AI choices that matter (Enarsson et al., 2022). HITL incorporates human oversight in decision-making, especially in high-stakes circumstances when errors or biases could be disastrous. To maintain justice and reduce AI limits, a human authority could analyze cases highlighted for more inspection if an AI system evaluates loan eligibility or assigns social service benefits. HITL systems improve accountability by engaging human judgment, allowing for nuanced decisions that algorithms may miss.

Legislation and policy frameworks are essential for AI accountability (Novelli et al., 2024). AI-driven public services need openness, justice, and responsible laws from governments. Laws may mandate recording decision-making, exposing data sources, and auditing regularly. Public administration can hold AI accountable, like human decision-making, by setting explicit legal criteria.

6. CASE STUDIES OF AI IN PUBLIC ADMINISTRATION

6.1 AI in Public Health Administration

Public health management is rapidly using AI to manage healthcare data, anticipate disease outbreaks, and allocate resources (Piccialli et al., 2021) (Alowais et al., 2023). AI's analytical capability helps public health authorities work more efficiently, respond proactively to health issues, and optimize resource allocation, increasing population health.

AI's ability to organize and analyze massive healthcare data has a major impact on public health. Public health systems create huge patient, treatment, and epidemiological databases daily. AI-driven systems can efficiently organize and analyze this data, discovering trends and providing insights that would be difficult to detect manually (Majeed & Hwang, 2021) (Aminizadeh et al., 2024). Machine learning algorithms can identify risk factors, predict illness progression, and suggest preventative measures using patient data patterns. Public health officials may make informed judgments and plan focused treatments on addressing the most important health issues by analyzing data at scale.

AI is crucial for disease epidemic prediction and monitoring. AI models can predict disease outbreaks by analyzing hospital records, social media trends, climate data, and travel patterns (Zhao et al., 2024) (Butt et al., 2023). AI technologies helped track infection rates, anticipate hotspots, and analyze COVID-19's spread across areas. Governments use predictive analytics to prepare healthcare facilities, deploy resources, and adopt containment measures. Beyond COVID-19, AI predicts seasonal flu trends, tracks mosquito-borne infections, and monitors other public health hazards to safeguard communities and reduce the burden of infectious diseases.

AI optimizes the distribution of scarce healthcare resources like medical staff, hospital beds, and necessary supplies. Machine learning algorithms use demand, patient demographics, and geography data to distribute resources depending on real-time demands. AI can recommend staffing adjustments and prioritize resource deployment in regions with healthcare provider shortages. AI can also foresee healthcare demand spikes, allowing hospitals to reallocate workers, expand facilities, or buy more medical supplies. This tailored resource allocation reduces healthcare system load and assures timely care.

AI can manage healthcare access for marginalized groups in public health administration (Koski et al., 2022). Artificial intelligence can discover healthcare access gaps and plan outreach campaigns to improve rural or low-income healthcare. AI chatbots and virtual assistants can also answer frequently asked questions, provide remote health counsel, and do pre-screening evaluations, making healthcare more accessible, especially in areas with inadequate infrastructure.

AI helps public health research and development speed up medicine and vaccine development. Machine learning models can find interesting drug candidates and forecast their efficacy and safety using biochemical data, speeding up development (Dara et al., 2022). AI models helped researchers study virus architecture and simulate immune responses in silico to build COVID-19 vaccines quickly. This ability to speed up research is crucial for responding to health crises and getting remedies to patients fast.

6.2 AI in Law Enforcement and Public Safety

By improving predictive policing, crime prevention analytics, and resource distribution, AI is improving law enforcement and public safety. AI's analytical and predictive powers help law enforcement avoid crime, respond quickly, and optimize resource allocation, making communities safer and public safety operations more efficient (Faqir, 2023).

Predictive policing is a major AI use in law enforcement. Machine learning algorithms examine historical crime data to detect patterns and predict crime hotspots in predictive policing. These algorithms use time of day, location, previous events, and environmental factors to predict crime hotspots. Law enforcement can deploy resources to increase patrol presence in areas with higher expected crime rates and deter crime by using these data. Predictive policing technologies have reduced crime in Los Angeles and Chicago by allocating police to strategic places based on data and optimizing patrol efficiency.

Advanced analytics from AI help law enforcement detect trends and causes of crime (Blount, 2024) (Faqir, 2023). AI-driven crime prevention analytics can detect violence, fraud, and organized crime by evaluating social trends, economic indicators, and past criminal activity. AI models analyze transaction patterns for abnormalities that may suggest financial fraud, allowing early intervention. These insights enable public safety organizations to identify high-risk locations or persons and take preventive measures like community engagement or increased presence in high-crime districts. These precautions make communities safer and more trustworthy.

Law enforcement is also benefiting from AI resource deployment (Faqir, 2023). Using demand, past crime statistics, and emergency call trends, AI systems can recommend staff and resource allocation. AI-driven dispatch systems can predict emergency service needs using real-time data, speeding response times. AI also recommends the best routes for police, ambulances, and firefighting units to improve response times. AI can also adapt staffing schedules to ensure adequate coverage during peak hours and important events, boosting public safety without overburdening resources.

Law enforcement also relies on facial recognition and surveillance. AI-powered facial recognition systems can compare surveillance footage to databases to identify criminals and missing people. In high-traffic public spaces, this software helps law enforcement track suspects and identify culprits quickly. However, to balance public safety and citizens' rights, facial recognition technology needs tight rules and control.

The New York Police Department uses AI to manage public safety during large events (Mahor et al., 2023) (Urquhart & Miranda, 2022). The department can anticipate security threats and allocate resources via real-time surveillance and predictive analytics. UK police use AI to forecast and prevent knife crime, a major issue in urban areas. By targeting hotspots and risk factors, authorities can reduce violent crime in these areas.

6.3 AI in Urban Planning and Smart Cities

AI is changing urban planning and smart city development by improving city design, management, and citizen well-being (He & Chen, 2024). Public administrators can develop more efficient, sustainable, and responsive urban settings that meet rising urbanization challenges by employing AI to evaluate urban data, manage resources, and engage residents. AI-driven solutions enable smart city potential in traffic management, energy conservation, and more.

AI systems evaluate sensor, camera, and GPS data to enhance traffic flow and reduce congestion, making traffic management a major AI application in urban planning. Using traffic data patterns, machine learning systems estimate peak congestion and dynamically change traffic signals to reduce bottlenecks (Kumar and Raubal2021). This real-time analysis cuts travel time, idle emissions, and road safety. Singapore and Barcelona have pioneered AI-driven traffic management technologies, improving commuter experiences and roadway efficiency. Growing urban populations face infrastructural issues, but AI can predict and manage traffic patterns.

AI is vital to smart utility management, especially water and energy saving (Egbemhenghe et al., 2023). Cities can monitor resource consumption in real time, optimize distribution, and minimize usage without sacrificing service with smart meters and AI analytics. AI can estimate water consumption at different times of day and power surges, modifying utility distribution to maximize efficiency and minimize waste. AI manages renewable energy sources and ensures their integration into smart networks to balance energy supply and demand. AI helps Amsterdam and San Diego reduce resource waste and government and resident costs.

AI supports data-driven environmental management decision-making, boosting sustainability initiatives. AI can monitor pollutants, predict environmental repercussions, and help city planners choose eco-friendly infrastructure. Based on city garbage levels, AI-driven waste management systems optimize collection routes, lowering fuel usage and emissions. AI also monitors air and water quality, helping towns manage pollution hotspots. Urban planners can improve city sustainability and livability by incorporating AI into these activities (Alahi et al., 2023).

Smart cities also require citizen engagement, and AI-driven solutions make governance more inclusive. Through chatbots, virtual assistants, and smartphone apps, AI lets residents report issues and provide real-time feedback to local services. AI-enabled systems let citizens report infrastructure issues, request public services, and learn about local projects. This real-time involvement helps residents and local authorities collaborate on urban planning decisions that meet neighborhood requirements. AI platforms in Helsinki and Toronto provide transparent and inclusive citizen interactions, allowing the community to shape their urban environment (Yigitcanlar et al., 2021) (Kinder et al., 2023).

CONCLUSION

Finally, AI can alter public administration by improving efficiency, accessibility, and decision-making. AI decreases administrative duties, allowing public servants to focus on more complicated, value-added operations that improve citizen involvement and satisfaction. This shift makes the public sector more agile and responsive to modern needs. AI's predictive insights into resource allocation and policy planning allow governments to anticipate public needs, improving service delivery and resource use.

Public services become more inclusive and accessible to various groups, especially those with linguistic or physical limitations, with AI. AI chatbots and virtual assistants provide 24/7 help, improving public involvement and government service responsiveness. Predictive analytics also enable data-driven healthcare, urban planning, and public safety decisions by public institutions, increasing governance and outcomes.

However, public administration AI integration presents substantial ethical and operational concerns. Given that AI systems process so much sensitive citizen data, data privacy and security are crucial. Public trust requires strong cybersecurity and government transparent data processing. In addition, bias in AI systems can perpetuate disparities, necessitating careful model design and continual monitoring to assure fairness and accountability in decision-making. AI's full potential in public administration will require a balanced strategy that balances efficiency and ethics. Policymakers, engineers, and public administrators must work together to create an AI-driven public sector that serves all residents fairly by protecting privacy, minimizing bias, and ensuring accountability. As AI evolves, it could make public administration more efficient, accessible, and transparent, integrating technology with public service objectives.

REFERENCES

Abid, S. K., Sulaiman, N., Chan, S. W., Nazir, U., Abid, M., Han, H., & Vega-Muñoz, A. (2021). Toward an integrated disaster management approach: How artificial intelligence can boost disaster management. *Sustainability*, 13(22), 12560.

Ahn, M. J., & Chen, Y. C. (2020, June). Artificial intelligence in government: potentials, challenges, and the future. In *Proceedings of the 21st Annual International Conference on Digital Government Research* (pp. 243-252).

Al-Besher, A. & Kumar, K. (2022). Use of artificial intelligence to enhance e-government services. Measurement: Sensors.

Al-Hawari, F., & Barham, H. (2021). A machine learning based help desk system for IT service management. *Journal of King Saud University. Computer and Information Sciences*, 33(6), 702–718.

AL-Mashaqbeh. (2023). The Relationship Between E-Government and Job Performance.

Alahi, M. E. E., Sukkuea, A., Tina, F. W., Nag, A., Kurdthongmee, W., Suwannarat, K., & Mukhopadhyay, S. C. (2023). Integration of IoT-enabled technologies and artificial intelligence (AI) for smart city scenario: Recent advancements and future trends. *Sensors (Basel)*, 23(11), 5206. PMID: 37299934

Alowais, S. A., Alghamdi, S. S., Alsuhebany, N., Alqahtani, T., Alshaya, A. I., Almohareb, S. N., & Albekairy, A. M. (2023). Revolutionizing healthcare: The role of artificial intelligence in clinical practice. *BMC Medical Education*, 23(1), 689. PMID: 37740191

Aminizadeh, S., Heidari, A., Dehghan, M., Toumaj, S., Rezaei, M., Navimipour, N. J., & Unal, M. (2024). Opportunities and challenges of artificial intelligence and distributed systems to improve the quality of healthcare service. *Artificial Intelligence in Medicine*, 149, 102779. PMID: 38462281

Andersson, C., Hallin, A., & Ivory, C. (2022). Unpacking the digitalisation of public services: Configuring work during automation in local government. Government Information Quarterly.

Ang, K. L. M., Seng, J. K. P., Ngharamike, E., & Ijemaru, G. K. (2022). Emerging technologies for smart cities' transportation: Geo-information, data analytics and machine learning approaches. *ISPRS International Journal of Geo-Information*, 11(2), 85.

Bankins, S. (2021). The ethical use of artificial intelligence in human resource management: A decision-making framework. *Ethics and Information Technology*.

Batko, K. & Ślęzak, A. (2022). The use of Big Data Analytics in healthcare. Journal of big Data.

Belenguer, L. (2022). AI bias: exploring discriminatory algorithmic decision-making models and the application of possible machine-centric solutions adapted from the pharmaceutical …. AI and Ethics.

Bhumichai, D., Smiliotopoulos, C., Benton, R., Kambourakis, G., & Damopoulos, D. (2024). The convergence of artificial intelligence and blockchain: The state of play and the road ahead. *Information (Basel)*, 15(5), 268.

Blount, K. (2024). Using artificial intelligence to prevent crime: Implications for due process and criminal justice. *AI & Society*.

Bracci, E. (n.d.). The loopholes of algorithmic public services: An "intelligent" accountability research agenda. Accounting.

Bragazzi, N. L., Dai, H., Damiani, G., Behzadifar, M., Martini, M., & Wu, J. (2020). How big data and artificial intelligence can help better manage the COVID-19 pandemic. *International Journal of Environmental Research and Public Health*, 17(9), 3176. PMID: 32370204

Buhmann, A. & Fieseler, C. (2021). Towards a deliberative framework for responsible innovation in artificial intelligence. Technology in Society.

Busuioc, M. (2021). Accountable artificial intelligence: Holding algorithms to account. Public Administration Review.

Butt, M. J., Malik, A. K., Qamar, N., Yar, S., Malik, A. J., & Rauf, U. (2023). A survey on COVID-19 data analysis using AI, IoT, and social media. Sensors.

Cheong, B. C. (2024). Transparency and accountability in AI systems: Safeguarding wellbeing in the age of algorithmic decision-making. Frontiers in Human Dynamics.

Cortés-Cediel, M. E., Segura-Tinoco, A., Cantador, I., & Bolívar, M. P. R. (2023). Trends and challenges of e-government chatbots: Advances in exploring open government data and citizen participation content. *Government Information Quarterly*, 40(4), 101877.

Dara, S., Dhamercherla, S., Jadav, S. S., Babu, C. M., & Ahsan, M. J. (2022). Machine learning in drug discovery: A review. *Artificial Intelligence Review*, 55(3), 1947–1999. PMID: 34393317

Dunleavy, P. & Margetts, H. (2023). Data science, artificial intelligence and the third wave of digital era governance. Public Policy and Administration.

Edwards, R., Gillies, V., & Gorin, S. (2022). Problem-solving for problem-solving: Data analytics to identify families for service intervention. Critical Social Policy.

Egbemhenghe, A. U., Ojeyemi, T., Iwuozor, K. O., Emenike, E. C., Ogunsanya, T. I., Anidiobi, S. U., & Adeniyi, A. G. (2023). Revolutionizing water treatment, conservation, and management: Harnessing the power of AI-driven ChatGPT solutions. *Environmental Challenges*, 13, 100782.

Enarsson, T., Enqvist, L., & Naarttijärvi, M. (2022). Approaching the human in the loop–legal perspectives on hybrid human/algorithmic decision-making in three contexts. *Information & Communications Technology Law*, 31(1), 123–153.

Faqir, R. S. A. (2023). Digital Criminal Investigations in the Era of Artificial Intelligence: A Comprehensive Overview. International Journal of Cyber Criminology.

Guo, Y. (2024). *Digital Government and Public Interaction: Platforms, Chatbots, and Public Satisfaction: Platforms*. Chatbots, and Public Satisfaction.

Han, X., Xiao, S., Sheng, J., & Zhang, G. (2024). Enhancing Efficiency and Decision-Making in Higher Education Through Intelligent Commercial Integration: Leveraging Artificial Intelligence. *Journal of the Knowledge Economy*.

He, W. & Chen, M. (2024). Advancing Urban Life: A Systematic Review of Emerging Technologies and Artificial Intelligence in Urban Design and Planning. Buildings.

Ittarat, M., Cheungpasitporn, W., & Chansangpetch, S. (2023). Personalized care in eye health: Exploring opportunities, challenges, and the road ahead for chatbots. *Journal of Personalized Medicine*, 13(12), 1679. PMID: 38138906

Jackins, V., Vimal, S., Kaliappan, M., & Lee, M. Y. (2021). AI-based smart prediction of clinical disease using random forest classifier and Naive Bayes. *The Journal of Supercomputing*, 77(5), 5198–5219.

James, A. & Whelan, A. (2022). 'Ethical' artificial intelligence in the welfare state: Discourse and discrepancy in Australian social services. Critical Social Policy.

Jiang, Y., Pang, P. C. I., Wong, D., & Kan, H. Y. (2023). Natural Language Processing Adoption in Governments and Future Research Directions: A Systematic Review. Applied Sciences.

Jnr, B. A. (2024). User-centered AI-based voice-assistants for safe mobility of older people in urban context. AI & Society.

Johnson, B. A., Coggburn, J. D., & Llorens, J. J. (2022). Artificial intelligence and public human resource management: Questions for research and practice. *Public Personnel Management*, 51(4), 538–562.

Khurana, D., Koli, A., Khatter, K., & Singh, S. (2023). Natural language processing: state of the art, current trends and challenges. Multimedia Tools and Applications.

Kinder, T., Stenvall, J., Koskimies, E., Webb, H., & Janenova, S. (2023). Local public services and the ethical deployment of artificial intelligence. *Government Information Quarterly*, 40(4), 101865.

Kingsly, S. R., & Archana, T. (2025). Understanding AI and Machine Learning Concepts. In AI and Machine Learning Applications in Supply Chains and Marketing (pp. 371-392). IGI Global.

Koski, E., Scheufele, E. L., Karunakaram, H., Foreman, M. A., Felix, W., & Dankwa-Mullan, I. (2022). Understanding Disparities in Healthcare: Implications for health systems and AI applications. In *Healthcare Information Management Systems: Cases, Strategies, and Solutions* (pp. 375–387). Springer International Publishing.

Kulal, A., Rahiman, H. U., Suvarna, H., Abhishek, N., & Dinesh, S. (2024). Enhancing public service delivery efficiency: Exploring the impact of AI. *Journal of Open Innovation*, 10(3), 100329.

Kumar, N., & Raubal, M. (2021). Applications of deep learning in congestion detection, prediction and alleviation: A survey. *Transportation Research Part C, Emerging Technologies*, 133, 103432.

Mahor, V., Rawat, R., Kumar, A., Garg, B., & Pachlasiya, K. (2023). IoT and artificial intelligence techniques for public safety and security. In *Smart urban computing applications* (pp. 111–126). River Publishers.

Majeed, A. & Hwang, S. O. (2021). Data-driven analytics leveraging artificial intelligence in the era of COVID-19: an insightful review of recent developments. Symmetry.

Marzo, R. R. (2024). Bridging the Digital Divide: AI Solutions for Health Literacy in Underserved Populations. In Modern Management Science Practices in the Age of AI (pp. 151-180). IGI Global.

McDonald, B. D.III, Hall, J. L., O'Flynn, J., & van Thiel, S. (2022). The future of public administration research: An editor's perspective. *Public Administration*, 100(1), 59–71.

Mhlanga, D. (2020). Industry 4.0 in finance: the impact of artificial intelligence (ai) on digital financial inclusion. International Journal of Financial Studies.

Mubarik, M. S., & Khan, S. A. (2024). Disruptive Digital Technologies and Contemporary Supply Chains. In The Theory, Methods and Application of Managing Digital Supply Chains (pp. 15-39). Emerald Publishing Limited.

Mushtaq, S. & Shah, M. (2024). Critical Factors and Practices in Mitigating Cybercrimes within E-Government Services: A Rapid Review on Optimising Public Service Management. Information.

Nicolas, C., Kim, J., & Chi, S. (2021). Natural language processing-based characterization of top-down communication in smart cities for enhancing citizen alignment. Sustainable Cities and Society.

Nirala, K. K., Singh, N. K., & Purani, V. S. (2022). A survey on providing customer and public administration based services using AI: chatbot. Multimedia Tools and Applications.

Nordström, M. (2022). AI under great uncertainty: implications and decision strategies for public policy. AI & society.

Novelli, C., Taddeo, M., & Floridi, L. (2024). Accountability in artificial intelligence: what it is and how it works. Ai & Society.

Ntoutsi, E., Fafalios, P., Gadiraju, U., Iosifidis, V., Nejdl, W., Vidal, M. E., & Staab, S. (2020). Bias in data-driven artificial intelligence systems—An introductory survey. *Wiley Interdisciplinary Reviews. Data Mining and Knowledge Discovery*, 10(3), e1356.

Osasona, F., Amoo, O. O., Atadoga, A., Abrahams, T. O., Farayola, O. A., & Ayinla, B. S. (2024). Reviewing the ethical implications of AI in decision making processes. *International Journal of Management & Entrepreneurship Research*, 6(2), 322–335.

Pahlka, J. (2023). Recoding America: why government is failing in the digital age and how we can do better.

Paul, M., Maglaras, L., Ferrag, M. A., & Almomani, I. (2023). Digitization of healthcare sector: A study on privacy and security concerns. ICT Express.

Pencheva, I., Esteve, M., & Mikhaylov, S. J. (2020). Big Data and AI–A transformational shift for government: So, what next for research? *Public Policy and Administration*, 35(1), 24–44.

Piccialli, F., Di Cola, V. S., Giampaolo, F., & Cuomo, S. (2021). The role of artificial intelligence in fighting the COVID-19 pandemic. *Information Systems Frontiers*, 23(6), 1467–1497. PMID: 33935585

Salem, A. M., Eyupoglu, S. Z., & Ma'aitah, M. K. (2024). The Influence of Machine Learning on Enhancing Rational Decision-Making and Trust Levels in e-Government. Systems.

Sarker, I. H. (2021). Machine learning: Algorithms, real-world applications and research directions. SN computer science.

Shahin, M., Chen, F. F., & Hosseinzadeh, A. (2024). Machine-based identification system via optical character recognition. *Flexible Services and Manufacturing Journal*, 36(2), 453–480.

Shao, Z., Zhao, R., Yuan, S., Ding, M., & Wang, Y. (2022). Tracing the evolution of AI in the past decade and forecasting the emerging trends. *Expert Systems with Applications*, 209, 118221.

Shawon, R. E. R., Rahman, A., Islam, M. R., Debnath, P., Sumon, M. F. I., Khan, M. A., & Miah, M. N. I. (2024). AI-Driven Predictive Modeling of US Economic Trends: Insights and Innovations. Journal of Humanities and Social Sciences Studies, 6(10), 1-15.

Shrestha, Y. R., Krishna, V., & von Krogh, G. (2021). Augmenting organizational decision-making with deep learning algorithms: Principles, promises, and challenges. Journal of Business Research.

Steen, R., Haug, O. J., & Patriarca, R. (2024). Business continuity and resilience management: A conceptual framework. *Journal of Contingencies and Crisis Management*, 32(1), e12501.

Urquhart, L., & Miranda, D. (2022). Policing faces: The present and future of intelligent facial surveillance. *Information & Communications Technology Law*, 31(2), 194–219.

Van Noordt, C., & Misuraca, G. (2022). Artificial intelligence for the public sector: Results of landscaping the use of AI in government across the European Union. *Government Information Quarterly*.

Vieira, A. D., Leite, H., & Volochtchuk, A. V. L. (2022). The impact of voice assistant home devices on people with disabilities: A longitudinal study. *Technological Forecasting and Social Change*, 184, 121961.

Vogl, T. M., Seidelin, C., Ganesh, B., & Bright, J. (2020). Smart technology and the emergence of algorithmic bureaucracy: Artificial intelligence in UK local authorities. *Public Administration Review*, 80(6), 946–961.

Wang, C. W., Hsu, B. Y., & Chen, D. Y. (2024). Chatbot applications in government frontline services: Leveraging artificial intelligence and data governance to reduce problems and increase effectiveness. *Asia Pacific Journal of Public Administration*, 1–24.

Willems, J., Schmid, M. J., Vanderelst, D., Vogel, D., & Ebinger, F. (2023). AI-driven public services and the privacy paradox: Do citizens really care about their privacy? *Public Management Review*, 25(11), 2116–2134.

Wirtz, B. W., Weyerer, J. C., & Sturm, B. J. (2020). The dark sides of artificial intelligence: An integrated AI governance framework for public administration. *International Journal of Public Administration*, 43(9), 818–829.

Xia, L., Semirumi, D. T., & Rezaei, R. (2023). A thorough examination of smart city applications: Exploring challenges and solutions throughout the life cycle with emphasis on safeguarding citizen privacy. *Sustainable Cities and Society*.

Yendluri, D. K., Ponnala, J., Tatikonda, R., Kempanna, M., Thatikonda, R., & Bhuvanesh, A. (2023, November). Role of RPA & AI in Optimizing Network Field Services. In 2023 7th International Conference on Computation System and Information Technology for Sustainable Solutions (CSITSS) (pp. 1-6). IEEE.

Yigitcanlar, T., Corchado, J. M., Mehmood, R., Li, R. Y. M., Mossberger, K., & Desouza, K. (2021). Responsible urban innovation with local government artificial intelligence (AI): A conceptual framework and research agenda. *Journal of Open Innovation*, 7(1), 71.

Yigitcanlar, T., Kankanamge, N., Regona, M., Ruiz Maldonado, A., Rowan, B., Ryu, A., & Li, R. Y. M. (2020). Artificial intelligence technologies and related urban planning and development concepts: How are they perceived and utilized in Australia? *Journal of Open Innovation*, 6(4), 187.

Yigitcanlar, T., Senadheera, S., Marasinghe, R., Bibri, S. E., Sanchez, T., Cugurullo, F., & Sieber, R. (2024). Artificial intelligence and the local government: A five-decade scientometric analysis on the evolution, state-of-the-art, and emerging trends. *Cities (London, England)*, 152, 105151.

Zhang, Y., & Kimathi, F. A. (2022). Exploring the stages of E-government development from public value perspective. *Technology in Society*.

Zhao, A. P., Li, S., Cao, Z., Hu, P. J. H., Wang, J., Xiang, Y., ... Lu, X. (2024). AI for science: predicting infectious diseases. Journal of Safety Science and Resilience.

Zuiderwijk, A., Chen, Y. C., & Salem, F. (2021). Implications of the use of artificial intelligence in public governance: A systematic literature review and a research agenda. Government information quarterly.

Chapter 4
Educational and Public Administration Transformation Projects:
The Role of Polymathics Based Artificial Intelligence (RPBAI)

Antoine Toni Trad
https://orcid.org/0000-0002-4199-6970
IBISTM, France

ABSTRACT

Advanced educational and public administration transformation projects (EPTP) are crucial for academic, public sector (PS), and business institutions. Unfortunately, such EPTPs are complex and have high failure rates, because of the various issues like the lack of experienced personal which should have polymathics and artificial intelligence (AI) capabilities and skills and should avoid the simplistic accountants' instant profits approach, which has long-term negative effects. The RPBAI needs to propose a holistic academic, educational, coaching, and research concept (and curriculum/roadmap), which starts in the primary and secondary schools or cycles (PSC), then is monitored in the university cycles (UC) (Bachelor, Master, and Doctorate) and continues in the professional career's upskilling activities. Such a concept and roadmap can be also applied to the PS (especially in the education/academic and industrial ministries) and business enterprises, which makes a synergy of these three majors and hard-linked sectors and domains.

DOI: 10.4018/979-8-3373-2272-8.ch004

INTRODUCTION

Today there is the lack of experienced AI professionals who have Polymathic capabilities and unfortunately today's business' reality privileges simple accountants' profiles who aim only the fast Return On Investment (ROI). PSCs are the jumpstart for RPBAI, because during this period AI-basics and Polymathics capable students can be detected. RbICC ensures educational sustainability and future professional and operational excellence for future project managers and specialists. The RbICC includes various AI and common domains and topics related to AI, algorithmics, data-management, data-architectures, mathematical models, PS' (re)organization, Information and Communication Systems (ICS), Enterprise Architecture (EA), societal changes, business/financial, and geopolitical contexts, and other (simply Fields). This chapter is related to the Role Team-Based Learning in Polymathics For University Cycle (RTBLP4UC) work (Trad, 2023a, 2024a). The RPBAI uses a Polymathic approach that promotes interdisciplinary Roadmap for managers, analysts, or architects (simply Persons). This chapter uses the author's Applied Holistic and Poly-Mathematical Model (AHMM) for Polymathics and AI (AHMM4PAI). The AHMM4PAI based RPBAI, combines various academic, educational, and professional (simply Project) Fields which also include Agile Project Management (APM), Geoeconomics, and distributed ICS. This RDP is linked to all the previous author's works and findings that are used to prove RPBAI's feasibility and to offer an RbICC for academic and professional cycles (simply Cycle) (Trad, 2023a, 20234). RbICC's have mandatory subjects which Persons must go through. All the author's works have a multi-dimensional concept to RDPs and Projects, because it includes: 1) An adapted research and development concept; 2) Shows how to build an in-house transformation framework, and to avoid locked-in Projects; 3) Uses a methodological approach that is based on Polymathic, AI, EA and complex organisations like PS; and 4) A AI Polymathic and Interdisciplinary Group Work In Complex Projects (simply Groupwork) (Trad, & Kalpić, 2023a). Groupwork is built on the AI-Team-Based Learning's Concept (AITBLC, simply Learning) and is its main component; which supports the RbICC, as shown in Figure 1.

Figure 1. RbICC and RPBAI related cycles

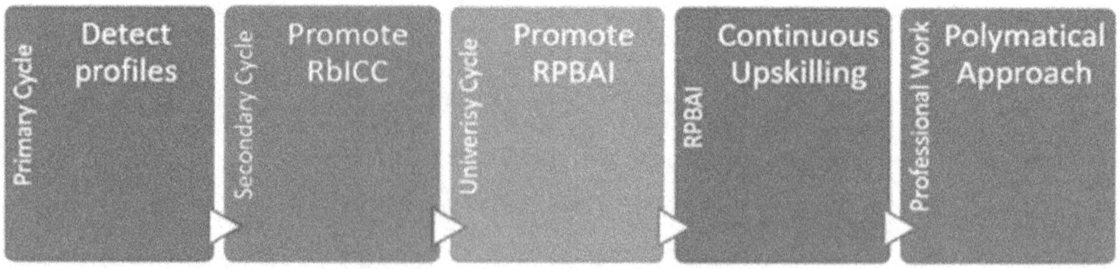

The Learning and RPBAI use integrated: Critical Success Areas (CSA), Critical Success Factors (CSF), Key Performance Indicators (KPI), Concrete ICS variables (CSAs, CSFs, and KPIs, are referred to as simply Factors), An authentic research and transformation framework, and an integrated heuristics-based Decision-Making System (DMS). The Learning supports all types of Cycle's activities, and uses current RbICC technics, standards, methodologies, personal habits, and Legacy Siloed Common Academic/Educational and Coaching System or Learning practices. RPBAI links various Fields and can add Business Analysis (BA), Business Engineering (BE), to enforce the RbICC. RbICC has mandatory topics like AI-subdomains, Project's strategy's analysis, Business, Economy, ICS, and other; so that Persons can work in transformation and innovation environments, knowing that such initiatives have eXtremely High Failure Rates (XHFR). Projects fail because of the lack RPBAI profiles, which are rare and when detected they have to have a well-deigned RbICC and Learning, because they are *very hard to spot* and most of them never finish a Cycle... They are very rare because the majority of Persons are forced to specialize and are blocked in upskilling their Polymathical capabilities, which also needs a tolerant multi-cultural vision. Where Polymathical capabilities are authentic human characteristics that some Persons are simply born with and Learning just makes it transparent… This chapter uses the author's In-House Implemented (IHI) Polymathical Transformation Framework (IHIPTF) that shows how to build an IHI framework that can include: 1) ICS, Groupwork, AI-subdomains, and integration patterns; 2) The DMS4PAI and KMS4PAI (simply Intelligence); 3) RPBAI and RbICC patterns; and 5) An RDP, which is the 1st CSA and its heading are in fact the initial set of CSFs.

THE RESEARCH DEVELOPMENT PROJECT

An Innovative Approach

Figure 2. The interaction between the project, RbICC, RPBAI, and RDP

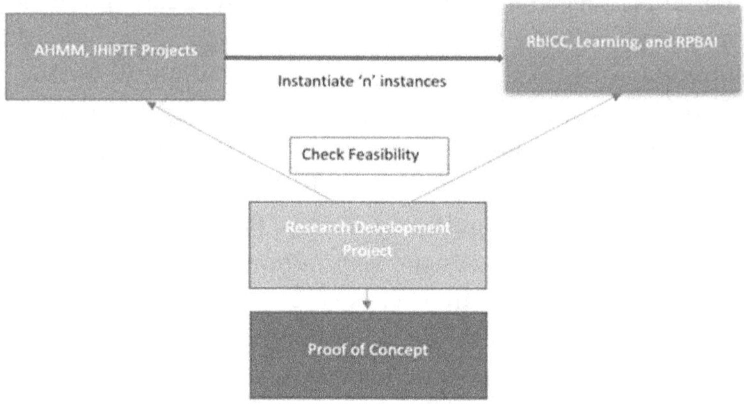

RPBAI capability is to find solutions and to improvise in Project's complex undertakings, which is not supported by traditional Cycles. RPBAI qualities and predispositions concern a limited number of Persons who are basically *Technocrats* who can develop related Fields with time, like Intelligence. The Learning, RPBAI and RbICC need an Action Research (AR) based PAI (ARbPAI) that solves various types of Cycles problems and optimize Persons' schedules. Knowing that AR is heavily used in education. This RDP and chapter's main facts are:

- Complexity, Polymathical concepts, and fast ICS-evolutions, provoke XHFRs.
- This RDP is based on a established and repetitive metamodel, and this chapter is just one of its bricks.
- This RDP is supported by IHIPTF with uses a set of interrelated concepts and methodologies; and it does not use simplistic quantitative research methods, which are the origins of XHFRs.
- To understand this RDP and approach there is the need for experiences and knowledge in various domains. Polymathic concepts need deep knowledge in many domains. Otherwise, the reader can refer to the recommendations and conclusion.

- The reader can use the references, links and related works to access more information on various topics.
- Here the main focus is to offer an RPBAI and upskilling Roadmap.
- All similar domains and methodologies, use a huge set of abbreviations, it is the nature of such a beast…
- Probably the main reason for XHFRs is that Persons expect simple approaches and reject complexities; which is logical but unfortunately Projects are complex…

IHIPTF*'s* and RDP's iterative approach are recurrent usages of Factors, and this RDP is unconventional, pioneering, and is not aligned to "very standardized quantitative" academic/educational dictated "recommendations"; but that is the essence of innovation... The reuse of IHIPTF, RDP, and other research concepts, which use IHIPTF approach can be considered by primitive tools as possible duplications or cases of similarities… Which is not the case and Project*s'* very high rate of failures, justify RDPs that deliver an adapted methods for such Projects… Entities can build their IHIPTF to support innovation, vision, and reuse most of the existing Learning' components to deliver RPBAI blueprints… The next step is to identify the Researched Literature Review (RLR) and RDP's Gap.

The RLR and RDP's Gap

Projects' complexities and XHFRs are due to the lack of cross-functional AI (and common) knowledge and Polymathic skills. Projects and Project recommends the usage of the AHMM4PAI with the ARbPAI based Heuristics Decision Tree (HDT), to support Intelligence's operations (Trad, & Kalpić, 2014a). This chapter's Research Question (RQ) is: "Which RPBAI and RbICC characteristics, and skills, are needed to support the Project?" The RQ is related to a set of hypotheses, where hypothesis (or assumption) corresponds to an RDP CSA, and this chapter's main-topic (or RPBAI) corresponds to the main CSA. RQ's feasibility is related to the evaluation of all CSAs and the set of hypotheses/assumptions. RQ's main hypothesis (or assumptions) are that the following transformational-activities were finalized successfully:

- Project's vision and roadmap define the right services' architecture-granularity (Trad, 2015a, 2015b).
- The budget was accepted and there is a sufficient level of political-support.
- The Entity has a robust and longterm RDP.
- The Refinement and automated choreography strategies were established.

- The Unbundling Process (UP) and Refinement Process (RP) (and thus Unbundling processes) were successful.
- Has implemented its own EA methodology, Polymathic Ratings and Weighing Concept (PRWC), and IHIPTF.
- The DataBase Centric Concept (DBCC) and Integration (DBCI) implementations.
- The Manager/Persons have Advanced Modelling Skills (AMS), ICS, and AI skills

The PRLR is based on IHIPTF's knowledge repository and authors' related works, like:

- A Mathematical Model (MM) for Building Blocks based Organizational UP (Trad, 2023e). Where The UP that is followed by a RP (simply Disassembling).
- The use of the Polymathic Rating and Weighting Concept (Trad, 2024b).
- The Role Team-Based Learning in Polymathics (RTBLP) (Trad, 2023d).
- The Educational Transformation Project's Remote Group Work (BTPRGW) (Trad, & Kalpić, 2023e).
- The Transformation framework-The role security in the global education system (Trad, 2021a).
- The role of artificial intelligence in the global business education (RAIGBE) (Trad, 2021b).
- The Societal and Educational Transformation Projects: The Evolution of the Lebanese Diverse Education (ELDES) (Trad, 2023c).
- The Role of Information and Communication Systems' Standards on Diversity in Educational Environment (Trad, 2023g).
- The Role of Skills in Academic Polymathics Fields (RSAPF) (Trad, 2024f).
- Societal Transformation Projects and the Role and Influence of Human Factors on Natural Resources (Trad, 2024g).
- The Role of Upskilling and Reconversion (RUR) (Trad, 2024h).
- Business transformation project's holistic agile management (BTPHAM) (Trad, & Kalpić, 2022c).
- Machine Learning Integration for Projects (MLI4P) (Trad, 2022).

The RDP confirms an important gap for the RQ, which is due to the following facts: 1) There are no similar RDP and IHIPTF approaches; 2) XHFRs; 3) No adequate RbICC; 4) The exclusive use of accountant's profiles as Managers, which is the cause of major problems like Resistances to Change (R2C); 5) AI-subdomains are siloed and dissociated from ICS Components (ICSC); and 5) There are no professional profiles' description(s) of the needed Polymathic AI-skills. The mentioned RDP's gap was located by using professional projects experiences, existing educational/coaching methods/curriculums, literature on Projects and AI, XHFRs, Groupwork, and RPBAI like concepts that do not exist. This RDP checks RPBAI's feasibility, which is built on existing: AI-subdomains; APM based Groupwork; RbICC; PS/Organizational, educational, and ICS standards. The RPBAI uses critical-thinking that aligns: 1) AI based Groupwork; 2) AHMM4PAI, ARbPAI and HDT based Intelligence; 3) RPBAI patterns; 4) PS (re)engineering for improving used ARbPAIs (Smith, 1987); 5) Provides a universal RbICC; 6) Uses EA blueprints for AI; and 7) RPBAI's integration Factors.

Factors' Management

The IHIPTF supports any type of Project and its subsystems, like the RPBAI, which selects the needed CSAs that in turn contain sets of CSFs. A selected CSF is in turn a set of KPIs, and where each KPI maps to a single Project requirement. Each KPI can map to a concrete ICS programming-language variable, so Project's evaluation delivers real-values/statuses. A requirement maps to a column of the ARbPAI based HDT evaluation CSA Decision Tables (CSA_DT) (Putri, & Yusof, 2009). Project's 1st phase (or feasibility phase), checks the selected sets of Factors, are processed and tuned by applying the following IHIPTF rules: 1) RPBAI-related references have to be credible and are estimated by the researcher by using the Intelligence, and have to be conform to IHIPTF*'s* classification-structure; 2) Project*'s* iterations are dependent on CSA_DTs; 3) The used EA modelling capacities and their mappings to KPIs and ICS' variables; 4) To use an Architecture Development Method (ADM) to manage RPBAI and Project phases; 5) The ADM manages IHIPTF*'s* iterations and Factors' evaluations; and 6) If the aggregations of all CSA_DTs exceed the initially defined Project's minimum, then the Project continues to Proof of Concept's (PoC) execution (or the 2nd phase), which uses the selected Project*'s* Applied Case Studies (ACS).

The Selected ACSs

The ACSs are combined with a common EA/ADM oriented ACS that originates from the Open Group, covers Project basic EA, modelling, linking KPIs, and basic transformation technics with ICS variables; that is the insurance ACS (Jonkers, Band, & Quartel, 2012a). Other ACSs present AI-subdomains. The PRWC is used the 1st Project's iteration and then (re)evaluated by using subsequent ADM coordinated iterations. The selected Factors (and especially CSFs) are linked to ACSs which are:

- A list of problem types must define especially when using Groupwork teaching environments. The response to quality mass education is to integrate cross-functional student groups and the RPBAI supports Polymathic teaching and learning. This ACS is related to Entity's approach by offering Groupwork based combined courses. Educators of Groupwork based courses must be (re) skilled with needed core capabilities. The usage of Groupwork was successful and the students and educators did find it complex (Postle, 2003).
- The use of Polymathic/cross-functional skills and Cycles cases curriculum (Clark, Johnson, Turner, 2004; Crittenden, & Wilson, 2006; D'Souza, Bement, & Cory, 2022; Fitzgerald, 2005).
- ACSs from various companies (AT&T, 2. Migrato, Prime Therapeutics, Tchibo, Zavarovalnica Triglav...) using AI/RPBAI to solve problems and challenges; where they have generated and stored huge data-volumes on their customers… It is complex to manage data over distributed ICS. AI supports such configurations and transforms Entities practices (Savage, 2024).

The Use of the ADM for the Project

Figure 3. ADM's phases (The Open Group, 2011a, 2011b; Holilah, Girsang, & Saragih, 2019)

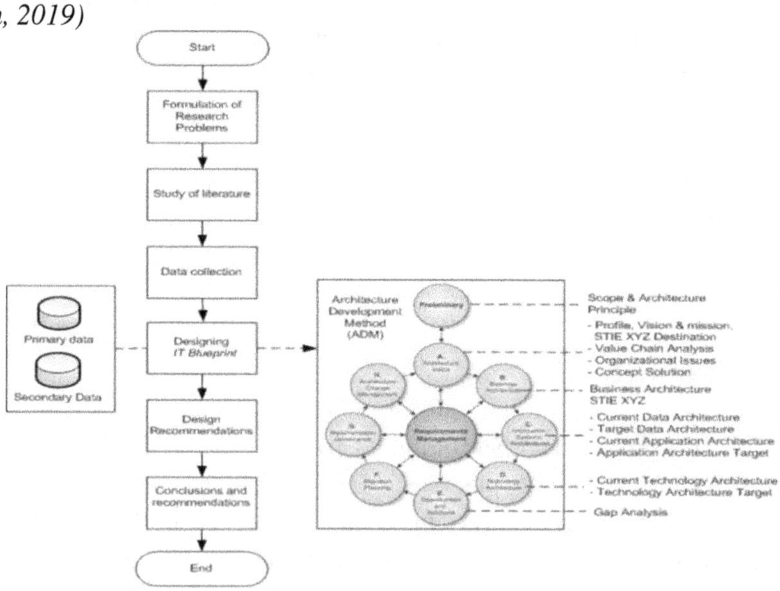

This RDP checks the RQ that is related to RPBAI's integration and activities. The ARbPAI based Learning, Groupwork, and ICS infrastructure, need an ADM to be coordinated. Intelligence delivers RPBAI solution types, recommendations, action sets, and optimal RbICCs. The IHIPTF synchronizes Project's with ADM activities as shown in Figure 3. The generated RbICCs support future Polymath profiles, who had experienced various AI-domains. The RPBAI operations and Project's structure can be modelled by using the AHMM4PAI.

The AHMM4PAI

The PRWC assesses critical Factors (and risks) to check Project's and RPBAI's coherencies, by using AHMM4PAI. This RDP uses the Empirical Engineering Research Model (EERM) (Easterbrook, Singer, Storey, & Damian, 2008) and a Polymathic-Mathematical Model (PMM) which is Project's limited reality. A PMM provides abstractions of Project*'s* physical system(s) or module(s) (Hinkelmann, 2016).

Figure 4. AHMM's nomenclature (Trad, & Kalpić, 2020a)

Basic Mathematical Model's (BMM) Nomenclature

Iteration	= An integer variable "*i*" that denotes a *Project/ADM iteration*	
microRequirement	= (maps to) KPI	(N1)
CSF	= Σ KPI	(N2)
Requirement	= (maps to) CSF = $\bigcup$ microRequirement	(N3)
CSA	= Σ CSF	(N4)
microMapping microArtefact/Req	= microArtefact + (maps to) microRequirement	(N5)
microKnowledgeArtefact	= $\bigcup$ knowledgeItem(s)	(N6)
neuron	= action->data + microKnowledgeArtefact	(N7)
microArtefact / neural network	= $\bigcup$ neurons	(N8)
microArtefactScenario	= $\bigcup$ microartefact	(N9)
AI/Decision Making	= $\bigcup$ microArtefactScenario	(N10)
microEntity	= $\bigcup$ microArtefact	(N11)
Entity or Enterprise	= $\bigcup$ microEntity	(N12)
EntyIntelligence	= $\bigcup$ AI/Decision Making	(N13)
BMM(*Iteration*) as an instance	= EntityIntelligence(*Iteration*)	(N14)

The Generic AHMM's Formulation

AHMM	= $\bigcup$ ADMs + BMMs	(N15)

AHMM's Application and Instantiation for RPBAI

Domain	= **RPBAI**	(N16)
AHMM4(*Domain*)	= $\bigcup$ ADMs + BMMs(*Domain*)	(N17)

AHMM4PAI's basic elements are used in Intelligence and RPBAI's requests-processing; and AHMM4PAI's nomenclature is presented in Figure 4:

- The symbol $\sum$ indicates summation of PRWC's actions, denoting the importance of the set members selected as relevant. Ratings and weightings as integers ranging in ascending importance from 1 to 10.
- The symbol $\underline{U}$ indicates sets union.
- The AHMM4PAI defines the Project and RPBAI as models, using Factors and PRWC.

The PRWC

An IHIPTF needs an internal and generic PRWC (like in IHIPTF) which can be implemented in various manners; and it can choose a standard external PRWC. The PRWC uses the following rules and definitions:

- The weighting for a CSA ϵ { 0.00% ... 100.00% } are floating point percentage values, which are derived from decision Tables. Each CSA has one decision Table.
- A weighting is defined for each RPBAI's CSF, and a rating for each KPI.
- The selected corresponding weightings for CSFs ϵ { 1 ... 10 } are integer values.
- The selected corresponding ratings to KPI ϵ { 0.00% ... 100.00% } and is derived from: 1) An ICS application/module variable(s); or 2) Estimated by the IHIPTF.
- The AHMM4PAI applies the HDT, which uses the PRWC.

The AHMM4PAI applies the HDT which is mainly qualitative specific quantitative methods. For a selected and known RPBAI problem type, RQ, or Factor, the HDT solves by relating breadth and depth tree processing; and the results/findings are persisted in ARbPAIs.

CYCLES AND POLYMATHICS FOR RPBAI

Fundaments

Cycles and Polymathic can support RPBAI by offering (Pushpakumara, Jayaweera, & Manjulan, 2021; Trad, & Kalpić, 2017a, 2020a, 2021a, 2022a, 2022b; Aksoy, & Ceylan, 2021):

- The RbICC is independent of Cycles and the PSC can detect Polymathic Persons.
- Agile environments, patterns, best practices, and interactive infrastructure.
- The RPBAI needs experienced Polymath Coaches to manage RbICC topics.
- The RbICC links complex AI-topics and defines their relationships, like in Architecture (in civil engineering) that makes Persons capable of designing complex towers design.
- Coaches who can support different types of strongly related courses, activities, and complexities.
- RPBAI based on: 1) EA models; 2) IHIPTF and AHMM4PAI; 3) Unbundled services pool; 4) Various Cycles templates, and patterns; 5) A scalable ICS for agile Groupwork; 6) An APM; and 7) A dynamic RbICC (based on the Business Transformation Project's Architect's Profile-BTPAP).
- Intelligence, Factors, and AR/ARbPAI based HDT that is optimal for evolutive education, and problem solving.

Cycles' Interactions

In the Project*'s* 1st phase there is the need to define: 1) Groupwork interfaces and RbICC mandatory subjects; 2) AI, EA, ICS and PS/organizational change frequencies-steps; 3) Common/related topics and activities; and 4) Coaches profiles and needed skills. Project*'s* complexities are due to the transformation of the Learning into dynamic and agile Groupwork based academic/educational system for UCs. RPBAI, RbICC, and Cycles' evolution needs EA methodologies, Intelligence, and experiences/skills. In the author's previous works, he has identified Project*s'* important research gap(s), which is due to management's incapacities and the need for BTPAP. Identified Polymathic Persons must be traced through all Cycles as shown in Figure 5. Unfortunately, today Project*s* are managed by business schools' graduates-based profiles (who have an accountants' profiles). Cycles require Coaches having Polymathic skills, who can coordinate and uses RbICCs/RPBAI. RbICCs has to incorporate also multi-cultural, Multi-technical, and cross-functional education for Persons (EURSC, 2022).

Figure 5. RbICC's organisation of cycles and project's evolution

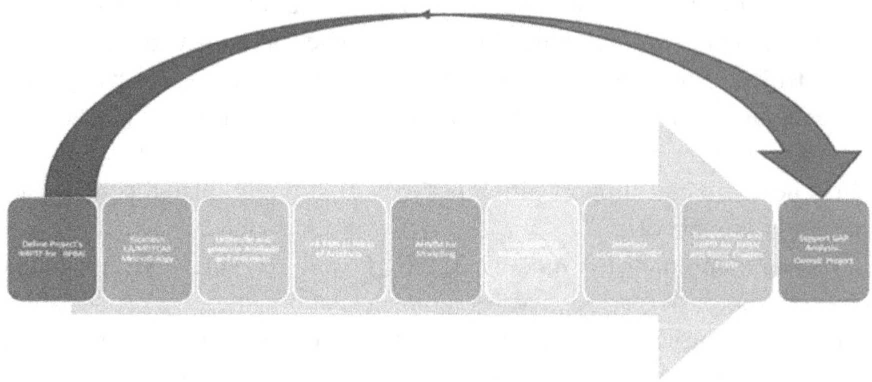

Polymathical Capacities and Profiles

Figure 6. The relation between polymathic groups (Cotellessa, 2018)

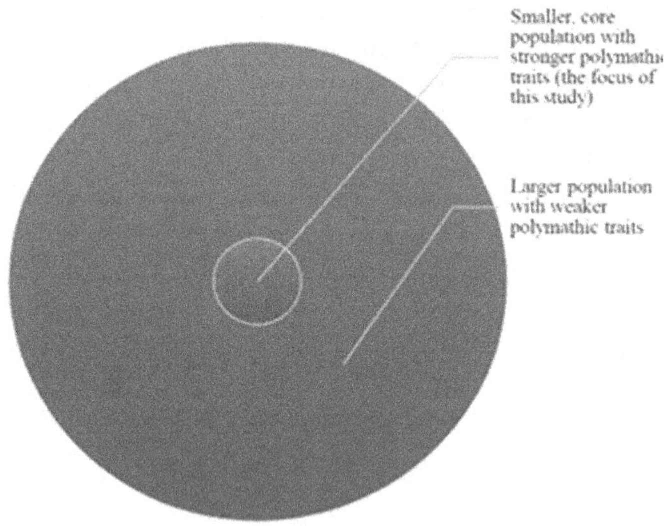

Polymathic capacities are crucial for AI-Fields and hence RPBAI. As AI is advancing and is capable of performing complex-tasks that brings great benefits, and also challenges for Persons with limited skills and where polymath-thinking play a major-role (Brayer, 2023). Polymathics are open to experiences, autonomous upskilling, multi-disciplinarity, cross-functional thinking, and diversity. Where identity Theory and social identity theory are important Factors. Since the age of the Renaissance that started in the 14th (AC) brought Polymathic personalities who exceled in cross-functional domains like: 1) Nikola Tesla an inventor, engineer, writer, mathematician, philosophy…; 2) Michelangelo a painter, sculptor, architect, poet, engineer, scientist; 3) Thomas Jefferson a politician, scholar, lawyer, philosopher, naturalist, astronomer, archaeologist, horticulturist, linguist, and inventor); 4) Albert Einstein a physicist and violinist; and many others. They share a common feature that is that they were all exceptional mathematicians (which is optimal for RPBAI); and they all different, unique and they have transformed Intelligence. The majority of Persons have Polymathic capacities and a smaller category has full Polymathic-capacities (Cotellessa, 2018). But Polymathics has also disadvantages, like the time (and resources) needed to know various Fields and interconnecting them; and Polymathicians are underestimated and even marginalized, because Entities give value to single-discipline expertise. There are common Polymathic features like (Cotellessa, 2018): 1) Experts across Fields; 2) Have complex identities; 3) Have Return on Experiences (ROE); 4) Have a clear career paths; 5) Shaped by society; 6) Voracious learners; 7) Confident; 8) Highly-creative; and 9) Never satisfied. RPBAI professions are related to transformations and innovations-oriented practices, which needs AI/ICSC implementation, refactoring/refinement, analyse/design, develop, and transform legacy Entity's parts. ACSs and experiences show the lack of the use of AI Polymathic concepts that are needed for Projects that also need continuous ARbPAI/Learning evolutions (Crittenden, 2005). The RbICC' can include: 1) Concept of evolutive AI-quality; 2) Cross-functional AI implementation-teams; 3) Use reference Projects and AI-solutions; 4) Cycles' bridging; 5) Persons' reorientation, upskilling, and renewal; 6) Linking Projects to all AI-topics; and 7) Use RPBAI interfaces. RbICC's, RPBAI's evolutions end Learning Process (LP) depend on ROE, ICSCs' evolutions, Speed of Changes (SoC), Agility/APM, Literature/references, and Cycles implications. Polymathic AI-teams need to be prepared and evaluated by Factors (Satterlee, 1996). There are different viewpoints on Polymathics and Learning, and there is the need to offer a suitable RbICC (Crittenden, & Wilson, 2006). Learning methodology is to teach *like-minded* Persons within t Cycle's majors. RPBAI specific Factors link to: 1) AI-modules outcomes; 2) AI-Groupwork fields; 3) Intelligence features, 4) Problem solving; and 5) Managing ROEs.

Managing ROEs

ROEs enable and supports AI-Groupwork. RPBAI uses an LP Database (LPD) that manages ROEs and interfaces Intelligence. RPBAI's requests to the LPD are used to enhance RbICCs, where a RbICC shows how Cycles topics are interconnected, where RbICCs are built on templates. An important ROE category is related to design and creativity which foster Persons' skills in EA, Intelligence, Business Process (BP), modelling. Groupwork based design and modelling supports complex problem-solving and can enhance their creativity in Groupwork based brainstorming activities that include Mind mapping; Strength, Weakness, Opportunity and Threat (SWOT), Unified Modelling Language (UML)… (Ahmad, 2020; Cress, Moskaliuk, & Jeong, 2016). ROEs can also relate to academic Cycles to connect to studying, practicing, and gaining architecture and design skills (Cambridge Dictionary, 2023, Trad, 2023a, 2024b), that need agility.

Agility and APM

The RPBAI needs agility to: 1) Delivers AI-Groupwork scenarios; 2) Supports quality upskilling; 3) Enables agile RPBAI- practices; and 4) Manages ROEs. AI agilization is based on (Trad, Kalpić, 2022c; Kersten, 2021; Burke, 2022; IBM, 2024):

- Defining granularity-levels and ensuring design team's Work-Flows (WF).
- Avoid eXtremely Agile Management (XAM) and use APM; adapt the right SoC.
- Manage AI-complexities by collaboration to change Entity's structure.
- The APM can use a Scaled Agile Framework (SAFe), for RPBAI.
- Supports complex AI based BPMs (intelligent BPM or iBPM)
- Coined by Gartner, AI for ITOps (AIOps), is the application of AI capabilities to automate and streamline ICS service management and operational WFs.
- AIOps uses big-data, analytics, and Machine Learning (ML) to: 1) Collect and aggregate the huge- volumes of data; 2) Identifies significant events and patterns related to performance and availability; and 3) Diagnoses root causes and report them.
- Integrating various tools into a single, AIOps enables ICS operations to be proactive and decrease outages in all AI-Fields and APplication Domains (APD).

THE AI-FIELDS AND APDs

AI's APDs

AI main APDs are (GiniMachine, 2022):

- Banking and Finance Technologies (FinTech) where AI offers data-analytics, conversational-AI, no-code-AI, and metaverse for Projects.
- Healthcare uses AI for disease prediction, risk assessment, pandemics management, insurance, and digital healthcare solutions.
- E-commerce implements use-cases of AI and ML, predictive-analytics, demand-forecasting, demand-patterns, internal-decisions, and external-factors.
- Sales and marketing use predictive-marketing/analytics, statistical-techniques, predictive-modelling, customer-segmentation, churn-prediction, and data-mining.
- Lending solutions use contract-type, mobile-Internet, streaming, total-day-charge, monthly-charges, Payment-methods, Total-day/night-minutes, Account-length, Voice-mail, Area-code…
- Agriculture uses computer-vision, historical-data/predictive-models, lending-insurance…
- Industry uses predictive-analytics in manufacturing, ML-tools, identifying-trends, detect-issues, planning, Internet of Things (IoT), optimizes-resource-planning, predicting-demand, and credit-risks.
- Insurance uses forecasts for risk-profiles, decision-making, predictive-analytics, onboarding, data- models for lending-decisions, devices-tracking driving, cognitive-technologies for customers' behaviours…
- Business decision-making uses ML, patterns, risks-management, predictive-models…
- Travel and hospitality use face-recognition (in airports), costs-optimizations and travel-booking, travel-disruptions management, customer-churn prediction, risks of cancelling, analyzing visitors' sentiments…

AI's Fields

AI has many branches like linguistics, prejudice, vision, planning, Robotic Process Automation (RPA), Natural Language Processing, decision science… As shown in Figure 7, AI main Fields are (Rancho Labs, 2021; Garanhel, 2023, Riedl, 2023):

- ML techniques and algorithms are trained so the machine can use Supervised, Unsupervised or Reinforcement Learning. And can used in self-driving cars, image and speech recognition…
- Neural Network (NN) incorporates cognitive science into machines to execute tasks. NN mimics the human-brain, which has an infinite number of neurons, to code brain-neurons into a system. Is used to identify elemental correlations among large amounts of data.

- NLP is a method of computational-analysis of human-languages, by mimicking human-natural-language, and it can interpret data by searching, analysing, and extracting information from text.
- Deep Learning (DL) learns by analysing data and identifying an acceptable-output; and is referred to as self-learning. It uses a variety of random programmes and algorithms, that includes: 1) Detection of human emotions-expressions; 2) Identify humans and animals based on pictures...; 3) Recognize and memorise voices of different people; 4) Video and audio conversions into text-data; and 5) Identification of right and wrong gestures...
- Cognitive computing enhances Human-Machine Interaction (HMI) to achieve complex tasks and solve problems. Cognitive thinking combined with AI creates a product with human-like actions and skills.
- Computer vision identifies, and interprets visual inputs from pictures and captures. It uses DL and pattern-recognition to extract visual-information from any data.
- Expert systems specialize in singular tasks, like human-experts, they are designed with human-like decision-making capabilities. They use inference rules to solve complex problems like in loan-analysis.
- Robotics is about programmed-machines that can automatically execute a series of actions, where Persons control them. Humanoid-robots which recognize human faces and understands emotions and gestures...
- Fuzzy Logic is a technique used to solve issues that can either be true or false, which copies human-decisions by considering all possibilities. And it has four parts: 1) Base for rules and conditions; 2) Fuzzification that convert inputs; 3) Inference engine matches rules and fuzzy inputs; and 4) Defuzzification, converts fuzzy sets into crips-values.
- Large Language Models (LLM) are trained on the internet of any type of text against people, like making stereotypical assumptions, conspiracy theories, political misinformation... And such terms can be generated...

Figure 7. AI fields (Rancho Labs, 2021)

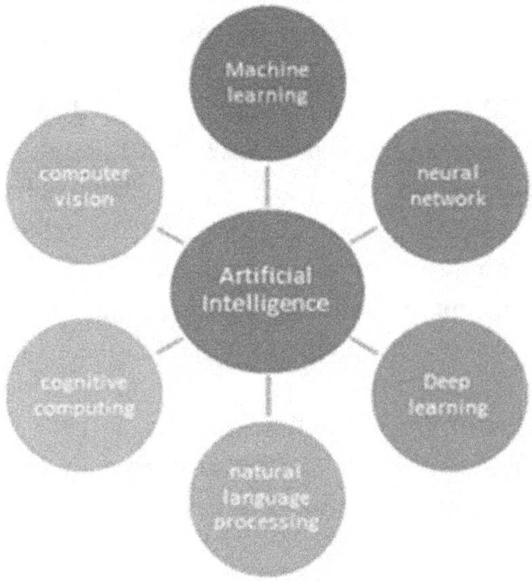

AR for RPBAI

AR is crucial in education and offers an AI teaching concept that is based on (Heinze, Haase, & Higgins, 2010; Trad, 2013; Dick 2002; Nijboer, Morin, Carmien, Koene, Leon, & Hoffman, 2009):

- AR can be used to improve Learning and ROEs.
- The improvement of educational outcomes in sciences and mathematics, and needs a corresponding syllabus based on AI-Fields.
- Introducing basic concepts, vocabulary and history of science generally and AI specifically in a manner that emphasises Persons' engagement.
- Adding AI to the Curricula and practices, and it is important to integrate problem-solving concepts in broader educational activities.
- The AI syllabus is a part of a whole of curricula approach to studies that integrates, various Fields and enriches experiences through empirical-evidence or ROE.
- AR improves and tunes the RbICC in and incremental manner.
- Such an RbICC fits PS' policy guidelines.
- IHIPTF's HDT applies a spiral model which implements AR steps.

- The spiral model matches perfectly with RPBAI's iterative approach, which is an empirical reasoning algorithm, and fits education; hence Cycles.
- AR = action and research corresponds to HDT's (tree) nodes process and calls to services.
- The AR based HDT implementation is cyclic (and spiral) where each cycle corresponds to the creation (or modification) of an Intelligence tree-node.
- Iterations extend across HDT's processing; where each cycle (or new node) defines the set of problems (related to Factors and actions) to be solved.
- These problems are processed-solved by a defined set of actions.
- That mapping concept defines analytical AR's inter-related actions/steps.
- AR based HDT can be considered as a Qualitative AI Field; and that should be added to the AI bas RbICC.
- The HDT based RPBAI and Intelligence.
- The HDT problem-solving process is supported by Intelligence and uses a dynamic tree algorithm.

THE AI BASED RBICC

The Roles of Complexities and Uncertainty

RbICC must take into account forging Polymathics preparing students to manage complexities. Complexities are related to cross-functional AI-Fields integration, AMS, (re)engineering, and ICSCs' implementation. Student's intellectual capabilities for cross-functional AI-Fields is determinant Factor. Factors related to complexity are (Bryce, 2015): 1) The volume of topics and tasks; 2) The characteristics of AI-component; and 3) Students AI's abstraction, architecture and modelling capacities. A Project can use Complexities Management Strategies (CMS) to detect complexities and to apply accountability (Heywood, Hillar, & Turnbull, 2010). CMSs can support AI which are difficult to predict and can exceed student's cognitive limits; and it relates various AI topics, and tasks which are autonomous (even siloed). The IHIPTF manages complexity and offers: 1) A cohesive AI strategy; 2) Using the HDT; 3) Using the *Global Simplicity Index,* for reducing complexities; and 4) Quantitative, Qualitative or Mixed Approach(s) for AI (QQMA4AI).

The QQMA4AI

QQMA4AI's features and constraints are (Marchese, 2023):

- AI-Fields like LLMs offer new possibilities in AI research, and understanding differences between these two major streams.
- Data-collection methods differ, and a quantitative-study depends on surveys/polls, whereas a qualitative-study uses AR-processing, interviews…
- The scope wider with qualitative research.
- It is simpler to structure data in quantitative-methods, whereas qualitative-data originate from unstructured databases. ML can be used to support formatting data.
- The final-goals are different, and a quantitative-study measures the relationship between variables, whereas qualitative-research tries to answer *why* questions or explore a specific subject.
- Statistical Analysis (SA) is popular quantitative-methods, whereas qualitative-methods use thematic analysis, synthesis, AR/grounded theory…
- Qualitative-research aims to get insights in open-ended questions; where formats can include: Focus groups, Interviews, ACSs, Observations, Diaries and journals, Comments and emails, Feedback and reviews, Support tickets…
- Quantitative-research is numerical and can include: SA from the web, Purchase data, Financial reports, Quasi-experimental research, A cross-sectional survey…
- Qualitative approaches reflect ROEs and answer the *why* questions and shows unique insights and lead to a new theory/recommendation; like this RDP. It is optimal for educational structures and RbICC core.

The RbICC Core

RbICC's Core includes the following features and constraints (Clark, Johnson, & Turner, 2004; Woudenberg, & Unis, 2023; Hayashi, Shibata, Inoue, Adachi, & Iba, 2022; Pisonia, Gijlersc, Nguyend, & Chene, 2021):

- Explaining quantitative, qualitative or mixed approaches in AI-Fields.
- Explaining data-structures, interfaces, algorithms and MMs.
- Explaining ICS topics for AI like programming.
- Explaining AI-Fields and their diffrences.
- Time constraints limit the number and type of elective subjects/courses.
- Implement cross-functional domains (ICS, purchasing/marketing/sales, innovation, manufacturing, …).
- Polymathic subjects, need collective-actions to deliver solutions, which brings-up new paradigms limiting creativity.
- Promote interaction and diversity that is inspired by the industry and incorporate adequate coursework.

- Create Polymathic cross-functional teams to benefit from cross-discipline diversity.
- Offer diverse disciplines in graduate/undergraduate courses from different Entity's departments; that encourages AI-Polymathism.
- Offer various topics AI-Fields, ICS, business, human-sciences, media to learn from each other's ROEs.
- Review courses' outcomes to find new opportunities and apply changes.
- Interactions and relations between topics can enable the optimal use of resources across all classes.
- Interaction with external partner's interactions by using projects and applying system's thinking.
- Polymathic system's thinking that includes: Holistic systemized-model; Solving complex problems as shown in Figure 8; Different viewpoints; and IHIPTF.
- Use of evolving advanced ICS/technologies and AI, have created an important transformation paradigm-shift.
- AI-Fields are integrated in ICSs, that needs Polymath thinking that relates to multiple disciplines.
- Includes skills, like: Critical thinking, AMS, Creativity, Adaptability, adaptability… (Orayer, 2023).
- Apply Leaning and managing ROEs.
- Use APM, EA models and Groupwork based LPs.
- Enable the implementation of Polymathic student projects.
- Supporting students' Polymathic capacities from persisted ROEs.
- Sharing collective ROEs/experiences and enforcing ethical principles.
- Includes topics like STEM, and other complex topics.
- Groupwork interactions by: Brain-storming, Managing, Modelling, Planning, coordinating actions, ...
- Modelling of complex inter-related AI-topics and problem-solving activities.
- Use AR/HDT to improve teaching technics.

Figure 8. Complex projects can support autonomous systems (Woudenberg, & Unis, 2023)

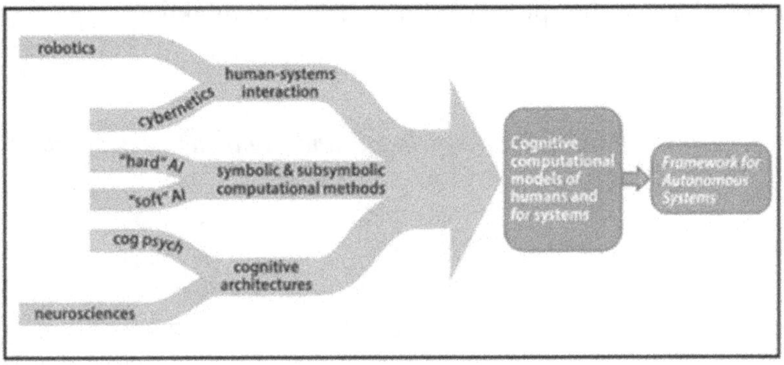

RbICC's Specific Issues

RbICC's specific issues (Fitzgerald, 2005; Tuononen, Hyytinen, Kleemola, Hailikari, Männikkö, & Toom, 2022; Page, Schagen, Fallus, Bron, De Coninck, Maes, Sleurs, & Van Woensel, 2005; Banks, & Barlex, 2021):

- Define policies and related professional domains, that include AI-Fields, Critical-thinking, Collaboration/Communication, Modelling, and problem-solving skills.
- Complex AI-topics must be controlled and related to cross-functional topics.
- Apply Polymathics based Project Oriented Learning for AI (PPOL4AI), which includes ROEs and Groupwork.
- PPOL4AIs uses real-world problems to be solved by AI.
- PPOL4AIs supports students in planning, modelling and implementing AI-modules.
- PPOL4AI is an organized development process that enhances students' empiric experiences.
- PPOL4AI's strategy is to minimize unpredictability, by modelling problem types and assignments.
- RPBAI needs adapted RbICCs, in which Polymathic topics are dynamically inserted in an RbICC, as shown in Figure 9.
- A Dynamic RbICC (DRbICC) can be adapted to students having exceptional Polymathical capacities.
- The DRbICC supports: 1) Cycles especially disseminating technological/ ICS development; 2) Integrate quality STEM ; 3) Use concrete projects; 4)

Critical thinking; 5) Enforce responsibility; and 6) Confronting complexities/ uncertainty.

- Didactics for interdisciplinary critical deductive thinking.

Figure 9. A case of Polymathic knowledge and competency curriculum/project (Banks, & Barlex, 2021)

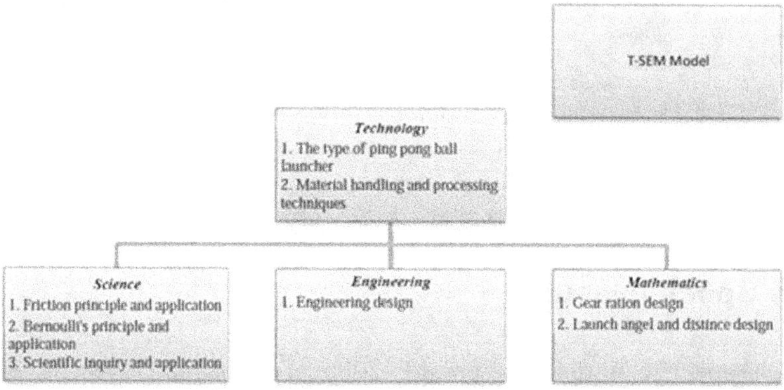

THE AI-FIELDS' ADVANCED TOPICS

EA, AMS, and Granularity

For AI-Fields and Groupwork based courses, limited students-group concept is optimal, but groups' granularity/size has to be defined. Granularity is related to class-size, the available period… Like *Virtual learning teams* which can have a class has any size, any time frame and its main purpose is to enforce relationships between students, and to increase their confidence. Creativity is essential for Intelligence which supports problem-solving, innovation initiatives. The RPBAI supports creativity that is associated with AI-Fields, AMS, and is considered a valuable characteristic in RbICC. EA has defined phases, predefined artefacts, and includes iterative ADM synchronizations. The ADM supports AI-modules development, and maintenance phases/processes. RPBAI uses market frameworks (like TOAGF) to implement complex AI-models, and that needs AMS.

AI based iBPM's Integration

iBPM's automation characteristics are (Brañas, 2024; IBM, 2024a, Trad, & Kalpić, 2017b):

- Combines BP's redesign, RPA, BP Automation (BPA), AI/ML to automate BPs.
- Reduces costs and supports productivity, quality…
- Minimizes human-labour and resource utilization.
- Improves quality and consistency of outcomes by applying standardized rules BPs.
- Enhances compliance with regulations by ensuring adherence to best practices.
- Monitors and measures performances by using DA.
- Integrates AI-Fields in ICSCs, to provide competitive advantages.
- Analyses huge amounts of data that enables real-time decision-making and optimization of BPs.
- Discovering bottlenecks, predicting nodes' failures and adapt to dynamic-market trends.
- Detecting incomplete (or inconsistent) data, leading to precise insights, forecasting…
- Applying ML for predictive analytics to support planning and streamline WFs.
- Supply chain optimization by performing routing, flexible scheduling, and streamlining BPs.
- Predictive maintenance to minimize downtime, extend assets' lifespan, and reduce operational costs.
- Supporting staff by using chatbots, providing data and answering common queries.
- RPA uses bots to automate routine tasks that are rule-based and repetitive tasks.
- AI for ITOps (AIOps), automates and streamlines ICS services' management and operational WFs.
- iBPM uses AI-as-a-service (AIaaS) platform that replaces legacy solutions.
- AIaaS is a 3rd-party solution of AI outsourcing, and it enables Entities to PoC AI-Fields without investing.
- Decision-making is data-driven by analysing large datasets, providing insights, enhancing Intelligence.

The Intelligence

A Project and the RPBAI are supported the HDT based Intelligence that manages ROEs. Intelligence delivers solutions for Project problems and these solution(s) are in the form of recommendations which propose transformational changes, and how to minimize important risks. Intelligence enhances stored ARbPAIs and supports RPBAI's integration risks' management (Hussain, Dillon, Chang & Hussain, 2010). At ADM's first iteration is to setup Learning transformation conditions and use the ARbPAIs to manage Educational Knowledge Items (EKI), where and ROE is a set of interlinked EKIs and enhanced Intelligence... Intelligence supports Entity's underlying mechanics to manage ARbPAIs and linked EKIs. The Project interfaces Intelligence and its stored EKIs, where an EKI is linked to Factors. The RPBAI interfaces Intelligence to offer an RbICCs. Intelligence offers patterns/templated to support encountered problems, like: Insufficient Polymathic capacities; Bad communication/coordination, Non-Autonomous conditions, and Lack of motivation. Intelligence supports project's goals and that was the ultimate strategic educational goal.

RPBAI and Intelligence's Main AI-Fields or Blocks

RPBAI and Intelligence's main AI-Fields or blocks incorporate AIaaS for (Trad, 2022; Schmelzer, 2021; Veneberg, 2014):

- EA supports: 1) Traceability and monitoring subsystem using standard patterns; 2) Operational and historic data to be used; 3) Data Base Management System (DBMS) that is a collection of inter-related data; and 4) DBMS' various technologies.
- DS supports: 1) Extraction of insights in the context of vast amounts of data; includes, statistics, visualization, DLI and ML concepts; 2) Finding hidden patterns from raw data (structured or unstructured), and translates problems into solutions; and 3) Discovery, preparation, model-planning/model building and predicting solutions.
- ML supports: 1) Learning from experience and helps machines to identify learning patterns; 2) Abstracting Learning from samples of data-models; and 3) Different types of LPs: Supervised, Unsupervised, and Reinforcement learning.
- Composite AI Model supports: 1) Combining DS, ML, and other for generating insights from massive data; 2) Predictive analytics forecasts of customers' behaviour...; 3) Conversational systems; 4) Anomaly detections; 5) Hyperpersonalization for advertising, product recommendation...; 6) Financial crimes detection.

- Data-Warehousing (DW) supports: 1) Store operational and historical data can be used in ML; 2) Decision support for Entity's knowledge-workers; and 3) Operational Data Store (ODS) is the data updated from an OnLine Transaction Processing (OLTP).
- Big-Data (BD) supports: 1) Massive, fast or complex accesses; 2) Now-mainstream definitions or the three V's: Volume, Velocity, and Variety.

AI-Based Transformations

AI based Transformations depend on (Kohli, 2024 ; Krysik, 2024 ; Hayes, & Downie, 2024):

- A Human-Centric Blueprint by putting emphasis on understanding user perspectives, behaviors and challenges.
- Identifying CSAs, where the transformation starts with understanding stakeholders' needs.
- Aligning requirements with objectives, by developing clarity of problems by using the IHIPTF.
- Apply iterative and successful steps, by prioritizing solutions, potential impacts, and feasibility.
- The hyper-evolution of tools like ChatGPT, DALL-E, LLMs, Theano are becoming popular.
- AI-Fields should be incorporated in BPs.
- Establishment of a strategic initiative where AI is embedded in operations, products and services.
- Optimization of organizational WFs by using AI-models and BPA.
- Modernize Apps, provide data-driven insights, improve ROEs.
- Prepare an AI-paradigm shift which: 1) Defines the strategy and value; 2) Technology and data that need well-designed models, and deployment strategies; 3) ROEs' design and operating models; and 4) Upskilling and adaptation.
- Is a dynamic process and follows the following planning processes: 1) Information gathering by performing research to gain an understanding of AI-Fields; 2) Assessing current resources and limitations; 3) Defining objectives that are measured by PRWC; 4) Implementing a roadmap by choosing AI based Project's components based on practical requirements.
- When Project's strategic planning has been completed, then transformation (designing, implementing, training/validating, and tuning) of AI-model starts.

- AI-deployment Factors include: Collecting and managing data, Organizing data, Building (training and tuning) of AI models, Automating WFs, and Infusing AI in whole of the ICS.
- Forsee AI-transformation challenges, where a robust, responsible AI based Project and RPBAI improve performance and enable significant competitive advantages. Having in mind Projects' XHFRs.
- Use EA-modelling and using modelling languages like Archimate.

EA-Modelling and Modelling Languages

EA-modelling and using modelling languages for AI-Fields, includes (Takeuchia, Yamamotob, 2019; Granger, 2024; Richards, 2024):

- Modelling AI Service Systems (AISS) based on business services that explicitly define exposed business behaviors.
- AISS' Business process that is a sequence of business behaviors achieving specific goals.
- AISS' Business object that is a concept used within a particular APD.
- AISS' Application service that is a defined application behavior.
- AISS' Application component that is an encapsulation of application functionalities.
- AISS' Data object that is a data structure used for automated processing.
- AISS' uses concepts, with defined model's Archimate's elements and relationships as shown in Figure
- Generative AI (GAI) for EA modeling has become the foundation of EA frameworks where models represent control.
- An LLM is both a dynamic process and a form of GAI and Intelligence's representation.
- GAI has upended various APD's assumptions around Intelligence.
- GAI is a major paradigm shift due to the improvements of LLM's performance, new database technologies, that makes information architecture of EA modeling, becomes more fluid. And that is transforming the language barriers.
- LLM based GAI for EA supports: 1) Risk assessment; 2) Risk mitigation; 3) Anti-Patterns; and 4) Decision-making. That can support Entity's Full Automation (EFA).

Figure 10. Elements in AISS (Takeuchia, Yamamotob, 2019)

AI Service System Model Element	Element in ArchiMate	
New business service		Business service
Business process preparing AI engine		Business process
Develop AI resource for a target business.		
Generate a model from AI resource.		
Business process using AI application		
Source(e.g., business data and business document)		Business object
AI resource (e.g., training data)		
Runtime input		
Runtime output		
Application service for developing AI resource		Application service
Application service for training a model		
AI application service		
Tool for developing AI resource		Application component
AI training engine		
AI runtime engine		
AI Model		Data model

THE EFA

Common-Grounds, Evolution, and Standards

RPBAI and EFA sub-domains lack common grounds, coordinated-evolution, standards and governance. The mentioned AI-Fields are in an excessive chaotic state, but they are in a process of hyper-evolution. But fields like RPA are quickly progressing and the more BPA is needed, the more important is the role of GAI and RPBAI. Important Factors are repeating transformational successes across iBPM and achieving EFA, that need mature AMS and GAI skills. Therefore, there is the need for a formalized central AMS paradigm to support EFA and RPA related transformations. RPBAI needs a Polymathic view for AI-Fields, ICS and APD, to support the following characteristics and roles as shown in Figure 11 (Sied, 2018):

- Speeds-up that EFA in a scalable manner.
- Business-outcome orientation needs GAI based EA/TDM (GEA) to support Polymathic concept for growth, productivity, cost improvements…
- Agile-vendor evaluation cannot solve all unautomated operations therefore, GEA to support different vendor-specific architectures and patterns.
- ICS' strategy needs enablers because RPAs fail due the lack of clear, documented strategy for Projects.

- Standards and governance frameworks like TOGAF enforce standards and governance across security, platforms, integration, and vendors.
- Integration strategy based on Platform-as-a-Service (PaaS), AIaaS, and today there are a lot of tools to integrate siloed systems.
- Modular reusability based on fit-gap analysis to transform legacy ICSCs.

Figure 11. The GEA increases success rates for RPA (Sied, 2018)

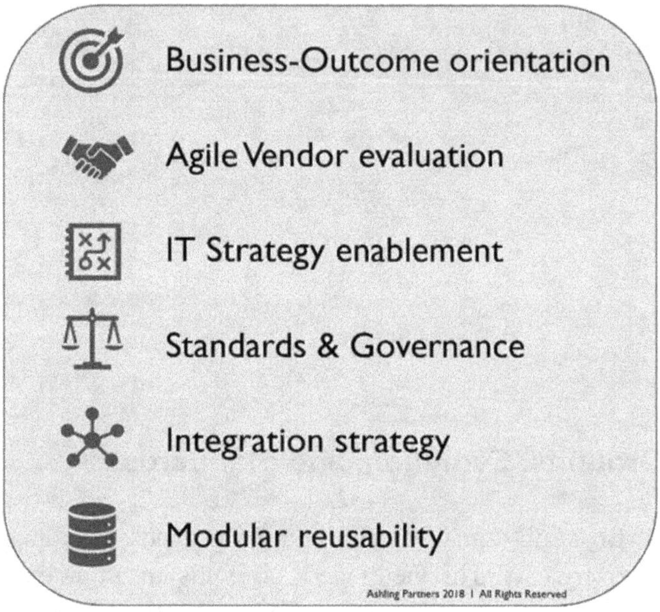

Scalability, Reusability and Optimization

Evolution and standards need a well-organized Entity and the GEA guides it through Cycles identification and prioritization across EFA related AI-Fields as shown in Figure 12. That implies that there is the need for testing and scaling RPA, intelligent process automation, and AI modules. These facts improve the ROI but there is also the need to use RPBAI in a coordinated manner with GEA.

Figure 12. EFA's fields needed for optimization (Sied, 2018)

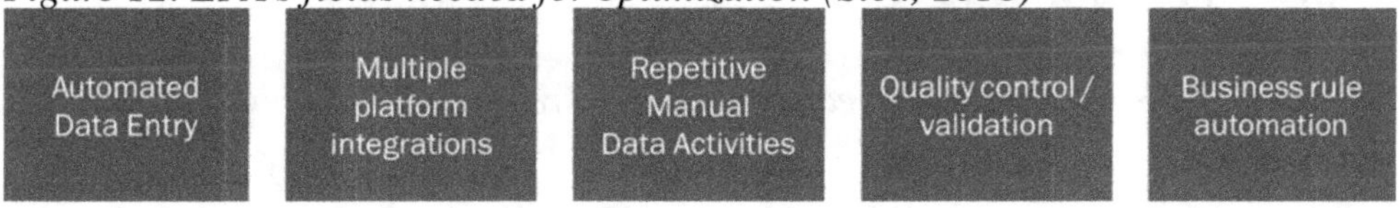

These facts support Projects and Disassembling processes for EFA, but can face difficulties because of heterogenous fields (Trad, 2023e). This can be improved by the use of the Audit, Control and Monitoring Design Patterns (ACMDP) (Trad, 2005).

The ACMDP and EFA

The ACMDP can be used for support Autonomous and Robust Systems (ARS), Mobile Robot Systems (MRS). This set of patterns can be used also for other Mission Critical and Complex Systems (MCCS) (Trad, 2005). The ACMDP supports Project managers and engineers in building, designing, and estimating Project's gaps. Furthermore, it offers the possibility to solve encountered problems with the help of: Audit, monitoring and controlling components; Adjustments of Project's management pathways; Define the problem sources as well as their possible solutions; and Establish an Architectural Design Pattern for EFA (ADP4EFA). The ADP4EFA is also applicable for autonomous complex systems and offers the possibility to detect in advance the potential GEA problems with the help of monitoring and controlling systems. The ADP4EFA improves the manufacturing of EFA solutions. Increasingly competitive Automated Manufacturing Environments (AME) are the main drivers for investments and evolution in the development of agile and efficient GAI, ICS, EFA and RPBAI. The AME is also specialized in delivering control and monitoring solutions for Industrial Robots (IR). Robust ICSCs' development, implementation and maintenance capabilities influence AME's improvements. Many Factors influences AME's business evolution and Entity's iBPMs, where these Factors are also dependent on the Entity's production infrastructure. The AME needs the GEA for planning and implementing production infrastructures based on IRs. The GEA uses different components (known also as Design Patterns) which promote an iterative development process for AMEs, based on a high-level of reusability of transformed components. These components include RPBAI interfaces, IRs' interfaces, internet protocols and interfaces… And can be managed Real-Time Object-Oriented Modelling (ROOM).

Applying ROOM in EFA

Figure 13. The component-based exploration architecture (Gobillot, Lesire, & Doose, 2019)

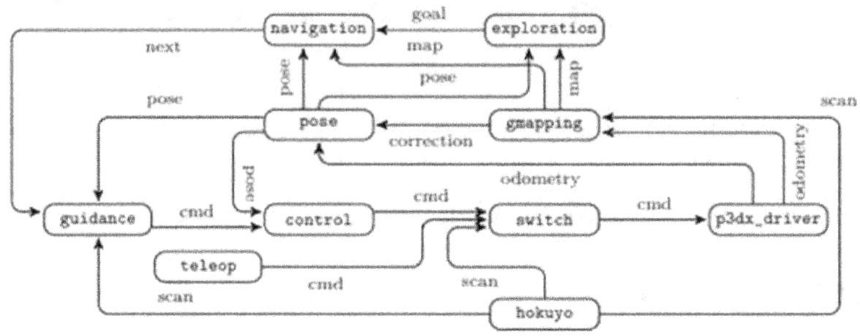

ROOM can support the design and analysis methodology for EFA components as shown in Figure 13. EFA components integration in ICS applications is a real challenge because it is based real-time implementation skills and an adapted methodology like ROOM. ROOM supports: 1) The design of component-based EA models using the Domain Specific Language; 2) Code generation and execution; 3) Design Robotics interfaces; and 4) Supports RPA complex activities as shown in Figure 14.

Figure 14. RPA's activities (IBM, 2024b)

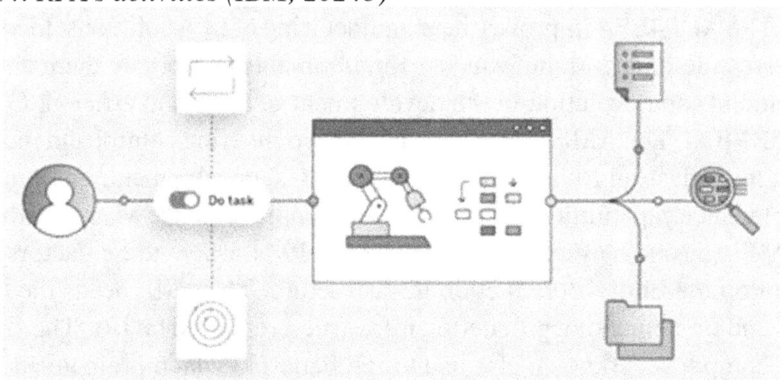

ROOM can support RPA by (IBM, 2024b): 1) Intelligent and efficient automation with help of NLP scripts; 2) Support EFA with AI and ML modules; 3) Minimizing human intervention; 4) Less programming by using drag-and-drop features; 5) Reduces workload of Project Teams; 5) Enhances customer satisfaction; 6) Enhances employee morale; 7) Enhances accuracy and compliance; 8) Complex technical issues and scaling; 9) Offering adaptability in EFA based DTs; 10) Specialized Use Cases.

THE PROOF OF CONCEPT

Introduction and Used ACSs

Figure 15. Transformation goals (Jonkers, Band & Quartel, 2012)

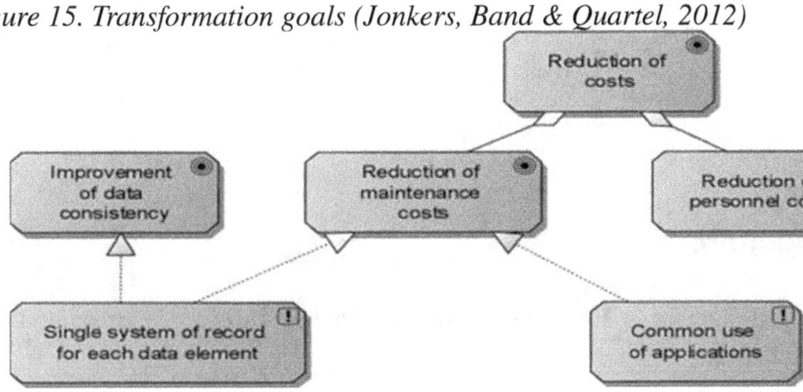

This RDP and PoC uses various ACSs, where a common EA based ACS (ArchiSurance) from the Open Group (Jonkers, Band, & Quartel, 2012a); and AI in Robotics that describes a cloud-platform for Robotics' processes ACS (IFR, 2021). ArchiSurance's transforms a legacy ICS that has a claim files-services manager, and a customer file-services manager. The ACS explains how to manage, register, accept, valuate, and invoice claims related activities. The ArchiSurance presents a merger of multiple ICSs. The transformed ICS has to improve data-quality and Factors evaluations, as shown in Figure 15. Also uses ACSs related to Learning and AI. PoC's objective is to show that the RPBAI and AI-Fields can be integrated in RbICCs. The Project manages the selected Factors and the used ACSs use a common EA based concept as shown in Figure 13, which tunes the Factors. RPBAI's actions in ADM phases, are: 1) Phase A: To setup Groupwork services' roadmap; 2) Phase B: To setup RPBAI's target architecture; 3) Phase C: To model Groupwork's application landscape; 4) Phase D: Manage the gap analysis and design the infrastructure; and 5) Phases E/F: Verifies RPBAI's implementation and evaluate Project's status.

Evaluating RDP's CSA_DTs

The RPBAI interfaces the Intelligence/PRWC which are presented and evaluated in Table 1, and using the CSA_DT's Tables Weighting and Rating Enumerator (CTWRE) that is shown in Figure 16.

Figure 16. The CTWRE's values

CTWRE Label	Limit's Value	Description	Color
Proven, Mature	9.01-10.00	Success	Green
Possible, Feasible	8.51-9.00	Success	Green
Risky	8.01-8.50	Important Risk	Yellow
Complex	7.01-8.00	Unclear	Red
VeryComplex	5.01-7.00	Will probably fail	Red
Impossible	0.00-5.00	Failure	Red

PoC's Execution

The RPBAI interfaces Intelligence and its Factors which are presented and evaluated in Table 1.

Table 1. The RPBAI RDP's outcome is 8.20

CSA Category of CSFs/KPIs	Transformation Capability	Average Result	CSA_DT
The RDP's Integration	Mature	From 1 to 10. 9.20	1
Cycles and Polymathics	Risky	From 1 to 10. 8.20	2
AI-Fields and APDs	Risky	From 1 to 10. 8.40	3
AI based RbICC	Risky	From 1 to 10. 8.10	4
Advanced Topics	Risky	From 1 to 10. 8.30	5
EFA	VeryComplex	From 1 to 10. 7.0	6
Phase's 1 Outcome	Complex	From 1 to 10. 8.20	7

Evaluate First Phase

The RPBAI has mappings to Project's resources; and the RPBAI defines relationships between the AI-Fields and RbICCs. The PoC was implemented using IHIPTF and the initial activity was to setup Factors, then the scripting interface was launched to implement the needed programs to process the Factors/CSAs. After initializing IHIPTF*'s* client, Factors/CSFs were linked to a specific node of the HDT. The programs linked the AHMM4PAI instance to the set of HDT actions which uses Intelligence's actions. Table 1 presented results conclude PoC's first phase, which shows that the RPBAI can be used in Projects. RPBAI is not an independent component and is bonded to all the Project*'s* overall RbICC, and Groupwork concepts. IHIPTF and its AHMM4PAI's main constraint to implement the RPBAI is that CSAs having an average result below 8.0 will be ignored. This work's conclusion with the result of 8.20 implies that RPBAI's integration is complex and due to the fact that AI-Fields are complex and a new hype.

CONCLUSION AND RECOMMENDATIONS

This RDP proposes a set of recommendations on how to use RPBAI where AI-Fields support various Project's phases. The most important recommendation that was generated by the previous research phases was that the Manager must be a BTPAP, which can describe a Coach or educator. The recommendations for the RPBAI are based on the processing of Factors to assert its capabilities, coordination, and effectiveness. RPBAI characteristics are needed to be integrated in the RbICC. Because of the low score, 8.20, from Table 1, shows that RPBAI's integration is complex but can be made possible; and the resultant recommendations are:

- The author uses his IHIPTF to show how and Entity can build an inhouse framework for Projects.
- This RDP uses an innovative concept, which includes: 1) An RDP; 2) The IHIPTF; and 3) A methodological approach to EA.
- The RLR proved the existence of an important RPBAI knowledge gap.
- To use an MM (like the AHMM4PAI) and HDT, to support Intelligence's operations.
- The HDT supports the RDP is used to create the initial RPBAI concept.
- The APD is the PS, but the RPBAI can be applied to any other APD.
- Entities and Cycles are dominated by single-disciplinary experts and concept, and this fact has very negative implications on Projects, RbICC, EFA, GAI, and RPBAI.
- Academia and hence Cycles must encourage the development of interdisciplinary and Polymathic experts.
- Cross-functional/Polymathic skills building is mainly based on common and AI-Fields.
- The Learning cannot cope with complexity of modern heterogeneous ICS and AI-Fields.
- There is a need for a cross-functional RbICC.

- A RbICC's content and sequence of Polymathic common, EFA, GAI, and AI-subjects taught and assessed.
- Intelligence is based on RPBAI.
- The RPBAI coordinates RbICCs integration to deliver educational blueprints, patterns, …
- Students learning concepts that are recurrent in all Cycles (primary, secondary, university…).
- Educators must have the needed set of skills and experience (academic, pedagogic, and professional).
- As RPBAI was modelled and the PoC checked its feasibility, and it can replace the Learning.
- The RbICC promotes Polymathism, critical-thinking, and opinion-based concepts.
- The RPBAI integration is complex.
- The PoC proved RDP's feasibility and delivered the recommendations on how to integrate the RPBAI.

REFERENCES

Ahmad, G. (2010). *Domain-Oriented Modeling of Indian Education System Through UML*. IUP.

Aksoy, M., & Ceylan, T. (2021). An Action Research on Improving Classroom Communication and Interaction in Social Studies Teaching. /.DOI: 10.1155/2021/9943194

Banks, F., & Barlex, D. (2021). *Teaching STEM in the Secondary School-Helping Teachers Meet the Challenge* (2nd ed.). Routledge.

Brañas, A. (2024). Intelligent Process Automation Costs: Saving with Efficiency. https://qflowbpm.com/intell-auto-costs/

Brayer, O. (2023). Is Polymath Thinking the Answer to Thriving in the AI Era? Medium. https://medium.com/@opher.brayer/is-polymath-thinking-the-answer-to -thriving-in-the-ai-era-d269000163a3

Bryce, T. (2015). Managing Complexity. Modern Analyst Media LLC. https://www .modernanalyst.com/Resources/Articles/tabid/115/ID/3354/Managing-Complexity .aspx

Burke, J. (2022). Group Work in the Classroom: Types of Small Groups. CENTRE FOR TEACHING EXCELLENCE. University of Waterloo. https://uwaterloo.ca/ centre-for-teaching-excellence/

Cambridge Dictionary. (2023). Academic. https://dictionary.cambridge.org/ dictionary/english/academic

Clark, W., Johnson, K., & Turner, C. (2004). Cross-Functional Student Teams as a Teaching Tool for Enhanced Learning. East Tennessee State University, Johnson City.

Cotellessa, A. (2018). In Pursuit of Polymaths: Understanding Renaissance Persons of the 21st Century. Department Human and Organizational Learning and International Affairs. The Faculty of The Graduate School of Education and Human Development of The George Washington University, USA.

Cress, U., Moskaliuk, J., & Jeong, H. (2016). *Mass Collaboration and Education. Computer-Supported Collaborative Learning Series* (Vol. 16). CULS.

Crittenden, V., & Wilson, E. (2006). An Exploratory Study of Cross-Functional Education in the Undergraduate Marketing Curriculum. *Journal of Marketing Education*, 28(1), 81–86. DOI: 10.1177/0273475305284643

D'Souza, D., Bement, D., & Cory, K. (2022). Cross-functional integration skills: Are business schools delivering what organizations need? Empirical Research. DOI: 10.1111/dsji.12262

Dick, B. (2002). Action research: action and research. Available at https://www.scu.edu.au/schools/gcm/ar/arp/aandr.html

Easterbrook, S., Singer, J., Storey, M., & Damian, D. (2008). *Guide to Advanced Empirical Software Engineering-Selecting Empirical Methods for Software Engineering Research*. Springer.

EURSC. (2022). Organisation of studies. Office of the Secretary-General of the European Schools. https://www.eursc.eu/en/European-Schools/studies/studies-organisation#:~:text=The%20European%20School%20system%20consists,seven%20years%20of%20secondary%20education

Fitzgerald, J. M. (2005). A case study of a high school's development of teacher collaboration through interdisciplinary curriculum planning (Publication No. 3173664) [Doctoral dissertation, Boston College]. ProQuest Dissertations and Theses Global.

Garanhel, M. (2023). What are the top 7 branches of artificial intelligence? AI Accelerator Institute. https://www.aiacceleratorinstitute.com/tag/artificial-intelligence/

GiniMachine. (2022). *10 Fields that Use Artificial Intelligence and Machine Learning*. GiniMachine.

Gobillot, N., Lesire, Ch., Doose, D. (2019). A Design and Analysis Methodology for Component-Based Real-Time Architectures of Autonomous Systems.

Granger, E. (2024). Artificial Intelligence-Generative AI and Enterprise Architecture: Modeling the Enterprise. Ardoq. https://www.ardoq.com/blog/ai-enterprise-architecture-modeling

Hayashi, K., Shibata, S., Inoue, E., Adachi, S., & Iba, T. (2022). Online Education Patterns, Part 1: Patterns for Linking Separate Worlds. EuroPLoP'21: 26th European Conference on Pattern Languages of Programs. DOI: 10.1145/3489449.3490003

Hayes, M., & Downie, A. (2024). What is AI transformation? IBM. https://www.ibm.com/think/topics/ai-transformation

Heinze, C., Haase, J., & Higgins, H. (2010). An Action Research Report from a Multi–Year Approach to Teaching Artificial Intelligence at the K–6 Level. *Proceedings of the Twenty-Fourth AAAI Conference on Artificial Intelligence (AAAI-10)*. DOI: 10.1609/aaai.v24i3.18830

Heywood, S., Hillar, R., & Turnbull, D. (2010). *Insights into organization-How do I manage the complexity in my organization? Organization Practice*. McKinsey & Company.

Hinkelmann, K. (2016). *Modelling in Enterprise Architecture. University of applied sciences northwest Switzerland*. Business School.

Holilah, H., Girsang, A., & Saragih, M. (2019). *Designing IT Blue Print Academic System on Higher Education with Togaf. Journal: Advances in Science*. Technology and Engineering Systems Journal. DOI: 10.25046/aj040232

Hussain, O., Dillon, Th., Chang, E., & Hussain, F. (2010). Transactional risk-based decision making system in e-business interactions. *International Journal of Computer Systems Science & Engineering*, 2010(1), 15–28.

IBM. (2024). What is AIOps? IBM. https://www.ibm.com/topics/aiops#:~:text=IBM-,What%20is%20AIOps%3F,service%20management%20and%20operational%20workflows

IBM. (2024a). 10 ways artificial intelligence is transforming operations management. IBM. https://www.ibm.com/blog/ai-in-operations-management/

IBM. (2024b). What is robotic process automation (RPA)? IBM. https://www.ibm.com/topics/rpa

IFR. (2021). Cloud Platform for Robotics Operation and Maintenance and Process Management Based on Industrial Internet. IFR. https://ifr.org/case-studies/cloud-platform-for-robotics-operation

Jonkers, H., Band, I., & Quartel, D. (2012a). *ArchiSurance Case Study*. The Open Group.

Kersten, M. (2021). *Introducing SAFe® 5*. Your Operating System for Business Agility. Scaled Agile Inc.

Kohli, P. (2024). AI Transformation: A Three-Step Blueprint For Organizations. Forbes. https://www.forbes.com/councils/forbesbusinesscouncil/2024/02/05/ai-transformation-a-three-step-blueprint-for-organizations/

Krysik, A. (2024). All You Need to Know About AI Transformation in 2024. Stratoflow. https://stratoflow.com/ai-transformation/

Marchese, M. (2023). Thought Leadership AI Research Qualitative Vs Quantitative Data Research. Tempesta. https://tempestamedia.com/2023/08/30/ai-research-qualitative-vs-quantitative-data-research/

Nijboer, F., Morin, F., Carmien, S., Koene, R., Leon, E., & Hoffman, U. (2009). Affective brain-computer interfaces: Psychophysiological markers of emotion in healthy persons and in persons with amyotrophic lateral sclerosis. *3rd International Conference on Affective Computing and Intelligent Interaction and Workshops*. IEEE. DOI: 10.1109/ACII.2009.5349479

Orayer, O. (2023). Is Polymath Thinking the Answer to Thriving in the AI Era? Medium. https://medium.com/@opher.brayer/is-polymath-thinking-the-answer-to-thriving-in-the-ai-era-d269000163a3

Page, M., Schagen, S., Fallus, K., Bron, J., De Coninck, Ch., Maes, B., Sleurs, W., & Van Woensel, Ch. (2005). *Cross-curricular themes in secondary education-Report of a CIDREE collaborative project*. Consortium of Institutions for Development and Research in Education in Europe.

Pisonia, G., Gijlersc, H., Ha Nguyend, T., & Chene, H. (2021). Collaboration patterns in students' teams working on business cases. CEUR Workshop Proceedings (CEUR-WS.org).

Postle, G. (2003). Online Teaching and Learning in Higher Education: A Case Study. Department of Education, Science and Training. University of Southern Queensland, USQ. Canberra. Australia.

Pushpakumara, H., Jayaweera, P., & Manjulan, W. (2021). Using the Open Group Architecture Framework (TOGAF) for Quality Assurance in Higher Education Teaching and Learning. DOI: 10.2139/ssrn.3808691

Putri, N., & Yusof, S. M. (2009). Critical success factors for implementing quality engineering tools and techniques in malaysian's and indonesian's automotive industries: An Exploratory Study. *Journal Proceedings of the International Multi-Conference of Engineers and Computer Scientists.*, 2, 18–20.

Rancho Labs. (2021). *6 Major Sub-Fields of Artificial Intelligence*. Rancho Labs. Meduim.

Richards, M. (2024). The Use of AI in Software Architecture. Neueda. https://neueda.com/enterprise-learning/resources/blogs/ai-in-software-architecture/

Riedl, M. (2023). A Very Gentle Introduction to Large Language Models without the Hype. Meduim. https://mark-riedl.medium.com/a-very-gentle-introduction-to-large-language-models-without-the-hype-5f67941fa59e

Satterlee, B. (1996). Continuous Improvement and Quality: Implications for Higher Education. Warner Southern College (FL). USA.

Savage, N. (2024). 5 AI Case Studies. VKTR. https://www.vktr.com/ai-disruption/5-ai-case-studies/

Schmelzer, R. (2021). Data science vs. machine learning vs. AI: How they work together. TechTarget. https://searchbusinessanalytics.techtarget.com/feature/Data-science-vs-machine-learning-vs-AI-How-they-work-together?track=NL-

Sied, M. (2018). Enterprise Architecture: The Great Process Automation Enabler. Ashling Partner. https://www.ashlingpartners.com/enterprise-architecture-the-great-process-automation-enabler-rpa/

Smith, A. (1987). Educational Engineering: Heuristics for Improving Learning Effectiveness and Efficiency. Engineering Education.

Takeuchia, H., & Yamamotob, Sh. (2019). AI Service System Development Using Enterprise Architecture Modeling. *23rd International Conference on Knowledge-Based and Intelligent Information & Engineering Systems*. Elsevier. DOI: 10.1016/j.procs.2019.09.259

The Open Group. (2011a). Architecture Development Method. The Open Group. USA. The link was reviewed and extracted in February 2018, https://pubs.opengroup.org/architecture/togaf9-doc/arch/chap05.html

Trad, A. (2013). The Selection and Training Framework for Managers in Business Innovation and Transformation Projects-Overview of the development of the empirical model. Recent Advances in Business Administration, Marketing and Economics. *Proceedings of the 2013 International Conference on Business Administration, Marketing and Economics (BAME 2013).*

Trad, A. (2015a). *A Transformation Framework Proposal for Managers in Business Innovation and Business Transformation Projects-Intelligent aBB architecture.* Centeris.

Trad, A. (2015b). *A Transformation Framework Proposal for Managers in Business Innovation and Business Transformation Projects-An ICS's atomic architecture vision.* Centeris.

Trad, A. (2021a). The transformation framework-The role security in the global education system. Journal: International Journal of Higher Education Management.

Trad, A. (2021b). The business transformation enterprise architecture framework for innovation: The role of artificial intelligence in the global business education (RAIGBE). Journal: The Business & Management Review.

Trad, A. (2022). *Business Transformation and Enterprise Architecture Projects: Machine Learning Integration for Projects (MLI4P). Book: Unmanned Aerial Vehicles and Multidisciplinary Applications Using AI Techniques*. IGI Global.

Trad, A. (2023a). *Academic and Educational Transformation Projects-The Role Team-Based Learning in Polymathics (RTBLP)*. IGI-Global.

Trad, A. (2023c). *The Societal and Educational Transformation Projects: The Evolution of the Lebanese Diverse Education (ELDES). Book: Global Perspectives on the Internationalization of Higher Education*. IGI Global.

Trad, A. (2023d). *The Role Team-Based Learning in Polymathics (RTBLP)*. IGI Global.

Trad, A. (2023e). *Organizational and Digital Transformation Projects-A Mathematical Model for Building Blocks based Organizational Unbundling Process*. IGI-Global.

Trad, A. (2023g). *The Education Transformation Project: The Role of Information and Communication Systems' Standards on Diversity in Educational Environment. Book: Global Citizenship and Its Impact on Multiculturalism in the Workplace*. IGI Global.

Trad, A. (2024a). *Academic and Educational Transformation Projects-The Role Team-Based Learning in Polymathics For University Cycle (RTBLP4UC)*. IGI-Global.

Trad, A. (2024b). *Enterprise Transformation Projects- The use of the Polymathic Rating and Weighting Concept (PRWC)*. IGI-Global.

Trad, A. (2024f). *Academic and Educational Transformation Projects-The Role of Skills in Academic Polymathics Fields (RSAPF)*. IGI Global.

Trad, A. (2024g). *Societal Transformation Projects and the Role and Influence of Human Factors on Natural Resources (RIHFNR). Natural Resource Management Issues in Human-Influenced Landscapes*. IGI-Global.

Trad, A. (2024h). *Educational and Continuous Learning Transformation Projects-The Role of Upskilling and Reconversion (RUR)*. IGI Global.

Trad, A., & Kalpić, D. (2014a). The Selection and Training Framework for Managers in Business Innovation and Transformation Projects-An applied mathematics hyperheuristics model. *Proceedings of the 2014 International Conference on Mathematical Methods, Mathematical Models and Simulation in Science and Engineering (MMSSE 2014)*.

Trad, A., & Kalpić, D. (2017a). *An Intelligent Neural Networks Micro Artefact Patterns' Based Enterprise Architecture Model*. IGI-Global.

Trad, A., & Kalpić, D. (2017b). The Business Transformation Framework and Enterprise Architecture Framework for Managers in Business Innovation The role of legacy processes in automated business environments. Journal: The Proceedings of E-Leader.

Trad, A., & Kalpić, D. (2020a). *Using Applied Mathematical Models for Business Transformation. IGI Complete Author Book.* IGI Global. DOI: 10.4018/978-1-7998-1009-4

Trad, A., & Kalpić, D. (2021a). Business transformation project's architect's profile (BTPAP). *The Business & Management Review.*, 12(2), 137–153. DOI: 10.24052/BMR/V12NU02/ART-11

Trad, A., & Kalpić, D. (2022a). Business Transformation *Projects* based on a Holistic Enterprise Architecture Pattern (HEAP)-The Basics. IGI.

Trad, A., & Kalpić, D. (2022b). Business Transformation *Projects* based on a Holistic Enterprise Architecture Pattern (HEAP)-The Implementation. IGI.

Trad, A., & Kalpić, D. (2022c). *Business Transformation Project's Holistic Agile Management (BTPHAM).* CBER.

Trad, A., & Kalpić, D. (2023a). *Educational Transformation Project's Remote Group Work (ETPRGW). Book: Shaping Online Spaces Through Online Humanities Curricula.* IGI Global.

Trad, A., & Trad, C. (2005). Audit, control and monitoring design patterns (ACMDP) for autonomous robust systems (ARS). *International Journal of Advanced Robotic Systems*, 2(1), 4. DOI: 10.5772/5805

Tuononen, T., Hyytinen, H., Kleemola, K., Hailikari, T., Männikkö, I., & Toom, A. (2022). Systematic Review of Learning Generic Skills in Higher Education—Enhancing and Impeding Factors. Frontiers in Education. Systematic Review. DOI: 10.3389/feduc.2022.885917

Veneberg, R. (2014). *Combining Enterprise Architecture And Operational Data-To Better Support Decision-Making. University of Twente.* School of Management and Governance.

Woudenberg, M., & Unis, C. J. (2023). Systems Thinking-Skills and Insights to Resolve Wicked Problems. Systems Thinking. https://www.polymathicbeing.com/p/systems-thinking

Chapter 5
AI and Social Networks:
A Transformative Partnership for Education

Ken Lui
https://orcid.org/0009-0004-2651-3776
Guizhou Institute of Technology, China

ABSTRACT

The advent of social networks has undoubtedly changed the way we disseminate information, communicate, and interact with one another. The ways in which AI and social networking are beneficial for higher education have come under much scrutiny. This chapter examines multifaceted roles that AI and social networks play. The chapter starts with the historical context of the social learning theories, reflects the birth and rise of digital networking and differentiates between social networks as used in teaching practices. It also elaborates on possible advantages of the integration of social networks and AI in the context of education as well as the risks it could bring. It also provides a series of case studies in which social networks have been used in successful ways and across different educational contexts. This examination offers insights and strategies for educators, administrators, and policymakers to more successfully implement social networks within education creating richer, more engaging, collaborative, digitally fluent learning contexts.

1. INTRODUCTION

In the rapidly evolving landscape of education, two powerful forces have emerged recently as game-changers: Artificial Intelligence (AI) and Social Networks. Both of them have contributed immensely towards shaping learning and communication within educational environment. AI, with its proficiency to examine big sets of

DOI: 10.4018/979-8-3373-2272-8.ch005

data and learn from what it sees, is used to make learning better for each student, handle admin tasks, and boost student interest (Chen, Chen, & Lin, 2020). Social Networks, on the other hand, give ways for working together in learning, sharing knowledge, and connecting globally (Whitworth & Ahmad, 2013b). This chapter will look into how AI and Social Networks are brought into education showing their possible efficacy and challenges.

Online social networks allow people to communicate, interchange ideas and wisdom, and work together regardless the distance between them (Samreen et al., 2020b). They have given the communities venues for effective peer-to-peer education, information exchange, and joint problem solving on a scale that has never been seen before (Golubeva et al., 2020). Form learning groups on social sites such as Facebook to professional development groups on business sites such as LinkedIn, social networks have stretched the paradigm of a class well into the 21st century (Ahmad et al., 2019). It therefore becomes effortless for students make groups to enable them carry out a particular topic of study, in group discussions and even group projects or assignments irrespective of classroom settings. This has enabled students to become more proactive in their learning and self-acquisition of materials that best suits their individually learning styles (Whitworth et al., 2012).

In the same way that ML has done for ordinary interactions, AI has enabled learners to enjoy personalization, partially automated, and data driven learning (Forero-Corba & Bennasar, 2024). The systems that are being developed have the capabilities of responding adequately to user learning styles, presenting feedback to the users and presenting learning routes in real time. As such, every child is able to have a personalized education which in turn can boost his learning ability and memory. Analyzing the educational data, they are able to find the trends and forecast the outcomes (Ahmad et al., 2021). Based on education data processes and analyses, AI, therefore, has the potential of revealing patterns that may help in curriculum design and instructional approaches. This in result creates and leads to more efficient and evidence based educational practices into consideration.

The combination of integrating artificial intelligence and social networks in learning process has become a popular topic of discussion as well as research. Such a convergence can only go along way into the creation of educational experiences that are improved in terms of their relevance, student attenuation, and accessibility (Ng & Chu, 2021). Some techniques that AI can bring are intelligent content recommendations, more meaningful connections between learners and better ways to connect learners with learning resources/tool and collaborators. On the other hand, social networks can offer AI systems accurate and realistic data about how people learn and communicate translating into the improvement of such systems and the enhancement of human orientation (Whitworth et al., 2006).

The comprehensive comprehension of such breakthrough subjects as AI and social networks in the context of learning requires an understanding of the transformation of the domains that underlie the learning process (Ahmad et al., 2017). The integration of technology, cognitive science, neuroscience, and other fields has led to significant shifts in our understanding of learning and teaching practices (Li et al., 2024):

- Cognitive Science: The work accomplished by those working in cognitive science has advanced knowledge in the areas of learning, memory, thinking and problem solving. This has precipitated various effective teaching practices that include; spacing techniques, practice retrieval, and metacognition (Hasanah & Shimizu, 2020). To this end, the findings of cognitive psychology learning theorist (CLT) has been integrated into educational software and Learning Management Systems (LMS) to improve their functioning and increase their compatibility with brain structures.
- Neuroscience: Recent development in the theories of brain imaging and neurology has enlightened the understanding of the neural processes which occurs during learning processes. This has affected education by changing how students attend, how the brain stores information and also to do with emotional states (Gkintoni et al., 2023). Findings from research in neuroscience have facilitated the development new technologies in learning which includes the applications in brain training and neurofeedback all designed to improve the brain performance.
- Psychology: Motivational theory; self-efficacy theory; and growth theory, these theories have played a huge contribution towards the development of education. These have helped the educators in addressing students' engagement, feedback, and assessment in light way (Siann & Ugwuegbu, 2024). They've also shaped the learning technologies where the latter feature program components of game design and positive instruction to promote motivation and tenacity.
- Computer Science: The discipline of computer science has not only contributed to creating the technological framework for technology enhanced learning but has also brought into the discourse of education of the twenty-first-century skills of computational thinking. Coding bootcamps and online programming courses are some of the examples of how computer science has impacted the educational domain (Ahmad et al., 2020b).
- Data Science: The capacity to obtain, process and parse big volumes of data has given rise to learning analytics and educational data mining. These practices enable more accurate accountability for students' performance, timely identification of the learners who may be struggling, and evidence-based de-

cision making for learners and educational policies and practices (Imran & Ahmad, 2023).

- Human-Computer Interaction (HCI): HCI research has impacted on the development of educational software and e-learning environments such that they better meet the users, accessibility, and efficiency needs. This has been especially crucial in the creation of application for learning, e-learning and adaptive learning (Bilal et al., 2024).
- Information Science: The sheer volume of information coming in has forced changes in how information and digital literacy is approached. Information science thus has a role of having provided for frameworks and tools for conduct of information search, assessment and utilization within learning settings (Stancin, Poscic, & Jaksic, 2020).
- Economics: Economic theories and models have been axiomatic in education policy in fields relating to, school choice for example; the distribution of educational resources as well as the estimation of educational intercessions. The idea of human capital has also influenced matter related to its value and importance in a society (Burgess, 2016).
- Sociology: Sociological perspective has described social structure, social justice, and culture in educational process. This has led to emergent concerns with equity and representation in educational technologies and pedagogical practices, and new frameworks of culturally sustaining pedagogy (Musgrave, 2017).

This integration has created the background for the present revolution in education with such key elements as artificial intelligence and social networks. With its system design, AI is more equipped to analyze information from various fields and apply to different areas in order to tailor an even better learning process. Social networks, in contrast, offer the platform for the allocation of collective learning, exchange of knowledge and formation of various learning communities which can take advantage of these multiple discipline findings. Speaking of the symbiotic relationship between AI and social networks in learning, we have to address how they can enhance the advancements made by the listed domains. It is with this confluence that the capability to dramatically reshape education has emerged – toward an education that is more proactive, responsive, interactive, and diverse (Williamson, 2024).

This chapter will explain the concept of social learning in theoretical aspects, analyze the historical development of social networks in the learning environment, and discuss the adoption of artificial intelligence in learning. We will then examine the nature of this intersection and the possibilities which can usher in new dynamics to education. Moreover, the effective strategies of incorporating AI-assisted environments to support social learning will be illustrated by cases. We also will discuss the impact and, specifically, the pros and cons of this convergence and the ethical questions that appear with it such as, data privacy and protection, bias of the algorithms, and the digital divide question. Further, the chapter will then make predictions toward the future and the possible projections about the future state of pedagogy and the educational practices. Last, but not the least; we will present an applied research in which we will discuss the development of an educational social network that harnesses the power of AI and guidelines which educators and technologist can follow.

2. SOCIAL LEARNING THEORIES

It is important to understand that social learning started way back in the early 20th century. Knowledge of these theories is important because they serve as the base to which all more contemporary notions of learning in social contexts – including contemporary social networks – are referred to.

2.1 Social Learning Theory by Bandura

Among popular theories, Albert Bandura's Social Learning Theory (Bandura, 1977) is an important exploration to outline this process. In observation, imitation, and modeling, Bandura asserted that people learn through observation. His theory can be considered as an integration of the behaviorist and cognitive learning theories because he incorporated attention, memory, and motivation.

Key principles of Bandura's theory include:

1) Observational Learning: Observing behaviors and the outcomes that result from these behaviors can be a way of learning for people.
2) Modeling: The likelihood is higher when the modeled behavior is performed by one who is similar to the observer and who is admired.
3) Self-efficacy: Self efficacy means individual's perception of achievement and self confidence in activities that may be relevant to learning.

2.2 Vygotsky's Sociocultural Theory

Lev Vygotsky's Sociocultural Theory (Marginson & Dang, 2017), developed in the 1930s but gaining prominence later, emphasizes the fundamental role of social interaction in cognitive development. According to Vygotsky, community plays a central role in the process of "making meaning."

Key concepts include:

1) Zone of Proximal Development (ZPD): The gap between what a learner is able to accomplish independently, and what he or she is able to accomplish with supervision of a more competent teammate.
2) Scaffolding: The care provided to the student in the course of learning with the view of assisting her achieve her learning objectives.

2.3 Lave and Wenger's Situated Learning Theory

In the late 20th century, Jean Lave and Etienne Wenger introduced the concept of Situated Learning (Lave, 1991). This theory holds it that learning is integrated into the activity as well as culture and context. They envision it out in terms of what is known as “legitimate peripheral participation” and here the learner joins a “community of practice”.

2.4 Connectivism: A Learning Theory for the Digital Age

As we entered the 21st century, George Siemens and Stephen Downes proposed Connectivism as a learning theory that addresses learning in the digital age (Duke, Harper, & Johnston, 2013). Connectivism sees knowledge as residing in connections and learning being the development of bridging as well as transitioning in those connections.

Key principles include:

1) Transfer of learning and knowledge are found in different opinions.
2) Education is a process of linking of specific nodes or information resources.
3) Readiness to know is more important than what is currently known.
4) By so doing, there is always need to maintain relationships so as to cultivate more learning.

2.5 Relevance to AI and Social Networks in Education

These theories provide a crucial backdrop for understanding the potential of social networks and AI in education:

1) Connectivist principles align well with social networks where there are multiple views to gather info and linking strangers together.
2) AI can support social learning in a way that helps learners stay engaged in interactions with other members of the learning community while drawing on additional resources provided by the AI system, thus extending the role of the “more knowledgeable other” defined by Vygotsky.

3) The two principle parts of Bandura's theory, observational learning and modeling, can be boosted by SNSs, where AI may pinpoint relevant models.
4) Based on situated learning theory we understand how to put together online communities of practices, with AI, potentially enhancing the legitimate peripheral participation.

While advancing through this chapter, it will be demonstrated how these theories underpin and are advanced by the introduction of AI and the social network in the learning environment.

3. THE EVOLUTION OF SOCIAL NETWORKS IN EDUCATION

It is a fact that has reached educations settings from small online communications tools in their evolution. This section describes their development and discusses the kinds of social networks in education and their benefits.

3.1 From Early Online Forums to Modern Social Platforms

The use of networks in education can be traced from the use of Early Bulletin Board System hence the use of social networks in education started from the 1990s. These platforms enabled the establishment of asynchronous discussions thereby enabling the continuation of classroom dialogues beyond the physical and calendar time (Berestova, Alizade, & Umirzakova, 2020).

As technology advanced, more sophisticated platforms emerged, including:

1) Learning Management Systems (LMS): Systems like Blackboard and Moodle incorporate social aspects into learning /teaching affairs software.
2) Educational Social Networks: Examples of such sites include Edmodo and Schoology, though the two sites blended social networking functions with education resources.
3) Mainstream Social Networks in Education: Some of the social platforms such as Facebook and Twitter are useful in the education intend where Facebook groups are useful in group discussions and collaborations.

3.2 Types of Social Networks in Education

Multiple different types of social networks have been found in education (Wiechetek & Pastuszak, 2022):

1) Professional Networks: Platforms like LinkedIn and ResearchGate facilitate connections between educators, researchers, and professionals.
2) Content-Sharing Networks: Platforms like YouTube, SlideShare, and Pinterest allow educators and learners to share educational content with each other.
3) Microblogging Platforms: Platforms like Twitter have become a useful tool for professional development and sharing educational resources.
4) Virtual Learning Environments: Platforms like Second Life have been used to create immersive educational experiences.
5) Question-and-Answer Networks: Sites like Quora and Stack Exchange that promote peer learning and knowledge sharing.

3.3 Advantages of Social Networks for Education

Social networks offer numerous advantages in educational contexts (Berestova, Alizade, & Umirzakova, 2020; Wiechetek & Pastuszak, 2022;). Some of them are outlined below:

1) They also give access to simple communication between students and teachers, as well as parents.
2) Social network technologies provide possibilities for collaborative learning (group assignments, peer mentoring and shared problem-solving).
3) It implies that educators and students can share any number of educational resources required.
4) The potential global reach of social networks is one of the most beautiful aspects in fostering international partnerships or cultural exchange.
5) They are an aid to the educational systems and makes the formal and non-formal learning process easier.
6) Teachers can communicate with other teachers around the world as well as learn about best practices being carried out in the world.
7) It also observes how social aspects cater to the issue of transforming learning into a more interactive process.
8) Social advertizing can be employed to coordinate regular special cases with community likes and organization.

3.4 Challenges and Considerations

While social networks offer many advantages, their use in education also presents challenges:

1) Privacy and Security: First and foremost is the protection of student information which is an issue of great concern in the current era.
2) Digital Divide: Not all learners are privileged to enjoy technology and internet of high speeds.
3) Distraction: It is found that social networks of students can actually cover their interest which act as a distraction to the students studying part.
4) Information Overload: This has made collection of information easier but on the same note it has remained a challenge to sort out this information for both students and educators.
5) Digital Citizenship: Education on acceptable use also becomes important.

Now, we will demonstrate how integrating AI with social networks mitigates such hitches while boosting other advantages thereby developing stronger and efficient learning cultures.

4. THE RISE OF AI IN EDUCATIONAL CONTEXTS

AI has found its way into the education sector bringing in method of enhancing learning process, handling administrative work and most importantly, in gaining insight about the process of learning. Now, we discuss artificial intelligence in the context of learning.

4.1 Historical Context

Machine-assisted learning can be traced back to the 1920 with the invention of teaching machines. Nevertheless, these were not possible until the use of computers dawned and the emergence of AI between the 1950s and 1960s. Key milestones of AI include:

1) 1960s: Formulation of the basic concepts of one of the earliest computer-assisted instruction systems known as PLATO computers (programmed-logic for automatic teaching operations).
2) 1970s: Utilizing of intelligent passenger systems (IPS) that could be tailored to the learner.
3) 1980s-90s: The emergence of new trends on the expert system and development of educational software.
4) 2000s onwards: Growth and expansion of technology in general and in particular to the use of online learning platforms and learning analytics, as well as AI applied to more complex tasks in learning.

4.2 Current Applications of AI in Education

Today, AI is being applied in various ways in educational contexts (Ahmad et al., 2022):

1) Personalized Learning: There is the ability to personalize the content, movement through it, the level of difficulty can be changed according to the learner.
2) Intelligent Tutoring Systems: These systems prepare personal lessons making provision for individual feedback and assistance (Hamid et al., 2020).
3) Automated Grading: It can help in marking multiple-choice questions as well as give first feedback to essay questions.
4) Learning Analytics: The major advantage of using AI in student admission and management is that the big data sets can be scanned to establish performance and engagement levels.
5) Administrative Tasks: The principles of AI can be applied to manage multiple administrative responsibilities hence reducing their workload from the educators.
6) Content Creation: To improve efficiency, lesson content can be created with the help of AI and the program can also be used for creating quizzes and summarizing texts.
7) Language Learning: The app for language learning with the use of AI helps learners practice in accordance with their level and offers feedback immediately.
8) Accessibility: AI can help make content accessible, i.e., transferring in real-time to captions or text-to-speech (Zeshan et al., 2020).

4.3 AI Technologies in Education

Several AI technologies are particularly relevant in educational contexts:

1) Machine Learning: Enables systems to show enhanced capability of doing a task by learning from their previous performance.
2) Natural Language Processing: Allows systems to interpret and synthesis human language important for facility of learning spaces.
3) Computer Vision: Applied into proctor systems and student interaction analysis in videoed classes.
4) Data Mining: Is useful in pattern analysis of massive amounts of student data.
5) Expert Systems: Applied in some ITSs to simulate an expert's decision-making capability (Hamid et al., 2020).

4.4 Challenges and Ethical Considerations

The rise of AI in education also brings different challenges. Some of them are outlined below:

1) Data Privacy: The collection and use of students' data bring privacy issues into the fore.
2) Algorithmic Bias: There is a main drawback in using AI decision making systems, that is they reinforce bias.
3) Teacher Role: Predicted consequences also raise certain questions about the part of human teachers as far as their work is regarded.
4) Digital Divide: The given AI-based education is not available for all students equally.
5) Transparency: Some of the systems involving the use of artificial intelligence are 'black box' like, this makes it hard to explain decisions that have been made.

The next section presents the integration of AI and social networking in the context of education.

5. INTERSECTION OF AI AND SOCIAL NETWORKS IN EDUCATION

The use of both AI and the social networks in education is one of the most amazing synergies that may transform the learning experiences in the foreseeable future. This intersection forms a rich intersection between social aspects of learning authored by human creativity and Intelligence incorporated into the learning process offered by AI (Huang et al., 2021).

5.1 Enhanced Personalization

AI can analyze data from social networks to provide more personalized learning experiences:

1) Content Recommendations: Since the social network may contain information about the learner's interactions, interests, and connections, the content recommenders can use those to provide suitable educational content to the learner. For example, if a student regularly comments on posts related to renewable energy, the AI might suggest courses or articles based on the same subject.

2) Learning Path Optimization: AI can predict the sequence of learning activities the same as similar users in the network based on the successful learning paths. This may for example entail guiding students on which course to take first or second, or what skills to build in order to meet the intended career goals given results of other learners who have accomplished similar goals.
3) Adaptive Group Formation: AI can create proper group for study or project working where participants have similar skills, learning approaches and social networks. For example, in a programming class, the AI might form groups for all students with strong theory knowledge, intermediate theory knowledge with some practical coding experience.
4) Personalized Feedback: Feedback based on analysis of comments, posts, shares, and performance of a student in the course of the social network. This could be recommendations that are directed toward some enhancement, acknowledgment of positives or encouragement towards interaction with specific type of content or activities.
5) Interest-Based Community Suggestions: According to the learner's interaction and preferences, AI can recommend the specific community or group of the greater social networking site which may consist of the similar learner's batch as well as the experts.

5.2 Intelligent Content Curation and Creation

The combination of AI and social networks can enhance content curation and creation (Bozkurt, 2023):

1. Crowd-Sourced Content Evaluation: The engagement, feedback, and overall interaction and activity history of a user in the network can be used by AI to filter good educational content. This could entail evaluating attributes like the rank users give to content, the amount of time users spends with content, tendencies of sharing and content creators' authenticity.
2. Automated Content Summarization: This way AI can generate summaries for discussions or the resources that were discussed in the course of the learning process so that the learner can easily go through it in case they missed on some discussions. For instance, during the forum where a complicated issue is being debated, AI could come up with an abstract that contains main notions, general opinion, and open questions after the debate.
3. AI-Assisted Collaborative Content Creation: By implementing AI, many learners can work collaboratively and the AI can notify the group about improvements or even gaps in content. This could entail live writing cooperation, proofing

and editing, as well as the capacity to contribute first writing concept from a discussion process of a group.

4. Dynamic Content Adaptation: AI can customize content that has been shared with a reader with respect to past knowledge, mode of learning and present learning objectives. For example, when a learner selects an article included in the shared network, the AI may modify the language used, include comments where necessary and provide examples that might suit the learner best.
5. Multimedia Content Generation: AI can assist in the transformation of user generated content into another type. For instance, it could translate a text explanation into a single image or create a visual presentation of the text of an article with a narration.

5.3 Enhanced Social Learning

Artificial Intelligence can be used to improve social learning networks (Ouyang & Jiao, 2021):

1) AI and chatbots support each other in an intelligent discussion by asking and answering queries for a more gripping conversation. The AI virtual assistant can also help oversee care and activate silent members as well as mediate if necessary.
2) AI can analyze patterns of interactions taking place within a social learning environment This will help to know what kind of social relationships facilitate learning most (good for designing better group activities and optimal network structures).
3) AI-based local student peer (with strengths and weaknesses instantly matched) learning optimization. It can also predict the optimal timing for collective learning events, analyzing both individual learning time slots and participant engagement histories.
4) AI can recognize experts and connect them with students in education forums. This offers a collaborative, peer-to-peer learning environment in which knowledge may be shared throughout the network.
5) AI can enable virtual learning buddies to contribute to group conversations, present alternate perspectives, and clarify complex topics. These AI friends can be customized to address each student's specific strengths and weaknesses.

5.4 Automated Administrative Tasks

Administrative tasks within educational social networks as we discussed earlier — all (or nearly) needless AI.

1) AI will help the new users in getting joined and knowing the network. For more detail, this includes: features launch, setup guide, and user experience doc.
2) It can help in Calendar planning, coordination with Work Groups, and Lesson Planning based on attendance. It will connect with its companion Calm app to provide smart alerts and suggest optimal times for learning activities based on a machine-learned model.
3) Use AI to monitor student or group progress with respect to learning goals. This may be through making periodic announcements, marking successes and alerting students or staff when intervention is required.
4) In schools using social learning, detecting which groups and usage patterns of resources (classrooms, laboratory equipment) fit would be possible with AI by looking at the network.

5.5 Emotional Intelligence and Support

With the help of AI and its integration in educational social networks, the students may experience mental support and promote happiness (Song, Tung, & Jeon, 2022):

1) Sentiment Analysis: A1 can detect students who may be depressed or anxious. This can be used to generate warning to the human instructor.
2) Psychological support: AI chatbots integrated into conversation can provide initial psychological support, provide resources, provide problem-solving ideas, or encourage connection to human mentors when needed.
3) Motivation and engagement: AI can provide personal motivation, small celebrations, and encourage participation in the learning community based on student interaction patterns.
4) Empathy Training: AI techniques can help students develop empathy by analyzing student interactions and providing communication feedback, and can come up with multiple responses in discussions.

5.6 Effective assessment and feedback

The combination of AI and social networks leads to new forms of assessment and feedback:

1) Peer Assessment: AI can guide students to give positive feedback to peers, offer suggestions for improvement, and maintain goals.
2) Collaborative Problem-Solving: In group projects, AI can analyze individual contributions and interaction patterns to assess collaborative problem-solving skills, providing insights into team and individual strengths.

3) Real-Time Assessment: As students interact in a social environment, Intelligence can continuously assess and identify areas where individuals or groups may need additional support or resources.
4) Competency-Based Progression: AI can assess the development of skills and knowledge by analyzing students' online participation and interactions; the potential nature leads to the ability to succeed in academics.

5.7 Cultural Exchange and Global Learning

On the positive side, social networks can also increase the quantity and quality of cultural and cross-cultural exchanges and expand learning opportunities globally (Kuleto et al., 2021).

1) Linguistic aid: ai can provide immediate language translation so that learners of different languages are able to easily communicate across the network.
2) Cultural context awareness: If people with diverse cultural backgrounds are talking together, the AI could provide cultural context to avoid misunderstandings or suggest other ways of phrasing things, (Filters Lead to Cultural Bias).
3) Global project matching: using ai to pair and connect learners around the world based on their mutual interests, complementary skills and projects needs.
4) Virtual cultural immersion: through data analysis via the social network, it is able to develop virtual personalized culture immersions that allow learner involvement in content and individuals/groups they would never otherwise gain access to AI.

5.8 Lifelong Learning Support

The synergy between artificial intelligence and social networking can support lifelong learning (Mhlanga, 2023):

1) AI can suggest probable career paths with this knowledge and the learning experiences they might have to undergo by factoring in information such as the learner's interactions, interest level, and skills within the network. 1
2) AI can analyze what skills are important in the field on a regular basis and match this with an evaluation of the learner's current skill set to suggest learning opportunities within the network that could help fill such knowledge gaps.
3) AI can help learners sustain and grow their learning network as they transition from formal education into a professional environment. It may suggest new connections and other communities to enable them to go further with their learning journey.

4) AI pinpointing short, tightly focused learning within his social network relevant to a hectic lifestyle fosters continuous professional development and lifelong learning.

5.9 Challenges

The mix of smart machines and social sites gives many benefits, but it also brings its own problems.

1) Privacy concerns: the huge flow of info made by social talk, when joined with machine brains study, brings up big privacy problems. It's very important to have clear and open data rules, and also strong safety steps, to keep safe private details.
2) Algorithm flaw: smart systems can unknowingly make bad beliefs in social groups worse. Doing checks often and putting together varied teams is important to deal with this danger.
3) Too much trust in technology: there is a chance of being too reliant on robot-made talks, maybe missing the need for real human ties. Finding the right mix between AI help and face-to-face chats is key.
4) Digital Divide: The new traits from this mix may not be the same easy to reach for all students, likely making learning differences worse.
5) Too much information exposure: while AI can help in sorting things out, the huge amount of info and talks in AI-boosted social learning places might still overawe some learners.
6) Realness of Talks: As fake brain (AI) gets more mixed in with social learning nets, it is key to make sure the realness of human talks and clearly tell apart ai-made stuff and human-made stuff.
7) Ethical use of analysis: the use of smart machines to guess student results or suggest job ways brings up worries about fate and the chances of making what we expect come true.

Integration of AI with social networks is changing the course of education. It opens an inventive line of creating learning experiences that will better be transformed in the world of learning. Here, the collaborative learning nature with the sophisticated abilities of AI can build more adaptive, interactive, and effective learning scenarios. Only then can the promise of these technologies be fully realized by considering challenges and ethical concerns while implementing in ways that are sure to ensure these technologies benefit all learners, consonant with the core values of education. There is a need to address these challenges while taking advantage of the benefits toward a successful amalgamation of AI and social networks.

6. CASE STUDIES: INTEGRATION OF AI AND SOCIAL NETWORKS IN EDUCATION

Integration of AI and social networks brings about novel ways by which learners learn and means through which they can interact with one another. This paper investigates the integration of AI tools using social networking applications in educational institutions, with particular reference to the effects on student participation, learning achievements, and the general learning process.

6.1 Case Study 1: Ho Chi Minh City University of Technology and Education (HCMUTE)

HCMUTE included the AI language model, ChatGPT, in their curriculum. The AI was applied to complement the learning resources of the students, provide insights, and fulfill assignments. There were 73 first and second-year students applied with a mixed-methods approach. Electronic surveys and semi-structured interviews were applied to gather data. Students believed that using ChatGPT was safe for them during the time of learning or even searching. However, overreliance on AI was observed, which could lead to a loss of ability to think independently and critically evaluate. The authors found that it was possible to use AI in a balanced manner and further strengthen policies for ethical use to foster independent learning (Nguyen, Lai, & Nguyen, 2024).

6.2 Case Study 2: Georgia Institute of Technology

Georgia Tech created an AI teaching assistant called "Jill Watson," built on IBM's Watson platform within one of its online Masters in Computer Science courses. Jill Watson had been trained on over 40,000 forum posts from runs of the course to generate answers with great success in common questions posed by students. Jill Watson greatly reduced response times and relieved the loads of student queries on human teaching assistants. Most routine questions were thus well addressed by the AI, hence delivering consistent and timely support to students. The project highlighted the importance of careful training data in the performance of an AI and how AI could be perceived as a non-intrusive tool in the educational sector (Digitaldefynd, 2024).

6.3 Case Study 3: Learning AI Through Social Networking in Hong Kong

This was another project on delivering online instructions through social networking sites with the application of AI tools to expand engagement. Semi-structured interviews, a motivational questionnaire, and observations of lessons assisted with data collection. The use of social networking sites for learning AI presented students with interesting and motivating learning experiences. The sites allowed the teamwork among the students, improving their learning. However, some of the students faced difficulties with regards to time management and concentration since the social networks were informal by nature (Ng, & Chu, 2021).

From these case studies, numerous lessons can be gleaned. AI ensures that educational content can be created according to the need and desire of the learning student. That will be able to provide high outcomes. Social networks give a source for interactive or collaborative learning, thus making education more fun. However, too much reliance on AI by students can break critical thinking and independent reasoning skills. The integration of AI and social networks also comes with ethics issues, for example, the violation of data privacy, the problem with academic integrity, and many more. Its successful integration mandates careful planning, monitoring, and establishment of policies as well as rules.

7. CHALLENGES AND ETHICAL CONSIDERATIONS

While the integration of AI and social networks into education brings numerous benefits, it also brings major challenges and ethical concerns that deserve due consideration:

7.1 Data and Privacy

It raises great concerns about privacy matters because gathering such scale data as required by AI-driven personalization. Then the question about ownership of data produced in the educational social networks will arise. How to inform the users, especially minors, about what happens to their data is another concern (Ahmad & Whitworth, 2011).

7.2 Algorithmic Bias

AI systems may inadvertently exacerbate already existing biases in the education framework. For example, some AI algorithms create opaque systems that cannot be discerned and corrected to overcome already prevailing biases. This calls for a need to have diverse sets of datasets that prevent the marginalization of a minority section (Samreen et al., 2020a).

7.3 Digital Divide and Equal Access

Different learners do not have equal opportunities with respect to access to devices and high-speed internet on which most AI-enhanced social learning activity dependencies are based. Digital literacy of the students as well as teachers creates inequality in the usage of technology; the complex nature of these technologies may deepen inequalities between well-resourced and under-resourced education institutions around the world (Ahmed et al., 2019).

7.4 Over-reliance on Technology

The potential threat that AI-mediated interactions may overshadow all aspects of interaction in schools is a reduction in authentic human connections. Relying on AI suggestions to create an idea or write a paper would fail to develop critical thinking skills. The changing nature of the role of educators will be another related concern, and, indeed, there is apprehension that technology may replace human instructors (Hamid et al., 2019).

7.5 Content Quality and Misinformation

AI systems should be able to effectively detect and screen out the misinformation that exists in social networks. Echo chambers created by AI recommendation can limit a student's exposure to other perspectives. This can also result in homogenized learning experiences -which can dampen creativity and original thought (Sarfraz et al., 2024).

7.6 Responsible Use of AI in Assessment

It should be ensured that AI-based tests and assessments do not inflict undue harm on specific groups of students and are fair. The use of AI for assessing the work of a student must be transparent to the student. Students should be allowed to appeal any outcome by an AI through due processes (Salman et al., 2022).

7.7 Psychological Impact

There is a higher chance of negative social comparison and increasing stress due to increased visibility of what peers are doing and achieving. The engaging quality of AI-facilitated social learning may result in addictive behavior. Constant connectivity and the obligatory participation might negatively impact students' mental health and general well-being (Whitworth & Ahmad, 2013a).

These are critical issues and ethical concerns in dealing with appropriateness and effective usage of AI and social networks in education. High standards and best practices that ensure maximum benefits while limit hazards for the appropriate usage of AI and social networks must be constantly achieved through collaboration from educators, technologists, policymakers, and ethicists.

8. FUTURE PROSPECTS AND POTENTIAL DEVELOPMENTS

As AI and social networks advance, its integration into education is likely to result in fascinating new innovations. This section looks at some possible future directions:

8.1 Immersive Learning Through AI and VR/AR

Artificial intelligence-driven virtual and augmented reality platforms could provide engaging social learning experiences, enabling students to join forces in simulated environments that mirror real-life situations. Learners could possess digital representations in the educational social network—AI-powered avatars that are capable of engaging in discussions and collaborative projects, even when the user is not actively online.

8.2 Cutting-Edge Natural Language Processing

The advancement of real-time AI translation technology could render language barriers nearly nonexistent in global educational partnerships. Highly advanced AI chatbots might function as personal teaching aides, accessible around the clock to answer inquiries, clarify concepts, and facilitate learning.

8.3 The Role of Predictive Analytics in Education

AI could examine a student's interactions, achievements, and social networks to forecast their learning path and proactively provide support or opportunities for advancement. Sophisticated AI systems could detect students who may be at risk of dropping out or facing challenges, making early intervention possible.

8.4 Integrating Blockchain and AI for Educational Credentials

The combination of blockchain technology and AI could enable the creation of secure, evolving records of a student's skills and knowledge based on their contributions and interactions within educational social networks. AI could autonomously award and verify micro-credentials, reflecting a learner's demonstrated capabilities and knowledge within the social learning ecosystem (Ahmed et al., 2024).

8.5 Dynamic Adaptive Learning Environments

AI could flexibly modify course materials and organization based on the shared learning patterns found within the social network. Each learner could enjoy a personalized, AI-curated educational experience that develops in response to their interactions, objectives, and the collective knowledge of the community.

9. EDUCATIONAL IMPLICATIONS AND BEST PRACTICES

The fusion of AI and social networks in education calls for a reevaluation of teaching methods. Below are essential implications and best practices:

9.1 Transition to Facilitative Teaching

Instead of the teacher-centered approaches emphasized in traditional models, educators may be led to focus their energies on creating learning experiences and on facilitating interactions rather than on direct instruction. One aspect of their work, therefore, will be to choose and make appropriate selections from those AI and social networking tools that can best complement their instructional setting.

9.2 Emphasis on Higher-Order Skills

Curricula should provide instruction on how to critically evaluate AI-generated content and suggestions. Learning experiences should utilize AI and social media to develop advanced skills for collaborative problem-solving.

9.3 Data Literacy Role

Educators and learners need to be trained in accessing and applying learning analytics that AI systems create. Curriculum conversation must contextualize issues related to ethical considerations in data collection and use in schools (Zeshan et al., 2019).

9.4 Balancing Technology With Human Interaction

Teachers need to consciously craft learning interactions that make human beings move, ideally from AI-rich social learning contexts both in and out of school. The more routine tasks become the responsibility of AI, the greater the experience needed to be developed to hone emotional intelligence and interpersonal skills.

9.5 Commitment to Inclusive Design

Implementing AI and social networks in a manner consistent with universal design principles will also ensure it is accessible to learners with a wide range of abilities. Educators need to be vigilant to those cultural biases that may arise from the implemented AI systems or the social network frameworks they use and work hard towards addressing and neutralizing the same.

10. DESIGNING AN EDUCATIONAL SOCIAL NETWORK: A CASE STUDY

To give a flavor of how the technology learned so far is practically applied, consider the following case study in building an AI-augmented education social network called GlobalEd Connect, with much attention paid to the architectural and software technical details (Hamid et al., 2022).

10.1 Features

Different features of such a system are outlined below:

1) It links students across different countries for project work by matching interested individuals based on their interest, skills, and goal objectives of studies.
2) The AI-based system also suggests relevant resources specific to the needs of the project as well as the individual's learning style.
3) Using AI, the platform provides real-time translation while providing cultural context to overcome language barriers and drive communication processes.
4) Students are supported through personalized learning paths which continually change based on the interactions, involvement in projects, and review by their peers in the network.
5) AI constructs virtual spaces that represent cultural exchange by automatically populating them with relevant artifacts, conversations, and activities that would reflect the experiences of students.

10.2 AI and Social Network Integration

AI observes the interaction pattern and does comment on the effectiveness of collaboration and individual contributions to the network.

1) AIs-powered chatbots enable discussions so that it makes them think deeply and so that all the participating ends are equal.
2) Micro-credentialing happens automatically through an AI system as one shows skills acquired in projects and peer reviews.
3) AI tools there are, that assist instructors in designing cross-cultural activities for curriculum in any given educational system.
4) The platform creates insights regarding whether students have engaged with the content and learning process, how they learn, and what is the dynamic unfolding of interactions.
5) An AI-based system suggests the best times and approaches for an educator to intervene or help out the student or group when they face any problem.

10.3 System Architecture

The system was built as a comprehensive online education platform that includes various educational activities. The system architecture follows the guidelines provided by (Muhammad & Ahmad, 2021). These include course management, content distribution, tests, and interactive experience for the students. Its designing involves multi-tier architecture to ensure scalability, flexibility, and reduced maintenance complexity. It is surrounded by the core logic, which is processed through the application server upon the invocation of a user request. The database server is responsible for communicating with it and holds all the information regarding courses, users, and learning activities. The relational database model provides data integrity and complex queries for convenient retrieval of data. The intuitive front-end is built using the modern web technologies with the help of HTML, CSS, and JavaScript and ensures responsiveness such that desktops, tablets, or mobile smartphones can access it without any hassle. The front-end application server of the RESTful APIs deals with communication to provide a smooth flow of information.

Trusted third-party service interfaces were added to make learning more delightful by offering a content management system and an assessment system with video conferencing tool. This can be represented by the middleware layer that acts as a connector between the application servers and external services of this type (Ahmad et al., 2020a). In this e-learning system, security is a top priority, with multiple layers of security, encryption of data at both rest and transit (Zeshan et al., 2024). Setting protocols regarding user authentication and authorization are programmed. Regular security auditing to ensure the system's integrity occurs. The system also adheres to relevant data protection directives to protect the information of users with secrecy and security. It is highly scalable, so it can serve a growing number of users and courses over a cloud-based infrastructure so that resources can be dynamically allocated on demand. Techniques applied include load balancing and caching to ensure performance and high availability. Features will be deployed through containerization technologies like Docker, ensuring that the deployment process is streamlined and uniform across different environments. The continuous integration and continuous deployment pipeline will allow for efficient automation of testing and the roll out of new features and updates.

High scalability, flexibility, and ease of maintenance can be ensured by embracing a microservices architecture in GlobalEd Connect. The system uses a cloud-native infrastructure that gives consideration to containerization and orchestration technologies. Some of the critical steps and interactions among different layers to consider while drawing data flow for the e-learning system are discussed below:

1) User Interaction: Each time users-students or instructors-log in, navigate to a course, or submit assignments, the front-end captures all this activity. It is created with HTML, CSS, and JavaScript for results responsive but friendly to the user across different devices.
2) API Requests: These enable the interaction between the frontend and the server hosting the application. The front-end sends this action as a request from an HTTP to the application server via RESTful APIs. For instance, a login request might comprise the credentials of a user. Responses are then sent back through the RESTful API by the application server to the front-end with whatever data was required or the status.

3) Business Logic Processing: Whenever a request arrives, the application server processes it according to the business logic in place. This could be checking the credentials being submitted with those in the database for a login request. Therefore, dealing with user requests can be considered as managing business logic.
4) Database Interaction: The application server communicates through a relational model that represents data about courses, users, and activities to the database server. When data access is required to read from or write to the database, it interacts with the database server. For example, it queries the database to confirm user credentials or update information about a student's course progress.
5) Response Generation: On the arrival of request, the application server gets prepared with a response. In case of valid log in then it starts creating session tokens and starts fetching data regarding that user which may contain courses enrolled by him.
6) Front End Update: Front end of the system receives the response and updates the User Interface accordingly like user's dashboard with courses listed if logging in is done properly.
7) Third-Party Integrations: Whenever the services outside of the application server are required for any action-like video conferencing setup, the application server communicates with these services by the help of the middleware. Such a service middleware assists in integration and is sure of proper, secure data exchange while making it manage the associations with the outside services through video conferencing and content management systems.
8) Different security measures are implemented through this process by encrypting, authenticating, and authorizing access. For instance, the data that is exchanged between the front-end and the application server is encrypted for avoiding illegal unauthorized access.
9) Scalability and Performance: Load balancing and caching strategies are used in this system to control data flow effectively. The system can process a lot of requests together without compromising its high-performance rate.

All these factors come together to provide a strong, secure, and scalable e-learning application that could process user actions efficiently and accurately, thus providing a smooth learning experience.

11. CONCLUSION

For the first time, artificial intelligence and social networks have been combined; it is so that this synergy is powered to change completely the view on teaching-learning processes entirely. Leverage social networks, along with the analytical power of AI, to change learning by making virtually connected an actual fact, while optimizing peer-to-peer learning relations to adapt education experiences according to individuals' needs so as to be most engaging and effective ever.

In this chapter, we discussed the theoretical underpinning of social learning and evolution of social networks in education environments and over-visualized the rise of AI especially noticeable in schools. A perfect intersection of these two technologies, we went quite in-depth on what this can offer with regard to personalized content delivery, robust grouping of content and social learning. The case studies could not be clearer in demonstrating the advantages of these technologies when they raise engagement, improve learning outcomes, and facilitate international cooperation. In tandem with this, we have captured the significant challenges and ethical concerns such convergence poses in regard to privacy, algorithmic bias, equality, and the evolving teacher landscape.

We expect the near term to be filled with exciting developments in immersive learning environments, sophisticated natural language processing and adaptive learning platforms. These may potentially raise the reach, immediacy, and quality of education for a far-reaching number of learners. However, in order to tap AI and social media in education at max, Gagné should be looked through a pedagogical lens. This will, therefore transform the role of an educator from one that is mainly focused on designing learning experiences as well as facilitating interactions. This would bring a complete change that would require first of all an emphasis on critical thinking and data literacy amongst other skills needed, as well as balance between copyright technology development and good old human interaction.

Take the case of GlobalEd Connect, for example. It is a great illustration of a platform that caters to these principles to provide globalization through collaboration, personalized learning, and interculture understanding. That means-as we go around experiencing the exciting amalgamation of AI and social lens in education-never an ammunition shortage in our pursuit to design more inclusive, immersive, and effective learning experiences. But that journey continues only through ongoing conversation, periodic ethical reflection, and a commitment not to betray the principles of learning upon which these technologies are based. The future of education rides not just on the promise of AI or the networked connectivity promised by social media, but how these tools are effectively integrated to support learning. By leveraging the scope and speed of innovation, that we will use in revolutionizing our digital world, with a global platform for scalable learning, we reimagine education as a new atelier.

REFERENCES

Ahmad, A., Alzahrani, A. S., Ahmed, N., & Ahsan, T. (2020a). A delegation model for SDN-driven federated cloud. *Alexandria Engineering Journal*, 59(5), 3653–3663.

Ahmad, A., & Whitworth, B. (2011, December). Access control taxonomy for social networks. In 2011 7th International Conference on Information Assurance and Security (IAS) (pp. 256-261). IEEE.

Ahmad, A., Whitworth, B., Zeshan, F., Bertino, E., & Friedman, R. (2017). Extending social networks with delegation. *Computers & Security*, 70, 546–564.

Ahmad, A., Whitworth, B., Zeshan, F., Janczewski, L., Ali, M., Chaudary, M. H., & Friedman, R. (2019). A relation-aware multiparty access control. *Journal of Intelligent & Fuzzy Systems*, 37(1), 227–239.

Ahmad, A., Zeeshan, F., Marriam, R., Samreen, A., & Ahmed, S. (2021). Does one size fit all? Investigating the effect of group size and gamification on learners' behaviors in higher education. *Journal of Computing in Higher Education*, 33, 296–327.

Ahmad, A., Zeshan, F., Hamid, M., Marriam, R., & Samreen, A. (2022). Application of Gamification in Modern Education. In *Handbook of Research on Promoting Economic and Social Development Through Serious Games* (pp. 60–75). IGI Global.

Ahmad, A., Zeshan, F., Khan, M. S., Marriam, R., Ali, A., & Samreen, A. (2020b). The impact of gamification on learning outcomes of computer science majors. *ACM Transactions on Computing Education*, 20(2), 1–25.

Ahmed, M., Ahmad, A., Zeshan, F., & Turab, H. (2024). Blockchain Basics: A Deep Dive Into the Blocks, Chains, and Consensus. In Decentralizing the Online Experience With Web3 Technologies (pp. 57-89). IGI Global.

Ahmed, S., Javaid, S., Niazi, M. F., Alam, A., Ahmad, A., Baig, M. A., & Ahmed, T. (2019). A qualitative analysis of context-aware ubiquitous learning environments using Bluetooth beacons. *Technology, Pedagogy and Education*, 28(1), 53–71.

Bandura, A. (1977). *Social learning theory.*

Berestova, A., Alizade, T., & Umirzakova, Z. (2020). The Role of Social Networks in the Educational Process. *International Journal of Emerging Technologies in Learning*, 15(22).

Bilal, A., Mirza, H. T., Hussain, I., & Ahmad, A. (2024). Investigating Influence of Google-Play Application Titles on Success. *Big Data Research*, 36, 100443.

Bozkurt, A. (2023). Generative artificial intelligence (AI) powered conversational educational agents: The inevitable paradigm shift. *Asian Journal of Distance Education*, 18(1).

Burgess, S. (2016). Human capital and education: The state of the art in the economics of education.

Chen, L., Chen, P., & Lin, Z. (2020). Artificial intelligence in education: A review. *IEEE Access : Practical Innovations, Open Solutions*, 8, 75264–75278.

Digitaldefynd, (2024). https://digitaldefynd.com/IQ/ai-in-schools-case-studies/

Duke, B., Harper, G., & Johnston, M. (2013). Connectivism as a digital age learning theory. *The International HETL Review*, 2013(Special Issue), 4–13.

Forero-Corba, W., & Bennasar, F. N. (2024). Techniques and applications of Machine Learning and Artificial Intelligence in education: a systematic review. RIED-Revista Iberoamericana de Educación a Distancia, 27(1).

Gkintoni, E., Dimakos, I., Halkiopoulos, C., & Antonopoulou, H. (2023). Contributions of neuroscience to educational praxis: A systematic review. *Emerging Science Journal*, 7, 146–158.

Golubeva, T. I., Kokhanovskaya, I. I., Fatykhova, A. L., Golovneva, E. V., & Terekhova, N. V. (2020). Social networks and education: the increase in student learning efficiency and the search for means of control. Revista Inclusiones, 7(S3-2), 48-60.

Hamid, M., Ahmad, A., & Aimeur, E. (2019). Factors contributing in failures of software projects. *International Journal of Computer Science and Network Security*, 19(5), 62–77.

Hamid, M., Zeshan, F., Ahmad, A., Ahmad, F., Hamza, M. A., Khan, Z. A., & Aljuaid, H. (2020). An intelligent recommender and decision support system (IRDSS) for effective management of software projects. *IEEE Access : Practical Innovations, Open Solutions*, 8, 140752–140766.

Hamid, M., Zeshan, F., Ahmad, A., Malik, S., Saleem, M., Tabassum, N., & Qasim, M. (2022). Analysis of software success through structural equation modeling. *Intelligent Automation & Soft Computing*, 31(3), 1689–1701.

Hamid, M., Zeshan, F., Ahmad, A., Munawar, S., Aimeur, E., Ahmed, S., & Yousif, M. (2020). An intelligent decision support system for effective handling of IT projects. *Journal of Intelligent & Fuzzy Systems*, 38(3), 2635–2647.

Hasanah, U., & Shimizu, K. (2020). Crucial cognitive skills in science education: A systematic review. Jurnal Penelitian dan Pembelajaran IPA, 6(1), 36-72.

Huang, J., Saleh, S., & Liu, Y. (2021). A review on artificial intelligence in education. Academic Journal of Interdisciplinary Studies, 10(3).

Imran, M., & Ahmad, A. (2023). Enhancing data quality to mine credible patterns. *Journal of Information Science*, 49(2), 544–564.

Kuleto, V., Ilić, M., Dumangiu, M., Ranković, M., Martins, O. M., Păun, D., & Mihoreanu, L. (2021). Exploring opportunities and challenges of artificial intelligence and machine learning in higher education institutions. *Sustainability*, 13(18), 10424.

Lave, J. (1991). *Situated learning: Legitimate peripheral participation*. Cambridge university press.

Li, L., Ma, Z., Fan, L., Lee, S., Yu, H., & Hemphill, L. (2024). ChatGPT in education: A discourse analysis of worries and concerns on social media. *Education and Information Technologies*, 29(9), 10729–10762.

Marginson, S., & Dang, T. K. A. (2017). Vygotsky's sociocultural theory in the context of globalization. *Asia Pacific Journal of Education*, 37(1), 116–129.

Mhlanga, D. (2023). Open AI in education, the responsible and ethical use of ChatGPT towards lifelong learning. In *FinTech and artificial intelligence for sustainable development: The role of smart technologies in achieving development goals* (pp. 387–409). Springer Nature Switzerland.

Muhammad, T., & Ahmad, A. (2021). A joint sharing approach for online privacy preservation. *World Wide Web (Bussum)*, 24(3), 895–924.

Musgrave, P. W. (2017). *The sociology of education*. Routledge.

Ng, D. T. K., & Chu, S. K. W. (2021). Motivating Students to Learn AI Through Social Networking Sites: A Case Study in Hong Kong. *Online Learning : the Official Journal of the Online Learning Consortium*, 25(1), 195–208.

Nguyen, T. N. T., Lai, N. V., & Nguyen, Q. T. (2024). Artificial Intelligence (AI) in Education: A Case Study on ChatGPT's Influence on Student Learning Behaviors. *Educational Process: International Journal*, 13(2), 105–121. DOI: 10.22521/edupij.2024.132.7

Ouyang, F., & Jiao, P. (2021). Artificial intelligence in education: The three paradigms. *Computers and Education: Artificial Intelligence*, 2, 100020.

Salman Khan, M., Ahmad, A., & Humayoun, M. (2022). Building an Effective Automated Assessment System for C/C++ Introductory Programming Courses in ODL Environment. arXiv e-prints, arXiv-2205.

Samreen, A., Ahmad, A., & Zeshan, F. (2020a, February). Searching for truth in the post-truth age. In 2020 3rd international conference on advancements in computational sciences (ICACS) (pp. 1-5). IEEE.

Samreen, A., Ahmad, A., Zeshan, F., Ahmad, F., Ahmed, S., & Khan, Z. A. (2020b). A collaborative method for protecting teens against online predators over social networks: A behavioral analysis. *IEEE Access : Practical Innovations, Open Solutions*, 8, 174375–174393.

Sarfraz, A., Ahmad, A., Zeshan, F., & Mirza, H. T. (2024). Synews: A synergy-based rumor verification system. *Social Network Analysis and Mining*, 14(1), 57.

Siann, G., & Ugwuegbu, D. C. (2024). *Educational psychology in a changing world.* Taylor & Francis.

Song, Y., Tung, P. H., & Jeon, B. (2022, August). Trends in Artificial Emotional Intelligence Technology and Application. In 2022 IEEE/ACIS 7th International Conference on Big Data, Cloud Computing, and Data Science (BCD) (pp. 366-370). IEEE.

Stancin, K., Poscic, P., & Jaksic, D. (2020). Ontologies in education–state of the art. *Education and Information Technologies*, 25(6), 5301–5320.

Whitworth, B., & Ahmad, A. (2013a). Polite Computing. In *The Social Design of Technical Systems: Building technologies for communities* (pp. 77–105). The Interaction Design Foundation.

Whitworth, B., & Ahmad, A. (2013b). The evolution of computing. In *The Encyclopedia of human-computer interaction* (2nd ed.). Interaction Design Foundation. Retrieved from https://www.interaction-design.org/literature/book/the-encyclopedia-of-human-computerinteraction-2nd-ed/socio-technical-system-design

Whitworth, B., Ahmad, A., & Soegaard, M. (2006). *Encyclopedia of Human Computer Interaction.* Interaction Design Foundation.

Whitworth, B., Janczewski, L., & Ahmad, A. (2012, July). A Logic of Creation in Online Social Networks. In *2012 World Congress in Computer Science, Computer Engineering and Applied Computing (WORLDCOMP 2012).*

Wiechetek, Ł., & Pastuszak, Z. (2022). Academic social networks metrics: An effective indicator for university performance? *Scientometrics*, 127(3), 1381–1401.

Williamson, B. (2024). The social life of AI in education. *International Journal of Artificial Intelligence in Education*, 34(1), 97–104.

Zeshan, F., dar, Z., Ahmad, A., & Malik, T. (2024). A fuzzy ontology-based context-aware encryption approach in IoT through device and information classification. *The Journal of Supercomputing*, 80(16), 23311–23356.

Zeshan, F., Ahmad, A., Abdel-Aty, A. H., Algarni, F., Mahmoud, E. E., & Ahmad, A. (2020). A hybrid semantic knowledge integration and sharing approach for distributed smart environments. *Sensors (Basel)*, 20(20), 5918. PMID: 33092118

Zeshan, F., Mohamad, R., Ahmad, M. N., Othman, M. B., Elhag, A. A. M., Hussain, S. A., & Babar, I. (2019). Context-Aware ontology and web services discovery for distributed embedded real-time systems. *Malaysian Journal of Computer Science*, 32(3), 186–208.

Chapter 6 Customer Relationship Management (CRM) Systems: Impact of AI on Post-COVID-19 Student Enrolment in Kerala's Higher Education Institutions

Limson Antony Puthur
Christ University, India

Meljo Thomas Karakunnel
Christ University, India

Vishnu Achutha Menon
https://orcid.org/0000-0003-4028-3685
Institute for Educational and Developmental Studies, Noida, India

ABSTRACT

This study investigates the influence of artificial intelligence (AI) on student enrollment in higher educational institutions in Kerala, with a particular emphasis on the mediating role of customer relationship management (CRM) systems. Employing a descriptive research design, a self-prepared questionnaire was administered to a purposive sample of 200 students, encompassing various educational stages. The findings reveal a significant positive correlation between AI usage and student enrollment, with AI usage accounting for 37.3% of the variance in enrollment outcomes. Furthermore, the analysis indicates that CRM systems partially mediate the relationship between AI and student enrollment, enhancing the effectiveness of

DOI: 10.4018/979-8-3373-2272-8.ch006

AI-driven strategies in the recruitment process. With high reliability demonstrated in the research instrument (Cronbach alpha = 0.827), the study underscores the necessity of integrating AI and CRM technologies to optimize enrollment strategies in the evolving educational landscape.

INTRODUCTION

Artificial Intelligence (AI) is transforming various sectors, including higher education. AI technologies are being adopted by higher educational institutions to streamline and enhance the student enrolment process. The use of AI in this context can be broadly categorized into predictive analytics, personalized communication, and process automation. AI-driven predictive analytics is a powerful tool used by colleges and universities to forecast enrolment trends, identify at-risk students, and optimize resource allocation (Cirelli et al., 2018; Gnoh et al., 2024). AI can predict which students are most likely to apply, accept offers, and ultimately enroll. This helps institutions allocate resources more efficiently, target their recruitment efforts, and make informed decisions about class sizes and program offerings. Predictive models, including logistic regression, neural networks, and decision trees, have shown accuracy rates of around 70% in predicting enrollment decisions(Ab Ghani et al., 2019) and can identify students who are likely to struggle academically and may need additional support, enabling institutions to intervene early and improve retention rates. AI applications in higher education extend to personalizing learning experiences, augmenting faculty capabilities, and improving administrative efficiency(Begamudra Rangavittal, 2024; Hannan & Liu, 2021). The integration of AI technologies offers benefits such as improved learning outcomes, increased retention, and decreased time to completion (Hutson et al., 2022). AI can help forecast the impact of changes in tuition fees, scholarship programs, or marketing campaigns on student enrollment, providing valuable insights for strategic planning. However, challenges remain, including ethical considerations, data privacy, and the need for infrastructure adjustments(Tarisayi, 2023). Recent research demonstrates that AI-based predictive models can achieve up to 95.7% accuracy in predicting student satisfaction, emphasizing the potential for personalized education (Gallastegui & Forradellas, 2024).

Personalized Communication

AI-powered systems enhance the recruitment process by providing personalized communication with prospective students. Chatbots and virtual assistants, driven by natural language processing (NLP) algorithms, engage students on various platforms such as college websites, social media, and emails, answering queries and guiding them through the application process (A et al., 2024; Fox et al., 2024; Lalwani et al., 2018). These AI tools analyze data from multiple touchpoints, such as interactions with the institution's website, social media activity, and responses to email campaigns to create tailored content, increasing engagement and improving conversion rates that resonates with prospective students based on their interests and preferences (Tasheva & Karpovich, 2024). This targeted approach can significantly increase engagement and improve the likelihood of conversion from inquiry to application. Studies have shown that AI-driven interventions can significantly increase on-time enrollment rates(Page & Gehlbach, 2017). AI chatbots also enhance efficiency in the recruitment process, freeing up administrative staff for more complex tasks (Nawaz & Gomes, 2020). While AI offers numerous benefits, including improved efficiency and better-quality hires, ethical considerations such as data privacy and potential algorithmic bias must be addressed (Albassam, 2023; Hutson & Plate, 2023).

Process Automation

Artificial Intelligence (AI) is transforming higher education by enhancing learning experiences, improving administrative efficiency, and supporting research (Al-Ka'bi, 2023; Begamudra Rangavittal, 2024). AI applications in higher education include personalized learning, automated assessments, predictive modelling, and intelligent tutoring systems(Crompton & Song, 2021; Salas-Pilco & Yang, 2022). The application process for higher education can be complex and time-consuming, both for students and administrative staff. AI can automate many routine tasks, such as data entry, document verification, and application status updates, reducing the administrative burden and minimizing errors. This not only streamlines the process but also allows staff to focus on more strategic activities, such as building relationships with prospective students and addressing their unique needs.

Machine learning algorithms can streamline admissions processes, reducing review time and improving efficiency (Waters & Miikkulainen, 2013). For instance, these algorithms can be used to screen applications and identify those that meet the institution's criteria, speeding up the review process and ensuring a more efficient selection process. Robotic process automation can further assist with admissions, registration, and evaluation processes (Roxana & MOS¸TEANU, 2022). Strategic leadership is crucial for responsible AI adoption, addressing technical, ethical, and cultural challenges while harnessing its potential (Tarisayi, 2023). Despite these challenges, AI has the potential to significantly improve teaching, learning, and administrative processes in higher education, enabling institutions to manage the influx of applications more effectively and focus on more strategic activities.

CRM Systems and AI Integration

Customer Relationship Management (CRM) systems integrated with Artificial Intelligence (AI) have become integral to the admissions process in higher educational institutions, transforming recruitment strategies and student engagement (Almahairah, 2023; Gavade, 2024). CRM systems provide a centralized platform for managing all interactions with prospective students, capturing data from various sources such as website visits, social media interactions, email communications, and event attendance. By consolidating this data, CRM systems enable institutions to have a comprehensive view of each prospective student, facilitating more informed decision-making (Ahmad & Pande, 2024; Janakova, 2023).

Integrating AI with CRM systems allows for the analysis of large volumes of data to identify trends and patterns. This can inform recruitment strategies by highlighting the most effective channels for reaching prospective students, the types of messages that resonate most, and the timing of communications. Institutions can use these insights to optimize their marketing efforts and improve the overall recruitment process(Ledro et al., 2022). AI can analyze data from previous recruitment cycles to identify characteristics of students who are most likely to enroll and succeed at the institution. This information can be used to refine targeting criteria and focus recruitment efforts on high-potential candidates.

In the education sector, CRM systems can improve student engagement, retention, and satisfaction(Seeman & O'Hara, 2006). They facilitate a student-centric approach, enhancing the overall recruitment process(Lavanya, 2011). AI-enabled CRM systems can automate routine tasks, personalize student interactions, and provide data-driven insights for recruitment strategies(Almahairah, 2023; Gavade, 2024). This automation not only streamlines processes but also allows staff to focus on more strategic activities, such as building relationships with prospective students and addressing their unique needs. While CRM was initially designed for the private sector, studies have shown that it can be successfully adapted for university recruiting environments (Barriento et al., 2003), making it a valuable tool for higher education institutions. By utilizing AI and CRM systems, institutions can manage the influx of applications more effectively, optimize their marketing efforts, and ultimately improve the efficiency and effectiveness of their admissions processes.

AI integration in CRM systems is revolutionizing customer engagement and student support in higher education. These AI-enhanced CRM systems enable personalized engagement with prospective students, transforming the recruitment and admissions processes (Gavade, 2024; Journal, 2024). By analyzing data from various touchpoints, institutions can create tailored communication plans that address the specific interests and concerns of each student.

AI-powered CRM tools facilitate critical thinking, offer real-time feedback, and improve the overall learning experience(Janakova, 2023). For instance, AI-powered chatbots and virtual assistants can provide instant responses to queries, guide students through the application process, and offer personalized recommendations based on their profiles. AcademiBot, an AI-driven college dialog system, demonstrates the potential for personalized assistance and strategic marketing in higher education (Fox et al., 2024). These AI chatbots are transforming student support by offering quick responses and personalized recommendations (Segovia-García, 2024).

CRM systems can automate follow-up communications, ensuring that prospective students receive timely and relevant information throughout the recruitment process. This level of personalized engagement can significantly enhance the student experience and increase the likelihood of enrollment. By analyzing data from various sources, institutions can create a comprehensive view of each prospective student, facilitating more informed decision-making and optimizing marketing efforts. However, implementing AI in CRM systems presents challenges such as data security and privacy concerns (Segovia-García, 2024). Organizations must assess their readiness for AI integration in CRM systems by evaluating various indicators and ensuring appropriate data management (Chatterjee et al., 2019). Despite these challenges, AI-integrated CRM systems have the potential to enhance customer satisfaction, streamline processes, and improve decision-making in various sectors, including higher education (Ahmad & Pande, 2024; Riyaz et al., 2023). Overall, the combination of AI and CRM systems in higher education admissions offers powerful tools for personalized engagement, efficient process management, and data-driven decision-making. These technologies have the potential to significantly improve the recruitment process, enhance the student experience, and ultimately contribute to the success of both students and institutions.

Artificial Intelligence (AI) is increasingly influencing higher education, particularly in areas of student enrollment, retention, and success. AI-enhanced Customer Relationship Management (CRM) systems provide valuable insights for strategic decision-making in educational institutions (Journal, 2024; Seeman & O'Hara, 2006). These systems can predict enrollment behaviour, identify at-risk students, and inform support programs (Shilbayeh & Abonamah, 2021). AI applications in higher education span student learning experiences, support services, and enrollment management (Hannan & Liu, 2021).Institutions can use predictive analytics to identify factors that influence student retention and success. This can inform the development of support programs and initiatives aimed at improving student outcomes. Additionally, AI can help institutions assess the effectiveness of their recruitment strategies and make adjustments as needed to achieve their enrollment goals.

Institutions are adopting AI-powered chatbots for student services and learning support(Khare et al., 2018). The integration of AI in education systems, mediated by smart learning, can enhance academic outcomes (Akour et al., 2023). However, the adoption of AI-integrated CRM systems depends on factors such as system quality and user satisfaction (Chatterjee et al., 2021). AI-based research methods, like chatbots, can also efficiently gather data on students' university choice factors (Cingillioglu, 2024).

The major research objectives of the study are to determine the extent to which AI influences student enrollment and to understand the role of Customer Relationship Management (CRM) systems as a mediator in this relationship. Therefore, the two hypotheses that have been formulated to be tested in this study are:

H1: AI influences student enrollment in higher educational institutions

H2: Customer Relationship Management (CRM) systems-enabled platforms mediate the influence of AI on student enrollment

METHODOLOGY

The current study employs a descriptive research design to comprehensively explore the intricate relationship between AI and student enrolment, with a specific focus on the distinctive context of the Kerala region. A self-prepared questionnaire was meticulously crafted following an exhaustive literature review, serving as the primary data collection tool. This questionnaire was systematically administered to a purposive sample of 200 students representing various educational stages – ranging from twelfth-standard students to college and university students, along with research scholars across Kerala. The selection of the Kerala region is underpinned by its unique socio-cultural and educational landscape, with its high literacy rates, progressive educational institutions, and widespread digital connectivity rendering it an ideal setting to investigate the dynamic interplay between AI usage and student enrolment. The region's diverse demographic composition, spanning a wide age range and encompassing varied educational backgrounds, contributes to a rich and textured canvas for exploring the subtleties of this relationship. Participants were judiciously chosen through purposive sampling, ensuring a representative cross-section across distinct educational levels. All respondents were either enrolled in a course or were in the process of enrolling in a college or university, thereby enhancing the study's relevance to its intended focus. The questionnaire was disseminated through both face-to-face interactions and digital platforms. Google Forms, distributed via email accounts, group chats, and messaging platforms, facilitated data collection from a geographically dispersed participant pool. The collected data underwent meticulous analysis using the Statistical Package for the Social Sciences (SPSS).Principal

Component Analysis (PCA) with Varimax rotation was employed to extract three distinctive factors – AI usage, information seeking, and content distribution – from the dataset. Subsequent Pearson's correlation analysis confirmed a significant positive relationship between AI usage and student enrolment. Multiple regression analysis revealed that AI usage substantially contributed to variance in student enrolment. To ensure ethical standards, participants were provided with comprehensive information regarding the study's objectives, potential risks, benefits of participation, confidentiality safeguards, and the unequivocal right to withdraw at any stage. Demographic insights derived from the sample distribution provided further depth to the study's contextual comprehension. Among participants, 64.5 percent were male and 35.5 percent were female. Examination of age distribution indicated that 30 percent fell within the 15 to 20 years age bracket, 39 percent belonged to the 20 to 25 years range, and 31 percent were above 25 years old. Geographical distribution highlighted over 70 percent of respondents residing in urban areas, while the remaining 30 percent hailed from rural locales. Regarding marital status, 75 percent of respondents were unmarried, while 25 percent were married.

RESULTS

Reliability of the Instrument: The research instrument comprised three sections. The first section comprised demographic statements, the second comprised statements about social media, and the third comprised statements about technology-based student enrolment. The Cronbach alpha value for the research instrument was 0.827, which is high, indicating good internal consistency between the items. The data pertaining to different AI usage activities were subjected to factor analysis-based segmentation. Factor analysis helps in classifying social media activities into broad underlying factors. Principal component analysis was carried out for factor extraction, and the method of rotation used was Varimax rotation.

Hypothesis 1: AI influences student enrolment in higher educational institutions

A correlation test was run between AI Usage and student enrolment, and it was found that there is a positive significant association between them at a 1% significance level. Pearson's correlation coefficient was found to be 0.775which indicates a high relationship between AI Usage and student enrolment.

Table 1. Descriptive statistics, model summary, analysis of variance (ANOVA) and coefficient values of social media and its influence on student enrolment

		AI Usage	**Student Enrolment**
	Mean	4.70	4.08
	SD	0.69	0.62
Model Summary	R2	0.373	
ANOVA	F	149.82	
	Sig	0.000	
Coefficient	B_0	0.159	
	$B_{(social\ media)}$	0.286	
	t	14.479	
	Sig	0.000	

The table 1 displays descriptive statistics and model summary for AI usage and student enrollment. AI usage shows a mean of 4.70 with a standard deviation (SD) of 0.69, while student enrollment has a mean of 4.08 with a SD of 0.62. The model summary indicates an R-squared of 0.373, suggesting that 37.3% of the variance in student enrollment is explained by the model. ANOVA results show a significant F-value of 149.82 ($p < 0.001$), indicating that the regression model is statistically significant. The coefficients reveal that AI usage ($B = 0.159$, $t = 14.479$, $p < 0.001$) and social media ($B = 0.286$, $t = 14.479$, $p < 0.001$) both significantly influence student enrollment.

Hypothesis 2: Customer Relationship Management (CRM) systems enabled platforms mediated the influence of AI on student enrolment

The goodness-of-fit index of the model investigating the mediator role of Usage of CRM between AI Usage and Student Enrolment is as follows: $\chi 2/df$ (chi-square/ degrees of freedom) is 4.043 (p= .001), lower than 5, which indicates a good fit. The RMSEA is .0241, which is in the range of 0.05–0.10, indicating thereby a good fit; the normed fit index (NFI) is .928, the comparative fit index (CFI) is .963, the goodness-of-fit index (GFI) is .983, which all are in the range of 0.90–0.99, reflecting thereby good fit again. Thus, it may be determined that the created model has a good fit and can be used for testing the mediation. The analysis results of the direct and indirect effect and the total effect of the mediator on the dependent variable have been shown in Table 2. All the values in the table are standardized beta coefficients.

Table 2. Standardized coefficients of mediator role of usage of CRM technology between AI usage and student enrolment

Variables	B	Direct effect	Indirect effect	Total effect	Decision
Use of CRM ←------AI Usage	.578**	.259**	.125**	.384**	Partial mediation
Student Enrolment ←-----AI Usage	.259**				
Student enrolment ←--------- Usage of CRM	.101**				

**The significance level of all the values is *p <.01*

Table 2 presents standardized coefficients that analyze the mediator role of CRM technology between AI usage and student enrollment. The findings indicate significant direct effects: AI usage strongly predicts increased CRM utilization (coefficient = .578, p < .01) and positively correlates with higher student enrollment (coefficient = .259, p < .01). The indirect effect shows that CRM usage partially mediates the relationship between AI usage and student enrollment, with a coefficient of .259 (p < .01). The total effect of AI usage on student enrollment, combining direct and indirect effects, is .384 (p < .01). These results suggest that while CRM technology enhances the impact of AI on student enrollment, other factors also contribute to this relationship.

DISCUSSION

The rise in the utilization of Customer Relationship Management (CRM) systems by educational institutions has significantly transformed the dynamics of student admissions, particularly during the tumultuous period of the COVID-19 pandemic. The pandemic necessitated a swift adaptation to digital communication and enrollment processes, compelling educational institutions to leverage technology to maintain engagement with prospective students. This transition not only facilitated the continuation of admissions processes amidst widespread disruptions but also highlighted the critical role that CRM systems play in managing relationships with prospective and current students. During the COVID-19 pandemic, traditional admission methods faced substantial challenges due to restrictions on in-person interactions and the closure of physical campuses. Educational institutions had to rapidly pivot to online platforms to conduct outreach, information sessions, and application processes. The implementation of CRM systems during this time allowed institutions to streamline communication, manage inquiries, and track engagement with prospective students more effectively. For instance, automated responses and personalized communication via CRM platforms enabled institutions to address student concerns regarding admissions, course offerings, and safety protocols in real time, thereby nurturing a sense of connection despite physical distancing measures. The impact of artificial intelligence (AI) on post-COVID student enrollment in Kerala's higher education institutions has been profound. As institutions transitioned to a more digital-centric approach, AI technologies became instrumental in analyzing student data, predicting enrollment trends, and optimizing marketing strategies. For example, AI-driven analytics could identify potential students based on their online behavior and engagement with institutional content, allowing universities to tailor their outreach efforts more precisely. This targeted approach not only improved the efficiency of recruitment campaigns but also enhanced the overall experience for prospective students by providing them with relevant information aligned with their interests and aspirations.

In the post-COVID context, the integration of AI within CRM systems has allowed institutions to maintain robust relationships with prospective students throughout the enrollment journey. Automated communication workflows, predictive analytics, and personalized marketing strategies have enabled institutions to keep prospective students informed and engaged, ultimately influencing their enrollment decisions. Additionally, AI can assist in assessing student preferences and concerns, enabling institutions to adapt their offerings and support services accordingly. This adaptability is essential in a rapidly changing educational environment where student expectations and needs may differ significantly from those in pre-pandemic times. The rise of CRM systems in educational institutions during the COVID-19 pandemic has fundamentally reshaped the processes of student admissions. The integration of AI technologies has further enhanced the effectiveness of these systems, facilitating improved communication, targeted recruitment strategies, and better relationship management with prospective students. As Kerala's higher education institutions navigate the post-COVID era, the strategic use of CRM and AI will continue to play a vital role in shaping student enrollment outcomes and addressing the evolving needs of the student population.

The study found that AI influences student enrollment in higher educational institutions and that Customer Relationship Management (CRM) systems-enabled platforms mediate this influence. Several reasons support these findings:

- Enhanced Decision-Making Through Data Analysis: AI technologies can analyze vast amounts of data quickly and accurately, helping institutions identify prospective students more effectively. For example, predictive analytics can forecast student enrollment trends based on historical data, allowing institutions to tailor their marketing strategies. If a college notices that students from certain demographics or geographic areas are more likely to enroll, they can focus their outreach efforts accordingly.

- Personalized Marketing and Communication: AI enables institutions to engage with prospective students through personalized communication strategies. Chatbots, powered by AI, can provide real-time information on courses, application processes, and financial aid options. For instance, a chatbot on a university's website can answer questions about admission criteria, making it easier for potential students to navigate their choices. This tailored approach increases the likelihood of student engagement and enrollment.
- Streamlined Enrollment Processes: AI can automate and optimize various administrative processes involved in student enrollment, making them more efficient and user-friendly. For example, AI-driven CRM systems can streamline the application and admissions processes by automatically sorting applications, tracking documents, and notifying students of their status. This not only reduces administrative burden but also improves the overall experience for prospective students, which can enhance enrollment rates.
- Improved Student Support Services: AI tools integrated into CRM systems can analyze student interactions and feedback, helping institutions provide targeted support services. For instance, if data indicates that students from certain backgrounds struggle with specific courses, the institution can implement tailored support programs or resources to address those needs. By proactively offering assistance, institutions can improve student satisfaction and retention, ultimately influencing enrollment decisions.
- Enhanced Engagement Through Social Media: AI-powered analytics tools can assess social media trends and engagement levels, allowing institutions to create content that resonates with prospective students. For example, universities can analyze which types of posts receive the most interaction and adjust their social media strategies accordingly. By using insights from AI, institutions can build a stronger online presence and engage more effectively with potential students, impacting their enrollment decisions.
- Strengthened Relationships Through CRM: CRM systems improve relationship management between institutions and prospective students. By tracking interactions and preferences, institutions can tailor their outreach efforts and follow-up communications. For example, if a student shows interest in a particular program, the CRM can flag this and ensure that relevant information is sent to them, creating a sense of personalized engagement. This proactive approach can positively influence a student's decision to enroll.

CONCLUSION

This study underscores the positive influence of AI on student enrollment in higher education institutions, supported by the reliability of the research instrument and statistical evidence. Factor analysis identified key segments within AI usage, including social media and technology-based enrollment practices, as influential components. Correlation analysis demonstrated a strong association between AI use and increased student enrollment, with Pearson's coefficient at 0.775. The model's analysis revealed that AI usage, along with social media, accounts for a notable portion of the variation in student enrollment. Additionally, the mediation analysis highlighted the partial mediating role of CRM technology, amplifying AI's effect on enrollment while suggesting that other factors may also contribute.

REFERENCES

A, S., V, M., V, R., & B, U. (2024). COLLEGEBOT: Virtual Assistant System for Enquiry Using Natural Language Processing. *2024 2nd International Conference on Intelligent Data Communication Technologies and Internet of Things (IDCIoT)*, 1407–1414. https://api.semanticscholar.org/CorpusID:268613686

Ab Ghani, N. L., Che Cob, Z., Mohd Drus, S., & Sulaiman, H. (2019). Student enrolment prediction model in higher education institution: a data mining approach. *Proceedings of the 3rd International Symposium of Information and Internet Technology (SYMINTECH 2018)*, 43–52.

Ahmad, R., & Pande, S. (2024). Examining the Integration of Artificial Intelligence in Customer Relationship Management. SSRN *Electronic Journal*. https://api.semanticscholar.org/CorpusID:269825841

Akour, I. A., Alshurideh, H. M., Alzoubi, H. M., Alshurideh, M. T., & Antouz, Y. A. (2023). Integrating Artificial Intelligence in Improving Educational System: The Mediating role of Smart Learning. *2023 International Conference on Business Analytics for Technology and Security (ICBATS)*, 1–5. https://api.semanticscholar.org/CorpusID:258728985

Al-Ka'bi, A. H. (2023). Proposed artificial intelligence algorithm and deep learning techniques for development of higher education. *Int. J. Intell. Networks*, 4, 68–73. https://api.semanticscholar.org/CorpusID:257574020

Albassam, W. A. (2023). The Power of Artificial Intelligence in Recruitment: An Analytical Review of Current AI-Based Recruitment Strategies. *International Journal of Professional Business Review*. https://api.semanticscholar.org/CorpusID:259639373

Almahairah, M. S. Z. (2023). Artificial Intelligence Application for Effective Customer Relationship Management. *2023 International Conference on Computer Communication and Informatics (ICCCI)*, 1–7. https://api.semanticscholar.org/CorpusID:258869492

Barriento, F., Cheng, W., & Gulledge, T. R. (2003). Customizing CRM for University Implementations. *International Journal of Electronic Business Management*, 1, 63–74. https://api.semanticscholar.org/CorpusID:38148250

Begamudra Rangavittal, P. (2024). Transforming Higher Education with Artificial Intelligence - Benefits, Challenges, and Future Directions. *International Journal of Scientific Research*, 13(5), 1635–1642. DOI: 10.21275/sr24525214415

Chatterjee, S., Ghosh, S. K., Chaudhuri, R., & Nguyen, B. (2019). Are CRM systems ready for AI integration? *The Bottom Line*. https://api.semanticscholar.org/CorpusID:197781292

Chatterjee, S., Rana, N. P., Khorana, S., Mikalef, P., & Sharma, A. (2021). Assessing Organizational Users' Intentions and Behavior to AI Integrated CRM Systems: A Meta-UTAUT Approach. *Information Systems Frontiers*, 25, 1299–1313. https://api.semanticscholar.org/CorpusID:238650817

Cingillioglu, I. (2024). What impacts matriculation decisions? Identifying students' university choice factors on a global scale with Artificial Intelligence. *Studies in Higher Education*. https://api.semanticscholar.org/CorpusID:267735802

Cirelli, J., Konkol, A. M., Aqlan, F., & Nwokeji, J. C. (2018). Predictive analytics models for student admission and enrollment. *Proceedings of the International Conference on Industrial Engineering and Operations Management,* 2018(SEP), 1395–1403.

Crompton, H., & Song, D. (2021). The Potential of Artificial Intelligence in Higher Education. *Revista Virtual Universidad Católica Del Norte*. https://api.semanticscholar.org/CorpusID:234234123

Fox, A., Stoner, J., & Wang, J. (2024). Revolutionizing Student Engagement and Enrollment through Personalized, AI-Driven Dialog Systems in Higher Education. *Proceedings of the 55th ACM Technical Symposium on Computer Science Education V. 2*. https://api.semanticscholar.org/CorpusID:268433080

Gallastegui, L. M. G., & Forradellas, R. R. (2024). Optimization of the Educational Experience in Higher Education Using Predictive Artificial Intelligence Models. *Revista de Gestão Social e Ambiental*. https://api.semanticscholar.org/CorpusID:270006202

Gavade, P. (2024). Enhancing Customer Relationship Management with Artificial Intelligence. *International Journal of Computer Science and Engineering*. https://api.semanticscholar.org/CorpusID:269081575

Gnoh, H. Q., Keoy, K. H., Iqbal, J., Anjum, S. S., Yeo, S. F., Lim, A. F., Lim, W. L., & Chaw, L. Y. (2024). Enhancing Business Sustainability Through Technology-Enabled AI: Forecasting Student Data and Comparing Prediction Models for Higher Education Institutions (HEIs). *PaperAsia*, 40(2b), 48–58. DOI: 10.59953/paperasia.v40i2b.86

Hannan, E., & Liu, S. (2021). AI: new source of competitiveness in higher education. *Competitiveness Review: An International Business Journal*. https://api.semanticscholar.org/CorpusID:238650032

Hutson, J., Jeevanjee, T., Vander Graaf, V., Lively, J., Weber, J., Weir, G., Arnone, K., Carnes, G., Vosevich, K., Plate, D., Leary, M., & Edele, S. (2022). Artificial Intelligence and the Disruption of Higher Education: Strategies for Integrations across Disciplines. *Creative Education*. https://api.semanticscholar.org/CorpusID:255298108

Hutson, J., & Plate, D. (2023). Enhancing Institutional Assessment and Reporting Through Conversational Technologies: Exploring the Potential of AI-Powered Tools and Natural Language Processing. *DS Journal of Artificial Intelligence and Robotics*. https://api.semanticscholar.org/CorpusID:268580168

Janakova, M. (2023). Artificial Intelligence in CRM Education. *Proceedings of the 17th International Scientific Conference INPROFORUM*. https://api.semanticscholar.org/CorpusID:268696021

Journal, I. (2024). A Study to Know Impact of AI on CRM. *Interantional Journal Of Scientific Research In Engineering And Management*. https://api.semanticscholar.org/CorpusID:267735383

Khare, K., Stewart, B., & Khare, A. (2018). Artificial Intelligence and the Student Experience: An Institutional Perspective. *IAFOR Journal of Education*. https://api.semanticscholar.org/CorpusID:150179486

Lalwani, T., Bhalotia, S., Pal, A., Bisen, S., & Rathod, V. S. (2018). *Implementation of a Chat Bot System using AI and NLP*. https://api.semanticscholar.org/CorpusID:69287458

Lavanya, T. (2011). Customer Relationship Management and Higher Education -A Vision. *Advances in Management, 4*. https://api.semanticscholar.org/CorpusID:167447950

Ledro, C., Nosella, A., & Vinelli, A. (2022). Artificial intelligence in customer relationship management: literature review and future research directions. *Journal of Business \& Industrial Marketing*. https://api.semanticscholar.org/CorpusID:248030053

Nawaz, N., & Gomes, A. M. (2020). Artificial Intelligence Chatbots are New Recruiters. *Organizational Communication EJournal*. https://api.semanticscholar.org/CorpusID:203646454

Page, L. C., & Gehlbach, H. (2017). How an Artificially Intelligent Virtual Assistant Helps Students Navigate the Road to College. *AERA Open*, 3. https://api.semanticscholar.org/CorpusID:53124313

Riyaz, M., Sawant, P. D., Raju, S., Nijhawan, G., Deepika, N. M., & B, M. L. (2023). Artificial Intelligence for Customer Relationship Management: Personalization and Automation. *2023 10th IEEE Uttar Pradesh Section International Conference on Electrical, Electronics and Computer Engineering (UPCON), 10*, 547–551. https://api.semanticscholar.org/CorpusID:268036115

Roxana, N., & Mos, T. (2022). Machine Learning and Robotic Process Automation Take Higher Education One Step Further. *Romanian Journal of Information Science and Technology, 25*. https://api.semanticscholar.org/CorpusID:264435310

Salas-Pilco, S. Z., & Yang, Y. (2022). Artificial intelligence applications in Latin American higher education: A systematic review. *International Journal of Educational Technology in Higher Education*, 19. https://api.semanticscholar.org/CorpusID:248234262

Seeman, E. D., & O'Hara, M. T. (2006). Customer Relationship Management in Higher Education: Using Information Systems to Improve the Student-School Relationship. *Campus-Wide Information Systems*, 23, 24–34. https://api.semanticscholar.org/CorpusID:62651864

Segovia-García, N. (2024). Optimizing Student Support. A Review of the Use of AI Chatbots in Higher Education. *European Public & Social Innovation Review*. https://api.semanticscholar.org/CorpusID:271026677

Shilbayeh, S. A., & Abonamah, A. A. (2021). Predicting student enrollments and attrition patterns in higher educational institutions using machine learning. *The International Arab Journal of Information Technology*, 18, 562–567. https://api.semanticscholar.org/CorpusID:235749412

Tarisayi, K. S. (2023). Strategic leadership for responsible artificial intelligence adoption in higher education. *CTE Workshop Proceedings*. https://api.semanticscholar.org/CorpusID:261206820

Tasheva, Z., & Karpovich, V. (2024). Transformation of recruitment process through implementation of AI solutions. *Journal of Management and Economics*. https://api.semanticscholar.org/CorpusID:268479962

Waters, A., & Miikkulainen, R. (2013). GRADE: Machine Learning Support for Graduate Admissions. *AI Magazine*, 35, 64–75. https://api.semanticscholar.org/CorpusID:212620573

Chapter 7

Improving Documentation Process With Data Mining and Machine Learning Methods: A Case Study in the Aviation Industry

Sümeyye Gündüz
https://orcid.org/0000-0003-3887-3440
Istanbul University-Cerrahpasa, Turkey

Ersin Namli
Istanbul University-Cerrahpasa, Turkey

ABSTRACT

Many businesses have to operate within the framework of national and international standards to meet customers' expectations, security requirements, and environmental regulations. Compared to other industries, the aviation industry has high-security requirements. However, the continuous publication of documents has resulted in document inflation over time, document-process structure that deviates from a simple philosophy. Given the problem at hand, this study aims to develop a streamlined document processing system that aligns with the lean philosophy in the aviation company under investigation. Documents with a similarity rate exceeding 50% were examined, and a proposal was made to either combine these documents or establish relationships between them. Various machine-learning algorithms are

DOI: 10.4018/979-8-3373-2272-8.ch007

used in this chapter. The accuracy rate of a hybrid model that included the support vector machine (SVM) and logistic regression techniques increased by 6% to 76%. Python was utilised during the research.

INTRODUCTION

The process approach in organizations is an effective management strategy that guarantees that all these processes work in harmony with each other after defining all processes from the proposal stage to after-sales support, thus making the company overall measurable, traceable and therefore improvable. Quality is meeting customer expectations in line with their wishes at the least cost. For this reason, companies should manage their processes by focusing on the quality perspective.

One of the issues required for the quality management of processes is the generation, updating, control, distribution and cancellation of documented information. Documentation management in the aviation industry is important in terms of configuration tracking, minimising and monitoring non-conformity rates, ensuring traceability, and ensuring that all stakeholders are assured of their responsibilities and rights towards customers and suppliers.

Aviation sector has high security requirements in addition to other sectors. Due to the basic quality principle of 'write what you do, do what you write' and the standard requirements, it is obligatory to interpret the activities performed from a process perspective and to document all processes. In order to fulfil this requirement, the aviation company, which is the subject of the research, has determined the processes related to the activities it performs and published documents detailing the processes in accordance with these processes. However, the document publishing activity caused document inflation in time and a document-process structure far from the lean philosophy was formed. This situation negatively affects the timeliness, traceability and understandability of the processes.

Within the scope of this study, the process documents of the aviation company, which is the subject of the research, written in English language, will be analysed within the framework of document similarity and determination of document classes. The aim of this study is to build a lean process document structure in terms of number and content by finding the similarity ratios of the documents used in the company in order to solve the mentioned problem, and to automate the data classification process by accurately determining the classes of the documents produced by document classification.

CONCEPTUAL FRAMEWORK

Concept of Process

Process is an approach that connects all parts of the organisation and enables employees to understand the whole system rather than focusing only on individual parts. This definition states that the big picture can be seen by defining the processes. In addition, this approach has helped managers to realise that problems are caused by processes, not people (Evans & Lindsay, 2019). To draw attention to the customer-serving side of processes, the process starts with internal and external customers and results in increased customer satisfaction as a result of process improvement activities (Besterfield-Michna, Besterfield, Besterfield-Sacre, 1998). Understanding and managing processes is important to improve organisational performance and quality. Companies with effective process management can be agile in adapting to new business needs and share what they learn across the organisation. This helps the company to grow and capture innovation (Evans & Lindsay, 2019).

The Development of the Quality-Driven Process Approach

The method, which is known as Taylorism in the literature, is a production method put forward by Frederick Taylor (1997) in his work 'The Principles of Scientific Management'. Taylorism handled planning and implementation activities under two separate headings, holding the manager and engineer group responsible for planning activities and the technician group responsible for production activities. Quality control activities are carried out by inspectors. In this period, quality was left to the responsibility of quality departments and this situation caused a crisis in which the manager and technician group moved away from the understanding of quality. This crisis was tried to be overcome with the Total Quality Approach.

Total Quality Management is defined as a new management system in the book 'My Life and Work' published by the American-born Henry Ford, founder of Ford Motor Company (Ford, 2008). Total in the term Quality Management means that every part of the system is important and contributes to the system; quality means the level of excellence of the product or service; and management means the art of administration, control and direction.

The Aerospace Industry has established the International Aerospace Quality Group with representatives from aerospace and defence companies in the Americas, Asia/Pacific and Europe for quality improvements and cost reductions. AS 9100 is an SAE certification developed in 1997 by ISO TC20 Working Group 11 and supported by the International Aerospace Quality Group.

In accordance with the article 7.5 'Documented Information' under the heading '7 Resources' of the internationally recognised AS 9100 aviation standards, the Quality Management System and its processes, documents and records are within the scope of information and must be documented.

AS 9100 quality system is a process management that starts from the procurement of raw materials and products, continues with the training of employees, adopts the principle of safety and reliability with the management of risks, and aims to ensure customer satisfaction.

Concepts of AI and Big Data

AI, Data Mining, Machine Learning, Deep Learning and Big Data are often used interchangeably and there is confusion in terms of the definitions of the concepts. In order to eliminate this confusion, it will be useful to explain these five concepts. AI is a term first used by John McCarthy in the 1950s and refers to the effort to develop computers that can imitate the human brain. AI is a general name given to technologies that perform prediction or decision making. In AI projects, Robotic Coding, Data Mining, Machine Learning, Deep Learning, Big Data, etc. one or more of the fields of study can be applied together. In essence, data mining describes the process that brings the data into a form that can be used by machine learning algorithms, including data collection, selection, pre-processing and visualization of the results. Machine learning is a method developed for problems that can be solved by classification, clustering and/or association analysis algorithms. Unlike algorithms called hard-coded, these methods are referred to as machine learning because they enable computers to perform computational operations by learning from data without being completely coded. Deep learning is a much more specific concept and is one of the machine learning algorithms. The learning method of the algorithm is based on Artificial Neural Networks. The word 'deep' used in the definition means that the number of Artificial Neural Network layers increases the complexity of the model. The concept of Big Data is a concept that should be evaluated in parallel with all these and is related to the data that is constantly being produced with the digital revolution. Big data deals with the following 5 basic dimensions of data and the problems produced by these dimensions: Volume, velocity, variety, veracity, and value. The relationship between AI and big data is as shown in Figure 1.

Figure 1. AI and big data concepts

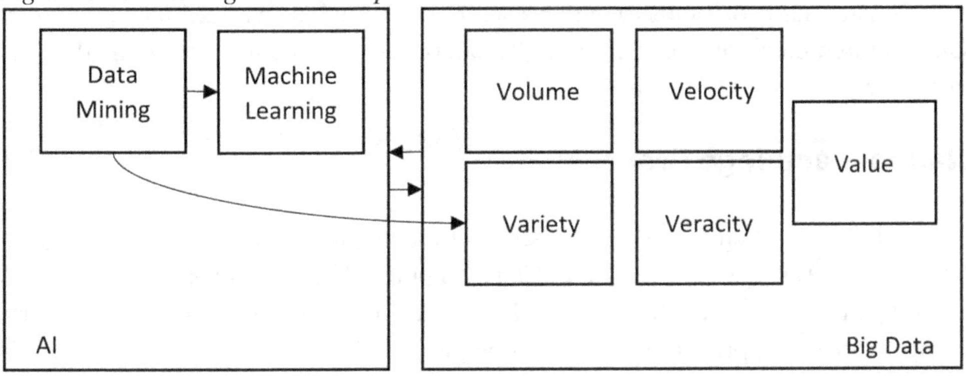

Data Mining Concepts

Data mining applications can be used for all kinds of data regardless of the sector. However, sector knowledge has an important place in data processing. The data mining cycle starts with pre-processing the data and ends with the interpretation of the results of the analysis within the framework of business knowledge.

Data mining is a method of producing prediction models from large amounts of data with software languages (Gürsoy, 2009). In Roiger's (2002) book 'Data Mining', data mining is defined as 'the process of using one or more computer learning techniques to automatically extract and analyze information from data in a database'. The information obtained as a result of the data mining process is a model or generalized version of the data studied. Although there are many techniques, all these techniques use the induction-based learning method. Induction-based learning is the process of forming general concept definitions by observing specific examples of the final concept to be learnt.

Dunham (2020) in his book 'Data Mining' defines data mining as the extraction of implicit knowledge in the database, while Miller (2004) in his book Data and Text Mining defines data mining as a research and analysis approach that covers the processes of accessing data, exploring data, establishing hypotheses and obtaining information.

One of the most important aspects of data mining is to understand the type of data used. Basically, data is divided into two main groups: structured and unstructured. Structured (tabular) data are quantitative data expressed in tables, with specific variables, which can be more easily understood by machine learning algorithms than unstructured data. Structured data is stored in tabular format such as Excel, SQL, etc., and since this type of data takes up relatively less space, storage costs are low and it is easier to apply machine learning methods to this data. Unstructured data is data that is difficult to express with tables, such as audio, image, text, etc. Unstructured data are stored in NoSQL databases with media extension files and take up relatively a lot of space.

Natural Language Processing

Looking at its historical development, natural language processing can be traced back to Alan Turing's (1950) article 'Can Computers Think?' and Noam Chomsky's (2002) generative grammar theory in 1956. Machine translation is one of the first computer-based applications of natural language.

The basic logic of natural language processing is the ability of computers to easily understand and operate on texts produced in human language, in a way to translate human language into machine language. In order to understand the meaning and structure of language, there are basically two different approaches to natural language processing problems: rule-based and model-based approaches. Rule-based approaches utilise modus ponens approaches. Rule 1: Penguin is a bird. Rule 2: Birds fly. When the modus ponens approach is used, the result of the rule that penguins can fly. In rule-based NLP (natural language processing), specific grammatical rules are used to analyse the input text. This approach does not evaluate non-rule possibilities and has difficulty in handling complex, non-standardised language structures. In contrast to the rule-based approach, model-based approaches learn the structural features and meaning of the language with machine learning methods. This approach uses statistical relationships based on data. Deep Learning and BERT are examples of model-based NLP.

Text Preprocessing Steps

Text preprocessing is like preparing the ingredients before cooking a meal. It is the process of preparing the data so that the computer can better understand the text (Indurkhya & Damerau, 2010). The methods used in text preprocessing are, elimination of spelling errors and stopwords, and case sensitivity, singularization of words, finding the roots of words. Elimination of spelling errors cause loss of meaning. Stopwords such as conjunctions, numbers, punctuation marks cause unreal commonalities and similarities between texts. Since most text mining software is case-sensitive, the same words are treated by the machine as two different words because of the case of the letter, and this leads to a loss of meaning. Therefore, spelling mistakes should be corrected, all words in the text must be converted to lowercase or uppercase and stopwords should be removed during data cleaning. Machines cannot distinguish between plural and singular words as different versions of the same word, This will result in the loss of an existing similarity between the texts. For this reason, plural words in the text should be singularized. Machines cannot distinguish between words with the same root but differentiated by a suffix. Stemming should be applied when words derived from the same root are to be combined into a single word. However, this can also result in divergence in the real cases, because construction suffixes are suffixes that change the meaning of words.

Another method used in text preprocessing is the tagging of words according to their function. Word tagging is the process of assigning labels such as subject, object, predicate, etc. to words based on their grammatical or semantic properties and their position in the sentence in which the word appears. It is an important topic in NLP and computational linguistics. Labeling words helps to learn the structure and meaning of sentences. It is used in various NLP applications such as information extraction, machine translation and text analysis (Bird, Klein & Loper, 2009).

Separation of Text into Words and Vectorization of Words

Since the machines are designed to work only with numeric input, texts must first be broken down into words (tokens) and then each word must be represented by a number. By combining these numbers, the texts are represented as vectors in multidimensional space.

Feature extraction is the process of extracting meaningful and useful features (variables) from raw data that machine learning models can process. This applies to numerical data, text, images or other types of data. The goal is to make the data analyzable so that it provides the best information for the model to learn from. For example, feature extraction for text data can be done in the following ways: Bag of Words, TF -IDF, Word Embedding.

In bag of words method, a document/ paragraph is considered as a bag of words. Each text becomes a vector of common length by assigning 1 to the words in the pool that are in the text and 0 to those that are not.

In the TF-IDF (Term Frequency-Inverse Document Frequency) method, the words in the text receive a value based on the number of times the word occurs in the relevant text divided by the number of times it occurs in all other texts. Equation (2) represents the term frequency, (3) the inverse document frequency and equation (4) the product of TF (Term Frequency) and IDF (Inverse Document Frequency). Term frequency (TF) can be defined as the relative frequency of a term (t) in a document (d). D is the document corpus and N is the total number of terms.

$$\mathrm{tf}(t,d) = \frac{f_{t,d}}{\sum_{t' \in d} f_{t',d}} \tag{2}$$

$$idf(t, D) = \log\frac{N}{|\{d \in D : t \in d\}|} \quad (3)$$

$$tfidf(t, d, D) = tf(t, d) \cdot idf(t, D) \quad (4)$$

In the word embedding method, unlike the first two methods, this method aims to extract the features of the text not only by linear numerical metrics of the constituent words but also by considering their semantic relations. By semantic relation, we mean that such algorithms interpret words not in isolation, but by considering the context in which they occur. Deep learning algorithms such as Word2Vec or GloVe can be used for word embedding.

Similarity Analysis in Natural Language Processing

After the words that make up the documents are converted into vectors, in other words, into numerical format, which is a computer language, with methods such as bag of words, word embedding, etc., the distance between these vectors is calculated. Some methods used for distance calculation are Cosine, Euclidean and Jaccard similarity.

In Cosine similarity, when the inner / dot products of the vectorized documents are found, the result is the parts of the two vectors that move together in the same direction. The dot product can be used to determine the degree of similarity or parallelism between two vectors. The dot product of two vectors is a measure of how similar the vectors are (Liu, Lin, Sun, 2020). The Cosine similarity is calculated as in equation (5).

$$\cos(\boldsymbol{\theta}) = \frac{\mathbf{A}.\mathbf{B}}{||\mathbf{A}||.||\mathbf{B}||} = \frac{(\sum_{i=1}^{n}\mathbf{A}_i + \mathbf{B}_i)}{\sum_{k=i}^{n}(\mathbf{A}_i^2)\sum_{k=i}^{n}(\mathbf{B}_i^2)} \quad (5)$$

When the vectors are 90° perpendicular to each other, the similarity between them will be 0. The Cosine value of a 90 degree angle is 0. The greater the similarity between documents, the closer the distance value is to 1 and the less similar the distance value is to 0.

Euclidean distance measures the linear distance between two points or vectors. It is used to find the shortest distance between two points and is usually calculated as the square root of the sum of the squares of the differences of the vectors. The greater the euclidean distance, the greater the difference. Euclidean similarity is calculated as in equation (6).

$$|AB| = \sqrt{(a_x - b_x)^2 + (a_y - b_y)^2} \tag{6}$$

Jaccard similarity treats vectors as sets and measures how similar or different two sets are. It does this by dividing the intersection of the two sets by their union. The higher the similarity between two texts, the closer the Jaccard similarity is to 1. Jaccard similarity is calculated as in equation (7).

$$J(A,B) = \frac{|A \cap B|}{|A \cup B|} = \frac{|A \cap B|}{|A| + |B| - |A \cap B|} \tag{7}$$

Machine Learning

Every machine learning project follows at least these five steps: defining the problem, data collection, data preprocessing, establishing the model, evaluation of the model.

Machine Learning Algorithms

In order to be able to use machine learning models, data sets should be made ready for use by going through data pre-processing steps. Machine learning algorithms are divided into two main categories according to the learning method: supervised and unsupervised, as shown in Figure 2. There are four different algorithm classes belonging to these two learning types.

Figure 2. Machine learning methods

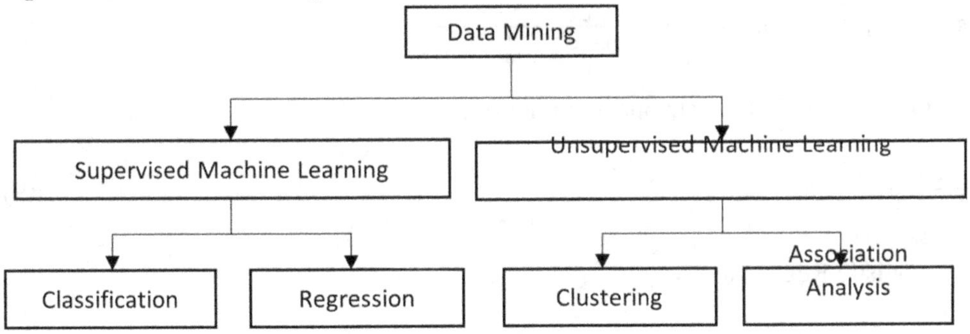

Supervised learning is a learning method applied in data sets where the data being studied has a dependent / target variable. Supervised learning algorithms are categorized under two main headings as classification and regression according to the problem type; and under six main headings as Frequency Distribution, Covariance,

Similarity, Ensemble Learning, Artificial Neural Networks and other according to the algorithms' approach to solving the problem (Güler et al, 2024)

Classification Algorithms. Classification algorithms for problems where the dependent variable is categorical. Classification algorithms enable computers to understand and organize data according to established patterns. These algorithms try to predict the category of new data by comparing the data to be predicted with previously learned examples, such as deciding whether an email is spam or not. (Chowdhary, 2020) Machine learning algorithms used for such problems are frequency table, covariance matrix (Güler & Namlı, 2024)

Logistic Regression is considered one of the oldest methods among classification algorithms. It was developed in the 1950s by David Cox, a statistician. It is a linear classifier. The outputs of logistic regression are probability values, not classes. (Kowsari, Meimandi, Heidarysafa, Mendu, Barnes & Brown, 2019) It takes its name from the logistic function, which takes all values given to it as 0 or 1. Logistic Regression examines the relationship between the dependent variable and the independent variable. The important difference between Linear and Logistic Regression is that the predicted value in Logistic Regression is categorical, while the predicted value in Linear Regression is numerical. This method calculates the probability of the desired situation. The Logistic Distribution function in equation (8) returns the input values to a probability value between 0 and 1. The logistic regression model is obtained by taking the odds of the logistic distribution function as in equation (9). In the logistic regression model in equation (10) β_0 denotes the bias value, β_p denotes the model coefficients and x_p denotes the input values.

Logistic Distribution Function:

$$\pi(x) = p(y = 1|X = x) = \frac{e^{(\beta 0+\beta 1x1+\beta 2x2+...+\beta pxp)}}{1+ e^{-(\beta 0+\beta 1x1+\beta 2x2+...+\beta pxp)}} \tag{8}$$

Odds of Logistic Distribution Function:

$$\frac{\pi(x)}{1 - \pi(x)} \tag{9}$$

Logistic Regression Model:

$$\mathbf{g(x)} = \ln\frac{\pi(\mathbf{x})}{1 - \pi(\mathbf{x})} = \boldsymbol{\beta}_0 + \boldsymbol{\beta}_1\mathbf{x}_1 + \boldsymbol{\beta}_2\mathbf{x}_{2+}\dots + \boldsymbol{\beta}_p\mathbf{x}_p \tag{10}$$

Regression Algorithms. Regression algorithms for problems where the dependent variable is numeric. Some of the machine learning algorithms used for such problems are Covariance Matrix and Multiple Linear Regression. Simple Linear Regression will be explained under covariance matrix. Simple linear regressionis a regression model expressed in simple terms because it consists of one independent variable. The main objective is to find the linear function that describes the relationship between the dependent and independent variables. What will be learned with machine learning methods is what the beta 0 and beta 1 values, coefficients and parameters are. The sampling model is as given in equation (11).

$$\mathbf{y_i} = \mathbf{b_0} + \mathbf{b_1 x_i} + \mathbf{e_i} \tag{11}$$

The estimation model is as given in equation (12). In equation, $\mathbf{y_i}$ the values to be estimated, $\mathbf{x_i}$ input values and $\mathbf{b_0}$ ve $\mathbf{b_1}$ refers to the coefficients to be found by machine learning.

$$\hat{y}_i = b_0 + b_1 x_i \tag{12}$$

The deviation / error equation is as given in equation (13). e_i refers to the deviation between actual values and predicted values.

$$e_{i =} y_i - \hat{y}_i \tag{13}$$

As expressed in Equation (14) for each input value, the difference between the predicted value and the actual values, i.e. e_i is aimed to be the smallest.

$$SSE = \sum_{i=1} (y_i - \hat{y}_i)^2 \tag{14}$$

Values to be learned with machine learning methods, e_i minimizes the value of $\mathbf{b_0}$ and $\mathbf{b_1}$ values, coefficients, parameters. $\mathbf{b_0}$ and $\mathbf{b_1}$ values are as shown in equations (15) and (16). In this equation $\bar{x}$ independent variables $\bar{y}$ is the mean of the dependent variables.

$$b_1 = \frac{\sum_{i=1}^{n}(x_i - \bar{x})(y_i - \bar{y})}{\sum_{i=1}^{n}(x_i - \bar{x})^2} \tag{15}$$

$$b_0 = \bar{y} - b_1\bar{x} \tag{16}$$

Multiple Linear Regression is a regression model expressed as multiple because it consists of more than one independent variable. The main purpose is to find the relationship between the dependent and independent variables and to determine which independent variable affects the dependent variable more.

Classification and Regression Algorithms. Under this heading, algorithms used in both classification and regression problems will be discussed. These algorithms will be analyzed under the headings of similarities functions, ensemble learning and others. Decision Three - Cart Models, KNN: K- Nearest Neighbors and Artificial Neutral Network algorithms are similarity-based approaches, functions.

Decision Three, CART algorithms answer sequential questions in the logic of "If so, then what?". They can work with numerical and categorical data. (Gürsakal, 2018) However, they give better results with categorical data and, it follows a hierarchical approach from top to bottom. Decision Trees consist of nodes (root), branches and leaves. For each input, a query is made at the nodes and branches according to the result, where the branching ends is called a leaf.

KNN is a distance-based algorithm. Prediction is made based on the distances of the observations in the data set to each other. For this algorithm, a value k is set, which indicates how many closest values to look at after calculating the distances of all data with the new input value. The new input value is then assigned to the class of the majority of these values. For large datasets, its performance can be degraded because all the data is reviewed to find the nearest neighbors. The value of k directly affects the result, and this is one of the disadvantages of this algorithm. (Manning & Schutze, 1999) In cases where k is chosen as an even number, the majority may not be achieved, so it is recommended that k is chosen as an odd number. Increasing k up to a certain value increases the success but then the success starts to decrease.

Neurons in the human brain receive the stimuli coming to them and transmit them to the target cell. In Artificial Neural Networks, parallel to the working principle of neurons, input values are transformed into target variables by exceeding the specified threshold value. It can be used for both classification and clustering problems. In its simplest form, Artificial Neural Networks consist of two layers, the input and output layers. Artificial Neural Networks are divided into single and multilayer according to the layer structure; feed forward networks and recurrent, feedback learning networks according to the learning method. Single Layer Artificial Neural Networks are an Artificial Neural Network model consisting of only input and output layers and no hidden (intermediate) layer. In Single Layer Neural Networks, input values are multiplied by the weights assigned to the values and these values are summed. If the sum exceeds a threshold value, an output is produced; if not, no output is produced. Perceptron is a Single Layer Artificial Neural Network algorithm.

Multilayer Artificial Neural Networks are an Artificial Neural Networks model that contains hidden (intermediate) layer(s) in addition to the input and output layer. Input values are multiplied by weights as in a Single Layer Artificial Neural Network and these values are summed. If the sum exceeds the threshold value, an output is produced; if not, no output is produced. In neural networks, weights are randomly assigned at the beginning of the model, then these weights are continuously updated to give the lowest error, called the delta rule.

Artificial Neural Networks are divided into two according to the learning method, feed forward learning (feed forward networks) and recurrent learning (recurrent, feedback learning networks). In feed forward learning (feed forward networks) learning, the neurons in the neural networks are fed only by the neurons of the previous layer. In other words, learning follows a linear path from the input value to the output value. In recurrent learning (recurrent, feedback learning networks) learning, in addition to the feed-forward learning method, the output of the neural cell is fed back to the network.

Ensemble learning refers to approaches that combine different learning algorithms or models to create a more powerful and generalizing classification model. Under this title, Random Forest Algorithm, Gradient Boosting Machine (GBM) Algorithm, XGBoost and Lightweight Gradient Boosting Machines (Light GBM) algorithms will be discussed. Random Forest Algorithm is an algorithm created by combining the bagging method, which aims to increase generalizability by randomly selecting observations from the data set, and the random subspace method, in which variables are randomly selected. Gradient Boosting Machine Algorithm is a combination of the AdaBoost method, which is based on the idea that weak learners can combine to form a strong learner, and the gradient descent algorithm, an optimization algorithm for finding the minimum (or maximum) value of a function. XGBoost is an algorithm created by improving the speed and performance of the gbm method in the estimation phase. It performs a horizontal search process. (Che, Hu, Zhao, Li & Lin, 2023) Light GBM algorithm is an algorithm created by improving the speed and performance of the XGBoost method in the prediction phase. it performs a vertical search.

The last group to be analyzed under the heading 'Classification and Regression Algorithms' is the group we call 'other', which excludes similarity functions and ensemble learning. In this group, SVM and hybrid models will be discussed. SVM is an algorithm proposed by Vapnik and Chervonenkis. It was created for binary classification problems, but it has also been used for many multiclass problems in the literature. It works on a divide and conquer basis, each problem is first divided into two classes. It is possible to separate the classes by drawing a boundary between the two groups. The boundary should be drawn where the members of the two classes are farthest apart. SVM determines how this boundary should be drawn. Compared to other methods, they are less prone to overlearning. Although the training process of the model is slow, it is a highly accurate method with the ability to model complex, non-linear data sets (Han, Kamber, Pei, 2011).

The one-class SVM cost equation is as shown in equation (17). The constraints of the equation are as in equation (18). In equation, w weight vector, $_i$ error term, p the number of bias coefficients, $\frac{1}{vl}$ refers to the coefficient of regularization.

$$\min \frac{1}{2} ||w||^2 + \frac{1}{vl} \sum_{i=1}^{n} {}_i - p \tag{17}$$

$$(w \cdot \Phi(x_i)) \geq p - {}_i \; i = 1,2..,l \quad \geq 0 \tag{18}$$

The SVM prediction model is as in equation (19).

$$f(x) = \text{sign}((w \cdot \Phi(x)) - p)) \tag{19}$$

The multiclass SVM prediction model is shown in equation (20). In equation (20), wj is the weight vector of the model, T is the transpose of the vector, b_j is the bias value for class j. Argmax is the operator that maximizes the expression in it.

$$\hat{y} = \text{argmax}\left(w_j^T \cdot x + b_j\right) \tag{20}$$

The cost function of the model is as in equation (21) and the constraints are as in (22) and (23). This cost function consists of weight vectors w for k classes and tries to minimize the penalty terms.

$$\min_{w_1, w_2, \ldots, w_k,} \frac{1}{2} \sum_{k}^{n} w_k^T w_k + C \sum_{(w_i, y_i)} P(i,j) \in D \quad {}_i \tag{21}$$

The constraints of the cost function are as shown in equations (22) and (23).

$$w_{y_i}^T x - w_k^T x \leq i - \quad {}_i \tag{22}$$

$$\forall (x_i y_i) \in D, k \in (1, 2, \ldots, K), k \neq y_i \tag{23}$$

Finally, hybrid models are a combination of different techniques to overcome the disadvantages of machine learning algorithms (Awasthi, Gupta, Bhogal, Anand & Soni, 2021).

Model Evaluation

Approaches to improve the generalization performance of the machine learning model to be used, that is, to make accurate predictions for examples that it has not encountered during the training process, are called model validation methods. Holdout, K-Fold Cross Validation and Leave One Out (LOO) methods will be discussed in this section.

In holdout method, the original data set is divided into training and test as shown in Figure 3. The model is trained with data from the training set and tested with data from the test set. This method is more effective in scenarios where the data set is rich because the probability of homogeneous distribution of training and test data increases in large data sets. The weaknesses of this method are the methods by which the data set is divided into training and test, and the inability to verify that the data are homogeneously distributed in the training and train set.

Figure 3. Holdout method

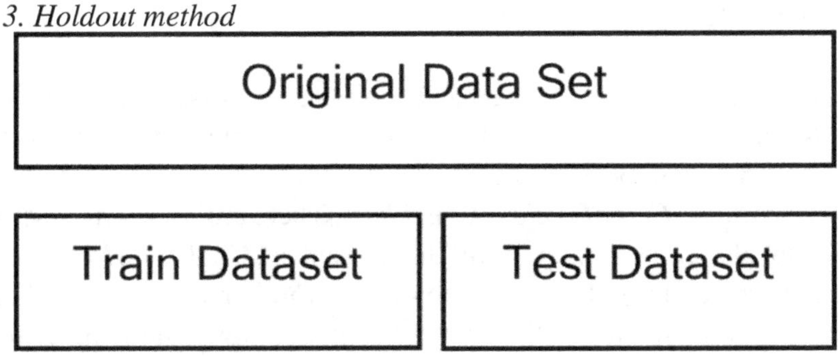

In the holdout method, the dataset is divided into two parts, training and test, once, while in the K-Fold Cross Validation method, the dataset is randomly divided into multiple parts and each part is used as test data in turn. The original data set is divided into k parts, each with k-1 different sets of training data and one set of test data. The average value of the resulting error values shows the performance of the model as shown in equation (24) (Ciner, et al, 2024).

$$f(x) = \frac{1}{k}\sum_{i=1}^{k} Performance_i \tag{24}$$

The K-Fold Cross-Validation method allows to observe how the model will perform on different datasets and is a useful method to avoid problems such as over-learning. (Witten, Frank & Hall, 2011)

The LOO method is a special variant of the K-Fold Cross-Validation method where instead of a dataset, each data point is excluded in turn and the model is trained on all the remaining data. For example, if you have 50 data points in your dataset, in the first iteration, 1 data point is left out for testing and the model is trained on the remaining 49 data points. In the second iteration, the second data point is left out for testing and the model is trained on the remaining 49 data points. This process is repeated for each data point in the dataset. The average value of the performance measures obtained in each iteration determines the overall performance of the model. The equation for the LOO method is as shown in equation (25), where n is the total number of samples in the data set.

$$f(x) = \frac{1}{n}\sum_{i=1}^{n} Performance_i \tag{25}$$

It is a model validation technique suitable for small datasets as the number of processing steps is equal to the number of samples.

Model Performance Measure

There are some error metrics that can be used for regression algorithms. in this context, R-Squared, Mean Squared Erros, Mean Absolute Deviation, Correlation Coefficient metrics will be examined.

Error Metrics for Classification Algorithms. There are some error metrics that can be used for classification algorithms. In this context, Confusion Matrix, Accuracy, Precision (Precession), Recall, F1 Score, ROC Curve metrics will be discussed. Confusion matrix is the metric that shows the extent to which the predicted class values agree with the actual class values. The confusion matrix is as given in Table 1.

Table 1. Confusion matrix

	Estimated Class Values	
Actual Class Values	**Class = 1**	**Class = 0**
Class = 1	TP	FP
Class = 0	FN	TN

TP = True Positive
TN = True Negative
FP = False Positive
FN = False Negative

Accuracy is the ratio of correctly predicted classes to all predicted classes. The mathematical notation is as follows: (TP+ TN) / (TP+TN+FP+FN). Precession is the metric that shows how many of the instances that the algorithm predicts as positive are actually positive. The mathematical representation is as follows: TP / (TP+FP). Recall expresses how many of the instances that are actually positive are correctly predicted by the algorithm. The mathematical notation is as follows: TP / (TP+FN). F1 Score is the harmonic mean of the sensitivity and susceptibility metrics. The mathematical notation is as follows: (2* (Precision*Recall)) / (Precision

+ Recall). It is a preferred accuracy metric when the data set is unbalanced. The complexity matrix uses a fixed threshold value of 50%. In the ROC curve approach, different TP and FP values are found for different threshold values. A curve is dawn through the intersection of these ratios and this curve is called the ROC Curve. The larger the area under this curve, the higher the accuracy rate. The integral of the area under the curve is calculated by Area Under Curve. The Area Under Curve value is a numerical expression of the ROC curve. In unbalanced data sets, it can be preferred instead of the complexity matrix in binary classification problems.

Bias

The concept of bias will be discussed in the context of overfitting and underfitting. In overfitting, model learns the data, not the data structure. In other words, as a result of memorization of the data, high success rates are obtained in the training data, but the success rates of the test data are very low. Inadequate data set and increasing complexity of the model are the two most important factors that cause overlearning. (Kumar, 2005) Underfitting is when the machine learning algorithm fails to learn the basic pattern in the model. To overcome this situation, the model complexity can be increased, the data set can be enriched.

Model Parameter / Hyperparameter Optimization (Model Tunning)

Model performances are directly related to hyperparameters and parameters. In order to increase the success of the model, it is necessary to find the optimum values of hyperparameters and parameters. Parameters are the weights that the models learn from the data. Coefficients b, w in linear regression models or c, penalty parameter in support vector machines are examples of model parameters; depth, learning coefficients in Decision Trees, number of layers in Artificial Neural Networks are examples of hyperparameters predetermined by the decision maker. Model performances are directly related to hyperparameters and parameters. In order to increase the success of the model, it is necessary to find the optimum values of hyperparameters and parameters.

LITERATURE REVIEW

Turing article (1950) He starts with the question "Can machines think?" and tests whether machines can think with the Turing test he developed. In the Turing test, a human and a computer are asked questions. It is argued that if it is not possible to distinguish which answer is given by the human and which is given by the computer, the computer is "able to think". The article also includes criticisms of the argument that machines can think and the Turing test, and Turing's responses to these criticisms.

A Logical Calculus of The Ideas Immanent in Nervous Activity, one of the first publications on data science (Mcculloch & Pitts, 1943) Neurons, the cells that carry information in our nervous system, communicate with each other by forming neural networks. A neuron that is stimulated does not stimulate all other neurons, but only the connected neurons in its own network. This excitation process has been likened to propositional logic because of its all-or-nothing logic. This is because neurons also assign weights to the stimuli they receive and collect the weight inputs, and if the resulting value exceeds a certain threshold, the neuron transfers the stimulus to the other neuron, i.e., it produces an output of 1. If the value does not exceed the threshold, the neuron does not transmit the stimulus to the other neuron, i.e., it produces an output of 0.

Tantug's (2016) his article is a theoretical study on text classification. Within the scope of the study, the reasons for the increase in the number of documents produced in electronic environment, the obstacles to text classification, the aims of text classification, the general definition of text classification, application areas and studies conducted for the Turkish language are mentioned.

Ateş (2021) in his research, the posts made on Twitter to fight against crime were analyzed with data mining techniques. It is aimed that the data obtained as a result of the thesis can be used in determining the usability of the security forces for crime prevention, predetermining the posts containing criminal content and analyzing the posts of security forces operating in the national/international arena.

Benedetti, Beneventano, Bergamaschi & Simonini (2019) The Contextual Semantic Analysis approach was used to calculate document similarity. The results show that Contextual Semantic Analysis improves the performance of KE4IR compared to traditional methods and is effective in information extraction tasks. However, it was also stated that Contextual Semantic Analysis did not make a significant difference on query time performance.

Lakkaraju, Gauch & Speretta (2008) in their study, the similarity between 50,100 documents was determined according to the tree classification method. In the proposed method, documents are represented as conceptual trees in the vector space, which have a more complex structure than traditional methods. This method showed 14-43% higher performance than traditional methods.

Borko & Bernick (1963) in this study, an automatic classification model was created for 405 documents using factor analysis and these documents were manually and automatically classified by five people according to the derived categories. The accuracy of the automatic classification was evaluated over the manual classification. Although this evaluation proves the accuracy of automatic classification for this sample, it is mentioned that much more work needs to be done to make a general judgment.

Thielman (2020) in his article, he proposes a hybrid model with SVM and Latent Dirichlet Allocation (LDA) classification algorithms for an imbalanced dataset. With the proposed method, more than 80% of the documents were correctly classified.

Ünlü & Xanthopoulos (2022) in this article propose an approach for combining ensemble learning algorithms inspired by modern portfolio theory and considering variance optimization results. And this approach achieves higher accuracy rates compared to traditional combining methods.

Yildirim, Çetin, Eryiğit, Temel (2014) this is the first paper in the literature to investigate the effect of natural language processing steps (normalization, stemming, etc.) on sentiment analysis of Turkish texts in social media. The rate was increased with the proposed preprocessing steps and a success rate of 78% was achieved. Within the scope of the article, sentiment analysis was performed on 1290 Turkish tweets with SVM algorithm.

Bilgin, Çetinoğlu, Oflazer (2004) The paper chronologically describes the steps in the process of developing a wordnet for Turkish as part of the Balknet project and discusses methodological issues in the process. The article also contributes to the field of wordnet development by providing resources for wordnet builders.

Ingole, Bhoir, Vidhate (2018) Sentiment analysis was performed on 25000 tweets about the problems experienced by engineering students in education. When the results are compared with the individual results of Naïve Bayes and Support Vector Machines, an increase in the accuracy of the hybrid model is observed. In addition, the training time was significantly reduced.

Ünlü (2022) in his article, instead of manually detecting anomalies in control data, various methodologies such as Artificial Neural Networks (ANN), Support Vector Machines (SVM) and Fuzzy Logic have been proposed to identify anomalous patterns in control charts in real time. The authors also implemented a weighting strategy in combination with ANN and investigated the performance of the weighted ANN on various anomalous patterns and compared its effectiveness with that of the standard ANN.

METHOD

Under this heading, the data set used within the scope of the study is explained, the data preprocessing steps, the determination of document similarity with the cosine distance method, the establishment of the hybrid model that gives the highest accuracy rate for the classification problem after weighting the imbalanced data set are detailed. The framework of the study is as shown in Figure 4.

Figure 4. Study framework

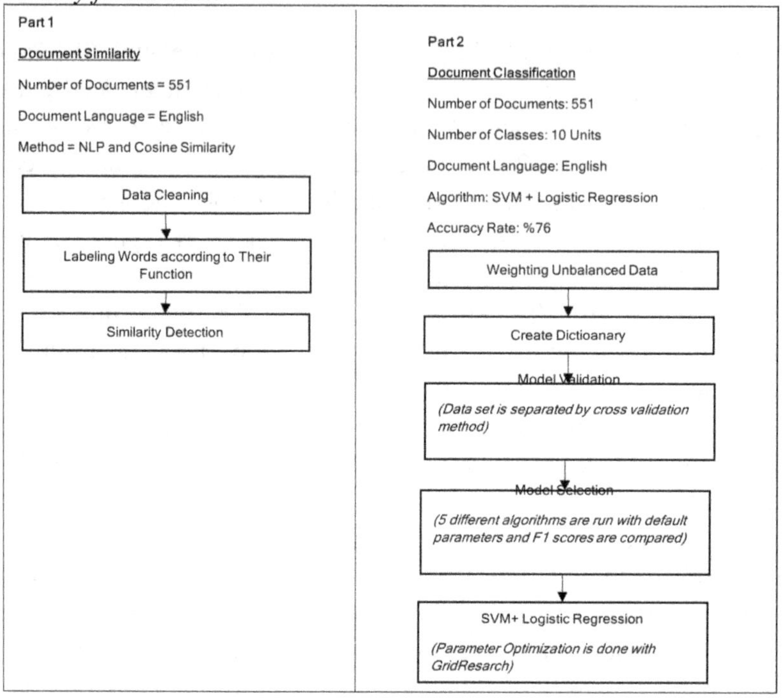

Data Set Analysis

The dataset subject of this study consists of 551 documents belonging to different process classes written in English. In the first stage, the similarity rate was determined for all 551 documents. Python software language was used in the application.

In the second stage, since the documents that make up the dataset are not homogeneously distributed among the classes, the imbalance in the dataset was tried to be controlled by weighting the dataset classes. The data set used in the application consists of 551 documents.

Similarity Detection

The basic approach to similarity detection is to count each word in a document as a token. The approach proposed in this study aims to add a semantic relation to the similarity detection between documents, and unlike the basic approach, the words in the document are tokenized with their function in the sentence (noun, fill, etc.) after determining their function in the sentence. Thus, even if the words in the documents are common, only those with the same function will be able to contribute to the similarity.

Some of the Python libraries used for similarity detection are string, nltk, glob, pandas, warnings, re, scikit-learn, collections, textblob. The NLTK library has many word tags as shown in Figure 5. Words labeled "CC", "CD", "DT", "IN", "LS", "NNP", "NNPS", "PTD", "POS", "PRP", "PRP$", "RP", "TO", "UH", "WDT", "WP", "WP$", "WRB" were removed from the word space.

Figure 5. NLTK word tags ("Nltk Tags," 2016)

CC	Coordinating conjunction	NNS	Noun, plural	UH	Interjection
CD	Cardinal number	NNP	Proper noun, singular	VB	Verb, base form
DT	Determiner	NNPS	Proper noun, plural	VBD	Verb, past tense
EX	Existential there	PDT	Predeterminer	VBG	Verb, gerund or present participle
FW	Foreign word	POS	Possessive ending	VBN	Verb, past participle
IN	Preposition or subordinating conjunction	PRP	Personal pronoun	VBP	Verb, non-3rd person singular present
JJ	Adjective	PRP$	Possessive pronoun	VBZ	Verb, 3rd person singular present
JJR	Adjective, comparative	RB	Adverb	WDT	Wh-determiner
JJS	Adjective, superlative	RBR	Adverb, comparative	WP	Wh-pronoun
LS	List item marker	RBS	Adverb, superlative	WP$	Possessive wh-pronoun
MD	Modal	RP	Particle	WRB	Wh-adverb
NN	Noun, singular or mass	SYM	Symbol		
		TO	to		

NLP methods were applied for similarity detection and the methods are as follows:

Step 1: The first step is to remove punctuation marks and numbers from the texts and convert all letters to lower case.

Step 2: The texts are stripped of non-English characters.

Step 3: Texts was cleaned of stopwords.

Step 4: In 4th step, all words in the texts was deduplicated.

Step 5: Spelling errors in the texts was removed.,

Step 6: Tasks of the words in the sentence was found.

Step 7: Words was counted together with the tags given to them in step 6.

Step 8: In last step, Cosine similarity between documents was calculated and a similarity matrix is created.

Classification Model

Each document that makes up the dataset used for text classification has a specific class. Over time, it has become difficult to determine which process code the documents fit into. Machine learning methods were used to make this selection more accurate and easier. The data set is the data cleaned by text preprocessing steps in the first part. Many Python libraries such as pandas, matplotlib.pyplot, sklearn.model_selection were used in the classification process.

Weighting of Data Set Classes

The dataset was numericalized by the TF-IDF method. The data set distribution is unbalanced as shown in Figure 6. Since it can be difficult for the model to learn from classes with fewer elements in unbalanced data sets, the classes in the data set are weighted. With weighting, rare classes are given larger weights and common classes are given smaller weights. This approach aims to increase the success of the model by making the classification algorithms work in a more balanced and objective way.

Figure 6. Distribution of documents to classes

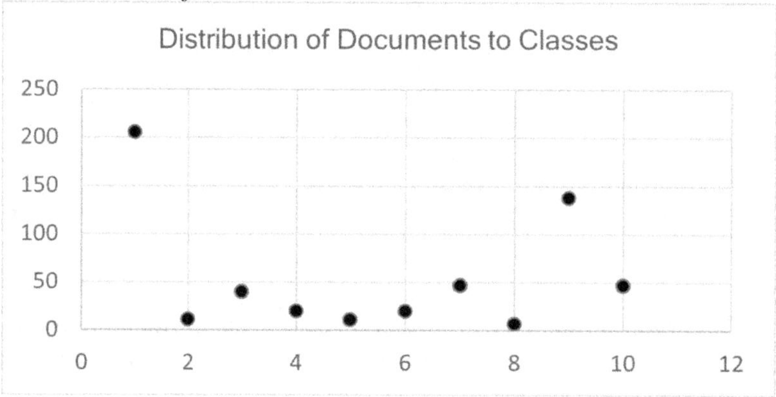

Model Validation

In this study, in the FFN algorithm, the Holdout Method was used as the model validation method and 80% of the dataset was divided into training and 20% as test. In the other algorithms, the K-Fold Cross-Validation Method was used as the model validation technique. The selected parameters of the K-Fold Class are as follows: n_splits=8, shuffle=True, random_state=42. In the Hybrid Model, the LOO method was used which gives better results for small data sets.

Creating a Dictionary

In text classification applications, texts are vectorized with numbers instead of words. A dictionary is used for vectorization, which may vary depending on the model, languages, etc. used. In this study, instead of a ready-made dictionary, an original dictionary was created based on the content of the documents that make up our dataset. In order to prevent data leakage, the dictionary was created on the training dataset after dividing the dataset into two parts as training and test. The steps followed while creating the dictionary are as follows:

1. 2 and words smaller than 2 letters have been removed.
2. Words greater than 15 and 15 letters have been removed.
3. The words that existed in each class were extracted.
4. Words not included in the English dictionary were removed.[1]

The dictionary obtained after these eliminations consists of 5208 words.

Establishing the Model

Five different models were built with SVM, Logistic Regression, Random Forests, CART and FNN machine learning algorithms. Python software language was used in the application. The Logistic Regression and SVM model were first run for the default parameters.

Model Evaluation

The five models were run with the assumed parameters and the complexity matrix was extracted for each model and the performance was evaluated according to the F1 Score value.

Parameter Optimization

Parameter optimization was performed with the Grid Search technique for Logistic Regression and SVM, the two algorithms with the highest accuracy.

FINDINGS

This chapter presents the findings obtained as a result of the methods developed in this study for similarity detection and classification problems.

In the first part, the similarity ratios of 551 documents written in English were determined and a similarity matrix with a section in table 2 was obtained, which includes the similarity ratios of all documents. 227 document samples were examined from 551 documents with 95% confidence interval and 5% error rate, and as a result of the examination, it was determined that the threshold value for similarity was 50%, and it was seen that documents with a similarity ratio above 50% had similarity and other relationships with each other. Relationships other than similarity helped to establish a hierarchical link between documents.

Table 2. Document similarity matrix

Document Name	1	2	3	4	5	6	7
1	1,00	0,28	0,16	0,20	0,21	0,29	0,34
2	0,28	1,00	0,15	0,11	0,14	0,18	0,17
3	0,16	0,15	1,00	0,16	0,14	0,15	0,21
4	0,20 0,21	0,11	0,16	1,00	0,24	0,20	0,26
5	0,21	0,14	0,14	0,24	1,00	0,21	0,16
6	0,29	0,18	0,15	0,20	0,21	1,00	0,25
7	0,34	0,17	0,21	0,26	0,16	0,25	1,00

In the second part, the disadvantages of the unbalanced dataset were minimized by weighting the dataset so that the classification algorithms could work effectively. K-Fold Cross Validation method was used as the model validation method. After the data separation process, classification was performed with machine learning algorithms. Classification algorithms were compared with each other based on F1 score. The reason for choosing this accuracy rate is that the F1 score takes the harmonic mean of the precision and recall parameters and provides a balance between these two values. In this study, SVM, Logistic Regression, CART, Random Forests and FNN machine learning algorithms were used and the F1 accuracy rates obtained for the default parameters are as shown in Figure 7:

Figure 7. Accuracy rates of algorithms

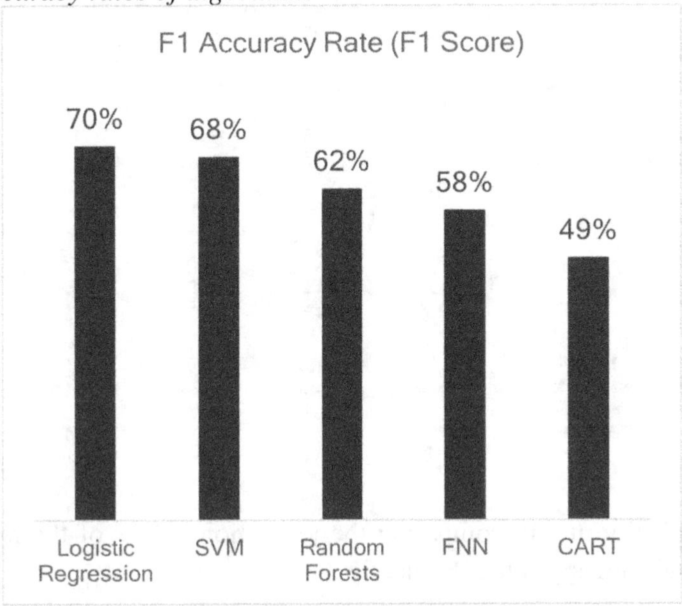

In order to increase the accuracy rates obtained, parameter optimization was performed with the Grid Research method for the Logistic Regression and Support Vector Machines (SVM) algorithms that gave the highest value. The parameters that give the highest accuracy rates for the two algorithms are as shown in table 3:

Table 3. Parameter optimization

Algorithm	**Ideal Parameters**
Logistic Regression	C: 5, max_iter: 100, random_state: 42, solver: saga, warm_start: True
Support Vector Machines (SVM)	C=3, kernel=poly, coef0=1.0, degree=2, gamma=0.1, random_state=42, probability= True

Logistic Regression and SVM algorithms, which yielded the highest F1 accuracy rate, were combined with the values obtained as a result of hyperparameter optimization with the voting method and a hybrid model was obtained. In the hybrid model, the LOO method, which gives more reliable results in small datasets, was used as a data validation method.

The F1, precision, recall accuracy rate values of the hybrid model and the normal and weighted average values for the accuracy rates obtained from these values are as shown in Figure 8. Values between 0-9 are numerical values representing the classes of documents.

Figure 8. Hybrid model accuracy results

	precision	recall	f1-score	support
0	0.79	0.95	0.87	216
1	0.40	0.36	0.38	11
2	0.75	0.59	0.66	41
3	0.91	0.45	0.61	22
4	0.90	0.82	0.86	11
5	0.69	0.45	0.55	20
6	0.68	0.61	0.64	46
7	0.00	0.00	0.00	7
8	0.77	0.84	0.81	135
9	0.50	0.31	0.38	42
accuracy			0.76	551
macro avg	0.64	0.54	0.57	551
weighted avg	0.74	0.76	0.74	551

The complexity matrix comparing the prediction values of the hybrid model with the actual data is given in Figure 9.

Figure 9. Hybrid model complexity matrix

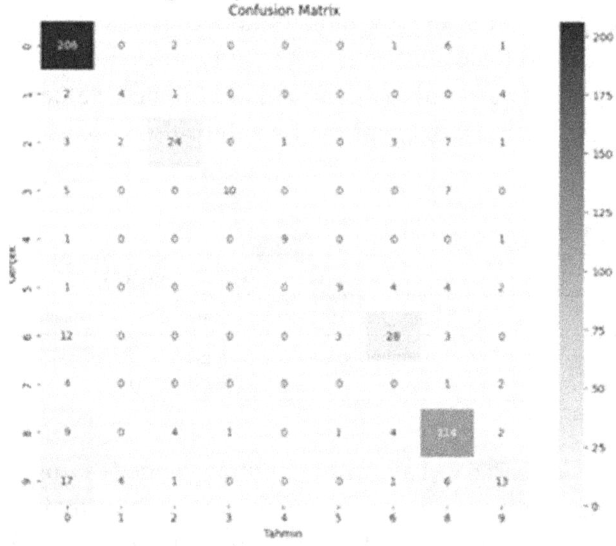

Of the two models that make up the hybrid model, Logistic Regression has an F1 accuracy rate of 70% and SVM model has an accuracy rate of 68% as shown in figure 7. The F1 accuracy rate of the hybrid model created with the ideal parameters obtained as a result of hyperparameter optimization with the Leave One Out model validation method is 76%, which is higher than the result of the single use of these two algorithms. The result obtained by comparing these algorithms is as shown in Figure 10.

Figure 10. Model comparison

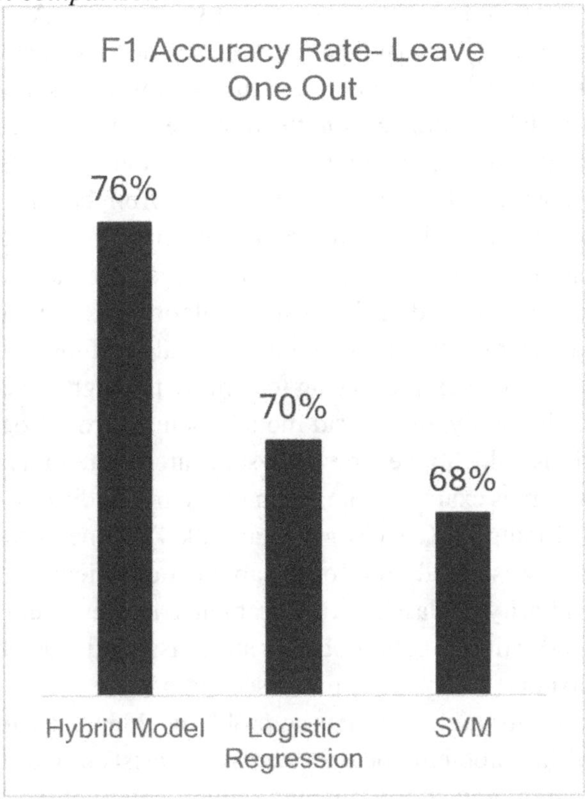

DISCUSSION

In the aviation company that is the subject of the study, document inflation has occurred over time and the documentation process has moved away from the lean philosophy. Within the scope of the study, the first approach to solve this problem is to determine the similarity ratios of the documents. The second approach is the establishment of a decision support system that will be used to predict the process classes of documents.

The most important difference of the similarity detection approach applied in the first part of the study from the applications in the literature is the method of tokenizing documents and texts. In the literature, texts have been parsed either in the most basic way, based on the gaps left between words (Ateş, 2021); or in a more complex way, through semantic approaches to identify relationships between words (Benedetti et al., 019). In our study, the texts were tokenized according to their sentence tasks, taking into account the role of each word in the sentence. This approach to tokenization is relatively more practical and easy to implement, but it is also intended to prevent the semantic relationship from being ignored.

There are several approaches to the choice of classification algorithms to be used in classification problems, which are the subject of the second part of the study. These approaches include using a single algorithm, selecting the algorithm with the highest accuracy rate after using multiple algorithms as in Yıldırım et al. (2014) and Ateş's (2021) thesis, or trying to achieve the highest accuracy rate with hybrid models. In this study, the hybrid model obtained from Logistic Regression and SVM algorithms, which gives the highest accuracy rate individually, is used.

When the literature is examined, it is seen that some studies focus on theory and literature review (Tantuğ, 2016), (Bilgin et al., 2004); some of them are practice-oriented. As far as it was found, most of the application-oriented studies addressed only one of the similarity or classification problems. However, unlike the others, in Lakkaraju et al. (2008) thesis, both problems are considered together and the results obtained in the first part can be used in the second part.

The strengths of this study are that the problem addressed within the scope of this study is a real-life problem, the data set used consists of real-life data, and the output obtained can improve the documentation processes of the company subject to the study.

Different software languages such as Weka, Python, Knime, R have been used in studies in the literature. The preferred software language for this study is Python.

CONCLUSIONS AND RECOMMENDATIONS

Within the scope of the study, two main real-life problems are addressed and the first one is the detection of similarity between documents. In the context of similarity detection, a sample of 227 documents out of 551 documents was analyzed with a 95% confidence interval and a 5% error rate, and it was concluded that documents with a similarity rate of more than 50% have similarities and other relationships with each other. It was suggested that documents with a similarity rate of 50% and above should be examined and these documents should be merged, and a relationship between documents should be established.

The second problem addressed is the classification of documents. In the context of the classification problem, a hybrid machine learning approach combining SVM and Logistic Regression models was preferred. With this model, the success rate of the two algorithms when used individually was increased and an accuracy rate of 76% was achieved. With this result, the process of finding the processes of documents, which is currently done manually, has been automated. Automating the process has benefits such as facilitating decision making and saving time in cases where there is no experience in the subject.

In this study, English texts were used and it would be useful to evaluate Turkish and English texts together in future studies. In the determination of the similarity rate in the first, a semantic dimension was added by considering the functions of the words in the sentence. This dimension can be deepened in terms of depth of meaning by adding different approaches.

In the second part, the dataset used for classification was inadequate for deep learning methods, so these models, which give high success rates on text data, could not be used effectively. By increasing the complexity of the hybrid model, higher accuracy rates can be targeted and the dictionary structure can be improved.

REFERENCES

Ateş, E. C. (2021). *Önleyici Kolluk Faaliyetleri Kapsamında Sosyal Medyada Veri Madenciliği: Suçları Önlemek İçin Twitter Analytic'i Kullanma*. Ankara Üniversitesi, Sağlık Bilimleri Enstitüsü.

Awasthi, I., Gupta, K., Bhogal, P. S., Anand, S. S., & Soni, P. K. (2021). Natural Language Processing (NLP) based Text Summarization—A Survey. *2021 6th International Conference on Inventive Computation Technologies (ICICT)*, 1310-1317. DOI: 10.1109/ICICT50816.2021.9358703

Benedetti, F., Beneventano, D., Bergamaschi, S., & Simonini, G. (2019). Computing Inter-Document Similarity with Context Semantic Analysis. *Information Systems*, 80, 136–147. DOI: 10.1016/j.is.2018.02.009

Bilgin, O., Çetinoğlu, Ö., & Oflazer, K. (2004). Building a Wordnet for Turkish. *Romanian Journal of Information Science and Technology*, 7, 163–172.

Bird, S., Klein, E., & Loper, E. (2009). *Natural Language Processing with Python: Analyzing Text with the Natural Language Toolkit*. O'Reilly Media, Inc.

Borko, H., & Bernick, M. (1963). Automatic Document Classification. *Journal of the Association for Computing Machinery*, 10(2), 151–162. DOI: 10.1145/321160.321165

Carol, B.-M. H., Besterfield, G., & Besterfield-Sacre, M. (1998). *Total Quality Management* (Subsequent edition). Prentice Hall.

Che, C., Hu, H., Zhao, X., Li, S., & Lin, Q. (2023). Advancing Cancer Document Classification with Random Forest. *Academic Journal of Science and Technology, 8*(1), Article 1.

Chomsky, N. (2002). *Syntactic Structures*. De Gruyter Mouton.

Chowdhary, K. R. (2020). *Fundamentals of Artificial Intelligence*.

Ciner, M. N., Güler, M., Namlı, E., Samastı, M., Ulu, M., Peker, İ. B., & Gülbaz, S. (2024). The Forecast of Streamflow through Göksu Stream Using Machine Learning and Statistical Methods. *Water (Basel)*, 16(8), 1125.

Dunham, M. H. (2020). *Data Mining: Introductory and Advanced Topics* (1st ed.). Pearson.

Evans, J. R., & Lindsay, W. M. (2019). *Managing for Quality and Performance Excellence* (11th ed.). Cengage Learning.

Ford, H. (2008). *My Life And Work*. CruGuru.

Güler, M., Kabakçı, A., Koç, Ö., Eraslan, E., Derin, K. H., Güler, M., & Namlı, E. (2024). Forecasting of the Unemployment Rate in Turkey: Comparison of the Machine Learning Models. *Sustainability*, 16(15), 6509.

Güler, M., & Namlı, E. (2024). Brain Tumor Detection with Deep Learning Methods' Classifier Optimization Using Medical Images. *Applied Sciences (Basel, Switzerland)*, 14(2), 642.

Gürsakal, N. (2018). *Makine Öğrenmesi*. Dora Yayıncılık.

Gürsoy, U. T. Ş. (2009). *Veri Madenciliği ve Bilgi Keşfi*. Pegem Akademi Yayıncılık.

Han, J., Kamber, M., & Pei, J. (2011). *Data Mining: Concepts and Techniques* (3rd ed.). Morgan Kaufmann.

Indurkhya, N., & Damerau, F. J. (Eds.). (2010). *Handbook of Natural Language Processing* (2nd ed.). Chapman and Hall/CRC.

Ingole, P., Bhoir, S., & Vidhate, A. V. (2018). Hybrid Model for Text Classification. *2018 Second International Conference on Electronics, Communication and Aerospace Technology (ICECA)*, 450-458. DOI: 10.1109/ICECA.2018.8474920

Kowsari, K., Jafari Meimandi, K., Heidarysafa, M., Mendu, S., Barnes, B., & Brown, D. (2019). Text Classification Algorithms: A Survey. *Information (Basel)*, 10(4), 150. DOI: 10.3390/info10040150

Kumar, V. (2005). *Introduction to Data Mining*. Pearson.

Lakkaraju, P., Gauch, S., & Speretta, M. (2008). Document similarity based on concept tree distance. *Proceedings of the nineteenth ACM conference on Hypertext and hypermedia*, 127-132. DOI: 10.1145/1379092.1379118

Liu, Z., Lin, Y., & Sun, M. (2020). *Representation Learning for Natural Language Processing*. Springer.

Manning, C., & Schutze, H. (1999). *Foundations of Statistical Natural Language Processing*. MIT Press.

Mcculloch, W. S., & Pitts, W. (1943). A Logical Calculus of the Ideas Immanent In Nervous Activity. *The Bulletin of Mathematical Biophysics*, 5(4), 115–133.

Miller, T. W. (2004). *Data and Text Mining: A Business Applications Approach* (1st ed.). Pearson.

Roiger, R. (2002). *Data Mining: A Tutorial Based Primer* (1st ed.). Pearson.

Tantuğ, A. C. (2016). Metin Sınıflandırma. *Türkiye Bilişim Vakfı Bilgisayar Bilimleri ve Mühendisliği Dergisi, 5*(2), Article 2.

Taylor, F. W. (1997). *The Principles of Scientific Management.*

Thielmann, A. (2020). Unsupervised Document Classification Integrating Web Scraping, One-Class SVM and LDA Topic Modelling. *Journal of Applied Statistics*, 50(3), 574–591. PMID: 36819086

Turing, A. M. (1950). Computing Machinery and Intelligence. *Mind*, LIX(236), 433–460.

Ünlü, R. (2022). An Assessment of imbalanced control chart pattern recognition by artificial neural networks. İçinde *Research Anthology on Artificial Neural Network Applications* (pp. 683-702). IGI Global. https://www.igi-global.com/chapter/an-assessment-of-imbalanced-control-chart-pattern-recognition-by-artificial-neural-networks/288982

Ünlü, R., & Xanthopoulos, P. (2021). A reduced variance unsupervised ensemble learning algorithm based on modern portfolio theory. *Expert Systems with Applications*, 180, 115085.

Witten, I. H., Frank, E., & Hall, M. A. (2011). *Data Mining: Practical Machine Learning Tools and Techniques*. Elsevier.

Yıldırım, E., Çetin, F. S., Eryiğit, G., & Temel, T. (2014). The Impact of NLP on Turkish Sentiment Analysis. *Türkiye Bilişim Vakfı Bilgisayar Bilimleri ve Mühendisliği Dergisi, 7*(1), Article 1.

KEY TERMS AND DEFINITIONS

Machine Learning: Machine learning is a method developed for problems that can be solved by classification, clustering and/or association analysis algorithms. Unlike algorithms called hard-coded, these methods are referred to as machine learning because they enable computers to perform computational operations by learning from data without being completely coded.

Natural Language Processing (NLP): Natural language processing is a field of study in artificial intelligence that is used for computers to gain the ability to translate human languages into computer language, analyze, interpret, and generate data.

Process: Process is an approach that connects all parts of the organisation and enables employees to understand the whole system rather than focusing only on individual parts.

ENDNOTE

1 https://raw.githubusercontent.com/dwyl/english-words/master/words.txt

Chapter 8
Classification of Fraud Detection in Call Centers Using Machine Learning Techniques

Ayşe Nur Adıgüzel Tüylü
https://orcid.org/0000-0002-3640-976X
Istanbul University-Cerrahpaşa, Turkey

Kaan Zengin
https://orcid.org/0009-0001-7945-1677
Istanbul University-Cerrahpaşa, Turkey

ABSTRACT

As a result of the transition of many systems to the digital age with the developing technology, it has been observed that fraud reports have increased, and this increase requires banks to develop strong systems against these threats. The inadequacy and slowness of the manual method currently used for the solution has led us to address this problem. As a solution to the fraud problem, this chapter presents an innovative method for periodic data analysis and automatic classification of fraud reports using text mining methods using machine learning algorithms. In this study, the authors aim to automate the labeling of incoming fraud reports as "social engineering" and "phishing" with the developed model. By comparing the performance of different algorithms, the random forest algorithm is selected as the most effective model. These results are valuable in terms of practical applicability.

DOI: 10.4018/979-8-3373-2272-8.ch008

INTRODUCTION

An examination of the historical development of banking worldwide reveals that Jewish financiers from Lombardy emerged as notable early bankers. These individuals conducted monetary transactions in public markets, specifically at a building known as Banco Rosso, utilizing tables and a wooden platform, or "banci," set up behind them for their operations. The origins of banking trace back to ancient civilizations, including the Sumerians and Babylonians.

The Ottoman conquest of Istanbul in 1453 facilitated the transfer of knowledge and literature from Italy, contributing to the advancement of Western civilization. The Renaissance saw an increased interest in lending practices, leading to the normalization of interest, while the Age of Exploration spurred significant changes in Europe's financial infrastructure.

In the Ottoman Empire, banking developed gradually due to the closed economic system. Institutions resembling modern banks did not emerge until the Tanzimat era. The introduction of paper currency, known as "kaime," in 1840 complicated foreign trade, ultimately leading to the establishment of Istanbul Bank in 1847. The Ottoman Bank, founded in 1856 with foreign capital, initially operated under foreign influence, which met with public discontent, prompting the formation of the Ottoman National Credit Bank. With the establishment of the Republic, Turkish banking entered a new era, leading to the foundation of various national banks. Turkey Is Bankası, established in 1924, was the first private bank, and the Central Bank was created in 1930 to support economic growth. The 1980s marked a pivotal shift in the banking sector, driven by the rise of private banks, leading to a more diverse economic structure (Kılıc, 2020). From the 1930s onward, the establishment of private banks alongside state-owned ones prompted rapid expansion within the sector, shifting from single-branch banks to multi-branch networks and transitioning from local to national banks. Reports indicate that, in 1944, there were 43 banks with 405 branches, which grew to 60 banks with 1,759 branches by 1959 (Cosar, 2009).

Banking is a critical sector for national economies, supporting both national and global economic growth. Recently, the banking industry has undergone digital transformation, with fintech companies introducing innovations such as online and mobile banking. The growing popularity of digital payment solutions and cryptocurrencies has reduced demand for cash and increased credit card usage. This trend aligns with consumers' preference for quick and secure services, enhancing customer transaction behaviors and optimizing banking services (Nurjanah et al., 2023). Retail banks, in particular, are at the forefront of this technological shift, facilitating the proliferation of these digital services and the innovations transforming traditional banking (Diener and Špacek, 2021).

Technological advancements within digital transformation have enabled the banking sector to establish more efficient distribution channels. Customer Relationship Management (CRM) is crucial for banks as it supports strategies for customer acquisition and retention. Additionally, call center services play a vital role in meeting customer demands promptly (Chitra and Subashini, 2013). In commercial banks, call centers handle customer inquiries, complaints, and information requests. Due to advancements in information technology, the operational capacity of call centers has significantly increased (Cao et al., 2011).

When bank customers experience issues such as losing, damaging, or having their ATM cards stolen, they can report these incidents to call centers, where representatives promptly address their concerns and perform necessary actions, including account blocking. Additionally, call center representatives assist customers with balance inquiries and efficiently resolve transaction-related complaints. These services are integral to banks' strategies for delivering optimal service to clients. By addressing customer issues through a structured approach, banks can better achieve their goals of providing quality service and convenience to clients. This leads to increased customer satisfaction, which, in turn, supports customer loyalty and alignment with organizational objectives (Karliadi and Erawati, 2023). In the banking industry, addressing customer complaints, needs, and requests requires attentive and swift service delivery, with solutions that are prompt, flexible, and responsive to customer issues.

Today, financial fraud is a significant global issue, especially prevalent in rapidly growing economies. Auditors often rely on data mining techniques to detect fraud while managing their workload effectively (Ravisankar et al., 2011).

Fraud Detection in the Banking and Finance Sector

While traditional data analysis methods have long been used to detect fraud, these approaches involve complex and time-consuming processes that span various disciplines such as finance, economics, business applications, and law. Recent advancements in information technology have provided significant support to the banking sector in overcoming challenges posed by the evolving economy. Although fraud cases often exhibit similarities in structure and content, each incident may present unique characteristics. Notably, fraud incidents are more prevalent in developing countries. Successful predictive models developed through data mining techniques are particularly effective when fraud alerts are analyzed and visualized in report form, offering users meaningful insights (Chitra and Subashini, 2013).

In our study, we examine the process by which a technology firm, specializing in the creation of innovative and value-added products and solutions for the financial sector, stores call center records in a database in text format for a bank it serves. This study investigates the categorization of fraud reports submitted to the call center by assigning two distinct labels, "Social Engineering" and "Phishing." However, as the company deemed the manual labeling process unsustainable, it aimed to develop a solution that would minimize the need for employee intervention. To this end, we detail our prototype application that leverages data mining and text mining methods to automatically label fraud reports.

There are a small number of text mining studies in the literature for fraud detection. Some of these are briefly described below.

The Sarbanes–Oxley Act requires that companies archive email, creating an untapped resource for deterring fraud. Holton (2009) developed a text mining application that uses a Naive Bayes algorithm to predict whether messages contain disgruntled communications for employees who are likely to commit fraud.

Ngai et al. (2011), in their study, provided an overview of typical text mining techniques used in the financial industry and analyzed these studies according to the type of data sources used as well as typical business applications. The study includes data mining applications such as classification, clustering, visualization, outlier detection, regression in financial fraud detection.

Gupta and Gill (2012) present a text mining approach to detect fraudulent financial reporting by analyzing hidden clues in the text of financial statements. Finally, in this paper they try to answer the question: "What features are necessary for correct pattern classification of a given class?"

Kumar and Ravi (2016) conducted security applications focusing on FOREX, stock market forecasting, customer relationship management applications and cyber security. In their analysis, they worked on text mining algorithms such as decision trees, neural networks, linear regression and logistic regression.

Dong et al. (2016), aiming to harness the power of largely ignored textual content in financial statements, developed a systematic text analytics model for financial statement fraud detection, guided by Systemic Functional Linguistics (SFL) theory. Finally, in an application to fraud detection with data from 1610 US listed companies, the developed model outperformed the baseline methods using financial ratios with an accuracy of 82.36%.

Pejić Bach et al. 2019 conducted a qualitative literature analysis on data mining in the financial sector using a systematic literature review, citation and co-citation analysis to answer the research questions: "what is the intellectual core of the field; what techniques are used for text mining in the financial sector, especially in the age of the internet, big data and social media; which data sources are most frequently used for text mining in the financial sector and for what purposes?".

Yadav and Sora (2021) used Deep Belief Network (DBN), an optimized classification technique to achieve better accuracy in their study with the aim of detecting frauds and protecting public investments using various text mining techniques.

The study also contributed to analyze various state-of-the-art techniques related to financial fraud detection; resolve the contradictions between different financial statement frauds; analyze various unsupervised learning algorithms for the clustering process of financial statements; and achieve better classification accuracy for financial statement fraud by extracting several optimal features under the feature selection process.

Li (2023) presented a deep learning approach to perform a natural language processing (NLP) binary classification task to analyze financial fraud texts. First, fraudulent companies are identified, then the sentences in the reports are labeled and organized, and different types of neural network models are used to classify the text, including Recurrent Neural Network (RNN), Recurrent Neural Network (RNN), Recurrent Multilayer Perceptron with embedding layer, Long-Short Term Memory (LSTM), and Gated Recurrent Unit (GRU), and a comprehensive comparison of their accuracy in detecting financial fraud is made.

When we examine the machine learning algorithms used in the literature, the preferred algorithms for text classification are Support Vector Machine, K-Nearest Neighbors, Decision Tree, Naive Bayes, Regression-based algorithms. In this study, we will discuss the categorization of fraud reports received by the call center with two different labels after reading the texts and manually evaluating them.

CONCEPTUAL FRAMEWORK

Machine Learning

The rapid increase in data volume today has further underscored the importance of data mining. The expanding mass of data holds immense potential benefits for organizations and individuals alike. Data mining is a process aimed at extracting hidden insights from data repositories and warehouses through systematic analysis. This process serves to interpret data and to generate forecasts for future trends. Data mining encompasses a wide array of techniques designed to uncover and define structural patterns within data. These techniques integrate a range of disciplines, including statistics, mathematics, artificial intelligence, and database management (Witten and Frank, 2005). Recent advances in machine learning have led to the development of intelligent systems that possess cognitive capabilities resembling human intelligence, impacting both professional and personal aspects of life (Janiesch et al., 2021).

Machine learning has emerged as a subfield of computer science within the realm of artificial intelligence. As intelligence cannot be achieved without the ability to learn, machine learning forms a foundational component of artificial intelligence.

For computers to think critically and solve problems as humans do, machine learning relies on algorithms and systems engineered to "learn" from previous experience. Processing and analyzing vast quantities of data manually are neither efficient nor practical. The structure and complexity of large datasets make manual analysis nearly impossible. Consequently, machine learning focuses on enabling computer programs to automatically recognize complex patterns and make data-driven, intelligent decisions. Through identifying and understanding patterns embedded in raw data, machine learning empowers computers to derive explanatory information and make predictions about future events. Algorithms developed through learning from experience or training data aim to detect meaningful patterns and progressively improve their performance, thereby generating more accurate predictions (Thomas and Gupta, 2020).

Machine learning, which involves acquiring knowledge and enhancing it through algorithmic processes without human intervention, has found extensive applications across a variety of fields (Janiesch et al., 2021; Thomas and Gupta, 2020). To enhance performance and generate accurate predictions, machine learning incorporates several computational techniques, which are broadly categorized into four types: Supervised Learning, Unsupervised Learning, Semi-Supervised Learning, and Reinforcement Learning (Mohri et al., 2018).

Figure 1. Machine learning techniques (Bonaccorso, 2017)

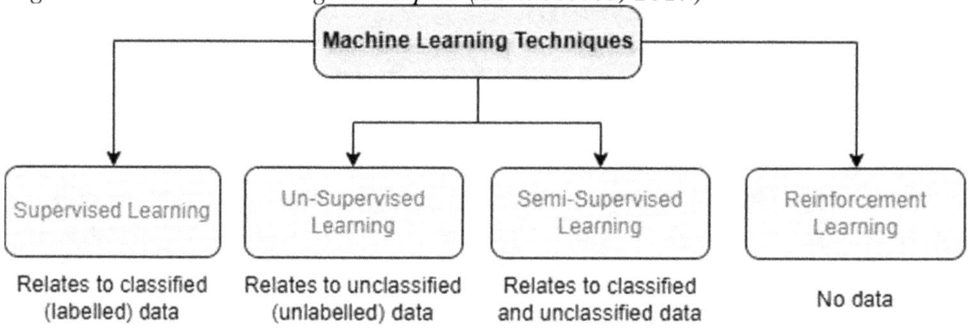

Classification

Classification is a data analysis method that utilizes models developed to identify key data classes. These models are designed to predict which categorical class within a dataset an item belongs to based on the characteristics it exhibits. The attributes and number of these classes are predefined, and the values identifying these classes within the dataset are known as labels. For instance, a classification model may be used to categorize customer feedback as either positive or negative, where the class labels are set as "positive" and "negative."

The classification process typically involves supervised learning. The data is split into training and testing sets, where the training set includes observations labeled with class information. The classes within the training set are specified and used to develop a model. Classification algorithms then analyze the relationships between the class labels and other attributes within the training set, enabling the model to "learn." This model is subsequently tested on data not included in the training set to measure its accuracy. Ultimately, the trained and tested model is used to determine the class of new items as they arrive. In contrast, in unsupervised learning, class labels are not known for the training data; instead, this process aims to form clusters based on shared characteristics of the data, without predefined classes. Here, the dataset is entirely comprised of training data, and the number of clusters is often unknown.

Figure 2. Classification (Han et al., 2011)

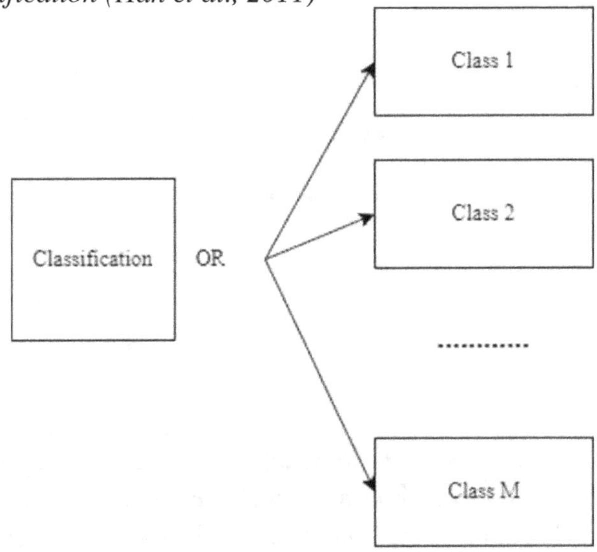

Classification analyses enable a deeper understanding of data and assist in developing more effective strategies. Various applications exist for classification, including fraud detection, sentiment analysis, targeted marketing, performance forecasting, production processes, and medical diagnosis (Han et al., 2011). By employing classification algorithms derived from machine learning, pattern recognition, and statistical disciplines, data can be interpreted more effectively.

Classification Algorithms

Decision Trees

Decision trees map relationships between independent and dependent variables by dividing them into branches, making it easy to interpret and visualize solutions. Each node in the tree represents an attribute, with branches extending from each node to represent the possible values of that attribute. An example of this structure for a decision tree is illustrated in Figure 3 (Bahety, 2014).

Figure 3. Decision tree diagram (Bahety, 2014)

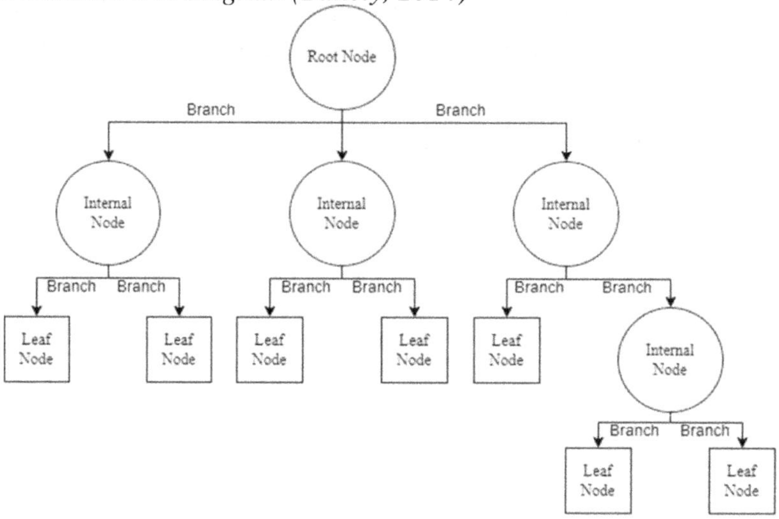

In classification problems, impurity reaches a minimum when all examples belong to the same class and a maximum when classes are equally represented within the analyzed data. The concept of entropy is used to measure class diversity, and the resulting metric is known as information gain. The entropy of a dataset L, with learning data, is expressed by the following formula (Kretowski, 2019):

$$Entropy(L) = -\sum_{c_i \in C} \frac{|c_i(L)|}{|L|} * \log_2 \frac{|c_i(L)|}{|L|} \# \quad (1)$$

where C = {c1, ..., cK} is a set of classes, c_i (L) is the set of examples in L belong to class ci.

In constructing a decision tree, we aim to make splits that minimize entropy, thereby identifying the most distinguishing features. By using information gain, we can identify the optimal branch for each split. The information gain for an attribute S within the dataset L is calculated using the following formula (Bahety, 2014):

$$Information\ Gain(S, L) = Entropy(S) - \sum_{v \in Values(L)} \frac{|S_v|}{|S|} Entropy(S) \# \quad (2)$$

Bayesian Classification Methods

Bayesian classifiers are statistical methods that predict the likelihood of specific instances belonging to particular classes. This classification approach is based on Bayes' Theorem, and studies have shown that Bayesian classifiers perform with high accuracy and speed in large databases (Han et al., 2011).

Named after Thomas Bayes, an 18th-century mathematician who worked on probability and decision theory, Bayes' Theorem uses probability theory and statistical principles to calculate the probability of an event based on prior conditions. Bayes' Theorem describes how the probability of an event is affected by the occurrence of another related event. The independent probabilities of events A and B are denoted as P(A) and P(B). Additionally, P(A|B) represents the conditional probability of A occurring given that B has occurred, and P(B|A) denotes the conditional probability of B occurring given that A has occurred. Bayes' Theorem is expressed as follows (Dimri et al., 2023):

$$P(A|B) = \frac{P(B|A)P(A)}{P(B)} \# \quad (3)$$

The Naive Bayes method, a probabilistic classifier, is one of the simplest forms of Bayesian classification, deriving its name from this simplicity. To determine a series of probabilities, the Naive Bayes method counts the frequency and combinations of values within a given dataset (Gripsy and Divya, 2023). ThAe classifier algorithm is trained on a subset of known values in the dataset and is then used to predict unknown values in future data. When applied to large datasets, Naive Bayes has shown good performance in terms of both accuracy and speed (Suhud et al., 2023).

Artificial Neural Networks (ANN)

An Artificial Neural Network (ANN) is a computational system consisting of interconnected processing units that work together to solve complex problems. Its primary objective is to emulate the human brain by identifying patterns between input and output data (Guler et al., 2024). The foundational concept of ANNs is derived from the brain's neural architecture. A basic ANN architecture includes several layers of interconnected neurons. The first layer, known as the input layer, contains neurons corresponding to the number of features in the data (including bias values). The next layer, termed the hidden layer, is crucial for capturing non-linear relationships. There is no definitive rule for determining the number of neurons in the hidden layer; instead, heuristic and statistical approaches are commonly recommended. The final layer, or the output layer, has neurons equal in number to the output classes (Unlu, 2022).

Furthermore, ANNs share certain characteristics with biological neural networks. A neural network comprises numerous basic processing units, called neurons, which form weighted connections with other neurons. ANNs have substantial advantages over traditional statistical methods, notably due to their minimal dependency on assumptions and their ability to model non-linear interactions effectively via suitable activation functions. Like humans who make reasoned decisions based on accumulated knowledge, trained ANNs can generate outputs even with incomplete data. Since data is distributed across the network, the removal of a few neurons does not lead to data loss (Guler et al., 2024).

The primary purpose of an ANN is to identify non-linear relationships between inputs and outputs (Namlı et al., 2022). The essential process involves feeding each layer with the weighted sum of input values, where each neuron receives a value based on a linear combination of the previous nodes. The network then adjusts weights to minimize errors through a technique known as backpropagation. Backpropagation is a widely used algorithm for training ANNs, as it calculates both the overall error in the output and the contribution of each neuron to that error.

As illustrated in Figure 4, ANNs consist of fully connected, layered stacks with a specified number of nodes (neurons). The main goal of ANNs is to reveal non-linear associations between input and output variables. Each layer receives the weighted sum of input values, where each neuron receives a linear combination of prior nodes, a structure known as a feedforward neural network. The weights are optimized using backpropagation, which minimizes errors by iteratively adjusting weights (Namlı et al., 2022).

Owing to its ability to execute the learning process using backpropagation and concurrently adjust connection weights across multiple layers, an ANN possesses an innate capability to perform non-linear mappings between input and output vectors, a hallmark of artificial intelligence systems.

Figure 4. The ANN structure for the classification problem (Han et al., 2011)

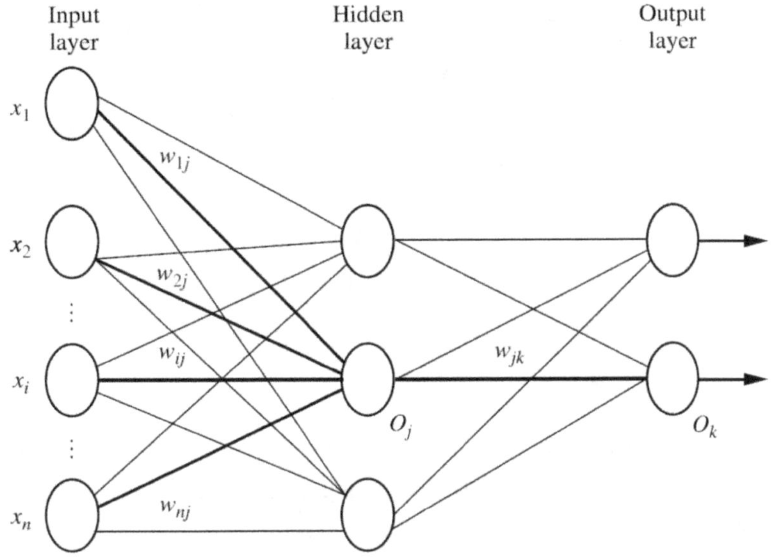

Support Vector Machines (SVM)

Support Vector Machines are classification algorithms designed for both linear and non-linear data (Han et al., 2011). The primary objective of SVMs is to separate multidimensional data into two distinct classes using a hyperplane. In this method, kernel functions are employed to map data into a space where it can be separated into two classes. Instead of working with the transformed data directly, SVMs rely on inner product formulations, which help prevent issues related to computational complexity and overfitting (Campbell and Ying, 2011). Various factors require careful consideration when training SVMs, including data processing techniques, kernel function selection, and parameter tuning (Ramazanov, 2020).

As shown in Figure 5, the objective is to identify the optimal hyperplane that can divide the data groups into two classes. To determine this, a hyperplane is drawn through data points closest to the optimal separating plane on either side. These two planes are parallel to each other. Support Vector Machines maximize the distance between these points and the separating surface in the training set, establishing a clear boundary between the two classes (Dogan, 2006).

Figure 5. Support vectors on linearly separable data (Dogan, 2006)

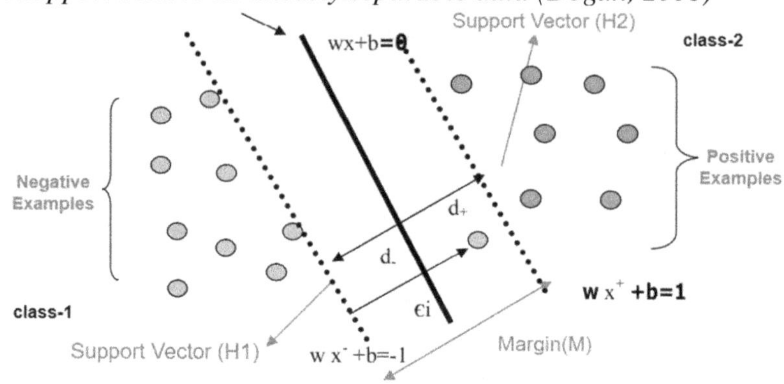

The Support Vector Machine seeks to find the hyperplane that maximizes the margin, or distance, between positive and negative examples and the hyperplane (Dogan, 2006).

K-Nearest Neighbor (k-NN) Algorithm

This algorithm is among the most easily understandable classification methods and operates using heuristic techniques. In this approach, unlabeled objects are classified by assigning them to the class of similar labeled examples. The class labels for the input features are determined by their closest neighbors. The fundamental rule in this classification method is based on the distance between the input feature to be assigned and the features in the training set, commonly using distance measured. Frequently used distance measurement methods (Guler and Namli, 2024):

- Euclidean Distance Measure: Euclidean distance is the linear distance between two points. The i value in the algorithm is selected in advance; a high value will cause dissimilar points to be grouped together, while a very small value will cause some points to be placed in separate classes, or separate classes to be opened for such points, even though they are similar to each other, that is, points of the same class (Algorabi and Namli, 2022).
- Cosine Similarity Measure: After all documents are expressed as vectors, the relationship between the training and query vectors is calculated with the formulas below. The document is assigned to the category of the n vectors whose "Similarity" ratio is closest to 1 (Seckin, 2011).
- Weighted Distance Method: In this method, the closer a neighbor is, the more weight it has when determining a class (Kesgin, 2007).

The k-Nearest Neighbor algorithm is highly resistant to noisy training documents and is effective when there are many documents. However, it has disadvantages such as the need for k parameters and the unknown distance measure to be used.

Random Forests Algorithm

Random Forest (RF) is an ensemble learning algorithm introduced by Breiman in 2001, primarily designed to enhance Classification and Regression Trees (CART). This algorithm operates through the aggregation of a substantial number of decision trees utilizing a bagging mechanism (Unlu, 2021). Furthermore, it allows for the construction of subtrees that integrate randomly selected features. Notably, the algorithm does not apply a pruning process to the trees it generates. The random tree algorithm can achieve a high accuracy rate in evaluations due to the extensive number of random trees generated. One of the most significant advantages of this algorithm is its capability to effectively address the overfitting problem commonly associated with decision trees (Ciner et al., 2024). However, the primary limitation of the RF algorithm lies in the fact that a large number of trees may render the algorithm slow and inefficient for real-time predictions (Unlu, 2021). Random Forest employs techniques such as bagging (bootstrap aggregating) and random feature selection to reduce overfitting and improve prediction accuracy. Its operating principles are as follows (Breiman, 2001):

- From the training dataset, n samples are randomly selected with replacement to create B bootstrap samples.
- Each bootstrap sample contains n data points selected randomly and with replacement from the original dataset.
- A decision tree T_b is trained on each bootstrap sample.
- At each node, the best split is determined using m features randomly chosen from the p available features.
- Each tree makes its own prediction, and the class with the most votes across all trees becomes the model's final prediction.

$$\hat{y} = mode\left(\{\hat{y}_b : b = 1,2,\ldots,B\}\right) \# \quad (4)$$

where:

$\hat{y}$: Represents the classification prediction made by the Random Forest model.
$\hat{y}_b$: Represents the individual prediction made by tree b.
b=1,2,…, B: Indexes the trees, with B representing the total number of trees.

mode: A statistical measure that selects the most frequently occurring value, thus choosing the most commonly predicted class among all trees.

Evaluation of Classification Models

Model evaluation is a process that employs various metrics to analyze a model's performance. As is well-known, model development is a multi-step procedure that involves assessing how well the model generalizes future predictions. Thus, model evaluation plays a crucial role in assessing a model's effectiveness. Additionally, evaluation aids in identifying fundamental weaknesses within the model. The evaluation metrics used depend on the specific machine learning algorithms in question.

The effectiveness of a machine learning technique for an unbalanced dataset may be evaluated using a variety of performance metrics. On the basis of the confusion matrix, several assessment metrics may be computed either directly or indirectly (Unlu, 2022; Unlu and Xanthopoulos, 2021). The accuracy (ACC) measure is the most often used criterion in classification issues. However, when applied alone, the accuracy requirement does not necessarily yield certainty. A more accurate and trustworthy analysis requires the use of additional measuring parameters. In addition to the accuracy measurement metric, the studies in the literature were found to employ the precision (Prec), sensitivity (Recall), and F1 score (F1) measures. The confusion matrix may be used to compute these values in matrix form (Guler and Namli, 2024).

Confusion Matrix

A confusion matrix provides a detailed breakdown of correct and incorrect classifications for each class. In this matrix, rows correspond to actual class labels, while columns represent predicted classes (Zheng, 2015).

The confusion matrix is essentially a table that records the number of instances within a dataset that belong to a specific category. For binary classification tasks, each class label has two potential values: a positive class and a negative class. During training, the model determines which two classes in the dataset are assigned as the positive and negative classes. The structure of the Confusion Matrix is shown in Table 1.

For datasets with string-based class labels, these labels are sorted alphabetically, with the first level designated as the negative class and the second level as the positive class. For class labels in boolean or integer format, examples marked with "1" or "true" are automatically assigned as the positive class (Shobhal and Rangaswamy, 2018).

Table 1. Confusion matrix (Han et al.., 2011)

		Predicted Class		
		Positive	**Negative**	*Total*
Actual Class	True	TP	FN	*P*
	False	FP	TN	*N*
	Total	*P'*	*N'*	*P+N*

P is the number of positive tuples and N is the number of negative tuples. For each tuple, the classifier's class label prediction is compared to the tuple's known class label. The terms used in the confusion matrix are:

- True Positives (TP): These are positive tuples that are correctly labeled by the classifier.
- True Negatives (TN): These are negative records that are correctly labeled by the classifier.
- False Positives (FP): These are negative tuples that are incorrectly labeled as positive.
- False Negatives (FN): These are positive tuples that are incorrectly labeled as negative.

The confusion matrix is used to analyze how well the classifier can recognize tuples belonging to different classes. TP and TN tell that the classifier got things right, while FP and FN tell that the classifier is labeling incorrectly (Han et al., 2011).

Accuracy

Accuracy measures how often the classifier makes the correct prediction. It is defined as the ratio between the number of correct predictions and the total number of predictions (the number of data points in the test set) (Zheng, 2015). It gives the percentage of test set groups that are correctly classified by the classifier (Han et al., 2011).

$$Accuracy = \frac{TP + TN}{P + N} \# \quad (5)$$

Precision

Precision is a measure to use when there is a high cost of false positives. The closer the value is to 1, the more certain the positive predictions are (Mishra, 2019).

$$Precision = \frac{TP}{TP + FP}\# \tag{6}$$

Recall

It shows what percentage of positive tuples are labeled this way. Recall has the same formula as precision (or true positive rate) (Han et al., 2011) Recall is the opposite of precision. It is less about answering questions correctly and more about answering all questions that are "correct" with the answer "correct". So if the models always give the answer "correct", it is 100% recall (Shobhal and Rangaswamy, 2018).

$$Recall = \frac{TP}{TP + FN} = \frac{TP}{P}\# \tag{7}$$

Precision can be defined as a measure of accuracy. In other words, what percentage of tuples that are labeled positive are actually so. But recall is a measure of completeness (Han et al., 2011).

F Measure (F1 Score)

In statistical analysis of binary classification, F score (or F measure) is a measure of the accuracy of a test. In general, it is a measure of the precision and robustness of the model. It takes into account the precision and recall of the test to calculate its score. It can have a maximum of 1 (perfect precision and sensitivity) and a minimum of 0. It is difficult to compare two models with low precision and high sensitivity and vice versa. So, F1 score is used to make them comparable. (Shobhal and Rangaswamy, 2018)

$$F1 - Score = \frac{2 \times Precision \times Recall}{Precision + Recall}\# \tag{8}$$

Text Mining

With technological advances and developments in information systems, a large amount of data is generated today. Public institutions, private businesses and other organisations create and store various types of data in their databases. Most of this data is in text format. These texts, which are produced both in research and in daily life, increase over time and turn into large piles of documents. However, when these documents are not processed, they remain only as a pile in databases. Therefore, these texts need to be processed in order not to lose important information and to access valuable data. The discovery of relationships, associations and patterns between data has led to the need to reveal hidden information (Dolgun et al., 2009).

In this context, text mining is an important method to reveal hidden information in unstructured text data (Jo, 2019).

Structured data refers to the type of data that has a specific format and an organised structure, while texts from sources such as blog posts, social media posts, forums, feedback forms, surveys and call centre interviews are defined as unstructured data. This unstructured data contains valuable information for businesses. Businesses need to analyse these data for purposes such as identifying relationships in texts, analysing consumer sensitivities and extracting text summaries. In this context, text mining can be defined as a tool of data mining and is used to obtain structured data from text sources (Dolgun et al., 2009).

Text mining benefits greatly from data mining studies and feeds on advances in this field; therefore, there are important similarities between both systems (Feldman and Sanger, 2006). Text mining includes analysis techniques such as classification, regression, clustering and association (Jo, 2019).

Text Mining Study and Application Areas

Information Extraction from Texts: In text mining, texts are analysed for meaningful entities and relationships in order to extract information from documents. Knowledge extraction reveals the elements in the text and the relationships between entities. These relationships can be a representation of facts or events contained in the entities. While static facts do not change, events have a dynamic structure depending on a certain time (Feldman and Sanger, 2006).

There are four basic types of information that can be extracted from texts:

- Entities: Basic building blocks, such as people, companies, places, genes or products.
- Attributes: Refers to the characteristics of entities, such as the title of a person or the geographical location of a place.
- Facts: Concrete information representing relationships between entities, such as the relationship between a company and its employees.
- Events: Events or actions mentioned in the text, such as a product launch or a merger.

These elements are important for analysing texts and building knowledge-based models. These processes often utilise natural language processing (NLP) and machine learning techniques.

Categorisation of Texts: Text categorisation is a process that involves assigning documents to predetermined categories (Jo, 2019; Sahami and Srivastava, 2009). Text categorisation has two main objectives (Massung and Zhai, 2016):

- Enriching text representation: Making the text more understandable by adding meaningful explanations
- Inference of entity properties: Inferring the properties of entities associated with the text, e.g. determining the native language of an author according to the language of the text

Text categorisation studies have diversified due to the variety of data to be classified.

Clustering of Texts: Clustering enables the grouping of objects according to predefined groups. These objects can be documents, sentences or words. Clustering is used to explore large datasets and allows text documents to be grouped under multiple subheadings. This method identifies bidirectional relationships between texts and it is important to define similarity metrics correctly in the text clustering process. For example, clustering of customer emails can help identify important customer complaints about the product (Gupta and Lehal, 2009; Massung and Zhai, 2016; Jo, 2019).

Summarisation of Texts: Text summarisation is the process of bringing texts into a shorter and more comprehensible form. The aim of summarisation is to provide a short version of the main content of the text. However, since manual summarisation is a challenging process, automatic summarisation techniques have been developed (Jo, 2019; Massung and Zhai, 2016). Automatic summarisation can also be used to improve the effectiveness of information retrieval and other text mining activities.

Sentimental Analysis: People often express objective information (facts) and subjective evaluations (opinions) in their writing. Sentiment analysis aims to classify the emotional content of texts and generally focuses on sentimental polarity, which categorises texts as positive, negative or neutral (Atılgan and Yogurtcu, 2021; Seker, 2016; Turkmenoğlu, 2015). For example, businesses can measure brand reputation or identify customer needs by analysing social media data (Atılgan and Yogurtcu, 2021; Seker, 2016).

Text mining enables the extraction of valuable information from large volumes of text, enabling use in many areas such as decision support systems and information management.

Fraud Detection and Text Mining

Rapidly developing technology has enabled users to perform their daily activities quickly and effectively in a virtual environment (Wales, 2003). However, many systems have been moved to the internet environment. Especially in the banking sector, users have turned to online systems because they facilitate their transactions. With the transition to the online system, the tendency of customers to prefer smartphones for ease of use has increased (Thomas et al., 2004). Thus, developing technology has not only provided customers with ease of use but also caused them to face fraudulent activities. Examples of fraudulent activities include data collection, social engineering and phishing. Fraudsters use these methods to obtain bank customers' information and manipulate them for their own benefit (Brause et al., 1999).

Social engineering is a type of cyber attack. The human factor is seen as the weakest link in the system. For this reason, social engineering is a form of attack that targets people. With various psychological methods and deception, the attacker can obtain information that people would not normally give. Accordingly, the concept of social engineering is defined as any action that influences a person to take an action, whether it is in his/her interest or not, and accordingly, confidential or privileged information can be obtained through both technical and non-technical means (Ozdenizci Kose, 2022). This information can be bank, credit card, identity information or confidential information about the company. Looking at the incidents that have occurred in recent years, it has been seen that the weakness of organizations is not only their information systems, but on the contrary, they are victims of social engineering due to the end user, that is, the human factor. Therefore, in order to prevent economic and social losses caused by social engineering attacks, it has become important to take the necessary precautions and predict the attacks in advance (Ozdenizci Kose, 2022). There are several different social engineering techniques. These are Shoulder Surfing, Garbage Mixing, Trojans, Role Playing, Phishing, Reverse Social Engineering.

Phishing attack is an act of deception in which the attacker tries to obtain information from the target by assuming a certain identity (Arslan, 2021). Phishing attacks start by throwing a bait to the target, as in fishing. Attacks usually start with a fake e-mail, message or website link from an unreliable source that appears to be a trusted source, such as a bank or a social network, but in fact comes from an unreliable source prepared by the attacker to obtain information from the target. Often these links lead to a fake website. Since the user thinks that this source is trustworthy, he/she provides the requested information and the attacker gets the information he/she wants from the target.

With the increase in reports to the bank's call center, it has become important for the bank to analyze fraudulent activities and to plan the measures to be taken in order to analyze how these activities are carried out and which category they fall into.

Figure 6. Phishing attack schematic (Arslan, 2021)

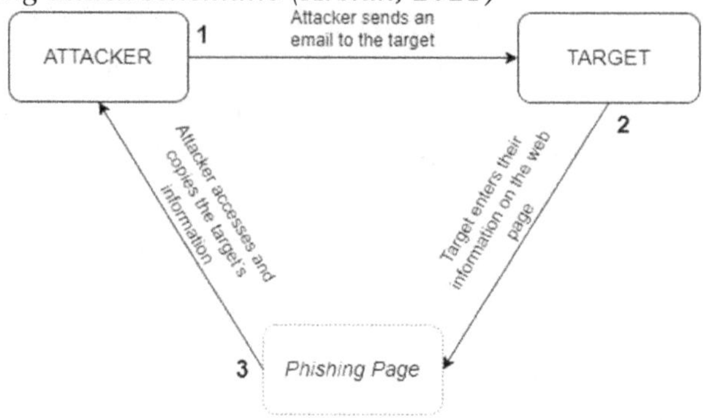

MATERIAL AND METHOD

System Description

In this text mining study, a text mining study in the banking sector is analysed. The bank in question will be referred to as Bank A from now on and the company providing technology services will be referred to as A Technology company. Here, Bank A is the customer and A Technology is the service provider.

Bank A, one of the leading banks in Turkey, serves its customers through its head office in Istanbul and nearly 800 branches covering all regions of Turkey and employs approximately 16 thousand employees. Thanks to its extensive branch network and innovative approaches to digital banking, 98% of all banking transactions were carried out through non-branch channels in the first nine months of 2023. A Bank offers retail banking, commercial banking, investment banking, payment systems, digital banking and customer-oriented financial solutions. The bank also draws attention with its efforts in mobile banking and digital payment systems.

A Technology is a leading company that provides technology-oriented solutions in the banking sector with the services it provides to Bank A. It provides consultancy services to Bank A in the fields of data analysis, customer experience supported by artificial intelligence, information security solutions and digital processes. In addition to traditional banking services, Bank A cooperates with A Technology in the field of digitalisation and technology.

Bank fraud has become an increasing threat with methods such as 'social engineering' and 'phishing' in 'Bank A', which is served by a technology company that offers innovative, high added value, innovative products and solutions in the financial sector. Such attacks, which abuse the trust of victims, are generally carried out to obtain personal information or seize financial assets. It causes not only financial loss but also psychological and spiritual losses.

Social engineering and phishing attacks usually make victims think that they come from sources they trust. Victims' weaknesses and information deficiencies are targeted. Victims have to cope with psychological problems such as feeling guilty, lack of trust, anxiety, stress and depression. Due to trust issues, they may become overly sceptical in order to avoid similar fraud attempts in the future. Fraud cases often involve legal procedures. Victims have to re-establish their identity, liaise with financial institutions and cooperate with law enforcement agencies to report the fraud. The process can be stressful, time-consuming and costly for victims.

Banks have to detect and prevent fraud cases to ensure the financial security of their customers. Therefore, it is of great importance to classify fraud reports quickly and accurately. The company attaches importance to the concepts of customer satisfaction, market competition and building trust, and in order to prevent this situation, it performs ‘phishing’ and ‘social engineering’ labels, which cause loss of time, money and labour, by manual labelling. Traditional manual classification methods are time-consuming and error-prone. At this point, machine learning models come into play.

Machine learning models can automatically classify fraud reports by processing large amounts of data quickly. By learning from past fraud cases and related data, these models can classify new reports with specific labels. Machine learning models can analyse the content of reports using natural language processing and text mining. In this way, it becomes accurate and consistent in classifying fraud reports. Thanks to accurate classification, banks can quickly intervene in fraud cases and take necessary measures. By reducing manpower, they can both get more accurate results in a short time and direct their human resources more effectively. In addition, classification results help to analyse fraud trends and develop preventive strategies.

Therefore, the adoption of machine learning applications in the banking industry is becoming increasingly important. As a result, this study proposes to minimise human errors in the classification of fraud reports and speeds up the processes.

Elements of the System

The elements of the system constitute the basic building blocks of a machine learning system used to automatically classify fraud calls to a bank call centre. The combination of these components ensures efficient and reliable operation of the system and provides better protection against fraud attacks. This section describes the definitions of system elements, variables, constants, parameters and constraints.

- Bank Call Centre: This system aims to receive fraud calls to the bank call centre. A call centre is a centre where calls are received and routed for the purpose of providing customer service.
- Customer Database: It is a database where the information of the bank's existing customers is stored and maintained. This database enables the call centre personnel to access the necessary information about the customer.
- Fraud Database: It is the database where previously detected fraud calls are recorded and the model is trained. This database enables the system to recognise fraud calls and provide better protection against such calls.
- Data Collection Tool: It is a special tool used to record fraud calls from the bank call centre. This tool can receive both text transcripts and audio recordings of calls. Thus, the content of the calls can be obtained in both written and audio format.
- Data Pre-Processing Module: It is a module used for cleaning, organising and formatting incoming data in a meaningful way. This module includes the removal of unnecessary information, tokenisation of texts, word normalisation and other pre-processing steps. Thus, the data is made ready for the machine learning model for use.
- Feature Engineering Module: This is a module for creating and selecting the features you need to develop your machine learning models. This module is used to extract and transform various features of calls such as content, duration, tone and call duration. The correct selection and processing of features will train the model correctly and give more accurate results. For example, features such as whether certain keywords appear in the content of a call, how long the call lasts, or the tone of the speaker's voice are taken into account by this module.
- Machine Learning Model: It is a model used to classify fraud calls into certain categories such as phishing or social engineering. This model includes various classification algorithms, such as decision trees, support vector machines, deep neural networks, etc. The model is pre-trained using training data, which is usually made available and then used to analyse calls in real time.
- Training Data Set: It is the labelled data set used for training the machine learning model. This dataset contains sample fraud calls with the correct categories. The data pre-processing module feeds it. It is very important for training the model correctly.
- Validation Data Set: It is a separate data set used to evaluate the performance of the machine learning model. This data set may be different from the training data set and is used to test the generalisation ability of the model. It is necessary to make sure that the model can generalise correctly.

- Model Training and Evaluation Tool: It is a tool or software used to train the machine learning model and evaluate its performance. This tool ensures that the model is trained correctly and supports the monitoring and improvement of its performance.
- Inference Module: It is a module used for applying the model on new calls and extracting the results. This module can determine whether the call is included in categories such as phishing or social engineering. It allows bank employees or system administrators to access these results and take necessary actions. For example, it can determine whether a call is categorised as a fraud call and forward this information to the relevant people.
- User Interface: It is the interface that allows bank employees or system administrators to manage the system and view the results. This interface is used to process new calls, review model results and intervene when necessary.
- Monitoring Module: It is a module used to monitor system activities and performance. This module is used to record system logs, report errors and intervene when necessary. Thus, it ensures the proper functioning of the system and provides a mechanism for detecting problems. It can also collect various metrics to monitor system performance and can perform analyses on these metrics.

Customer information, details of the incoming call, the device on which the customer was attacked, the number of incoming calls per day and the keywords used are variables for this system.

The constants of this systems are as follows:

- The software development standards, security policies and other organisational guidelines set by the company are fixed. These standards and policies are set at the beginning of the project and apply throughout the entire project.
- It targets the customer database in the bank. Anyone who needs to be protected against fraudulent activities is the target audience of this programme.
- Labelling criteria are defined as 'Social Engineering' and 'Phishing'.
- Data warehouse and business intelligence department tasks and definitions are fixed.
- The problem solution performance criteria to be used to evaluate the success of the model are fixed. Metrics such as accuracy, sensitivity, specificity help to objectively evaluate the performance of the model.
- The weekly working hours are fixed as 09.00 - 18.00 and the working days are fixed.
- The data set used in the training of the model is fixed.

The parameters of this systems are as follows:

- Call Text or Audio Recording: The content of the tip, in the form of call text or voice recording, may be the main source for the evaluation of the tip. This data may contain details of the fraud attempt.
- Calling Number and Identity Information: The number or identity information of the person to whom the call was made can be used to determine the source of the call and to evaluate the degree of accuracy.
- Content and Details of the Notice: The content and details of the tip may be important in determining what the tip is about and which fraud method is used.
- Call Centre Staff's Assessment: Knowledge of how call centre staff assessed and classified the tip may be helpful in determining the accuracy and severity of the tip.
- Similar Prior Tips or Fraud Cases: Reports that are similar to previous similar reports or fraud cases can be a reference in determining the degree of accuracy and importance.
- Verification by Reliable Sources: Verification or corroboration of the tip by reliable sources may be effective in determining the importance of the tip.
- Type of Fraud to which the Tip is Relevant: Determining to which type or category of fraud the whistleblower belongs can ensure that the whistleblower is correctly categorised.
- Target Audience to Which the Notice Relates: Determining the target audience to which the report is directed can help to prioritise the report.

These parameters represent the basic information and evaluation points that can be used in the categorisation of fraud calls received by the call centre. Correctly analysing and evaluating this information allows for effective categorisation and handling of calls.

This study was carried out under certain constraints:

- The operation to be performed is carried out during business hours due to internal work.
- Only the 'Data Warehouse and Business Intelligence' team performs the relevant work.
- The number of employees is determined.
- Software development standards are not exceeded.
- There are legal and ethical obligations regarding the use of sensitive data belonging to bank customers for data privacy and security. Confidentiality and

security of customer data is of great importance. Therefore, strict security measures are targeted throughout the data processing and storage process.

- High quality, clean and reliable data is needed for the machine learning model to be successful. The data received on complaint calls usually has a complex structure. Pre-processing steps are planned to improve data quality. Data quality control is performed.
- As the model complexity increases, the risk of incorrect results will increase. It is of great importance that the model can recognise different fraud scenarios and be successful in different data sets. To increase the generalisability of the model, careful feature selection and the model needs to be editable.
- Fraudsters may develop new and more complex social engineering and phishing techniques. Therefore, the model needs to be continuously updated. So that the model can recognise new fraud methods.

Prediction and Assumptions

Under this title, the predictions made based on the performance of the algorithms in the classification of fraud reports received by the bank call centre using machine learning algorithms and the assumptions for the implementation of these algorithms are discussed.

An important first step in the design process of any system is the assumptions and predictions phase. Predicting the future behaviour or results of a system is the focus of this phase. The reliability of these predictions is crucial for an efficient system. When designing a system to classify fraud calls to a bank call centre, the accuracy of the prediction is very important. Depending on the machine learning techniques to be applied, various predictions are made on the data set before the model is developed. Steps such as data collection, data exploration and data segmentation are typically included in this phase. Pre-processing of text data, appropriate model selection, model training, validation, prediction and verification of prediction findings are typically included in the prediction step. The project will determine which machine learning algorithm provides the best results when the bank's call centre classifies fraud calls into phishing or social engineering categories.

- Data Quality and Cleanliness: In order to increase the accuracy and reliability of the model, the data should not be incomplete, inaccurate or misleading. For this reason, data cleaning, noise removal and completion of missing data were carefully performed. It is assumed that the data used for the successful operation of the model are clean, accurate and up-to-date after preprocessing.
- Representative Dataset: It is assumed that the training and test dataset used is diverse and sufficiently representative of the bank's fraud reports. This in-

creases the generalisation capacity of the model and enables it to accurately classify different types of fraud reports. The sufficient diversity of the training dataset ensures that the model is also successful in practice.

- Suitability of Algorithms: It is assumed that the machine learning algorithms used are suitable for the problem of classifying fraud reports and will perform adequately. Decision Tree, Random Forest, Naive Bayes, SVM, Neural Network and K-NN algorithms were selected and applied according to the characteristics of the data set. These algorithms were chosen according to their suitability for different data structures and classification problems.
- Feature Selection and Engineering: In the process of converting text data to vector, it is assumed that the text features that are important in the classification of fraud reports are correctly selected and integrated into the model. These features are the factors that directly affect the performance of the model. In the text preprocessing steps, text data were converted into numerical feature vectors, especially using the TF-IDF technique.
- Suitability of Training and Testing Processes: It is assumed that the methods used in the training and testing processes of the models are appropriate. It is assumed that the training and test data are balanced. It is aimed to measure how well the model can perform on data that it has not encountered before.

These approaches and assumptions are fundamental to the successful implementation of the system design and accurate classification of fraud reports. These assumptions were taken into account when developing the system to improve the accuracy and reliability of the study. By taking these assumptions into account at every stage of the project, the overall performance and reliability of the system was prioritised.

Explanation of the Solution Techniques Used and Reasons for Selection

The algorithms used in this study were chosen for their advantages and suitability to the project requirements.

Naive Bayes works with low memory and processor requirements in terms of resource usage and speed. It offers very fast training and prediction. This means that it can perform fast training and prediction for large datasets. The important advantages of the algorithm are simplicity, low resource utilisation and fast results. However, the assumption that the features are independent may negatively affect the accuracy of the model.

Support Vector Machine (SVM) is a powerful machine learning model used in classification problems. It needs high memory and processor when working with big data. It aims to find how each data is positioned relative to other data and to find the most optimal hyperplane. This causes time-consuming and resource-intensive use of big data. However, it has high performance and generalisation capacity. It aims to increase the generalisation capacity, thus minimising the possibility of overfitting. It has a flexible algorithm structure on non-linear datasets:

Decision Trees are actively used in classification and regression problems. It has an easy to understand structure. It works with moderate memory and processor requirements. Training and prediction times are at medium speed. It provides advantages thanks to its explainability and visualisable decision structure. However, the risk of overfitting may be high.

Random Forest is formed by the combination of many decision trees. It is a powerful method used in classification and regression problems. It is a model that requires memory usage, but thanks to its parallel processing advantage, it manages resource usage correctly. Prediction and training times are medium speed. The low risk of overfitting, explainability and stability are the advantages of the random forest algorithm. However, it can work slowly in large data sets.

Artificial Neural Networks (ANN) is a model with high complex problem solving capacity. They are known for their high processor and memory requirements in terms of resource utilisation and speed. They have long training times. However, they perform prediction processes quickly. Its advantage over other models is its high learning capacity in complex relationships. The application area is wide. However, it needs a lot of data. Explainability is low.

K-Nearest Neighbour (K-NN) algorithm is a simple and intuitive model used in classification and regression problems in machine learning. It uses low level resources in the training process. While forecasting, it uses high memory and processor. It is a flexible model. Flexibility is provided by parameter settings. It is easy to implement; it has a simple structure that does not need any model learning process, it can be coded in various programming languages in a simple way. However, it makes slow prediction in large datasets. Prediction time will increase in direct proportion to the size of the data set. Memory consumption is high, above average.

Figure 7. Flow chart of the system

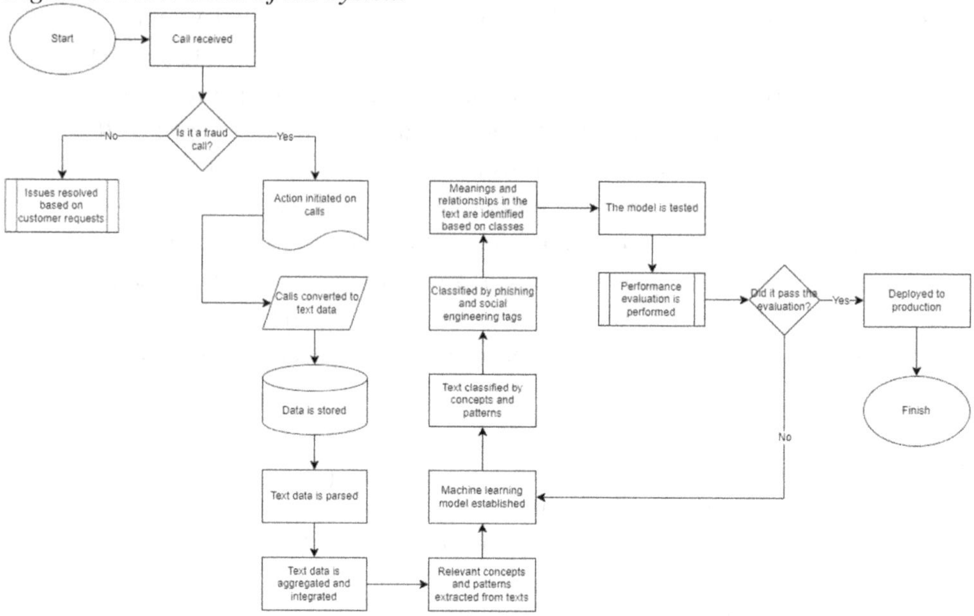

APPLICATIONS

In this study, Naive Bayes, Support Vector Machine, Decision Tree, Random Forest Algorithm, Artificial Neural Networks, KNN algorithms were used in fraud detection. Accuracy, Precision, Recall, F1-Score values were used to evaluate the model performances.

As a result of the studies, Random Forest Algorithm was selected as the model that makes the most accurate classification and performance evaluation in text data.

Furthermore, libraries such as Pandas, Numpy, Scikit-learn, Zemberek and Natural Language Toolkit were used in the study process. Python was preferred as the software language. Juptyer Notebook and Excel tools were used.

In this section, the process of model building with machine learning starting from the data preprocessing stage to obtaining the prediction model result is explained.

Acquisition of Text Data

The text data acquisition phase is one of the first and most critical steps of the data processing process. In this stage, the raw text data was collected using the dataset from the bank. The data relates to fraud reporting calls made to the bank. This data was stored in Excel file and read using pandas library to make it analysable. Pandas is a powerful Python library used for data manipulation and analysis. Reading the data and converting it into the pandas DataFrame format allows the data to be more easily processed and analysed. The aim of this stage is to obtain the raw data in an organised and accessible format.

Cleaning Text Data

The text data cleaning stage ensures that the raw data can be analysed through various pre-processing steps. The cleaning process aims to improve the accuracy and quality of the data, resulting in more reliable results.

Removal of Punctuation

Punctuation marks in text can often create unnecessary noise in the natural language processing process. Therefore, it is necessary to remove punctuation marks. In this step, the Python Re library was used to remove all punctuation marks from the texts. This process using regular expressions makes the texts more homogeneous and analysable. For example, the sentence 'Update your credit card details now!' is simplified to 'Update your credit card details now'. This process reduces the noise in the texts and allows more consistent analyses.

Conversion of Texts to Lower Case

Case sensitivity during text processing can cause different variations of the same word to be recognised as separate words. To avoid this, all texts are converted to lower case. Thus, words like 'Hello' and 'hello' are treated as the same. This step contributes to the deduplication of words in the dataset and more accurate analyses.

Removal of Numbers and Unwanted Elements

Numbers and unwanted elements in the texts (e.g. URLs, user tags) usually do not contribute to the analysis process and should therefore be removed. In this step, all numbers and unnecessary elements such as URLs and user tags are removed from the texts. This process makes the texts simpler and more meaningful. For example, '1000 TL was withdrawn from your bank account. Click for details: http://example.com' is simplified as "TL was withdrawn from your bank account Click for details". The aim of this step is to make the texts more readable and analysable.

Tokenization

The tokenisation phase separates the text word by word and treats each word as an independent unit (token). The Nltk (Natural Language Toolkit) library was used for this process. Tokenization is a fundamental step in text analysis and allows texts to be processed in more detail. At this stage, the aim is to divide the text into analysable parts (tokens) so that each word can be analysed separately. For example, the sentence 'TL was withdrawn from your bank account' is divided into 'Bank', 'from your account', 'TL', 'withdrawn'. Tokenization allows texts to be broken down into smaller pieces while preserving their meaning, so that more detailed and precise analyses can be performed. In this way, various analyses such as word frequencies, word vectors and natural language processing models can be applied more easily.

These steps cover the process of processing raw text data and making it analysable. Each step aims to improve the quality of the data and make more reliable analyses. Cleaning and tokenisation of text data are fundamental and critical processes in natural language processing projects. These processes provide a solid foundation for further analyses and machine learning models.

Removal of Stopwords (Ineffective Words)

Words that occur frequently in the texts but are not meaningful for the analysis are removed in the data preprocessing stage. These words may be frequently used conjunctions or pronouns such as 'and', 'or', 'but', 'that', 'this'. These words are not needed during the analysis as they cannot make sense on their own.

Stemming and Lemmatisation

Morphological analysis techniques such as stemming or lemmatisation can be used to transform words into their roots. This step reduces words that appear in different forms in the text to the same root form. For example, the words 'search' and 'searched' come from the same root although they occur in different forms in the text. In this case, we can use these two words for analysis by reducing them to the root form 'ara-'. This provides a more consistent semantic representation of the words. At this stage, the 'TurkishMorphology' class of the 'ZEMBEREK' library was used for morphological analysis. Thanks to this library, words were reduced to their roots and more consistent analyses were made.

Converting Text Data to Vector

Since the data set consists of texts, it is a stage used to convert text data into TF-IDF (Term Frequency-Inverse Document Frequency) vectors. TF-IDF is a technique used in many fields such as text mining, natural language processing, information retrieval and search engines, recommendation systems, natural language processing (NLP), clustering and segmentation, similarity calculation, document summarisation, social media analysis. Our goal is to convert text data into numerical feature vectors in order to put them in a format to perform machine learning.

TfidfVectorizer is provided as part of the scikit-learn library and is widely used. Define the TF-IDF Vectoriser by following the steps below.

- Import the scikit-learn library. It is a machine learning library often used in Python. It offers various tools for processing data.
- Create an instance of the TfidfVectorizer class. Create an object (tfidf_vectorizer) of class TfidfVectorizer. This object is used to convert text data into TF-IDF feature vectors.
- The parameters of the TfidfVectoriser are decided. The TfidfVectorizer class can take many parameters for processing text data. These parameters determine how the TF-IDF calculations are performed and which features are used. Below are a few important parameters:
    - max_df: Maximum document frequency of the term. For example, when max_df=0.85, if a particular term occurs in more than 85% of the dataset, it is ignored. Used to reduce the impact of very common terms.
    - min_df: The minimum document frequency of the term. For example, when min_df=5, if a given term does not occur in at least 5 documents, it is ignored. Used to reduce the impact of very rare terms.
    - max_features: The maximum number of features to convert. For example, when max_features=1000, 1000 terms with the highest TF-IDF scores are selected.
    - stop_words: A list of terms to be ignored. For example, when stop_words='english', English stop words (e.g. 'and', 'is', 'the') are ignored.
    - ngram_range: The phrase size to be used to create n-grams (multiple phrases). For example, when ngram_range=(1, 2), unigrams (single words) and bigrams (groups of two words) are considered.
    - use_idf: Determines whether you want to use IDF (Inverse Document Frequency) weighting. For example, when use_idf=True (default), IDF calculation is performed.

    - smooth_idf: Determines whether to add a constant to the IDF calculation. When smooth_idf=True (default), 1 is added to the IDF calculation to avoid zero division errors.
- Fit and transform operations are performed. The TfidfVectorizer object is used to transform text data into TF-IDF vectors. It is performed in two steps:
    - fit_transform: It performs fit (learning) and transform (transformation) operations on the training data together. It calculates the TF and IDF values of the terms in the training data. Accordingly, it transforms the values into data.
    - transform: Performs only transform operation on the test data. It transforms the test data based on the TF-IDF values learnt from the training data. It is performed according to the TF-IDF calculations learnt from the training data without fit operation on the test data.

Separation of Data into Train and Test Sets

The main objective is to measure how well the model can perform on data that it has not encountered before. To perform this step, we divide the data into two basic groups:

- Train Set: The data set used to train the model.
- Test Data (Test Set): The data set used to evaluate the performance of the model.

The distinction is used to prevent the model from overlearning and to test the generalisation ability of the model. Using the Scikit-learn library, we can divide the data into train and test sets. For this we use the train_test_split function. Usually 80% of the data is split for training and 20% for testing.

- x and y: x represents the text data that the model needs to learn and y represents the tags corresponding to these texts.
- train_test_split: This function randomly splits the data in the desired ratio. Since test_size=0.2, 20% of the data is split as test set and 80% as training set.
- random_state=42: Used for randomness control.

Training and Evaluation of the Model

Once we have created the training and test sets, we train our model on the training data and evaluate it on the test data. For example, we can do this using a TF-IDF vectoriser and a simple classifier.

Analysis and Evaluation of the Algorithms Used

Table 2 compares the accuracy, precision, recall and F1-score metrics of the models used in this study. Values for both Phishing and Social Engineering classes are given for each model.

Table 2. Comparison of machine learning model results

Model	Accuracy	Precision (Phishing)	Precision (Social Engineering)	Recall (Phishing)	Recall (Social Engineering)	F1-Score (Phishing)	F1-Score (Social Engineering)
Naive Bayes	0.861	0.90	0.80	0.86	0.86	0.88	0.83
SVM	0.889	0.95	0.81	0.86	0.93	0.90	0.87
Decision Tree	0.806	0.81	0.80	0.85	0.75	0.83	0.77
Random Forest	0.889	0.86	0.93	0.95	0.81	0.90	0.87
Neural Network	0.889	0.95	0.81	0.86	0.93	0.90	0.87
K-NN	0.833	0.90	0.75	0.82	0.86	0.86	0.80

Evaluation and Selection

While evaluating the performance of the models, basic performance metrics such as accuracy, precision, recall and F1-score as well as important parameters such as resource utilisation, speed, training time and model explainability were taken into account. The advantages and disadvantages of each model are detailed below.

The Naive Bayes model showed a high performance with an accuracy of 0.8611. In the phishing class, 90% accuracy, 86% recall and 88% F1 score were obtained. In the social engineering class, 80% precision, 86% recall and 83% F1 score were achieved.

Support Vector Machine (SVM) showed high performance with an accuracy rate of 0.8889. In the phishing class, 95% precision, 86% recall and 90% F1 score were obtained. In the social engineering class, 81% accuracy, 93% recall and 87% F1 score were achieved.

The Decision Tree model showed the lowest performance with an accuracy of 0.8056. In the Phishing class, 81% precision, 85% recall and 83% F1 score were obtained. In the social engineering class, 80% accuracy, 75% recall and 77% F1 score were achieved.

The Random Forest model showed high performance with an accuracy rate of 0.8889. In the Phishing class, 86% precision, 95% recall and 90% F1 score were obtained. In the social engineering class, 93% accuracy, 81% recall and 87% F1 score were achieved.

Neural Network shows a high level of performance with an accuracy rate of 0.8889. In Phishing, one of the classes, 95% precision, 86% recall and 90% F1 score were observed. In the social engineering class, 81% accuracy, 93% recall and 87% F1 score were obtained.

K-Nearest Neighbours (K-NN) showed moderate performance with an accuracy of 0.8333. In Phishing, one of the classes; 90% accuracy, 82% recall and 86% F1 score were observed. In social engineering, 75% accuracy, 86% recall and 80% F1 score were achieved.

After analysing the performance evaluations of each model, we can say that the Random Forest model is the most suitable model for this study when the following criteria are considered.

Accuracy and Performance: It has the same accuracy rate as SVM and Neural Network with an accuracy rate of 0.8889. Balanced performance and overall accuracy rate increases the reliability and generalisation capacity of the model. The information about the correct classification ability is given by the F1 score of 90% with 86% precision and 95% recall rate in the Phishing class. Considering the performance value, 87% F1 score with 93% precision and 81% recall in the Social Engineering class is a high performance indicator.

Explainability: Since it consists of decision trees, its explainability is high. The fact that each decision tree can be visualised makes it easier to understand and verify the results of the model. This is an important advantage, especially in areas where the model will be applied (e.g. security or financial applications).

Resource Utilisation: It can effectively manage resource utilisation through parallel processing. Parallel processing capabilities compensate for high memory usage. It achieves fast results. When working with large datasets, it offers good performance, albeit at medium speed of training and prediction times.

Speed: It performs moderately fast in training and prediction times. It provides enough speed in large datasets. Training time is shorter than models such as SVM and Neural Network. It is mostly used in practical applications.

In conclusion, the advantages of the Random Forest model that make it stand out are the following:

- High accuracy
- Balanced performance
- Explainability
- Effective resource utilisation

Random Forest provides superiority when these features are considered. It would be appropriate to choose Random Forest as the best performing model on the data set. This choice is supported by the model's generalisation capacity, resource efficiency and user-friendly structure.

CONCLUSION

In this study, the call centre records of Bank A, which is served by a technology company that produces innovative and high value-added products and solutions in the finance sector, were used. The calls received by the call centre are kept in the database as translated into text, and the fraud reports received by the call centre are read from these texts, evaluated and categorised with two different labels. The labels determined are divided into two as ‘Social Engineering’ and ‘Phishing’. Since the existing system is not sustainable and employees are labelling manually, it is aimed to develop a solution to eliminate this situation. Data mining and text mining methods were used to automate the labelling of textual fraud calls.

As a result of the labelling prediction made in line with the text data collected by the company, the performances of the algorithms were measured with Naive Bayes, Support Vector Machine, Decision Tree, Random Forest Algorithm, Artificial Neural Networks and K-NN methods. As a result of the measured performances, an accuracy rate of 0.8889 was obtained with Support Vector Machine, Random Forest Algorithm and Artificial Neural Networks methods. In addition to the accuracy rate, the Random Forest Algorithm provides a more balanced result when the methods are evaluated on the basis of training and prediction time, interpretability, overall performance and flexibility. The main reason for this is that although it is moderate in training and prediction time, it performs well in large data sets, provides interpretability and visualisation, and is also resistant to overfitting by coping well with data set imbalances.

In the system, the automatic categorisation of fraud reports received by the call centre into two different labels, social engineering and phishing, minimises the effort and time spent on manual labelling and allows the personnel to focus on more critical tasks. The fast record processing system minimises human-induced inconsistencies in the labelling process. This saves on personnel and training costs. Increases customer satisfaction and enables future growth plans to cope with increasing call volumes. In the long term, it supports the strategic goals of the company and offers competitive advantage. The level of operational efficiency and accuracy has increased with the automatic labelling of call centre records by using text mining methods. The developed system enables faster and more accurate evaluation of fraud reports. It increases the effectiveness of security strategies and prevents inconsistencies caused by human error. Thus, data analytics and insight capacity can utilise fraud prevention policy more actively. Savings in training and personnel costs optimise the company's cost structure. Improvement in customer service increases customer satisfaction and trust. This plays an active role in increasing the reputation of the company.

As a result of all these activities, the labelling system supports the operational and strategic objectives of the company. It will significantly increase the competitive advantage. In addition, it plays an active role in the sustainable growth process. It will be an innovative system that will increase security measures and will be effective in customer satisfaction.

REFERENCES

Algorabi, O., & Namli, E. (2022). An integrated machine learning-based decision support model for prediction of bank telemarketing success. *Verimlilik Dergisi*, (1), 94–109. DOI: 10.51551/verimlilik.748616S

Arslan, Y. (2021). Phishing Attacks Awareness Exercise Example. *Duzce Universitesi Bilim Ve Teknoloji Dergisi*, 9(3), 348–358. DOI: 10.29130/dubited.832862

Atilgan, K. O., & Yogurtcu, H. (2021). Sentiment Analysis of Twitter Posts of Cargo Company Customers. *Cag Universitesi Sosyal Bilimler Dergisi*, 18(1), 31–39.

Bahety, A. (2014). Extension and evaluation of ID3-decision tree algorithm. *Entropy (Basel, Switzerland)*, 2(1), 1–8.

Bonaccorso, G. (2018). *Machine Learning Algorithms: Popular algorithms for data science and machine learning*. Packt Publishing Ltd.

Brause, R. W., Langsdorf, T. S., & Hepp, H. (1999). Neural data mining for credit card fraud detection. *Proceedings 11th International Conference on Tools with Artificial Intelligence*, 103-106.

Breiman, L. (2001). Random forests. *Machine Learning*, 45(1), 5–32. DOI: 10.1023/A:1010933404324

Campbell, I. C. G., & Yiming, Y. (2011). *Learning with Support Vector Machines*. Morgan and Claypool., DOI: 10.2200/S00324ED1V01Y201102AIM010

Cao, S.-Y., Wang, W.-H., & Zhang, H.-F. (2011). Research and application on customer satisfaction degree evaluation system in call centers of commercial bank. In *2011 International Conference on Business Management and Electronic Information (BMEI)* (p. 803-807). IEEE.

Cebiroglu, G. (2002). Root reaching method without dictionary (Master's thesis, Istanbul Technical University). Istanbul Technical University, Institute of Science and Technology, Istanbul, Turkey.

Chitra, K., & Subashini, B. (2013). Data mining techniques and its applications in banking sector. *International Journal of Emerging Technology and Advanced Engineering*, 3(8), 219–220.

Ciner, M. N., Guler, M., Namli, E., Samasti, M., Ulu, M., Peker, I. B., & Gulbaz, S. (2024). The forecast of streamflow through Goksu Stream using machine learning and statistical methods. *Water (Basel)*, 16(8), 1125. DOI: 10.3390/w16081125

Cosar, N. (2009). *Historical Development of the Banking Sector in Turkey*. Yildiz Technical University, Department of Economics.

Diener, F., & Špaček, M. (2021). Digital transformation in banking: A managerial perspective on barriers to change. *Sustainability*, 13(4), 2032. DOI: 10.3390/su13042032

Dimri, S. C., Kumar, B., & Purohit, K. C. (2023). Application of Bayesian theorem for precise analysis of clinical test results. In 2023 6th International Conference on Information Systems and Computer Networks (ISCON) (p. 1-5). IEEE. https://doi.org/DOI: 10.1109/ISCON57294.2023.10112017

Dogan, S. (2006). Turkce dokumanlar icin n-gram tabanli siniflandirma: Yazar, tur ve cinsiyet (A new N-gram based classification for Turkish documents (Ng-ind): Author, type, and gender). (Master's thesis, Yildiz Technical University).

Dolgun, M. O., Guzel Ozdemir, T., & Oguz, D. (2009). Veri madenciliginde yapisal olmayan verinin analizi: Metin ve web madenciligi. *Istatistikciler Dergisi*, 2, 48–58.

Dong, W., Liao, S., & Liang, L. (2016). Financial statement fraud detection using text mining: A systemic functional linguistics theory perspective.

Feldman, R., & Sanger, J. (2006). *The text mining handbook: Advanced approaches in analyzing unstructured data*. Cambridge University Press., DOI: 10.1017/CBO9780511546914

Gripsy, J. V., & Divya, T. (2023). Lung cancer disease prediction and classification based on feature selection method using Bayesian network, logistic regression, J48, random forest, and naïve Bayes algorithms. In 2023 3rd International Conference on Smart Data Intelligence (ICSMDI) (pp. 335-342). IEEE.

Guler, M., Kabakci, A., Koc, O., Eraslan, E., Derin, K. H., Guler, M., Unlu, R., Turkan, Y. S., & Namli, E. (2024). Forecasting of the unemployment rate in Turkey: Comparison of the machine learning models. *Sustainability*, 16(15), 6509. DOI: 10.3390/su16156509

Guler, M., & Namli, E. (2024). Brain Tumor Detection with Deep Learning Methods' Classifier Optimization Using Medical Images. *Applied Sciences (Basel, Switzerland)*, 14(2), 642.

Gupta, R., & Gill, N. S. (2012). Financial statement fraud detection using text mining. *International Journal of Advanced Computer Science and Applications*, 3(12).

Gupta, V., & Lehal, G. S. (2009). A survey of text mining techniques and applications. *Journal of Emerging Technologies in Web Intelligence*, 1(1), 60–76. DOI: 10.4304/jetwi.1.1.60-76

Han, J., Kamber, M., & Pei, J. (2011). *Data mining: Concepts and techniques* (3rd ed.). British Library. DOI: 10.1016/C2009-0-61819-5

Holton, C. (2009). Identifying disgruntled employee systems fraud risk through text mining: A simple solution for a multi-billion dollar problem. *Decision Support Systems*, 46(4), 853–864.

Janiesch, C., Zschech, P., & Heinrich, K. (2021). Machine learning and deep learning. *Electronic Markets*, 31(3), 685–695. DOI: 10.1007/s12525-021-00475-2

Jo, T. (2018). *Text mining: Concepts, implementation, and big data challenge* (1st ed.). Springer International Publishing. DOI: 10.1007/978-3-319-91815-0

Karliadi, A., & Erawati, D. (2023). The influence of communication and problem handling on customer satisfaction in using call center services: A study on conventional banks in the city of Palangka Raya. Jambura. DOI: 10.37479/jimb.v6i2.19580

Kesgin, F. (2007). Topic detection system for Turkish texts (Master's thesis, Istanbul Teknik University).

Kilic, E. K. (2020). Banking crises and history in the world: The banking sector in the world. *International Journal of Financial Economics and Banking Practices*, 1(1), 1–31.

Kretowski, M. (2019). *Evolutionary decision trees in large-scale data mining* (1st ed.). Springer Cham. DOI: 10.1007/978-3-030-21851-5

Kumar, B. S., & Ravi, V. (2016). A survey of the applications of text mining in financial domain. *Knowledge-Based Systems*, 114, 128–147.

Li, Q. (2023). Textual Data Mining for Financial Fraud Detection: A Deep Learning Approach. arXiv preprint arXiv:2308.03800.

Massung, S., & Zhai, C. (2016). *Text data management and analysis: A practical introduction to information retrieval and text mining*. Association for Computing Machinery and Morgan & Claypool., DOI: 10.1145/2915031

Mishra, A. (2019). *Machine learning in the AWS cloud: Add intelligence to applications with Amazon SageMaker and Amazon Rekognition*. Sybex.

Mohri, M., Rostamizadeh, A., & Talwalkar, A. (2018). *Foundations of machine learning* (2nd ed.). The MIT Press.

Namli, E., Yucel, M., Unlu, R., & Adiguzel Tuylu, A. N. (2022). Smart estimation model for energy performance certificates of residential buildings. Journal of Engineering Research, 1-24. DOI: 10.36909/jer.17597

Ngai, E. W., Hu, Y., Wong, Y. H., Chen, Y., & Sun, X. (2011). The application of data mining techniques in financial fraud detection: A classification framework and an academic review of literature. *Decision Support Systems*, 50(3), 559–569.

Nurjanah, S., Shalshabilla, V., & Dari, A. (2023). Digital transformation in the banking industry: Challenges and opportunities. International Journal of Accounting. *Management and Economics*, 1(1), 64–71.

Ozdenizci Kose, B. (2022). Predicting individuals' susceptibility to social engineering attacks using machine learning methods.

Pejić Bach, M., Krstić, Ž., Seljan, S., & Turulja, L. (2019). Text mining for big data analysis in financial sector: A literature review. *Sustainability*, 11(5), 1277. DOI: 10.3390/su11051277

Pilavcilar, I. F. (2007). *Metin madenciligi ile metin siniflandirma(Text mining and text classification).* Yildiz Technical University, Institute of Science.

Ravisankar, P., Ravi, V., Raghava Rao, G., & Bose, I. (2011). Detection of financial statement fraud and feature selection using data mining techniques. *Decision Support Systems*, 50(2), 491–500. DOI: 10.1016/j.dss.2010.11.006

Seckin, K. (2018). Metin madenciliginde kullanilan yontemlerin karsilastirilmasi: Siyasi parti liderlerinin grup genel toplanti konusmalari ile bir uygulama [Sakarya University Institute of Social Sciences].

Seker, S. E. (2016). Duygu analizi (Sentimental analysis). *YBS Ansiklopedi*, 3(3), 21–36.

Shobha, G., & Rangaswamy, S. (2018). *Machine learning. Handbook of statistics.* Elsevier., DOI: 10.1016/bs.host.2018.07.004

Suhud, R., Febriandirza, A., Permatasari, I., & Ramadan, F. (2023). Recognizing Public Satisfaction Toward Kampus Mengajar Program with Naive Bayes. 2023 International Conference on Computer, Control, Informatics and Its Applications (IC3INA), Computer, Control, Informatics and Its Applications (IC3INA), 2023 International Conference On, 125–130. DOI: 10.1109/IC3INA60834.2023.10285769

Tanir, D., & Ramazanov, S. (2023). Analysis of factors affecting individuals' e-commerce use in Turkey using data mining methods. *KMU Journal of Social and Economic Research*, 25(44), 46–65.

Thomas, B., Clergue, J., Schaad, A., & Dacier, M. (2004). A comparison of conventional and online fraud. *Proceedings of the 2nd International Conference on Critical Infrastructures (CRIS 2004).*

Thomas, R. N., & Gupta, R. (2020). A Survey on Machine Learning Approaches and its Techniques. DOI: 10.1109/SCEECS48394.2020.190

Turkmenoglu, C. (2015). Sentiment analysis in Turkish text (Unpublished master's thesis). Istanbul Technical University, Institute of Science.

Ünlü, R. (2019). An assessment of imbalanced control chart pattern recognition by artificial neural networks. In *Artificial Intelligence and Machine Learning Applications in Civil* (pp. 240–258). Mechanical, and Industrial Engineering. DOI: 10.4018/978-1-7998-0301-0.ch013

Ünlü, R. (2020). An assessment of machine learning models for slump flow and examining redundant features. *Computers and Concrete*, 25(6), 565–574. DOI: 10.12989/CAC.2020.25.6.565

Ünlü, R., & Xanthopoulos, P. (2021). A reduced variance unsupervised ensemble learning algorithm based on modern portfolio theory. *Expert Systems with Applications*, 180. Advance online publication. DOI: 10.1016/j.eswa.2021.115085

Wales, E. (2003). E-commerce counts cost of online card fraud. *Computer Fraud & Security*, 9–11.

Witten, I. H., & Frank, E. (2005). *Data mining: Practical machine learning tools and techniques*. Elsevier.

Yadav, A. K. S., & Sora, M. (2021). Fraud detection in financial statements using text mining methods: A review. *IOP Conference Series. Materials Science and Engineering*, 1020(1), 012012.

Zheng, A. (2015). *Evaluating machine learning models*. O'Reilly Media.

Zinger, S. (2006). *Statistical Natural Language Processing: N-Gram Models*. Seminar in Methodology and Statistics.

ADDITIONAL READING

Gaikwad, S. V., Chaugule, A., & Patil, P. (2014). Text mining methods and techniques. *International Journal of Computer Applications*, 85(17), 42–45. DOI: 10.5120/14937-3507

Klopotan, I., Zoroja, J., & Meško, M. (2018). Early warning system in business, finance, and economics: Bibliometric and topic analysis. *International Journal of Engineering Business Management*, 10, 1–11. DOI: 10.1177/1847979018797013

Srivastava, A. N., & Sahami, M. (Eds.). (2009). *Text mining: Classification, clustering, and applications*. Chapman and Hall/CRC., DOI: 10.1201/9781420059458

Yehia, A. M., Ibrahim, L. F., & Abulkhair, M. F. (2016). Text Mining and Knowledge Discovery from Big Data: Challenges and Promise. *International Journal of Computer Science Issues*, 13(3), 54–61. DOI: 10.20943/01201603.5461

Zhang, S., Zhang, C., & Yang, Q. (2003). Data preparation for data mining. *Applied Artificial Intelligence*, 17(5–6), 375–381. DOI: 10.1080/713827180

Chapter 9
Assessing the Effects on General Government Health Expenditures With Machine Learning-Based Causality Analysis

Yeşim Altay
https://orcid.org/0009-0002-0964-3099
Istanbul University-Cerrahpaşa, Turkey

Ömer Algorabi
Istanbul University-Cerrahpaşa, Turkey

Ayşe Paksoy
https://orcid.org/0009-0003-6104-2693
Istanbul University-Cerrahpaşa, Turkey

ABSTRACT

This study uses machine learning-based causal analysis to analyze the relationship between government health spending and socioeconomic characteristics. The research aims to enhance public health and promote economic stability by allocating significant resources to healthcare. Conventional forecasting techniques may struggle to identify complex causal relationships within health data. Machine learning models like causal forest offer a robust analytical tool for understanding health spending dynamics. Data from developed countries between 1970 and 2021 is used, focusing on factors such as cigarette and alcohol use, net savings, average life expectancy, and rates of drug, alcohol, and suicide deaths. The results show

DOI: 10.4018/979-8-3373-2272-8.ch009

that healthcare spending is significantly influenced by life expectancy and income level, while other factors vary based on regional and demographic variations. The study provides valuable insights for policymakers to develop data-driven, equitable health interventions that address specific needs across diverse populations.

INTRODUCTION

The provision of healthcare represents a fundamental tenet of any society, exerting a significant influence on the quality of life and well-being of its population. Governments across the globe allocate a significant proportion of their financial resources to address the health needs of their citizens. The effective management of these expenditures is of the utmost importance for the long-term sustainability of the healthcare system and the maintenance of economic stability. The consequences of healthcare expenditure extend well beyond the improvement of individual health, exerting a significant influence on broader economic outcomes, including growth, labor productivity, and social stability. It is therefore imperative to gain an understanding of these expenditures and to implement effective management strategies, as they have a significant impact on not only health policies but also on the economic and social policies of nations. While Newhouse (1992) states that health expenditures have direct and indirect effects on economic growth, Barro (1996) reveals that health expenditures increase productivity and support long-term growth through their positive effect on the health of the workforce. In addition, the work of Bloom and Canning (2000) addresses the positive effects of health expenditures on the general well-being of society, showing that these expenditures provide a basis for economic stability and social peace. In recent years, the ability to accurately project healthcare costs has become a crucial element in the formulation of health policy and the management of budgets. Güler and Namlı (2022) Machine learning and deep learning models have shown success in biomedical image processing, particularly in diagnosing diseases early and reducing specialist shortages.While Obermeyer and Emanuel (2016) stated that machine learning increases budgeting accuracy by being used in health expenditure estimation, Chen and Guestrin (2016) stated that various algorithms used in this field (such as random forest and Gradient boosting) are more successful than traditional methods in predicting increases in health expenditures. Varian's (2014) study, which addresses the advantages of machine learning-based methods, especially for analyzing complex relationships in health data, shows that predictions made with machine learning are more reliable for political decision-makers. Effective financial planning in healthcare not only enables governments to deploy resources efficiently but also enhances their capacity to respond proactively to evolving health challenges. Traditional forecasting methods, frequently based on historical data, have constituted a fundamental element in expenditure forecasting. Nevertheless, novel methodologies employing machine learning and causal analysis now permit the identification and comprehension of intricate underlying factors that drive healthcare costs. These methods analyze the relationships within the data, thereby uncovering insights that enhance the precision of the forecasts and offer a deeper understanding for strategic health planning.

The influence of artificial intelligence on business processes is considerable, and its effects can be observed in a multitude of contexts. Furthermore, machine learning-based transformations are anticipated to have an impact on the healthcare sector (Habehh and Gohel, 2021). The capacity of machine learning to uncover patterns in large datasets is transforming health economics. When combined with causal analysis, which focuses on identifying the direct effects of one variable on another, machine learning provides policymakers with a multidimensional understanding of healthcare expenditure dynamics. This integrated approach reveals the crucial relationships between health spending and its underlying factors, thus offering a more sophisticated perspective for policy decisions based on concrete, data-driven insights.

Moreover, the quality, diversity, and reliability of the data are of paramount importance when forecasting healthcare expenditures. The incorporation of exhaustive datasets incorporating expenditure from both the public and private sectors, insurance costs, and individual out-of-pocket expenses provides a more comprehensive representation of the healthcare financial landscape. The prioritisation of reliable and diverse data sources facilitates more accurate policy analyses, which are less prone to bias and therefore contribute to the formulation of sounder policy decisions.

The shortcomings of conventional forecasting methodologies, which are predominantly based on historical patterns, render them incapable of discerning intricate interconnections and causal relationships among the myriad factors influencing healthcare expenditures. In this context, machine learning methods, particularly those designed for causal inference, offer a promising avenue for addressing the aforementioned limitations. Causal Forest is a machine learning method that builds upon the principles of decision trees and ensemble learning. It has been specifically developed for causal inference in observational data (Venkatasubramaniam et al., 2023). In contrast to traditional predictive models, which focus exclusively on correlation, Causal Forest seeks to ascertain causal relationships by modelling treatment effects across disparate subpopulations within a given dataset. This is of particular value in the context of healthcare expenditure analysis, where a range of factors, including age, income, geographic location, and lifestyle choices, can give rise to markedly divergent spending patterns. By identifying these subpopulations, Causal Forest assists policymakers in comprehending how healthcare expenditures might respond to particular interventions across disparate groups, thereby furnishing actionable insights into the optimal allocation of resources.

One of the most noteworthy attributes of Causal Forest is its ability to discern heterogeneous treatment effects (Miller, 2020). This allows for the identification of variations in the responses of different demographic or socio-economic groups to health policies or budgetary changes. To illustrate, Causal Forest can discern how preventive health spending affects younger versus older populations, or how healthcare access enhancements benefit urban versus rural areas in disparate ways. By accounting for these variations, policymakers can make data-driven decisions that tailor health interventions to the unique needs of diverse communities, thereby ensuring a more equitable and effective distribution of healthcare resources. Moreover, the utilisation of Causal Forest in the analysis of healthcare expenditure offers insights into the relative importance of economic, social, and demographic variables in determining healthcare costs. By focusing on causal relationships, this method allows for a more profound comprehension of the manner in which particular factors, such as economic growth, employment levels, or income inequality, exert an influence on health spending. This nuanced view is of critical importance for long-term planning, as it enables the anticipation of how shifts in these variables might influence future healthcare needs and budget requirements.

Finally, the deployment of Causal Forest in the construction of data-driven decision support systems is of paramount importance for the formulation of effective health policy. Decision support systems that integrate causal analysis empower policymakers to simulate a range of scenarios and assess the potential consequences of different budget allocations or health interventions. This enables them to make proactive, evidence-based decisions that optimize resource allocation and maximize societal health benefits. By elucidating causal insights, Causal Forest facilitates the development of a policy framework that is adaptable, equitable, and focused on long-term health outcomes.

LITERATURE REVIEW

A review of the literature reveals that there are many machine learning-based forecasting studies on the economy and government expenditures. Since causality analysis is still a new approach, studies in this field are very limited. Some of the studies conducted in these areas are given below.

For instance, Kamanda et al. (2022) employed a trivariate framework to investigate Granger causality and cointegration relationships among three variables. Using health outcome measures and a panel vector autoregressive model, they analyzed data from 45 sub-Saharan African countries between 1990 and 2018. Their findings revealed that no causal relationship existed between health expenditures, health outcomes, and economic growth in the short run, suggesting that in less developed countries, health improvements may contribute to economic growth over time.

In the context of emerging economies, Dinçer and Yüksel (2019) examined the causal relationship between health expenditures and economic growth among E7 countries. Utilizing the Pedroni panel cointegration method and the Dumitrescu-Hurlin panel causality analysis with data from 1996 to 2016, the study identified a long-run relationship between economic growth and public health expenditures but not with private health expenditures. Moreover, no causality was found from health expenditures to economic growth. Devlin and Hansen (2001) used Granger causality tests and cointegration methods to analyze the effect of health expenditures on economic growth in developed countries. The study revealed that health expenditures make a significant contribution to growth in developed countries, but this effect may vary across countries.

Atilgan et al. (2024) to investigate the Health-Led Growth Hypothesis (HLGH) in OECD countries and examine the impact of health expenditures on economic growth, considering different health financing systems. The researchers used advanced econometric methodologies and analyzed data from 38 OECD countries between 2000 and 2019. Second-generation panel data estimators (Dynamic CCEMG, CS-ARDL, AMG) and first-generation models (Panel ARDL with PMG, FMOLS, DOLS) were used to test the hypothesis. The study found significant variations in the ability of health expenditures to stimulate economic growth among different health financing systems, including the Bismarck, Beveridge, Private Health Insurance, and Transition System models. This suggests that the relationship between health expenditures and economic growth is influenced by the specific health financing system implemented in a country.

Wasim et al. (2023) examine the relationship between economic growth and health-development priorities in South Asian countries. This study examines the bidirectional relationship between economic development and public health expenditure. To this end, a three-stage least squares regression with the least squares dummy variable technique was employed to generate fixed effects over the period 1980-2022. The results demonstrate a positive correlation between economic growth and public health expenditures in South Asian countries. This indicates that the impact of economic growth on health expenditures is greater than the impact of health expenditures on economic growth.

Şentürk et al (2023) examined the causal relationship between health expenditures, human capital, and sustainable development in eleven EU member countries from 2000 to 2020. Results show that health expenditures and human capital are interrelated, but the interaction differs among new EU members. Sustainable development is a significant determinant of health expenditures and human capital.

Education and training programs should focus on improving sustainability and healthy life awareness.

Sart (2023) employs a panel data approach to examine the relationship between education and health expenditure during the 2000-2019 period, using a new member sample of the EU. The panel-level analysis of causality revealed that health expenditures exert an influence on the field of education. Nevertheless, the evidence does not support the hypothesis that education exerts an influence on health expenditure. The country-level analyses yielded analogous results for Estonia and the Slovak Republic. These findings indicate that health expenditures exert a significant influence on education, yet the opposite is not true, as education does not have a discernible impact on health expenditures.

In a more recent analysis, Wang et al. (2024) examine the persistent trends in health expenditures as a percentage of gross domestic product (GDP), identify the key drivers of this negative trend, and consider the necessity of urgent intervention to halt this accelerating negative trend. To predict future patterns, advanced machine learning algorithms, such as Random Forest and Support Vector Regression (SVR), are used in combination with traditional statistical methods. The research underscores the significance of health analytics in addressing the intricacies of the health system. The findings indicate the necessity for the expeditious development of efficacious policies to address these mounting challenges.

Lee et al. (2015) employ empirical data from 17 Organisation for Economic Co-operation and Development (OECD) countries, including Australia, Austria, Canada, Denmark, Finland, Germany, Iceland, Ireland, Japan, South Korea, New Zealand, Norway, Portugal, Spain, Sweden, the United Kingdom, and the United States. The diverse nature of the dataset permits a comprehensive analysis across different national contexts. The authors employ a panel Granger-causality test to analyze the data, the results of which indicate that public expenditure on health has a significant negative effect on private health expenditure. However, this effect is observed with a lag of 3 to 4 years in 16 of the 17 countries studied. The United States is noted as an exception, showing a different pattern that warrants further qualitative analysis.

Baltagi and Moscone (2010) conducted a panel data study encompassing 20 OECD countries with the objective of analyzing the long-run relationship between health expenditures and per capita income. In the study, panel data analysis, unit root, and cointegration tests were applied using data for the period 1971-2004. The results demonstrate the existence of a long-run cointegration relationship between health expenditures and income. Furthermore, the findings indicate that health expenditures exert a positive influence on economic growth.

Tao et al. (2024) conducted an investigation into the center of causal inference, examining the relationships between biodiversity and biomass in subtropical forests. This effective Bayesian causal inference method was employed, with the results supported by a causal forest. The study makes a significant contribution to the existing literature on biomass dynamics and carbon storage capacity.

In a recent contribution to the literature, La Mastra and Barchitta (2024) conducted an analysis of the causal forest narrative in the context of public health. The study emphasizes that causal analyses can be effectively presented in the context of public health by demonstrating how causal forest, graphical causal models, and network analysis methods can be employed to examine causal sources.

In a study published in 2024, they used causal forests to predict machinery failures in the agricultural sector. The study's objective was to predict failures in management machinery and analyze the causal changes between functional variables and problems. The causal forest offers an analysis of the potential to optimize maintenance strategies, thereby facilitating improvements in the management of the machinery in question (Reynoso-Meza & Hermont, 2024).

Carbo-Valverde et al. (2020) employed machine learning techniques to gain insights into customer digitalization in the banking sector and to identify the key factors driving this process. A variety of machine learning algorithms, including Random Forests, Conditional Inference Trees and Causal Forests, were employed to identify behavioral patterns associated with the digitalization process. The study examines the adaptation of traditional banking services to digital platforms, the diversity of usage patterns, and the complementarity between digital banking and FinTech/BigTech services. The Causal Forest model proved effective in demonstrating that the factors influencing customer decisions are the result of a causal process.

Türküz & Akay (2020) examined the relationship between qualitative preference models utilized in econometrics when dependent variables possess qualitative characteristics and classification algorithms in machine learning. The primary objective of the research is to investigate the potential for establishing a connection between econometrics and machine learning. In particular, the impact of big data on econometrics and the contributions of machine learning in this context are examined. Furthermore, given the reluctance of estimation-based classification algorithms to engage with causality research, the role of econometrics in this field is clearly demonstrated. Consequently, a more profound comprehension of the interplay between the two disciplines is sought.

Industrial processes pose challenges in building accurate causal models for abnormal event diagnosis, control, and maintenance. In the study prepared by Nadim, Ragab, and Ouali, Innovative data-driven causality modelling approach using interpretable machine learning and process mining techniques was developed. It focuses on capturing the complex dynamics of industrial systems by analyzing dependency relationships between events. The approach extracts trustworthy patterns from event data logs, generates a Petri net model, and provides real-time tracking of system dynamics. The model was successfully tested on a real industrial dataset in Canada (Nadim et al., 2022).

Elek and Bíró (2021) examined regional variations in diabetes prevalence across Europe, exploring the role of socio-economic conditions, comorbidities, health behaviors, and diabetes management in these differences. The authors employed data from the Survey of Health, Ageing and Retirement in Europe (SHARE), comprising responses from 15 European countries and 28,454 individuals who participated in waves 4 and 7 (2011 and 2017) of the study. Firstly, multivariable regressions were estimated in which the outcome variables were diabetes prevalence, diabetes incidence, and diet-related weight loss, which serves as an indicator of management. Secondly, the heterogeneous impact of demographic, socio-economic, health, and lifestyle indicators on regional differences in diabetes incidence was examined with causal random forests.

Ito and Biljecki (2024) employ the distribution of the causal forest in order to examine the impact of urbanization on cycling. The application of improvements to the analysis of time series street data using the causal forest method facilitated the examination of heterogeneous situations pertaining to dealership cycling. This work offers significant contributions to the planning of transport policies.

Taskaya & Demirkiran (2016) analyzed the causality between healthcare resources and health expenditure in Turkey from 1975 to 2013. Data from Turkstat, World Bank Indicators, and OECD Health Data revealed that the number of physicians per 1000 population affected health expenditures per capita and GDP per capita. This information is crucial for health policymakers to control limited resources.

Rossen & Faroque (2016) employ the Hartwig-Colombier method to analyze the growth rate of per capita health expenditure by province in Canada from 1982 to 2011. The findings indicate that Baumol's cost disease was a significant contributor to the growth of health expenditures in Canada, alongside traditional economic factors such as income growth and the impact of macroeconomic conditions.

Rose (2018) uses machine learning and regression to analyze the impact of medical conditions on health spending. It reveals that multiple sclerosis, congestive heart failure, severe cancers, major depression, bipolar disorders, and chronic hepatitis are the most costly medical conditions per individual. This suggests that current methods may underestimate the spending contributions of medical conditions, potentially leading to undesirable incentives related to care.

Shahraki & Ghaderi (2019) examine the causal relationship between public health expenditure and health status in upper-middle-income countries. The analysis of annual time series data revealed a positive correlation between public health expenditure and health status, indicating that increased spending leads to improved health outcomes. A panel vector autoregression (PVAR) model was employed to examine the data, which highlighted that investments in health contribute to enhanced health and that a higher health status is associated with lower public health expenditure.

Büyükkör & Doğan (2024) predict the direction of the Borsa Istanbul 100 (BIST-100) index using tree-based ensemble machine learning (ML) methods. Technical indicators calculated after applying exponential smoothing to daily opening, closing, high, low, and volume data obtained for three years are considered as input variables of the model. In addition, the window lengths of the technical indicators were increased, and the input variables were expanded. In the study, Random Forest, XGBoost, and CatBoost were preferred as ensemble machine learning methods based on decision trees. Model parameters were optimized by the Bayesian search method. According to the findings, all the methods used achieved an accuracy rate between 89.7% and 90.4%. Considering the other performance evaluation criteria, XGBoost was found to be the best performing method.

A study conducted by Hu and Wang (2024) across 33 OECD countries between 2001 and 2017 examined the influence of public health expenditure on economic growth. The findings of the study indicate that public health expenditures exert a constraining influence on economic growth. The effect in question varies depending on a number of factors, including household consumption, labour costs and physical capital investments. The results demonstrate that when the value of household consumption surpasses the threshold of 9.63, the effect is positive, and the impact of public health expenditures increases. Similarly, when employee wages exceed the threshold of 10.57 and physical capital investments exceed the threshold of 8.73, the impact of public health expenditures is positive. These findings illustrate that the impact of public health expenditures on economic growth is complex and may vary depending on various factors.

In a study that presents an analysis of artificial intelligence techniques for estimating per capita health expenditure in Turkey, a number of different techniques were employed, including random forest, artificial neural network, multiple linear regression, support vector regression and relevance vector machine. The effectiveness of all of the artificial intelligence models was enhanced by the use of a genetic algorithm-based feature selection process. The hybrid GAFS-RF model demonstrated the most favourable performance (Ceylan and Atalan, 2020).

Ozyilmaz et al. (2022) examine the impact of health expenditures on economic growth in 27 EU countries over the period 2000-2019. The results are presented in numerical form, and the regression problems are emphasized. Some classification issues are addressed. The bidirectional causality rates between health expenditures and economic growth are calculated. Health expenditures have a positive effect on economic growth, but the effects are widespread across countries. Government health expenditures are among the most important expenditures in terms of economic growth. Various regression models are designed to simulate the data and analyze the performance.

Gillani et al. (2021) examine the relationship between public health expenditure and health outcomes in nine Asian economies between 2000 and 2018. The findings indicate that immunization, GDP per capita, trade openness, and basic water service utilization are associated with a reduction in under-five and infant mortality in Asian economies. However, an increase in ecological footprint has been identified as a contributing factor to these deaths due to environmental damage. The results highlight the pivotal role of health in achieving sustainable development and the MDGs and SDGs.

The present study examines the interrelationship between oil revenue, health expenditure, and economic growth in Nigeria. The findings indicate that there is a bidirectional relationship between total health expenditure and real GDP, whereas a unidirectional relationship exists between oil revenue and GDP. The study proposes that the government should optimize the utilization of oil revenue, eliminate loopholes, and augment public expenditure on health in order to enhance productivity and stimulate economic growth (Awoyemi & Nwibe, 2022).

The objective of the study conducted by Satish et al. (2024) was to predict the surface water quality index using a causal forest. The study analyzes the causal status of variables on water quality by comparing the density of machine editing, artificial neural networks, and ensemble models.

Lee et al. (2024) use BPN-based causality analysis on Korean companies' HR practices to identify causal relationships between HR practices and firm performance. Results show compensation-related HR practices are most influential in predicting sales and employee turnover.

A novel method for identifying air quality in China was proposed using causality analysis-based significance tests and machine-learning algorithms. The study analyzed meteorological factors such as temperature, humidity, precipitation, wind speed, air pressure, sunshine duration, evaporation, and grand surface temperature, as well as industrial pollutants like NO2, SO2, CO, and O-3. Joint regression models were established to quantify the influence of different factors on PM2.5. Different classification models, including KNN, SVM, ensemble, and decision tree, were trained and tested. An accuracy of 90.2% was achieved with the ensemble classifier (Wang, 2019).

The automatic detection of abnormalities in control data is a more straightforward and efficacious process than manual detection. A variety of methodologies, including artificial neural networks (ANN), support vector machines (SVM), and fuzzy logic, are employed to identify anomalous patterns in real time. Researchers employed a weighting strategy with ANN to evaluate its performance relative to conventional ANN under diverse conditions. The weighting policy enhanced the prediction of minority class samples (Ünlü, 2019).

Yu and Reiff-Marganiec (2022), in their study, introduce a novel approach to developing causality-focused knowledge learning for machines, enabling them to gain causality and probability knowledge for inference and accurate prediction of diseases. This approach, built on a causal probability description logic framework, combines natural language processing, causality analysis, and extended knowledge graph technologies. The experimental work has processed 801 diseases, demonstrating the machine's efficient learning of comprehensive health causal knowledge and relations among diseases, symptoms, and other facts.

In their work, Zeng et al. (2021) put forth a multi-view deep learning framework for forecasting future healthcare expenditures at the individual level, based on historical claims data. The multi-view approach effectively models heterogeneous information, including patient demographics, medical codes, drug utilization, and facility utilization. The empirical results on a real-world pediatric dataset comprising over 450,000 patients demonstrate that the proposed method outperforms existing approaches in predicting medical expenditures.

METHODS

Random Forest Regression

Random forest (RF) is a classification and regression model introduced in 1984 by Breiman et al. Random Forest Regressor is an ensemble learning algorithm comprising multiple decision trees, with results generated according to the predictions of each tree. It is also a commonly employed method for determining the importance of variables.

This non-parametric model is a collection Classification and Regression Tree (CART). The model comprises a set of decision nodes and leaf nodes, which are connected in a tree structure. The decision nodes are responsible for evaluating the samples that are fed into them and then passing the sample information to the branches by a test function (Li et al., 2018). Let X be the input vector comprising m features and Y be the output variable. The training set A, consisting of t observations, is expressed as in Equation 1.

$$A_t = \{(X_1, Y_1), (X_2, Y_2), \ldots, (X_t, Y_t)\}, X \in R^m, Y \in R \quad (1)$$

In the process of training the RF model, a number of independent trees are created. Bagging is an ensemble technique that combines all the generated trees. The process of model aggregation is accomplished through the averaging of the outputs produced by all trees. The output Y is expressed as in Equation 2 (Li et al., 2018).

$$\hat{Y}_l = \frac{1}{p}\sum_{l=1}^{p}\hat{h}\left(X, A_n^{\theta_l}\right) \tag{2}$$

Where $\hat{Y}_l$ is the output of the lth tree, $\hat{h}$ is the prediction function, θ_l is the independent family and l =1, 2,..., p.

Machine Learning Based Causality Analysis

The integration of causality with machine learning is based on a number of theories from the fields of statistics and philosophy. Notable contributions in this regard include Judea Pearl's causal models and Rubin's causal inference framework. The majority of traditional machine learning models prioritize the identification of correlations between data. However, these models prioritize the identification of superficial relationships over the discovery of causal relationships. In his 2009 work, "Causality," Judea Pearl... The publication of "Models, Reasoning, and Inference" marked a significant turning point in this regard. Pearl posits that cause-effect relationships cannot be fully understood with observational data alone, and that a more comprehensive theoretical framework is necessary for their comprehension. In particular, he posits that causal relationships between variables should be modeled using causality graphs. Pearl's approach provides a fundamental framework for understanding causality in machine learning algorithms.

Causality is the scientific discipline concerned with the study of cause and effect. In particular, it seeks to elucidate the manner in which causes give rise to effects. In most cases, causality is associated with correlation. However, it is not possible to infer from the relationship or correlation between two variables that one causes the other (Naser and Tapeh, 2023).

Causality analysis is a method that is employed with the objective of elucidating the causal relationship between two or more variables. Causality analysis has a wide range of applications in various academic disciplines, including economics, the social sciences, and health. In the context of healthcare, it is of paramount importance to examine the impact of government health expenditures on health outcomes. This is a crucial step in understanding the effectiveness of health policies and the direct consequences of these expenditures on the healthcare system. Machine learning-based causal analysis represents a powerful tool for elucidating the effects of overall government health spending in the healthcare domain. By employing data from various datasets, this analysis enables an examination of the relationship between health spending and a range of influencing factors. The primary challenge in causality analysis is to accurately decompose the effects of independent variables on the outcome variable. It is frequently unfeasible to ascertain the precise causal relationships due to the influence of endogenous factors, potential biases, or other intervening variables. A variety of techniques are employed to examine the impact of health expenditures. In this study, causal forest algorithm is employed.

Causal Forest is a version of the Random Forest algorithm developed by Athey and Imbens (2016) adapted to causal inference.The Causal Forest method represents a significant contribution to the field of statistical inference, having been developed within the domain of machine learning. Causal Forest is a machine learning method that extends beyond traditional regression techniques, focusing on the estimation of heterogeneous treatment effects (HTE). This approach differentiates the impact of a specific treatment or intervention by accounting for subgroup differences within a data set. In particular, it is a method developed to elucidate cause-and-effect relationships in observational data sets. It is based on the classical random forest algorithm, but the objective is not classification or prediction, but rather the estimation of causal effects.

Causal forests are a data partitioning technique that estimate a separate treatment effect for each subsample, with the aim of minimizing the expected mean squared error (EMSE) between the predicted and actual treatment effects. In the context of a vector of covariates x and an unbiased estimator $\hat{\tau}(x)$ of a conditional average treatment effect $\tau(x)$, the EMSE is minimized by maximizing the quantity $Q=E[\tau^2(x)]-E[Var(\hat{\tau}(x))]$. Q can be predicted as in Equation 3 (Miller, 2020).

$$\widehat{Q} = \frac{1}{N_{tr}}\sum_i \hat{\tau}^2(x_i) - \left(\frac{1}{N_{tr}} - \frac{1}{N_{est}}\right)\sum_i \widehat{Var}\left(\hat{\tau}^2(x_i)\right) \qquad (3)$$

where; i indexes observations and N_{tr} and N_{est} represent the number of observations in training and prediction datasets, respectively

Placebo Tests for Causal Inference

A placebo test is a methodology employed to ascertain the veracity of the assumptions that underpin a research design. In a placebo test, a researcher seeks to identify an association that is more likely to be present if the underlying hypotheses are violated than if they are upheld. Consequently, this test offers substantial proof of a relationship exists and the validity of the assumptions and identifies the necessity for sensitivity analysis (Eggers et al., 2024).

Consider H_0 as representing the null hypothesis, which asserts that the foundational assumptions of the research design are valid. Conversely, let H_1 represent the alternative hypothesis, suggesting that these assumptions are violated in a specified manner. Assume there are nnn placebo tests conducted (with n=1 being a particularly significant case), each yielding a binary outcome: a "failing" test implies rejection of the null hypothesis, while a "passing" test indicates non-rejection. Let p_0 represent the likelihood of a failing test under the truth of H_0, and let p_1 signify the probability of a failing test when H_1 is true (indicating the true positive rate, sensitivity, or test power). For simplicity, we assume that all n tests share the same p_0 and p_1 and are conditionally independent, though this assumption can be readily extended (Eggers et al., 2024).

A common approach in causal inference is to conduct a placebo test using the difference-in-differences method. Equation 4 represent a placebo test in this context.

$$Y_{it} = \alpha + \beta Post_t + \gamma Treatment_i + \delta(Post_t \times Treatment_i) + \varepsilon_{it} \tag{4}$$

where; Y_{it} outcome variable for unit i at time t, α, constant term, β, coefficient for the post-treatment period, γ, coefficient for the treatment group indicator, δ, interaction term capturing the treatment effect, ϵ_{it}, error term. For a placebo test, create a "fake" treatment period where no real treatment was applied. If δ\deltaδ is significant in this context, it indicates potential bias or pre-treatment trends.

EXPERIMENTS AND ANALYZES

Study Design

The objective of the causality study on government health expenditures is to examine, in depth, the effects of inputs such as alcohol and cigarette consumption, the net savings rate, suicides per capita, alcohol and drug-related deaths, and life expectancy. The preliminary stage of the study entails the gathering of pertinent data. In this process, state statistical institutes, international reports, and survey results were employed as data sources, selected for their accuracy and reliability. The data used in the study and their explanations are given in Table 1.

Table 1. Description of features

Features	Data Type	Discription	Data Source
Time Period	Date	Years between 1970 and 2021	
Country	Nominal	Data from France, Germany, the United States of America, the United Kingdom and Japan were used	
Deaths	Numeric	Deaths per 100,000 people due to suicide, alcohol and drugs	OECD
Median Life Expectation of Individuals (Male)	Numeric	The average years a 60-year-old man is expected to live	OECD
Median Life Expectation of Individuals (Female)	Numeric	The average years a 60-year-old woman is expected to live	OECD
Net Savings	Numeric	Percentage of GDP saved by households, enterprises and government	OECD
Cigarette Consumption	Numeric	Total daily cigarette consumption of people over 15 years of age	OECD
Alcohol Consumption	Numeric	Annual sales in litres of pure alcohol per person aged 15 years and over	OECD
Income	Numeric	US dollars/capita	OECD
Health Spending	Numeric	Percentage of health spending	OECD

Missing or outlier data were removed to make the collected data suitable for analysis. Isolation Forest is an efficient, fast, and adaptive outlier detection algorithm. The Isolation Forest algorithm is based on random partitioning and isolation logic and provides effective solutions especially for large and complex data sets. In this study, the Isolation Forest algorithm is used for outlier detection.

Model Training with Random Forest Algorithm

A model was developed for forecasting health expenditure using the random forest regressor algorithm. In order to assess the performance of the model more reliably, the k-fold cross-validation method was used. In k-fold cross-validation, the data set is divided into k equal parts, and each time one part is used as test data, while the remaining parts are used for training. This process is repeated k times and each part is evaluated once as test data. This method is often used to measure the overall performance of the model and to avoid problems such as overfitting.

Table 2. Random forest regressor model evaluation

10-Fold Cross-Validation	20-Fold Cross-Validation
Average R^2: 0.8905 Standard Deviation (R^2): 0.0637	Average R^2: 0.8905 Standard Deviation (R^2): 0.0837

Table 2 shows that the average R^2 value as a result of the k-fold cross-validation process is 0.8905, which indicates that the model can explain 89% of the dependent variable. This high R^2 value indicates that the model performs well.

The model includes a dependent variable (outcome), a treatment variable (treatment), and several control variables. The correct results of the model depend on careful specification of the dependent, treatment, and control variables. This approach allows to reveal the true effect of the treatment variable on the dependent variable, thus obtaining reliable and valid results that are appropriate for the purpose of the study.

Causal Effects Results

The proportion of health expenditure within the total government budget was identified and subjected to analysis as an output variable. In the context of this analysis, each input variable is regarded as a treatment effect, with the objective of measuring its impact on health expenditures. The causal forest method, employed within the framework of the causality approach, was utilized to conduct a comprehensive analysis of the influence of each input variable on health expenditures. This approach allowed for a more detailed examination, encompassing both direct and potential indirect effects. Consequently, the factors that influence health expenditures and the extent of their effects have been determined.

In the Causal Forest model architecture, a random forest regressor was employed as the treatment model to estimate the treatment effect. Random forest regressor was similarly utilized to estimate the dependent variable (percentage of health expenditure). The random state parameter was set to 0 to guarantee that the treatments in the model yield identical results in each run. This parameter ensures the reproducibility of the model's results.

Results of treatment effects of inputs are given in Table 3. According to the results, the average treatment effect values of MLE (Male), MLE (Female), Net Savings, Cigarette Consumption, Alcohol Consumption, and Income inputs are -1.32, -2.8240, -0.3280, -0.3280, -0.0007, -0.1184, and 0.0021, respectively. It is evident that the MLE (Male) and MLE (Female) variables exert a considerable influence on health expenditure. Upon examination of the maximum and minimum effects, it becomes apparent that the treatment effect attains exceptionally high negative and positive values, particularly for a subset of individuals. Other variables were found to have a very low treatment effect.

Table 3. Treatment effect of inputs

Treatment Variables	Average Treatment Effect	Max Treatment Effect	Min Treatment Effect
Median Life Expectation of Individuals (Male)	-2.3666	5.7819	-31.4011
Median Life Expectation of Individuals (Female)	-2.8240	4.2204	-16.4545
Net Savings	-0.3280	1.8781	-1.6435
Cigarette Consumption	-0.0007	0.0028	-0.0046
Alcohol Consumption	-0.1184	1.1795	-2.0888
Income	0.0021	0.0080	-0.0085

Table 4 shows the findings of the placebo treatment effects of the inputs. Placebo treatment effect, indicates treatment effects obtained with a mock test in which the treatment variable is confounded (randomized).

According to the results; the placebo treatment effect for the MLE (Male) input was calculated as -0.055. The placebo effect is much smaller and negatively smaller than the original treatment effect. This indicates that the original treatment effect may be significant, while the placebo effect does not lead to a random change in the output. For the MLE (Female) input, the placebo test mean effect was positive (2.824), with the opposite sign and the same value as the treatment effect. This shows that the effect of the treatment variable provides strong evidence and can be considered significant in the model. The placebo treatment effect of the net savings and income variables were calculated as 0.011, and -0.0002, respectively. These values are close to zero and low, indicating that the placebo treatment effect is insignificant. The placebo test demonstrates that this effect is not random and that the model is reliable. It can be stated that net savings has a decreasing effect on health expenditures. While income was found to have a slightly increasing effect on health expenditures.

Table 4. Placebo treatment effect of inputs

Treatment Variables	Placebo Average Treatment Effect	Placebo Max Treatment Effect	Placebo Min Treatment Effect
Median Life Expectation of Individuals (Male)	-0.0550	0.4504	-0.5919
Median Life Expectation of Individuals (Female)	2.8240	16.4545	-4.2204
Net Savings	0.0110	0.2163	-0.2603
Income	-0.0002	0.0001	-0.0014

Heterogeneity Analysis by Country

The effect of life expectancy after 60 years of age for men and women on health expenditures by countries is given in Table 5. According to the results, the average life expectancy after 60 years of age in countries has been found to reduce health expenditures. The MLE (Male) treatment variable shows an effect that reduces health expenditures in France, USA, UK, Germany and Japan by 3.03%, 6.89%, 3.21%, 6.26% and 3.78% respectively. The effects of the MLE (Female) treatment variable on the health expenditures of the same countries are -1.73%, -3.47%, -2.49%, -5.4% and -0.79%, respectively.

The findings demonstrate that the impact of treatment variables varies across countries, with the USA and the United Kingdom exhibiting more pronounced effects. The discrepancies observed may be attributed to a number of factors, including country-specific characteristics, variations in health systems, and demographic differences.

Table 5. Treatment effect by country

Country	Median Life Expectation of Individuals (Male) Average Treatment Effect	Median Life Expectation of Individuals (Female) Average Treatment Effect
France	-3.026335712	-1.733524921
United States	-6.892262185	-3.472151939
Germany	-3.206846831	-2.494047676
United Kingdom	-6.27857501	-5.400232541
Japan	-3.781616853	-0.787030359

CONCLUSION

Predicting government health expenditure is essential for ensuring the sustainability and effectiveness of public healthcare systems. Accurate forecasts help policymakers allocate resources efficiently to address the growing demands of aging populations, emerging diseases, and healthcare innovation. By anticipating future costs, governments can plan for adequate funding of hospitals, medical research, and preventive care programs, reducing the risk of service disruptions or budget shortfalls. Predicting health expenditures also enables better preparedness for health crises, such as pandemics, by allowing for the timely investment in emergency response infrastructure. Moreover, accurate health expenditure forecasts contribute to equitable access to healthcare, ensuring that vulnerable populations receive necessary services without financial barriers. Overall, such predictions are key to fostering a resilient, accessible, and sustainable healthcare system.

The random forest regressor method offers several key advantages that make it a robust choice for regression tasks. Its ensemble approach, combining predictions from multiple decision trees, enhances accuracy and reduces the risk of overfitting compared to individual models. Additionally, it can handle both numerical and categorical data effectively and is resilient to noise, making it suitable for complex datasets. The method also provides insights into feature importance, aiding in better interpretability of the model. Moreover, its ability to parallelize tree construction ensures scalability and efficiency, even with large datasets, making it a versatile and reliable tool in predictive analytics.

Causal inference, also known as causality, is the methodology employed to ascertain the causal relationships between variables within a system. In other words, it is the scientific study of how alterations in one variable (the cause) influence another variable (the effect or treatment). Causal inference can play an important role in governments' strategies and government expenditure. In this study, the effects on health expenditures in France, USA, United Kingdom, Germany and Japan are investigated. According to the results of the random forest regressor algorithm, it was found that the inputs explained 89% of the health expenditure output. As a result of causality analysis, it was found that the average life expectancy of men and women over 60 years of age has a significant effect on health expenditures. When evaluated on a country basis, the life expectancy of men and women over the age of 60 in the USA has a negative impact on health expenditures, with a reduction of 6.89% and 3.47%, respectively. In the United Kingdom, these effects are -6.27% and -5.40%, respectively. Net Savings and Income variables were found to have a slight effect on health expenditures, while cigarette consumption was found to have no effect on expenditures.

The estimation of health expenditures represents a complex modeling challenge. Future research endeavors aim to enhance health expenditure forecasting and conduct causality analyses by incorporating additional variables beyond in this study utilized. Moreover, expanding the sample size to include a greater number of countries would enable a more comprehensive analysis of the determinants of health expenditures, particularly in developed, developing and underdeveloped nations. Examining the effects of expenditures in areas such as education, energy, law, transportation, and other sectors through causality analysis—an emerging area of study—has the potential to significantly contribute to understanding the pathways to national development.

REFERENCES

Athey, S., & Imbens, G. (2016). Recursive partitioning for heterogeneous causal effects. *Proceedings of the National Academy of Sciences of the United States of America*, 113(27), 7353–7360. PMID: 27382149

Atilgan, E., Ertuğrul, H. M., Baycan, O., & Ulucan, H. (2024). Health-led growth hypothesis and health financing systems: An econometric synthesis for OECD countries. *Frontiers in Public Health*, 12. Advance online publication. DOI: 10.3389/fpubh.2024.1437304 PMID: 39114507

Awoyemi, O. B., & Nwibe, D. A. (2022). A Causal Assessment of Nigeria's Crude Oil Revenue, Health Expenditure, and Economic Growth. *International Journal of Energy Economics and Policy*, 12(5), 420–424.

Baltagi, B. H., & Moscone, F. (2010). Health care expenditure and income in the OECD reconsidered: Evidence from panel data. *Economic Modelling*, 27(4), 804–811.

Barro, R. J. (1996). Health and Economic Growth. *Journal of Political Economy*, 94(5), S56–S71.

Bloom, D. E., & Canning, D. (2000). The Health and Wealth of Nations. *Science*, 287(5456), 1207–1209. PMID: 10712155

Breiman, L. (2017). *Classification and regression trees*. Routledge.

Büyükkör, Y., & Doğan, S. (2024). Borsa Endeks Yönünün Ağaç Tabanlı Topluluk Makine Öğrenmesi Yöntemleri ile Tahmini: BİST-100 Örneği. *Bingöl Üniversitesi Sosyal Bilimler Enstitüsü Dergisi*, 27, 324–335.

Carbo-Valverde, S., Cuadros-Solas, P., & Rodríguez-Fernández, F. (2020). A machine learning approach to the digitalization of bank customers: Evidence from random and causal forests. *PLoS One*, 15(10), e0240362. PMID: 33112894

Ceylan, Z., & Atalan, A. (2020). Estimation of healthcare expenditure per capita of Turkey using artificial intelligence techniques with genetic algorithm-based feature selection.

Chen, T., & Guestrin, C. (2016). XGBoost: A Scalable Tree Boosting System. *Proceedings of the 22nd ACM SIGKDD International Conference on Knowledge Discovery and Data Mining*.

Devlin, N., & Hansen, P. (2001). Health care spending and economic output: Granger causality. *Applied Economics Letters*, 8(8), 561–564.

Dinçer, H., & Yuksel, S. (2019). Identifying the Causality Relationship between Health Expenditure and Economic Growth: An Application on E7 Countries. DergiPark (Istanbul University). https://dergipark.org.tr/tr/pub/jhesp/issue/39338/413742

Eggers, A. C., Tuñón, G., & Dafoe, A. (2024). Placebo tests for causal inference. *American Journal of Political Science*, 68(3), 1106–1121.

Elek, P., & Bíró, A. (2021). Regional differences in diabetes across Europe – regression and causal forest analyses. *Economics and Human Biology*, 40, 100948. PMID: 33276258

Gillani, D. Q., Gillani, S. S., Naeem, M. Z., Spulbar, C., Coker-Farrell, E., Ejaz, A., & Birau, R. (2021). The Nexus between Sustainable Economic Development and Government Health Expenditure in Asian Countries Based on Ecological Footprint Consumption. *Sustainability*, 13(12), 6824.

Güler, M., & Namlı, E. (2022). Skin Cancer Detection with Deep Learning Methods Using Medical Images. *ROMAYA Journal Researches on Multidisiplinary Approaches*, (3), 1–10.

Habehh, H., & Gohel, S. (2021). Machine learning in healthcare. *Current Genomics*, 22(4), 291. PMID: 35273459

Hermont, R., & Reynoso-Meza, G. (2023). *Predictive Maintenance Strategies in agriculture using Survival Analysis*. Predictive Maintenance Strategies in Agriculture Using Survival Analysis.

Hu, Q., & Wang, L. (2024). Economic growth effects of public health expenditure in OECD countries: An empirical study using the dynamic panel threshold model. *Heliyon*, 10(4), e25684. DOI: 10.1016/j.heliyon.2024.e25684 PMID: 38370248

Ito, K., Bansal, P., & Biljecki, F. (2024). Examining the causal impacts of the built environment on cycling activities using time-series street view imagery. *Transportation Research Part A, Policy and Practice*, 190, 104286.

Kamanda, E., Lanpin, Y., & Sesay, B. (2022). Causal nexus between health expenditure, health outcome and economic growth: Empirical evidence from Sub-Saharan Africa countries. *The International Journal of Health Planning and Management*, 37(4), 2284–2302. DOI: 10.1002/hpm.3469 PMID: 35393680

La Mastra, C., Barchitta, M., Maugeri, A., & Agodi, A. (2024). Application of artificial intelligence to study the causality in public health: a systematic review. European Journal of Public Health, 34(Supplement_3)

Lee, M., Lee, G., Lim, K., Moon, H., & Doh, J. (2024). Machine Learning-Based Causality Analysis of human resource practices on firm performance. *Administrative Sciences*, 14(4), 75.

Lee, S., Lee, J., & Jun, C. (2015). Causality Analysis for Public and Private Expenditures on Health Using Panel Granger-Causality Test. *Industrial Engineering & Management Systems*, 14(1), 104–110. DOI: 10.7232/iems.2015.14.1.104

Li, Y., Zou, C., Berecibar, M., Nanini-Maury, E., Chan, J. C. W., Van den Bossche, P., & Omar, N. (2018). Random forest regression for online capacity estimation of lithium-ion batteries. *Applied Energy*, 232, 197–210.

Miller, S. (2020). Causal forest estimation of heterogeneous and time-varying environmental policy effects. *Journal of Environmental Economics and Management*, 103, 102337.

Nadim, K., Ragab, A., & Ouali, M. (2022). Data-driven dynamic causality analysis of industrial systems using interpretable machine learning and process mining. *Journal of Intelligent Manufacturing*, 34(1), 57–83.

Naser, M. Z., & Tapeh, A. T. G. (2023). Causality, causal discovery, causal inference and counterfactuals in Civil Engineering: Causal machine learning and case studies for knowledge discovery. *Computers and Concrete*, 31(4), 277–292.

Newhouse, J. P. (1992). Medical Care Costs: How Much Welfare Loss? *The Journal of Economic Perspectives*, 6(3), 3–21. PMID: 10128078

Obermeyer, Z., & Emanuel, E. J. (2016). Predicting the Future: Big Data, Machine Learning, and Clinical Medicine. *The New England Journal of Medicine*, 375(13), 1216–1219. PMID: 27682033

Ozyilmaz, A., Bayraktar, Y., Isik, E., Toprak, M., Er, M. B., Besel, F., Aydin, S., Olgun, M. F., & Collins, S. (2022). The Relationship between Health Expenditures and Economic Growth in EU Countries: Empirical Evidence Using Panel Fourier Toda–Yamamoto Causality Test and Regression Models. *International Journal of Environmental Research and Public Health*, 19(22), 15091. PMID: 36429808

Pearl, J. (2009). *Causality*. Cambridge University Press.

Rose, S. (2018). Robust Machine Learning Variable Importance Analyses of Medical Conditions for Health Care Spending. *Health Services Research*, 53(5), 3836–3854. DOI: 10.1111/1475-6773.12848 PMID: 29527659

Rossen, B., & Faroque, A. (2016). Diagnosing the Causes of Rising Health-Care Expenditure in Canada: Does Baumol's Cost Disease Loom Large? *American Journal of Health Economics*, 2(2), 184–212. DOI: 10.1162/ajhe_a_00041

Sart, G. (2023b). Education and Health Expenditures: Evidence From the New EU Member States. In Advances in healthcare information systems and administration book series (pp. 237–247)

Satish, N., Anmala, J., Varma, M. R. R., & Rajitha, K. (2024). Performance of Machine Learning, Artificial Neural Network (ANN), and Stacked Ensemble Models in Predicting Water Quality Index (WQI) from Surface Water Quality Parameters, Climatic and Land Use Data. *Process Safety and Environmental Protection.*

Şentürk, C., Sart, G., Şaşmaz, M. Ü., & Bayar, Y. (2023). Health Expenditures, Human Capital, and Sustainable Development: Panel Evidence from the New EU Member Countries. *Sustainability*, 15(19), 14514.

Shahraki, M., & Ghaderi, S. (2019). Investigating the Causal Relationship between Public Health Expenditure and Health Status; Panel Vector Self-Regression Model. *Health Research Journal*, 4(4), 220–226. DOI: 10.29252/hrjbaq.4.4.220

Tao, Y., Xia, Y., Zheng, X., Ding, H., Fang, Y., Tian, C., & Ma, P. (2024). Application of Bayesian Causal Inference in the Study of the Relationship Between Biodiversity and Aboveground Biomass of Subtropical Forest in Eastern China. *Forests*, 15(11), 1841.

Taskaya, S., & Demirkiran, M. (2016). The Causality between Healthcare Resources and Health Expenditures in Turkey. A Granger Causality Method. *International Journal of Academic Research in Accounting Finance and Management Sciences*, 6(2). Advance online publication. DOI: 10.6007/ijarafms/v6-i2/2075

Türküz, E., & Akay, E. (2020). Ekonometri ve Makine Öğrenmesi: Tercih Modelleri ve Sınıflandırma Algoritmaları Açısından Değerlendirmeler. *Social Sciences Research Journal*, 9(4), 181–194.

Ünlü, R. (2019). An assessment of imbalanced control chart pattern recognition by artificial neural networks. In *Artificial Intelligence and Machine Learning Applications in Civil* (pp. 240–258). Mechanical, and Industrial Engineering. DOI: 10.4018/978-1-7998-0301-0.ch013

Varian, H. R. (2014). Big Data: New Tricks for Econometrics. *The Journal of Economic Perspectives*, 28(2), 3–28.

Venkatasubramaniam, A., Mateen, B. A., Shields, B. M., Hattersley, A. T., Jones, A. G., Vollmer, S. J., & Dennis, J. M. (2023). Comparison of causal forest and regression-based approaches to evaluate treatment effect heterogeneity: An application for type 2 diabetes precision medicine. *BMC Medical Informatics and Decision Making*, 23(1), 110. PMID: 37328784

Wang, B. (2019). Applying Machine-Learning Methods Based on Causality Analysis to Determine Air Quality in China. *Polish Journal of Environmental Studies*, 28(5), 3877–3885.

Wang, J., Qin, Z., Hsu, J., & Zhou, B. (2024). A fusion of machine learning algorithms and traditional statistical forecasting models for analyzing American healthcare expenditure. *Healthcare Analytics*, 5, 100312.

Wasim, A., Hanif, U., & Kanwal, W. (2023). Economic Development and Public Health Expenditures Nexus for South Asian Countries. *Journal of Development and Social Sciences*, 4(IV). Advance online publication. DOI: 10.47205/jdss.2023(4-iv)40

Yu, H. Q., & Reiff-Marganiec, S. (2022). Learning Disease Causality Knowledge From the Web of Health Data. *International Journal on Semantic Web and Information Systems*, 18(1), 1–19.

Zeng, X., Lin, S., & Liu, C. (2021). Multi-View Deep Learning Framework for Predicting Patient Expenditure in Healthcare. *IEEE Open Journal of the Computer Society*, 2, 62–71. DOI: 10.1109/ojcs.2021.3052518

Chapter 10
Air Quality Index Prediction in Istanbul Based on Machine Learning Methods

Mustafa Güler
https://orcid.org/0000-0002-9289-5088
Istanbul University, Turkey

ABSTRACT

Istanbul, hosting millions of tourists annually, faces significant air pollution challenges, impacting both health and climate. The air quality index (AQI) is vital for assessing pollution and its health effects. This study predicts AQI levels in Istanbul using machine learning models (XGBoost and ANN), focusing on pollutants like PM10, NO2, CO, SO2, and O3, with data from 2021-2023. Ensemble methods incorporating meteorological data (temperature, pressure, wind) improved accuracy. Forecasted AQI levels range from "good" to "hazardous," offering actionable insights. The models achieved low error rates, underscoring their effectiveness in supporting air quality management and sustainable health policies through reliable AQI predictions.

INTRODUCTION

Air quality is a global issue with significant impacts on human health and the environment. Respiratory diseases are among the many health risks from polluted air. Each year, around 7 million people worldwide die from air pollution. Additionally, air pollution can lead to global warming, a process that traps heat in the

DOI: 10.4018/979-8-3373-2272-8.ch010

air, causing temperature increases, rising sea levels, and diseases associated with the hot climate (Simkovich et al., 2019). All countries are taking a global emergency position to avert the climate crisis. According to the Framework Convention on Climate Change proposed by the United Nations, there is a lot of work that each country has committed to (Lelieveld, et al., 2018). For instance, Turkey has committed to moving towards zero emissions and sustainable development goals. In this regard, Turkey has a lot of responsibilities. Especially in cities with large populations, such as Istanbul, Ankara, and Izmir, they have many responsibilities to protect the environment, such as the greenhouse gas effect, carbon emissions, and preventing water pollution.

The air quality index (AQI) is a pivotal metric for evaluating air quality. It plays a crucial role in assessing the cleanliness of the air by quantifying various pollutants and their potential health impacts. The AQI calculation provides a comprehensive understanding of air quality levels, facilitating informed decisions and actions to protect public health and the environment. Accurate calculation of AQI ensures timely implementation of measures to reduce the adverse effects of air pollution and protect public health. We can prevent pollution from affecting people by warning them whenever the AQI exceeds the maximum value. The AQI alerts people about the quality of the air they breathe, informs them about the groups it may impact, and provides them with preventive measures. Polluted air can have a variety of health effects within hours to days of being breathed (Kumar and Goyal, 2021).

One essential indicator for assessing air quality is the air quality index. It is essential for evaluating the quality of the air since it measures different contaminants and their possible effects on health. A thorough knowledge of air quality levels is obtained through the computation of AQI, allowing for the taking of well-informed choices and measures to protect the environment and public health (Plaia and Ruggieri, 2011). It is possible to shield individuals from the effects of pollution by alerting them anytime the AQI rises above the maximum level. People are informed about the AQI, including what groups are most vulnerable to air pollution and preventive measures they may take, as well as a warning about the quality of the air where they reside. Within hours to days of breathing it in, contaminated air can have a variety of negative health repercussions (Thurston, et al., 2016). The AQI is used to estimate the rate at which individuals might be impacted. Five pollutants are often used in the calculation of the air quality index: Carbon Monoxide (CO), Nitrogen Dioxides (NO_2), Ozone (O_3), Inhalable Particles (PM10), Sulfur Dioxide (SO_2), (Shend and Tang, 2016). Based on a random scale, AQI scores vary from 0 to 500. When the AQI is high, air pollution levels and health risks are often higher. It is regarded as excellent air quality when the index is 50 or below, and harmful when it is 300 or higher (Kumar and Goyal, 2021). According to the AQI, health issues are divided into six categories. To make the categories easier to understand, they are colour coded. The management and resolution of air pollution issues need time and work. Forecasts of air quality may be used to stop the harm that comes from air pollution. It is critical that air quality forecasts be completed on time in order to avert major pollution problems. For data prediction, there are several machine learning techniques accessible. Machine learning is the process of teaching an algorithm to recognize patterns in data and make choices based on this knowledge. Forecasting with machine learning methods has become very popular in recent years. Many researchers have successfully used machine learning methods in many different fields such as economics, health, military and security. However, there are successful studies in the literature on air quality measurement using machine learning methods (Yu et al., 2016). However, these studies have generally examined the time-dependent variation of particulate matter in the air or seasonal changes in air quality. In their study Almaliki et al., (2023), forecasted the air quality in the Mecca region. While calculating, five different parameters were used and three different machine and ensemble learning methods were used to find and compare the results. In another study, Paschalidou et al., (2011), used artificial neural networks and multiple regression models to predict airborne PM10 concentration in Cyprus using hourly data. In a similar study, Liu et al. (2019) estimated the air quality index in Beijing using random forest regression (RFR) and support vector regression (SVR). They obtained high accuracy from the comparative results. In another study, Yahya et al., (2014), focus on multi-year assessments of ozone (O_3) and fine particles PM2.5 using the WRF/Chem-MADRID model to predict air quality in the South-eastern US. They note that this model is successful for ozone, but has large biases for PM2.5. Finally, using deep learning models, Du et al. (2018) developed a deep learning model to improve PM2.5 forecasts. This model provides accurate forecasts by learning the spatial and temporal dependencies of time series data on air quality.

The main objective of this study is firstly to evaluate the air quality index in Istanbul, Turkey considering the main pollutants such as PM10, NO_2, CO, SO_2 and O_3. For this purpose, the values between 2021-2023 were used for the training and test set and models were created. XGBoost and ANN, which are machine learning methods, were used here. In addition, some optimization techniques and geographical values affecting air quality were used to increase the accuracy of the models used. Here, an ensemble forecasting approach is adopted by incorporating temperature, pressure and wind values that directly affect the particulate matter constituting the air quality index. Furthermore, the predicted AQI results are categorized into different levels from "good" to "hazardous". As a result, the study aims to contribute to reliable air quality management for the protection of health in order to understand how important AQI estimates are for human health and to continue sustainable health policies.

MATERIAL AND METHODS

Study Area and Data Used

This study was conducted in the region of Istanbul, Turkey. Istanbul is the most densely populated city among the 81 provinces of Turkey and is also one of the most important metropolises in the world. The following field was the focus of the study: The coordinates 41.0122 latitude and 28.976 longitude are between 41°0′44″ north and 28°58′34″ east. The total area of Istanbul is 5343.00 km^2. Istanbul is situated in the strait that separates the Black Sea from the Marmara Sea and connects the continents of Asia and Europe. Its strategic location has made it one of the world's most significant hubs for trade and transit throughout history. Due to the city's advantageous geopolitical position, several industrial and financial companies have established their Turkish headquarters there. The city offers every kind of transportation to facilitate business and industrial activity. Istanbul, having served as the capital of several civilizations over the ages, is a city rich in cultural and historical traditions. Because of this characteristic, the city welcomes millions of visitors each and consistently draws in both domestic and international visitors. Istanbul, home to over 18.5% of Turkey's total population, is growing more crowded due to increased commercial, cultural, and educational activity. As a result of this rapid population growth, unpreventable traffic density, industrial growth, wastes and fossil fuel consumption in the city result in high levels of exhaust and non-exhaust emissions and high amounts of dust clouds. The summer season in Istanbul has been very hot and dry, especially in recent years. Considering the four seasons, temperatures are around 22 degrees (Mutlu and Atahanlı, 2024). However, the average annual precipitation in Istanbul is around 800 mm. Although the highest precipitation is seen in winter and spring, this situation is inconsistent, especially due to global warming in recent years.

This study was conducted using 1095 data obtained daily between 2021 and 2023. These data are collected by the European statistical office for metropolitan cities to support zero emission, sustainability and carbon footprint studies in the world (URL-1). Since Istanbul is a very large city in terms of surface area, there are air quality measurement stations at many points of the city. The data used in the study are the data taken from Maslak district of Istanbul province. Maslak is one of the central districts of Istanbul. Air quality measurement stations measure many particulate matters in the air that are too small to be seen by the eye. Figures 1 and 2 show the study area from the maps of Turkey and Istanbul created in ArcGIS program.

Figure 1. Map of Istanbul, Turkey (ArcGIS view)

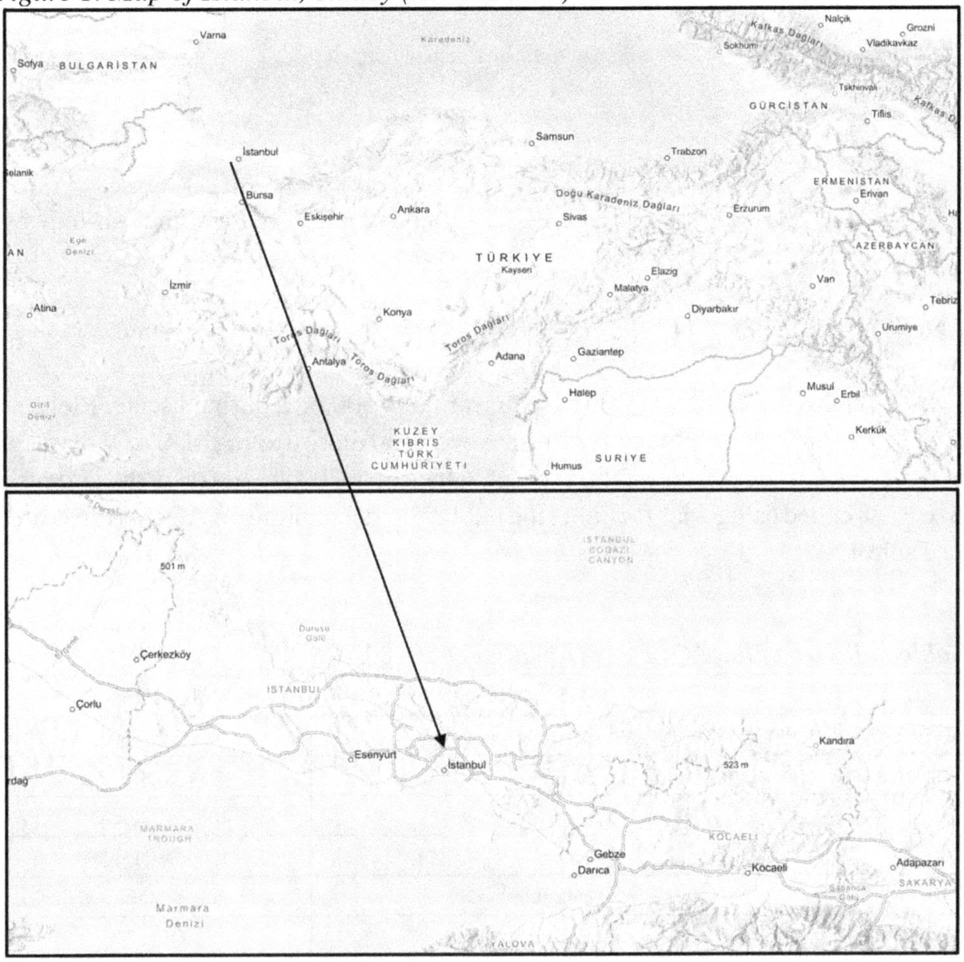

Air Quality Index Calculation

The air quality index (AQI) is an extensive metric of air pollution, including pollutants like NO_2, CO, SO_2, O_3, and PM10, recognized for their severe health effects. AQI is formulated to provide daily advice on preventing short-term health problems by transforming pollution concentrations through a piecewise linear function (Bruno and Cocchi, 2002). The AQI sub-index, represented as $I_{P,S}$, is calculated for each pollutant and station utilizing Equation (1), which takes into account concentration breakpoints (C_{High} and C_{Low}), pollutant concentration (C_p), and the associated breakpoint indices (I_{High} and I_{Low}).

$I_{P,S} =$

$$\frac{I_{High} - I_{Low}}{C_{High} - C_{Low}}$$

$$(C_p - C_{Low}) + I_{Low} \qquad (1)$$

The AQI for each station is calculated as the maximum value of the sub-indices, as show in below.

$$AQI_S = \max\,(I_{O3}, I_{Pm10}, I_{CO}, I_{SO2}, I_{NO2}) \qquad (2)$$

Air Quality Index (AQI) values span from 0 to 500 on a defined scale. Elevated AQI scores indicate heightened pollution levels and more health risks. AQI readings of ≤ 50 signify "good" air quality, whilst values of ≥ 300 are deemed "hazardous". Six color-coded categories facilitate the public's understanding of AQI, as illustrated in Table 1.

Table 1. Range of the AQI class (Almaliki et al., 2023).

Code	State	AQI Range
1	Good	AQI < 50
2	Moderate	50 < AQI < 100
3	Unhealthy for sensitive groups	100 < AQI < 150
4	Unhealthy	150 < AQI < 200
5	Very unhealthy	200 < AQI <300
6	Hazardous	AQI > 300

Figure 2 shows that flowchart depicting the functioning of the developed model for developing the predictive classification model. The model functions by calculating the AQI utilizing Equations (1). Consequently, the characteristics for each sample NO_2, CO, SO_2, O_3, and PM10 were utilized with the AQI as classifiers for the training data. The classifier that achieves the highest classification accuracy will forecast the new data and assess its robustness.

Figure 2. Model flowchart

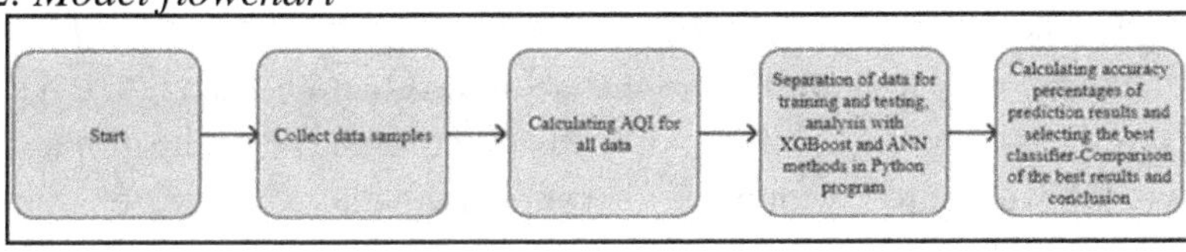

Data Classification and Models

Classification algorithms are employed in data analysis and machine learning to predict or categorize new instances based on the patterns and correlations observed in a labeled training dataset (Unlu and Xanthopoulos, 2021). Classification methods are advantageous when the target variable or intended outcome is discrete or categorical. Classification methods provide a systematic strategy to categorizing new occurrences based on historical patterns, facilitating decision-making, pattern detection, and prediction across numerous disciplines, including healthcare, finance, marketing, and engineering. However, prediction methods, just like classification methods, utilize past time series of data to perform validation and prediction processes. The methodology of this study is focused on estimating the AQI in Istanbul to study air pollution considering seasonal concentrations. In order to estimate the AQI, XGBoost and ANN method, which have given successful results in similar studies, are preferred. XGBoost and ANNs can be trained using Python's prediction learner package for predictive modeling. It may analyze the data, delineate attributes, establish validation processes, and evaluate outcomes. It displays the outcomes of multiple predictions, one or all of which have been selected. The models used utilize time series. In addition, the weight of particulate matter used in the calculation of the air quality index in the model and its effect on the result can also be analyzed in the python program. In this way, the error percentage of the predictions can be determined.

This procedure allows us to choose the most proficient model, which is then utilized to evaluate new data, leveraging its predictive capabilities to forecast results. The dataset used in the study includes meticulously collected air composition data from the pollution monitoring point located in the central district of Istanbul. The data were recorded daily in 2021-2023. The data included the concentration of several gases in the environment, utilized to determine the air quality index. These gases are NO_2, CO, SO_2, O_3, and PM10. The collected data included 1095 samples recorded daily from 1 January 2021 to 31 December 2023. This data is divided into two parts: the training part included 1035 data samples, and the testing part included 60 data samples. The data were employed to ascertain the air quality index (AQI), thereafter categorized into six classifications according to the AQI range presented in Table 1. The six classifications are good, moderate, unhealthy for sensitive groups, unhealthy, very unhealthy, and hazardous AQI status, designated as 1, 2, 3, 4, 5, and 6, respectively. In Table 2, AQI was calculated for each sample and each sample was classified into 6 groups. It also shows the classification examples of 15 randomly selected data samples.

Table 2. Random values and results

Date	NO_2	CO	SO_2	O_3	PM_{10}	AQI Value	AQI Category
15-Jan	54.56	7.16	17.83	11.30	27.26	54.56	Moderate
21-Jan	60.41	4.60	11.34	28.75	27.94	60.41	Moderate
5-May	49.37	3.02	48.96	39.41	51.88	51.88	Moderate
15-Jun	24.06	2.81	12.47	40.39	22.92	40.39	Good
1-Aug	38.47	0.76	7.44	37.87	35.42	38.47	Good
15-Oct	45.81	5.40	8.64	39.80	40.15	45.81	Good
5-Dec	42.58	5.75	17.06	23.17	38.13	42.58	Good
26-Feb	36.26	6.57	8.41	12.10	37.13	37.13	Good
6-Mar	66.93	4.92	7.67	17.56	46.94	66.93	Moderate
14-Apr	68.57	7.90	9.53	20.32	58.26	68.57	Moderate
27-Jul	24.04	3.01	8.54	29.56	21.89	29.56	Good
1-Sep	31.95	3.11	8.69	20.84	31.77	31.95	Good
10-Dec	59.76	2.48	9.71	9.06	37.82	59.76	Moderate
1-Jun	31.25	2.57	4.74	24.37	34.19	34.19	Good
15-Nov	59.13	5.55	12.64	9.27	57.81	59.13	Moderate

Extreme Gradient Boosting (XGBoost)

Artificial Neural Networks are widely utilized in multiple domains, particularly for applications involving classification, modeling, and prediction. The XGBoost method is an advanced algorithm within the field of artificial neural networks. It represents a state-of-the-art machine learning technique initially detailed by Chen and Guestrin. The published work garnered significant interest from data scientists. The XGBoost method represents an advanced iteration of the Gradient Boosting technique. The primary rationale for the widespread adoption of XGBoost is the significant advantages it offers compared to earlier versions. XGBoost utilizes the maximum depth parameter during the tree construction process. Pruning is performed when the tree shows signs of excessive downward growth. This method effectively reduces the occurrence of overlearning. XGBoost employs second-order functions for loss function calculation, whereas the Gradient Boosting method uses a first-order function to achieve the same goal (Chen and Guestrin, 2016).

XGBoost is a machine learning algorithm that falls under the category of boosting frameworks. Boosting is an ensemble technique that incrementally combines weak learners to create a strong learner. In the framework of XGBoost, decision trees are commonly utilized as the weak learners (Lewis, 1982). The core component of the methodology involves optimizing a regularized objective function that maintains a balance between the model's accuracy in representing the data and its overall complexity. (Eq. 3).

$$L(\theta) = \sum_{i=1}^{n} l\left(Y_i - \acute{y}_i\right) + \sum_{k=1}^{K} \Omega\left(f_k\right) \tag{3}$$

The variable, $L(\theta)$ represents the overall loss that needs be minimized, $\boldsymbol{l}$ represents a differentiable convex loss function measuring the discrepancy between the forecast $\acute{y}_i$ and the actual target Y_i, f_k denotes the term of regularization, defined as $\Omega, f_k = T + \frac{1}{2} \lambda \, ||W||^2$, with T representing the tree's number of leaves, The scores on leaves are denoted by W, is the complexity.

Artificial Neural Network (ANN)

An Artificial Neural Network (ANN) functions as a computational framework that employs interconnected processing units to collaboratively solve a specific problem. The objective is to replicate the operational mechanisms of the human brain through the identification of patterns between input and output data. Furthermore, artificial neural networks exhibit specific characteristics that are analogous to those of biological neural networks. A neural network is composed of multiple basic processing units referred to as neurons. Each individual neuron forms connections with other neurons, and these connections are assigned specific weights (Fausett, 2006). Artificial Neural Networks (ANN) have shown effectiveness in managing nonparametric data that exhibit nonlinear functions. This includes applications in employment prediction, credit scoring, stock market forecasting, business failure prediction, medicine, text mining, and image processing. Artificial Neural Networks (ANN) provide notable benefits over conventional statistical methods, mainly because of their diminished dependence on assumptions and their capacity to accurately model nonlinear relationships through the careful choice of activation functions. Acquiring knowledge about occurrences enables individuals to make informed decisions when faced with similar situations. Artificial neural networks (ANNs) that have undergone training can produce output despite insufficient data availability. Data is distributed across the network, and the elimination of certain brain cells does not lead to data loss (Xie et al, 2023). Multilayer Perceptron (MLP) is a prominent and extensively utilized type of artificial neural network (ANN). It is a general-purpose, adaptable, non-linear model composed of neurons arranged in multiple layers, enabling it to predict a variety of functions. The training of MLP is a commonly employed technique, attributed to the accessibility of numerous learning algorithms. MLP constitutes a category of neural networks characterized by the presence of an input layer, one or multiple hidden layers, and an output layer. The system operates using a feed-forward architecture. Each neuron within a specific layer establishes connections with all neurons in the following layer, leading to a one-way flow of information from the input layer to the output layer. The system functions based on a supervised learning approach, where both input data and their associated output values are provided to the network throughout the training process (Mutascu and Hegerty, 2023).

Figure 3. Multi-layer perceptron ANN structure

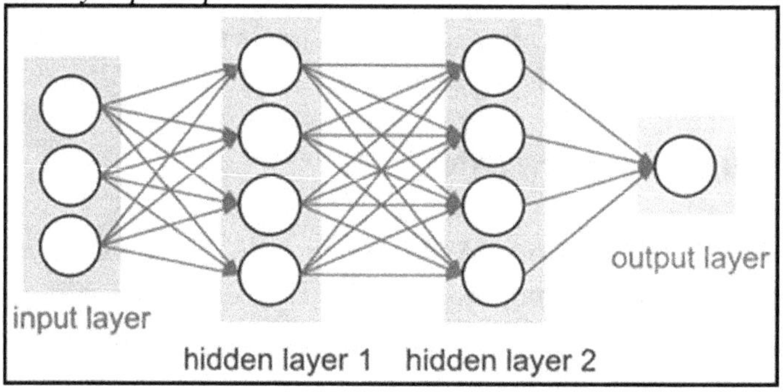

Model Performance Metrics

This study utilized performance criteria to demonstrate the adequacy of the models' fit the following metrics are used: Mean Absolute Error (MAE), Root Mean Square Error (RMSE) and Mean Absolute Percentage Error (MAPE). MAPE, represented by (Eq. 4), is a statistical metric used to quantify the accuracy of a prediction system. Additionally, it serves as a loss function in machine learning situations. MAPE quantifies the magnitude of the error as a percentage. Equation 1 also shows the numerical expression of MAPE.

$$MAPE = \frac{1}{N}\sum_{t=1}^{n}\left|\frac{A_t - F_t}{A_t}\right| \quad (4)$$

In this context, n represents the quantity of fitted points, A_t denotes the actual value, and F_t signifies the predicted value.

The MAE is the total of the absolute value of the differences between the actual values and the forecast values in the data set divided by the number of samples (Eq. 5). The mean absolute error is a continuous variable that ranges from 0 to infinity. Performance improves as the value decreases. MAE treats all errors equally and does not penalize large errors as severely as RMSE.

$$MAE = \frac{1}{n} = \sum_{i=1}^{n}|X_i - X| \quad (5)$$

RMSE is calculated by taking the sum of the squared differences between the actual and predicted values in the dataset, and then dividing it by the number of samples (as shown in Eq. 6). Presence of outliers can significantly increase the mean square error. RMSE is determined by taking the square root of the calculated value.

$$RMSE = \sqrt{\frac{1}{n}\sum_{i=1}^{n}x_t^2} \quad (6)$$

RESULTS AND DISCUSSION

Air Quality Index Results

Table 3. Statistics of air pollutants and AQI values

		NO_2	CO	SO_2	O_3	PM_{10}	Average AQI Value
2021	Min	13.73	0.23	1.19	2.11	7.70	49.91
	Max	91.16	11.16	65.39	97.16	72.62	
	Mean	44.45	4.16	18.55	28.78	35.06	
	S.d	13.82	2.32	16.03	14.70	15.77	
2022	Min	15.49	0.18	1.36	2.18	8.79	50.12
	Max	102.95	11.08	29.57	95.86	109.02	
	Mean	41.45	4.75	9.05	23.76	40.42	
	S.d	17.81	2.03	4.65	11.35	19.61	

continued on following page

Table 3. Continued

		NO_2	CO	SO_2	O_3	PM_{10}	Average AQI Value
2023	Min	8.86	0.15	1.79	2.40	8.01	49.33
	Max	105.60	10.16	66.34	40.30	96.84	
	Mean	41.73	3.53	12.03	19.28	43.46	
	S.d	16.38	2.03	9.59	8.07	17.72	

This research examines air pollution data obtained from the central station situated near the city center of Istanbul, Turkey, utilized to compute the air quality index based on essential criteria. This dataset contains observations from January 2021 to December 2023. Table 3 show that concise descriptive statistics for the pollutants (PM_{10}, NO_2, CO, SO_2, O_3) and the corresponding AQI results from this dataset. The three-year average AQI values are 49-50. These results mean that the air quality in Istanbul is considered good for three years. Considering that the standard deviation (S.d) increased by 17.81 in 2022, NO_2 levels fluctuated. Again, while the average level of CO was 4.16 $\mu g/m^3$ in 2021, this level increased to 4.75 $\mu g/m^3$ in 2022 and decreased significantly to 3.53 $\mu g/m^3$ in 2023. This decrease indicates an improvement in CO pollution. SO_2 levels also show a significant fluctuation over the years. Finally, there is a continuous upward trend in particulate matter pollution. This is a negative sign for air quality. However, fluctuations in the main sources of NO_2 and SO_2, such as industrial activities and vehicular traffic, lead to variations in the levels of these pollutants over the years. A significant decrease in SO_2 in 2022 is likely to be associated with the introduction of specific pollution measures. A significant increase in particulate matter (PM_{10}) levels was observed. This increase has a negative impact on air quality and indicates the need for more serious measures to address sources of PM_{10} (e.g. construction activities, dust generation). A steady decrease in O_3 levels indicates that ozone remediation measures have been successful, but periodic high O_3 values also indicate that this improvement is not fully stable.

Machine Learning Algorithms Results

Figures 4-5 and 6 show the actual and predicted AQI values for 2021-2023 using XGBoost and ANN models. This study compares the performance of XGBoost and ANN models in forecasting three-year air quality index (AQI) data. The graphs show the actual AQI values in all years (blue) and the AQI values predicted by two different models, XGBoost (red) and Artificial Neural Network (ANN, green). In terms of model parameters, XGBoost demonstrated a balanced and consistent prediction performance with a learning rate of 0.01, 5-layer decision trees, 200 decision trees and 80% data subsampling. However, the ANN model was trained with a learning rate of 0.01, momentum of 0.9, 100 hidden layer units and 500 iterations. In its predictions, XGBoost can learn pollution trends based on previous data and predict future values of AQI. However, ANN can be a powerful model for solving a problem with non-linear relationships such as air quality. It can learn complex relationships in the data and make more dynamic predictions.

Figure 4. 2021 Actual and predicted values

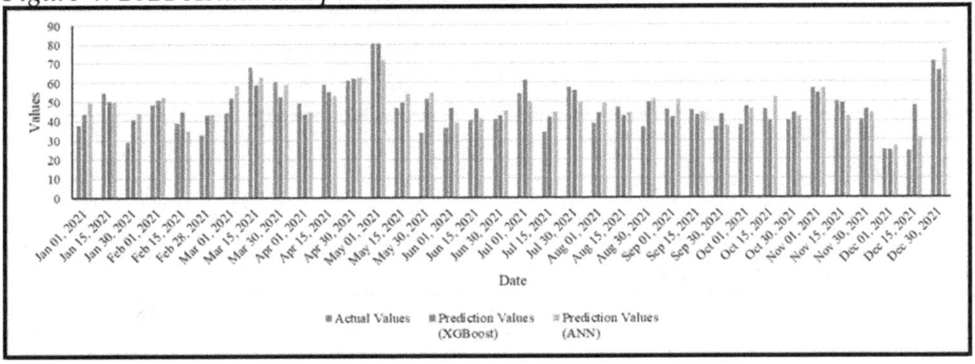

Figure 5. 2022 Actual and predicted values

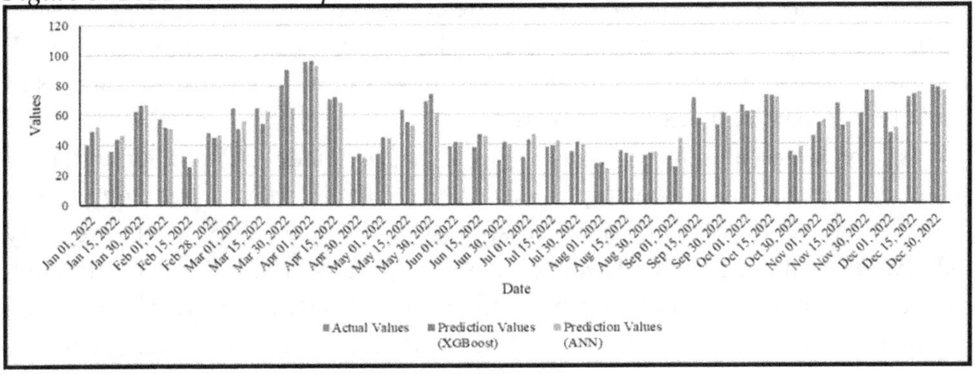

Figure 6. 2023 Actual and predicted values

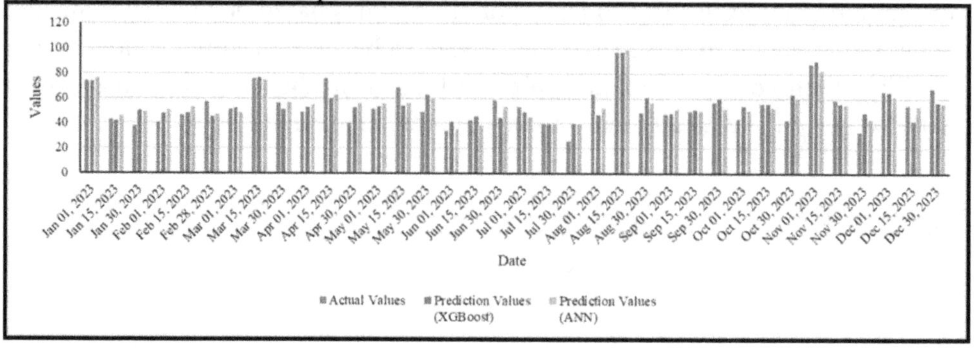

Table 4. Performance metrics

	XGBoost	ANN
MAE	10.96	11.03
MAPE	0.23	0.23
RMSE	14.33	14.38

When the predictions of both models are compared with the actual AQI values on the graph, it is seen that the models make successful predictions in general. The prediction performance of the XGBoost model shows a significant success in predicting air quality index data. In particular, the MAE (10.96) and RMSE (14.33) values, which indicate low error rates, reveal that the model can predict with high accuracy. The analysis on the graph reveals that the model shows a trend quite close to the actual values and is quite successful especially at medium level air quality index values (between 30-70). However, at high AQI values (80 and above), although deviations were observed from time to time, these deviations were more limited compared to the ANN model and did not negatively affect the overall prediction accuracy. An important factor explaining the strong performance of XGBoost is its high flexibility and tree-based structure. This structure, thanks to its capacity to capture complex data relationships, provided a forecast performance that was sensitive to seasonal and short-term weather changes.

Just like the XGBoost model, ANN's performance in air quality index forecasting, while generally successful, also reveals some challenges. Although graphical analysis shows that the ANN model generally provides a prediction accuracy close to the actual values, deviations are more pronounced, especially at high AQI values (80 and above). This can be considered as one of the factors limiting the performance of the ANN model at extreme values. When the error metrics of the ANN model are analyzed, it is seen that the MAE (11.03) and RMSE (14.38) values are slightly higher compared to the XGBoost model. However, these differences are not very large, indicating that both models have a similar overall accuracy level. The Mean Percentage Error (MAPE) is 0.23 for both models, indicating a 23% margin of error in the predictions. This error rate indicates that the models generally provide forecasts that are in line with the AQI data, but deviate in some periods, especially at high values. The fact that the prediction errors of the ANN model are more pronounced in certain periods can be explained by the model's inability to fully learn the complexity and variation in the data distribution. Depending on the structure of neural networks, the large number of parameters and hidden layers in the learning process of the model may lead to optimization problems such as overlearning or learning rate. However, the ANN model was able to successfully capture seasonal effects and long-term air quality changes and performed well at low and medium AQI values.

In addition to the model used in this study, air temperature, wind speed and pressure values were added to the model to make the forecasts more accurate. The use of such additional variables within the scope of feature selection has enabled the inclusion of environmental factors affecting air quality in the model, thus making the forecasts more comprehensive and sensitive. Variables such as air temperature, wind speed and pressure are often among the main factors affecting air quality. For example, low pressure conditions can often be associated with meteorological events that increase air pollution, while high wind speeds can help disperse air pollutants and thus reduce pollution levels. Incorporating such factors into the model provides a better understanding of the complex relationships between seasonal effects on air quality, local meteorological variations and the distribution of airborne pollutants. In both XGBoost and ANN models, these additional variables improved the prediction accuracy and contributed to obtaining results closer to the actual data. This improvement is reflected in the low levels of error metrics such as MAE and RMSE for both models. Meteorological variables such as pressure, air temperature and wind added to the model through feature selection also improved the performance of XGBoost and ANN models in extreme forecasts. However, in some cases, especially at high AQI levels, the variability of these factors may have made the model's predictions more complex.

CONCLUSION

This research spanned three years (2021–2023) to thoroughly evaluate air pollution levels in Istanbul. The application of the air quality index (AQI) functioned as an essential instrument, providing both the public and decision makers with a clear measure of air quality. Considering the complex and dynamic characteristics of pollution over time and in various locations, making precise predictions about air quality presents a significant challenge. Both models show significant promise in accurately forecasting AQI values using historical data and pollutant concentration levels. Our study effectively addressed this challenge by strategically applying advanced machine learning techniques, particularly utilizing the XGBoost and ANN models. These established and robust methodologies were utilized to develop predictive models for the AQI in the Istanbul region. XGBoost, with its tree-based structure, demonstrates a higher prediction accuracy, especially at mid-level AQI values, owing to its ability to capture complex patterns and seasonal variations. ANN, while also effective, encounters slight prediction limitations at high AQI values, suggesting that improvements in capturing extreme pollution events may enhance its accuracy. The close error rates of both models suggest that the parameters and data sets employed in the forecasting processes exert comparable influences. In summary, although both XGBoost and ANN models demonstrate effective forecasting capabilities, XGBoost appears to have a slight edge due to its lower error rates, making it a preferable choice for air quality index forecasting. Nonetheless, the error rates of both models suggest that the discrepancies between the actual data and the predicted data remain within an acceptable range, and the overall accuracy of the models is commendably high.

The inclusion of meteorological factors, such as temperature, wind speed, and pressure, contributes to the models' robustness by accounting for external environmental impacts on air quality. This integration not only reduces error metrics, as indicated by MAE and RMSE values, but also supports more nuanced predictions, especially for seasonal and daily fluctuations in AQI. This demonstrates that machine learning-based models for air quality prediction are a powerful tool for proactive environmental management and public health interventions. The study's findings underline the value of machine learning-based AQI prediction as a tool for proactive air quality management, providing a foundation for informed public health interventions and sustainable policy-making in urban areas with complex environmental dynamics like Istanbul. Therefore, air pollution management plays a critical role, especially in cities with a population of over 5 million. The clear success of the XGBoost and ANN models establishes them as fundamental to the reliability of forecasting the air quality index. This accomplishment highlights the effectiveness of machine learning in forecasting air quality and emphasizes the possibilities for addressing environmental challenges through creative solutions. We suggest a thorough examination of hourly data as a logical progression to improve predictive results and raise performance benchmarks. The findings obtained from our study have broad relevance, offering avenues to tackle air quality issues worldwide. This approach can be considered as an important step towards a cleaner and healthier future. By harnessing the collaboration between machine learning and environmental management, we create a pathway toward a sustainable and healthier future.

REFERENCES

Almaliki, A. H., Derdour, A., & Ali, E. (2023). Air Quality Index (AQI) Prediction in Holy Makkah Based on Machine Learning Methods. *Sustainability*, 15(17), 13168.

Bruno, F., & Cocchi, D. (2022). A unified strategy for building simple air quality indices. *Environmetrics*, 13, 243–261.

Chen, T., & Guestrin, C. (2016). Xgboost: A Scalable Tree Boosting System. *Proceedings of the 22nd acm Sigkdd International Conference on Knowledge Discovery and Data Mining*.

Du, S., Li, T., Yang, Y., & Horng, S. (2018). Deep Air Quality Forecasting Using Hybrid Deep Learning Framework. *IEEE Transactions on Knowledge and Data Engineering*, 33, 2412–2424.

Fausett, L. V. (2006). *Fundamentals of neural networks: architectures, algorithms and applications*. Pearson Education India.

Kumar, A., & Goyal, P. (2011). Forecasting of daily air quality index in Delhi. *The Science of the Total Environment*, 409, 5517–5523. PMID: 21962560

Lewis, C. D. (1982). *Industrial and Business Forecasting Methods*. Butterworths Publishing.

Liu, H., Li, Q., Yu, D., & Gu, Y. (2019). Air quality index and air pollutant concentration prediction based on machine learning algorithms. *Applied Sciences (Basel, Switzerland)*, 9, 4069.

Mutascu, M., & Hegerty, S. W. (2023). Predicting the contribution of artificial intelligence to unemployment rates: An artificial neural network approach. *Journal of Economics and Finance*, 47(2), 400–416.

Mutlu, N. M., & Atahanlı, E. B. (2024). Veri Madenciliği ile Hava Kalitesi Tahmini: İstanbul Örneği. *Bilişim Teknolojileri Dergisi*, 17(3), 139–158.

Paschalidou, A. K., Karakitsios, S., Kleanthous, S., & Kassomenos, P. A. (2011). Forecasting hourly PM10 concentration in Cyprus through artificial neural networks and multiple regression models: Implications to local environmental management. *Environmental Science and Pollution Research International*, 18, 316–327. PMID: 20652425

Plaia, A., & Ruggieri, M. (2011). Air quality indices: A review. *Reviews in Environmental Science and Biotechnology*, 10, 165–179.

Sheng, N., & Tang, U. W. (2016). The first official city ranking by air quality in China—A review and analysis. *Cities (London, England)*, 51, 139–149.

Simkovich, S. M., Goodman, D., Roa, C., Crocker, M. E., Gianella, G. E., Kirenga, B. J., Wise, R. A., & Checkley, W. (2019). The health and social implications of household air pollution and respiratory diseases. npj Prim. Care Respir. Med., 29, 12.

Thurston, G. D., Kipen, H., Annesi-Maesano, I., Balmes, J., Brook, R. D., Cromar, K., De Matteis, S., Forastiere, F., Forsberg, B., & Frampton, M. W. (2016). A joint ERS/ATS policy statement: What constitutes an adverse health effect of air pollution? An analytical framework. *The European Respiratory Journal*, 49, 1600419. PMID: 28077473

Ünlü, R., & Xanthopoulos, P. (2021). A reduced variance unsupervised ensemble learning algorithm based on modern portfolio theory. *Expert Systems with Applications*, 180, 115085.

Xie, X., Pu, Y. F., & Wang, J. (2023). A fractional gradient descent algorithm robust to the initial weights of multilayer perceptron. *Neural Networks*, 158, 154–170. PMID: 36450188

Yahya, K., Zhang, Y., & Vukovich, J. (2014). Real-time air quality forecasting over the southeastern United States using WRF/Chem-MADRID: Multiple-year assessment and sensitivity studies. *Atmospheric Environment*, 92, 318–338.

Yu, R., Yang, Y., Yang, L., Han, G., & Move, O. A. (2016). RAQ–A random forest approach for predicting air quality in urban sensing systems. *Sensors (Basel)*, 16, 86. PMID: 26761008

KEY TERMS AND DEFINITIONS

Air Pollution: Air pollution is the accumulation of pollutants in the atmosphere that can harm human health, ecosystems and the environmental balance. These pollutants are often released into the atmosphere as a result of industrial activities, fossil fuel combustion, agricultural practices and natural phenomena (e.g., volcanic eruptions). Major air pollutants include carbon monoxide (CO), sulphur dioxide (SO_2), nitrogen oxides (NO_2), particulate matter (PM_{10}) and ozone (O_3). Air pollution causes major environmental and health problems such as respiratory diseases, climate change, acid rain and ozone depletion.

Air Quality Index: The Air Quality Index (AQI) is an assessment system that provides a numerical measure of air pollution status by indicating the levels of pollutants in the atmosphere. The AQI is usually calculated separately for specific pollutants (e.g., particulate matter (PM_{10}), Ozone (O_3), sulphur dioxide (SO_2), nitrogen dioxide (NO_2) and carbon monoxide (CO) and the pollutant with the highest value is reported as the overall index. This index is categorized into categories ranging from "good" to "dangerous" to ensure that different segments of society (e.g., vulnerable groups, general population) are informed about the health impacts. The AQI is a critical tool for decision-makers and public health professionals in both air pollution management and awareness raising.

Artificial Neural Network: Artificial Neural Networks (ANN) are computational models inspired by the working principles of nerve cells in the human brain. ANNs consist of layers of interconnected artificial neurons and are used to learn complex relationships between data. These structures, usually consisting of an input layer, one or more hidden layers and an output layer, are a powerful tool for solving nonlinear problems. ANNs perform learning through optimization of weights and are widely applied, especially in areas such as image processing, natural language processing, prediction systems and biomedical engineering. These models form the basis of subfields such as deep learning.

Machine Learning: Machine learning is a subfield of artificial intelligence that enables computer systems to learn from data without being explicitly programmed and to make predictions or decisions using this learned knowledge. At its core is the ability of algorithms to generalize by extracting patterns from past data and applying these generalizations to new data. Machine learning, which has subtypes such as supervised learning, unsupervised learning and reinforcement learning, is used in various fields such as natural language processing, image recognition, recommendation systems and health diagnostics. This approach has become an important tool for solving complex problems in the data-intensive modern world.

Chapter 11

Assessing the Causal Impact of Trade Balance, Interest Rates, and Exchange Rates on Unemployment in the Euro Area: A Double Machine Learning Approach

Ayşe Paksoy
https://orcid.org/0009-0003-6104-2693
Istanbul University-Cerrahpaşa, Turkey

Yeşim Altay
https://orcid.org/0009-0002-0964-3099
Istanbul University-Cerrahpaşa, Turkey

ABSTRACT

This study employs three sophisticated econometric models based on the dual machine learning (DML) methodology to examine the causal effect of pivotal economic variables on unemployment rates within the Eurozone. The models analyse the impact of the trade balance, interest rates and real effective exchange rate on the unemployment rate, while controlling for complex interactions among macroeconomic variables such as exports, imports, and exchange rates. A sensitivity analysis of each model demonstrates the varying degree of dependence on the con-

DOI: 10.4018/979-8-3373-2272-8.ch011

trol variables. The results indicate that exchange rate and interest rate variables are pivotal in stabilising treatment effect estimates, emphasising the necessity to consider these factors for the development of reliable unemployment modelling. By employing machine learning-based causal inference, this chapter contributes to the field of labour economics and provides insights for policymakers aiming to achieve balanced economic growth and employment stability in the Euro area.

INTRODUCTION

The unemployment rates observed in the Euro Area have exhibited considerable volatility in recent years, reflecting a complex interplay between domestic and international economic forces. It is of the utmost importance to comprehend the causal relationship between these factors—in particular, the trade balance, interest rates, and exchange rates—and unemployment to develop effective labor market stabilization measures. This study employs the Double Machine Learning (DML) paradigm to examine the influence of key economic factors, namely the trade balance, interest rates, and real effective exchange rates, on employment levels.

A principal indicator of economic well-being with direct implications for employment is the trade balance, defined as the discrepancy between imports and exports. An increase in exports typically leads to an improved trade balance, which in turn stimulates domestic production, enhances labor demand, and may contribute to a reduction in unemployment (Krugman, Obstfeld & Melitz, 2018; Sachs & Warner, 1995). Conversely, increased imports may have the effect of reducing domestic employment, as they may precipitate changes in the labor market by replacing home-produced goods with imported items (Rodrik, 1997). However, other macroeconomic factors, such as borrowing rates and currency strength, which may influence local production and consumption decisions, are essential for understanding how shifts in the trade balance impact employment (Egger & Etzel, 2012).

The Euro Area offers a unique opportunity to examine these relationships due to its common currency and coordinated economic policies. Other factors influencing unemployment can be isolated in a controlled environment where there are no intra-regional exchange rate variations. Furthermore, the Euro Area's continued vulnerability to changes in international commerce and currency values introduces an additional layer of complexity to the analysis of the variables affecting unemployment (Blanchard & Katz, 1992; Ferrucci, Jiménez-Rodriguez, & Onorante, 2010). Some research has indicated that domestic policies and structural factors within economies may exert a greater influence than trade balance considerations, even though numerous studies have demonstrated that trade balance is a significant element in labor market adjustments (Bayoumi, Laxton, & Pesenti, 2004).

It is evident that interest rates exert a considerable influence on labor market outcomes, in addition to the trade balance. This is because they affect borrowing costs, consumer spending, and corporate investments. It is well known that higher interest rates have a stifling effect on economic activity, which in turn causes unemployment to rise. Conversely, a reduction in interest rates may lead to an increase in employment and economic activity (Blanchard, 2009; Stock & Watson, 2019). Moreover, the competitiveness of exports and the affordability of imports can be influenced by the real effective exchange rate, a parameter that modifies the nominal exchange rate in consideration of relative price levels. An increase in purchasing power resulting from a stronger home currency may lead to a reduction in unemployment. However, this could also result in a decline in the competitiveness of exports (Mankiw, 2016).

This study employs a DML approach that considers the potential endogeneity and confounding factors inherent in economic data, thereby enabling the precise identification of the causal effects of these variables on unemployment. The analysis considers the temporal dynamics of trade, interest rates, and currency impacts on unemployment using monthly data from 2002 to 2024. As DML is robust in identifying causal linkages where traditional econometric models may be inadequate, particularly in the presence of interacting macroeconomic factors, it is highly beneficial in this context (Chernozhukov et al., 2018). A comprehensive examination of these interrelationships and their impact on labor market dynamics within the Euro Area is made possible by the incorporation of controls, including inflation (HICP), real effective exchange rates, and long-term interest rates.

This study contributes to the existing literature on the Euro Area by employing machine learning-based causal inference to assess the joint impact of trade balance, interest rates, and currency volatility on unemployment. The results are intended to furnish policymakers with valuable insights for enhancing labor market stability through judicious modifications to trade and economic regulations.

CONCEPTUAL FRAMEWORK

The Purpose of Study

This paper aims to examine the causal effects of the trade balance, interest rates, and the real effective exchange rate on the unemployment rate in the Euro Area using a DML framework. The application of DML to account for potential endogeneity and complex interactions among macroeconomic variables provides a more precise understanding of the nuanced relationships between key economic indicators and employment. In contrast to conventional econometric methodologies, DML enables the identification of specific treatment effects within a complex system of interacting variables, thereby facilitating a comprehensive investigation of the impact of the trade balance, interest rates, and currency strength on unemployment.

The Impact and Importance of Study

The intricate interconnections between unemployment and pivotal economic indices, including the trade balance, interest rates, and real effective exchange rates, have garnered considerable scrutiny in macroeconomic research, largely due to their profound implications for employment policies and economic stability. This study employs DML to elucidate the intricate relationships between the unemployment rate and other macroeconomic variables, including inflation, exports, and long-term interest rates. The investigation aims to ascertain the causal effects of these variables on the unemployment rate within the Euro Area. The unique economic backdrop of the Euro Area, defined by a common currency and integrated policies, provides an ideal environment for examining these linkages while taking into consideration the possible confounding variables present in multi-country research (Blanchard, 2009).

The value of this study lies in its potential to contribute to both academic research and practical policymaking. From an academic standpoint, this research addresses a gap in the extant literature by employing machine learning-based causal inference techniques in macroeconomic analysis, where conventional approaches frequently encounter challenges in effectively managing endogeneity and confounding variables. Previous studies have examined the relationship between unemployment and individual economic factors; however, few have employed a combined model to comprehensively analyze multiple influential variables simultaneously. By examining three major economic factors and including control variables such as export, import, inflation (HICP), and long-term government bond yields, this study offers a more comprehensive analysis of the determinants of unemployment.

From a policy perspective, it is of the utmost importance to comprehend the causal relationships between these variables, particularly given that Euro Area member states share a single currency and coordinate economic policies yet experience disparate national economic conditions. The findings of this study provide insights into the factors that are most effective in reducing unemployment, thereby assisting policymakers in adapting economic policies in a more efficacious manner. To illustrate, if the model indicates a robust positive correlation between interest rates and unemployment, policymakers may contemplate modifying monetary policy, cognizant of the prospective influence on employment. Moreover, the analysis of the impact of trade balances and real effective exchange rates on unemployment demonstrates the impact of external economic relationships and thus informs the formulation of trade and monetary stability policies that support labor market stability.

In conclusion, this study contributes to our understanding of unemployment dynamics in the Euro Area by employing machine learning to identify complex economic relationships. In addition to advancing the theoretical understanding of macroeconomic linkages, the insights gained from this research provide valuable guidance for policymakers who aim to manage employment levels through informed adjustments in trade, monetary, and fiscal policies.

Theoretical Background

The relationship between employment and the trade balance is a topic of considerable interest within the field of economics. Transformations in a country's trade balance, defined as the net discrepancy between imports and exports, have the capacity to influence employment in a multitude of ways. According to Keynesian economic theory, an increase in net exports (a trade surplus) has the effect of boosting aggregate demand, which in turn has the effect of boosting domestic production and job opportunities (Krugman & Obstfeld, 2003). Conversely, in countries with a significant reliance on imports, an unfavorable trade balance may impede aggregate demand, resulting in an increase in unemployment (Mankiw, 2016). The theoretical framework posits a negative correlation between improvements in the trade balance and unemployment rates.

In the field of economics, there is considerable interest in the relationship between interest rates and employment. One of the principal factors influencing economic activity and, consequently, employment levels is the level of interest rates. An increase in interest rates will render borrowing more costly, which may act as a deterrent to corporate investment and consumer spending. Consequently, there is a possibility of an increase in unemployment and a slowing of economic growth (Blanchard, 2009; Stock & Watson, 2019). Empirical evidence indicating a correlation between rising interest rates and labor market contractions lends support to this theoretical proposition. This is due to the fact that a more restrictive monetary policy may result in an increase in redundancies and a reduction in hiring (Bartolini et al., 2014).

The relationship between employment and the real effective exchange rate is a significant factor to be considered. The real effective exchange rate (REER) has a significant influence on both imports and exports, which in turn affects a country's trade competitiveness. As a nation's currency appreciates, exports become comparatively more costly, which may result in a decline in demand from overseas consumers and, consequently, a reduction in the number of jobs created in industries that rely heavily on exports (Eichengreen, 2019). Nevertheless, a stronger currency also serves to reduce import prices, which may in turn stimulate local demand and domestic spending power, thereby benefiting employment, particularly in nations with significant import volumes (Mankiw, 2016).

Empirical Evidence

The inconclusive findings from empirical studies on the relationship between these macroeconomic factors and unemployment demonstrate the disparate effects they have on different economic environments. As evidenced by studies conducted in developed economies, such as those by Bussière et al. (2011), a reduction in unemployment rates is typically associated with an improvement in trade balances. Nevertheless, the interplay with other economic variables, such as interest rates and levels of domestic consumption, may influence the extent of this impact. Similarly, Baldwin and Di Mauro (2020) emphasize that a favourable trade balance plays a significant role in employment growth in regions with a robust export-oriented industrial base. In economies where the service sector is the dominant contributor to the economy, this effect is less pronounced.

The analysis will also consider the impact of interest rates, which have been demonstrated to exhibit a consistently positive correlation with unemployment in a variety of economic contexts. For example, Ferrucci, Jiménez-Rodriguez, and Onorante (2010) demonstrate that an elevated unemployment rate is associated with elevated interest rates. This is in accordance with the tenets of conventional monetary theory, which posits that elevated interest rates impede the processes of borrowing and spending. Conversely, the prevailing circumstances inform how the real effective exchange rate influences employment. As Eichengreen (2019) posits, augmented domestic demand resulting from reduced import costs may counterbalance the adverse impact of a stronger currency on employment, although it may impede export competitiveness.

LITERATURE REVIEW

As unemployment rates have a profound impact on people's financial circumstances and quality of life, they play a crucial role in the social structure. According to the literature, both individual characteristics and economic cycles have an impact on unemployment rates. In this regard, machine learning algorithms can achieve significant results in predicting unemployment (Xu et al., 2013; Cook and Hall, 2017). In the literature, machine learning algorithms for predicting unemployment rates are particularly useful for investigating the complex relationships between an individual's demographic and educational characteristics and unemployment (Kreiner and Duca, 2019).

In order to forecast unemployment in rural Europe, five distinct machine learning methods were employed in the joint study. These were classification trees, bootstrap aggregation, random forests, gradient boosting, and stochastic gradient boosting.

These techniques permitted a comprehensive examination of the principal factors influencing an individual's unemployment status. The utilisation of explainable machine learning methodologies, such as SHAP value analysis, elucidated the influence of age, parental educational attainment and educational achievement on unemployment, and demonstrated the way these variables exerted their effects upon distinct subgroups. Consequently, it has been established that access to educational programmes may serve to mitigate disparities in the labor force within rural regions (Celbiş, 2023).

The efficacy of machine learning and time series models for forecasting unemployment rates was evaluated in a study. In order to estimate the unemployment rates of different nations, a number of techniques were employed in the study, including long-memory time series models (such as FARIMA and FARIMA/GARCH) and machine learning techniques (such as artificial neural networks (ANN), support vector regression (SVR), and multivariate adaptive regression splines (MARS)). The performance of the models was evaluated using the mean absolute error (MAE) and root mean square error (RMSE) criteria. Furthermore, the impact of forecast horizons and geographic locations on the outcomes was investigated. The findings indicate that while artificial neural network methodologies demonstrated superior efficacy in long-term forecasting, FARIMA models yielded the most optimal results in short-term forecasting (Katris, 2020).

A subsequent study devised a technique for estimating unemployment rates through the analysis of social media content. The author employed natural language processing techniques to analyse Korean-language news, blogs and tweets on social media. In order to assess unemployment using the ARIMAX and ARX models, the data was subjected to a process of elimination, whereby the findings of the sentiment analysis and the frequency of keywords were removed. The generated model exhibited a 27.9% reduction in the mean absolute percentage error relative to Google search data. The study demonstrated that social media data can effectively capture rapid fluctuations in social events, thereby yielding more precise estimates than those derived from conventional time series models (Ryu, 2018).

In a different study, a range of techniques was employed for estimating the unemployment rate in Poland, including regression, Holt, ARIMA, and Winters models. The investigation, which employed data from 2008 to 2018, demonstrated that the Winters multiplicative model and the second-order regression model yielded the most precise results. The Winters multiplicative model was found to be the most effective in reflecting seasonal oscillations (Gostkowski & Rokicki, 2021).

In a study published in 2020, a hybrid model combining the nonlinear Autoregressive Neural Network (ARNN) model and the linear ARIMA model was proposed as a means of estimating unemployment rates. The initial stage of the analysis involved the examination of the unemployment data using the ARIMA model, with the objective of identifying linear patterns. Subsequently, the estimates were enhanced through the processing of the model's error terms using the nonlinear ARNN model. The hybrid model demonstrated superior performance in terms of estimate accuracy when tested on unemployment rate datasets from Canada, Germany, Japan, the Netherlands, New Zealand, Sweden, and Switzerland (Chakraborty et al., 2021).

One study demonstrated that accounting for the consensus among consumers regarding their expectations of unemployment resulted in more precise estimates of the unemployment rate. The researchers initially employed the ARIMA model to generate baseline projections for unemployment rates in eight European nations. Subsequently, the researchers incorporated measurements of consumer expectations regarding agreement and disagreement as independent variables into a dynamic regression model. The findings indicated that a high level of consensus among consumer expectations enhanced the precision of unemployment rate projections, particularly in anticipating turning points (Claveria, 2019).

A different study employed supervised artificial neural networks (ANNs) to estimate unemployment rates and evaluated the accuracy of the resulting models. The study combined conventional time series models, including the autoregressive moving average (ARMA) and the smooth transition autoregressive (STAR), with four distinct artificial neural networks: the multilayer perceptron (MLP), the feedback neural network (RNN), the psi sigma network, and the radial basis function neural network (RBFNN). The findings indicated that the most precise forecasts were generated when learning vector quantization (LVQ) and radial basis function neural networks (RBFNN) were integrated (Sharma and Singh, 2016).

In another study, manual detection of anomalies in control data was defined as a laborious task requiring expertise, and it was suggested that automatic detection could be simpler and more effective. For this purpose, real-time detection of anomalous patterns in control chart data was targeted using various methods such as Artificial Neural Networks (ANN), Support Vector Machines (SVM), Fuzzy Logic. Numerical results showed that the weighting strategy could provide better results in some cases in correctly classifying the samples belonging to the minority class. (Ünlü, 2019)

In a study conducted in 2022, the backpropagation technique was employed for the calculation of the unemployment rate in the Tuban region of East Java Province. The model was constructed using data from 2001 to 2021, which was divided into two subsets: 70% of the data was employed for training purposes, while the remaining 30% was utilized for testing. The 2-70-1-1 network structure was identified as the optimal model, exhibiting an accuracy rate of 91.6% and a mean absolute percentage error (MAPE) value of 8.36%. The model predicts that the open unemployment rate in the Tuban region will reach 4.7% by 2022 (Putri et al., 2022).

In a subsequent study, five distinct univariate time series models—SARIMA, SETAR, Holt–Winters (HW), ETS, and neural network autoregression (NNAR)—were evaluated for their ability to predict the Romanian unemployment rate for the period spanning 2021 to 2022. The researchers employed both in-sample and out-of-sample data, with the latter spanning the years 2000 to 2020. The findings revealed that the Holt–Winters multiplicative model demonstrated superior performance for in-sample forecasts, whereas the NNAR model exhibited the greatest accuracy for out-of-sample forecasts. Additionally, the Diebold–Mariano test indicated that the NNAR and SARIMA models exhibited particularly high precision in out-of-sample forecasts (Davidescu et al., 2021).

In 2020, a model was constructed using online search data to predict unemployment claims in the United States. The researchers examined the correlation between specific keywords derived from Google Trends data and unemployment claims, employing two predictive models: the Long Short-Term Memory (LSTM) model, which was based on Google Trends data, and the Vector Autoregressive (VAR) model, which utilized Google Trends data in conjunction with unemployment claims data. The findings indicated that the LSTM model demonstrated superior performance compared to the VAR model across a range of forecast horizons (Kundu & Singhania, 2020).

Another study employed supervised machine learning algorithms to forecast unemployment rates in India. The researchers employed a range of algorithms, including Decision Tree, k-Nearest Neighbour (kNN), Logistic Regression, and Support Vector Machines (SVM), to analyse unemployment rates across various states. They identified states with unemployment rates exceeding 5% as areas with urgent labor needs. The Decision Tree algorithm demonstrated the most optimal performance in the evaluation process, attaining a 100% accuracy rate (Sen et al., 2022).

In a different study, the potential of ARIMA and ANN models to predict Turkey's unemployment rate was evaluated. The researchers created two models using monthly unemployment data from 2008 to 2022 and a variety of independent variables, including the price of oil, the real exchange rate, and interest rates. The findings indicated that, overall, the ARMA (2,1) model demonstrated superior accuracy compared to the ANN model. However, in periods of economic uncertainty, such as the SARS-CoV-2 viral epidemic, the ANN model demonstrated superior efficacy. The findings indicated that the selection of ANN for complex periods and ARIMA for stable periods could enhance the accuracy of predictions (Yamacli & Yamacli, 2023).

In another study, the unemployment rate in Turkey was estimated through the application of machine learning techniques. TÜİK furnished the monthly unemployment statistics between 2005 and 2023, and two distinct models were constructed. The first model was constructed using XGBoost techniques, while the second employed support vector machines (SVM) and artificial neural networks (ANN). The second model incorporated a more comprehensive set of economic variables, including inflation, exchange rates, and the labor force, whereas the first model was based solely on unemployment statistics. The findings demonstrated that the XGBoost algorithm exhibited superior performance when a greater quantity of economic data was incorporated. The findings indicate a decline in Turkey's unemployment rate during the summer months, with significant economic occurrences exerting a detrimental influence on unemployment rates (Güler et al., 2024).

A few fields have witnessed significant developments because of machine learning, including recommendation systems, text categorisation, image identification and credit score prediction (Xu, 2013). Nevertheless, challenges persist due to the opacity of these models, particularly regarding explainability (Vowels, 2020). Conventional interpretable machine learning methodologies tend to eschew an emphasis on cause-and-effect relationships, instead focusing on the examination of correlations (Silva, 2021). This is regarded as a significant shortcoming, particularly in contexts where sensitive data is involved and where automated decision-making is a feature.

In a different study, a weighting scheme was devised with the objective of reducing the variability in the outputs of the clustering algorithms. The objective of the study was to achieve more balanced and low-variance findings through the application of the consensus clustering method, which involves the integration of the outputs from multiple clustering algorithms. The findings indicated that, in most cases, the proposed weighted consensus clustering approach yielded results with greater accuracy and reduced variance compared to conventional techniques (Ünlü and Xanthopoulos, 2021).

The increasing utilisation of causal machine learning (CML) in the healthcare sector offers significant potential for the prediction of treatment outcomes (Feuerriegel, 2023). Similarly, CML may prove invaluable in evaluating the efficacy of a given treatment. Nevertheless, several challenges persist, particularly regarding unstructured and high-dimensional data (Zhao, 2023). Similarly, the incorporation of causal knowledge is becoming increasingly crucial in the realm of business strategic decision-making processes (Hünermund, 2022). A more comprehensive understanding of the causal mechanisms underlying human-machine interaction is imperative, given that traditional machine learning models are predominantly oriented towards correlation and are inadequate for causal analysis (Moraffah, 2021).

A subsequent study examined the impact of the "Made in China 2025" agenda on China's urban green economic growth. The study employed a twofold machine learning approach. To overcome the limitations of conventional causal inference models, this approach was selected. DML approach addresses issues such as the "curse of dimensionality" and multicollinearity that arise in conventional regression models, while providing predictive accuracy under high-dimensional control variables. In order to evaluate the impact of the "Made in China 2025" plan on urban green economic growth, this approach was employed to enhance the accuracy and dependability of the results (Yuan and Liu, 2024).

In a separate study, the "double machine learning" approach is employed to investigate the influence of public services and local taxes on real estate values. The impact of local income taxes on property prices is estimated using a dataset comprising 947 time-varying local characteristics and variables pertaining to public services from Swedish municipalities between 2010 and 2016. The research indicates that tax capitalisation is more pronounced in regions characterised by heightened municipal competition. An increase in municipal income taxes is associated with a decline in house values (Grodecka-Messi and Hull, 2022).

METHODOLOGY

This study employs the Dual Machine Learning (DML) approach and sensitivity analysis to evaluate the causal impacts of macroeconomic factors (trade balance, interest rates, and real effective exchange rate) on the unemployment rate in the Euro Area. In circumstances where conventional econometric models are inadequate, the DML methodology, as developed by Chernozhukov et al. (2018), is particularly beneficial for addressing endogeneity and regulating complex relationships between economic variables, thereby facilitating more reliable causal inferences.

Double Machine Learning

The DML approach, developed by Chernozhukov et al. (2018), is particularly well-suited to causal inference in settings where endogeneity and confounding factors complicate traditional econometric methods. The robust design of DML permits the isolation of the treatment effect of each macroeconomic variable while accounting for complex interactions with control variables, including exports, imports, inflation (HICP), and long-term interest rates.

The general setup of the DML method is based on the partially linear model, where the main equation for estimating the impact of the treatment variable T on the outcome variable Y (unemployment rate) is formulated as follows:

$$\mathrm{Y} = \mathrm{T}\theta_0 + g(X) + \epsilon$$

Here:

- Y represents the outcome variable (unemployment rate),

- T is the treatment variable (either trade balance, interest rate, or real effective exchange rate, depending on the model),
- θ_0 denotes the parameter of interest, reflecting the average treatment effect (ATE),
- g(X) is an unknown function of the control variables X,
- ϵ is the error term, assumed to be independent of T and X.

The DML framework proceeds by first estimating the nuisance functions g(X) and m(X), where m(X) captures the expected values of T given the control variables X. By leveraging machine learning algorithms, such as Random Forest or Lasso regression, we estimate these nuisance functions non-parametrically to account for potential nonlinear relationships between T, Y, and X. This is particularly advantageous in this study, as it enables flexible modelling of complex interactions among variables without restrictive parametric assumptions.

Once the nuisance functions are estimated, the next step involves residualizing both the outcome and treatment variables. This process creates orthogonalized versions of Y and T, which allow for an unbiased estimation of θ_0, the causal effect of interest. The residuals are computed as follows:

$$\tilde{Y} = Y - g(X)$$

$$\tilde{T} = T - m(X)$$

In the final step, we estimate the causal effect θ_0 by regressing the residualized outcome $\tilde{Y}$ on the residualized treatment $\tilde{T}$:

$$\theta_0 = \frac{Cov(\tilde{Y}, \tilde{T})}{Var(\tilde{T})}$$

The two-step orthogonalization process, in conjunction with cross-fitting (the partitioning of the data into folds and the utilization of out-of-sample predictions for the estimation of nuisance functions), serves to minimize the occurrence of overfitting and thereby ensures the generation of more reliable and unbiased causal estimates.

For each of the three models—trade balance, interest rates, and real effective exchange rate—the Average Treatment Effect (ATE) is calculated, and its robustness is examined using sensitivity analysis. This entails a systematic elimination of control variables, one at a time, to ascertain their impact on the ATE estimates. The stability of the ATE across these variations provides insights into which control variables are most critical in explaining the causal relationship between the treatment and outcome variables, thereby enhancing the reliability of our findings.

The DML process is comprised of the following steps:

1. The estimation of nuisance functions is a crucial aspect of the DML process. To capture intricate interactions, machine learning algorithms such as Random Forest or Lasso regression are employed to ascertain the nonlinear relationships embedded within the control variables.
2. Persistence is a crucial element in this process. In order to provide an objective estimate of the ATE, the outcome and treatment variables are subjected to a process of residualization or orthogonalization, with the aim of removing any biases that may be associated with the control variables.
3. The final estimate is as follows: In order to ascertain the precise and isolated causal relationship between each treatment variable and unemployment, the ATE is calculated by regressing the residualized result on the residualized treatment.

This approach allows for the analysis and assessment of the unique impact of each economic component on unemployment, thereby enhancing the accuracy and reliability of the model.

Sensitivity Analysis

A sensitivity analysis examines the impact of modifying the coefficient values associated with a linear programming problem on the optimal solution to that problem. The extent to which the coefficients in the developed model are not fixed and will undergo alteration over time, thereby impacting the optimal outcome, is investigated. Should this modification result in a different ideal solution, the issue must be resolved once more. In the event of the introduction of a new variable and constraint, sensitivity analysis examines the impact of alterations to the objective function, constraint coefficients and source values on the optimal solution.

ANALYSIS

This section presents a detailed examination of the analytical procedure, illustrating the precise steps employed to ascertain the causal relationships between the Euro Area unemployment rate and the trade balance, interest rates, and the real effective exchange rate. The disparate effects of these macroeconomic factors are identified and quantified through the utilization of the DML approach. Moreover, a sensitivity analysis is performed to evaluate the reliability of the model and provide comprehensive insight into how each control variable affects the stability of the results.

Sample and Data

The dataset employed in this study encompasses monthly macroeconomic data for countries within the Euro Area, obtained from the Federal Reserve Economic Data (FRED) and the Organization for Economic Co-operation and Development (OECD) databases. The sample period extends from 2002 to 2024 and encompasses a range of pivotal economic variables, including the unemployment rate, trade balance, interest rates, real effective exchange rates, exports, and imports. The countries included in the sample of the Euro Area are Austria, Belgium, Cyprus, Estonia, Finland, France, Germany, Greece, Ireland, Italy, Latvia, Lithuania, Luxembourg, Malta, the Netherlands, Portugal, Slovakia, Slovenia, and Spain. The data from these sources have been harmonized to maintain consistency across variables and time periods, thereby ensuring that the analysis accurately reflects economic conditions within the Euro Area. The incorporation of data from both the Federal Reserve Economic Data (FRED) and the Organization for Economic Co-operation and Development (OECD) databases enhances the robustness of the analysis, as these databases provide reliable, high-quality macroeconomic indicators that are widely used in empirical economic research.

Table 1. Final dataset

Exports, US dollars, exchange rate converted, Billions, Calendar and seasonally adjusted	Imports, US dollars, exchange rate converted, Billions, Calendar and seasonally adjusted	Trade balance, US dollars, exchange rate converted, Billions, Calendar and seasonally adjusted	HICP-contributions to EA annual inflation (in percentage points)	Financial Market: Real Effective Exchange Rates	Currency Conversions: US Dollar Exchange Rate: Average of Daily Rates: National Currency: USD for Euro Area	Interest Rates: Long-Term Government Bond Yields: 10-Year: Main (Including Benchmark) for Euro Area	Unemployment Rates (OUTPUT)
85,77	79,3	6,47	0,3	102,84	1,05	5,16	8,6
86,99	79,74	7,25	0,27	104,68	1,01	5,03	8,7
87,16	79,13	8,03	0,29	104,25	1,02	4,73	8,7
87,96	80,24	7,73	0,31	104,39	1,02	4,52	8,8
86,86	82,09	4,77	0,28	104,82	1,02	4,62	8,8
.	.	.	.	.	.	.	.
.	.	.	.	.	.	.	.
.	.	.	.	.	.	.	.
255,14	236,82	18,31	0,29	105,46	0,93	3,17	6,5
259,2	242,43	16,77	0,26	105,93	0,92	3,11	6,4

Table 1 presents a summary of monthly data on the principal macroeconomic variables that exert an influence on the unemployment rate in the Euro Area. The variables employed in the study comprise exports, imports, the trade balance, contributions to inflation, the real effective exchange rate, the exchange rate and long-term interest rates. The unemployment rate represents the principal output in the analysis.

Data Cleaning

In order to ensure the requisite consistency and dependability for the derivation of precise causal estimates, a comprehensive data cleaning procedure was implemented.

1. **Outlier Detection and Treatment**: The objective of outlier detection and treatment is to identify and address instances where data points deviate from the norm. The Isolation Forest algorithm, a machine learning method with a reputation for efficacy in the context of high-dimensional data, was employed for the purpose of identifying outliers. This technique facilitated the reduction of excessive fluctuations that have the potential to distort model findings by differentiating data points that exhibited notable divergence from the mean. The identified outliers were subsequently removed from the model.
2. **Handling of Missing Data:** Missing values in the time series were addressed through the utilization of regression-based estimation for larger missing segments and linear interpolation for smaller gaps.
3. **Prediction Model:** In this study, the accuracy of the data set was evaluated by comparing the unemployment rate values estimated using the random forest model with the actual values. Metrics such as MAE, MAPE, RMSE and Correlation Coefficient (R^2) were used in this analysis. The low error rates and high R^2 obtained showed that the model made estimates that were quite close to the actual values.

A graph showing actual values and predicted values is given in Figure 1. According to the graph, it is observed that the predicted values are very close to the actual values.

Figure 1. Comparison of actual values and predicted values

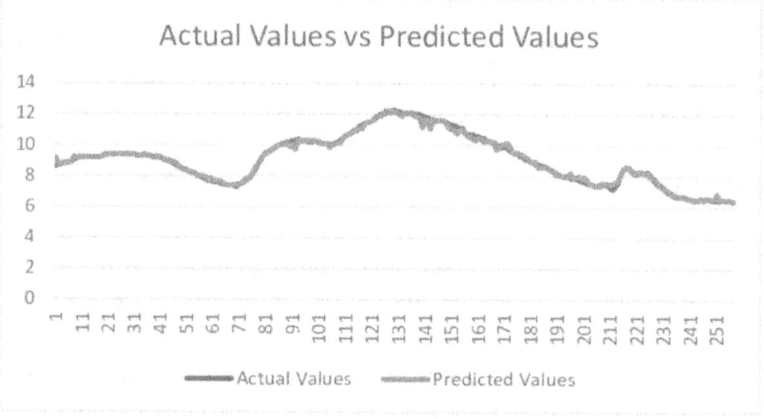

DML Approach for Causal Analysis

This study employs the primary analytical approach of DML, which is selected due to its reliability in addressing endogeneity and intricate inter-variable relationships. DML enables the estimation of the ATE of each treatment variable (trade balance, interest rates and real effective exchange rate) on unemployment, while accounting for potential biases arising from control variables.

1. **Model Structure:** Three discrete DML models were utilized in the analysis, each of which incorporated the others as control variables and focused on a single primary treatment variable (real effective exchange rate, interest rates, or trade balance). The additional control variables of long-term interest rates, imports, exports, and inflation (HICP) assist in differentiating the unique impacts of each treatment variable on unemployment.
2. **Estimation of Nuisance Functions:** The estimation of nuisance functions is a crucial aspect of any scientific investigation. The Random Forest machine learning technique was employed for the estimation of the nuisance functions associated with the control variables. The application of this method resulted in a reduction of biases in the estimated treatment effects, due to the model's capacity to capture complex non-linear patterns and relationships.
3. **Residualization Process:** In order to obtain unbiased estimates of the treatment effect, DML employs a revisualization process in which the outcome (unemployment) and treatment variables are orthogonalized. This process enables

the model to identify the causal effect of each treatment on unemployment by reducing the impact of confounding variables.

4. **Sensitivity Analysis for 3 Treatments:** Sensitivity analysis was performed for all three treatment models.

Figure 2. Flow chart

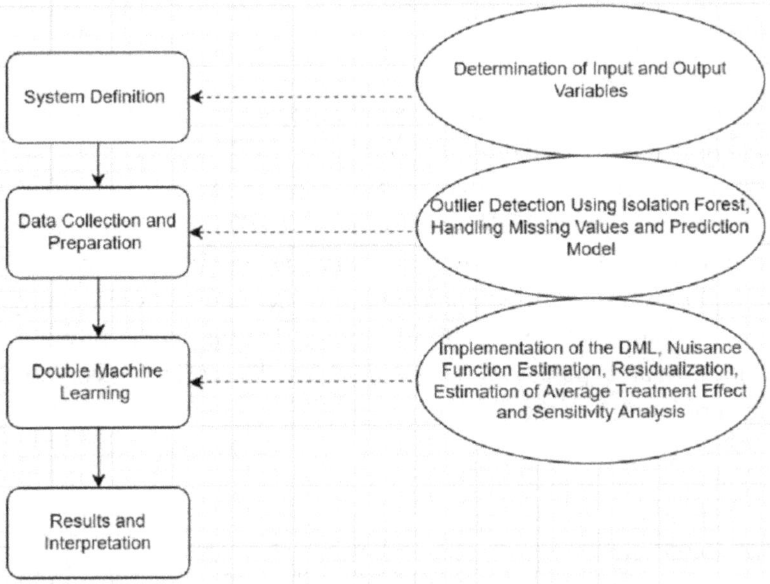

The overall process flowchart is presented in Figure 2. The process commences with the System Definition stage, which defines the input and output variables. It then proceeds to illustrate the primary steps of the analysis process. Subsequently, the process progresses to the phase of data collection and preparation. This involves the handling of missing values, the creation of predictive models, and the utilization of Isolation Forest for the identification of outliers. The dual machine learning process encompasses the application of DML, the estimation of nuisance functions, residualization, the determination of the ATE, and the conducting of a sensitivity analysis. The final step, Results and Interpretation, is dedicated to the analysis of the results, with the objective of deriving significant conclusions regarding the relationships observed in the study.

Results

The following section presents the findings for each of the three models, accompanied by baseline ATE values, sensitivity analysis outcomes, and interpretative insights. Results are supplemented with tables to demonstrate the stability and significance of treatment effects across scenarios. Model accuracy results are also given in this section.

Model Accuracy

Table 2 presents the evaluation of the model performance. The actual values of the unemployment output and the values predicted by the Random Forest algorithm are compared. The model performance evaluation shows that the model has high predictive accuracy as evidenced by the low MAE (0.077) and RMSE (0.13) values. The minimum error rate indicated by the very low MAPE value of 0.83% shows that the model produces results that are highly accurate and closely aligned with the true values. The R^2 value of 0.993 indicates that the model provides a strong fit to the data with an explanatory power of 99.3%. These findings demonstrate the accuracy and reliability of the model.

Table 2. MAPE and R2 results

MAE (Mean Absolute Error):	**0,077**
MAPE (Mean Percent Error):	0,830
RMSE (Root Mean Square Error):	0,130
Correlation Coefficient (R^2):	0,993

Treatment 1: Trade Balance and Unemployment

In the trade balance model, the baseline ATE was found to be 0.033, indicating that an uptick in the trade balance exerts a modest yet favorable influence on unemployment. This demonstrates that an increase in the trade balance may result in a slight rise in the unemployment rate in certain instances.

A sensitivity analysis was conducted to ascertain the impact of varying key parameters on the baseline ATE. The removal of the exchange rate resulted in a notable shift in the ATE, indicating the crucial role of the exchange rate in maintaining the model's stability.

Table 3. Trade balance model sensitivity analysis

Removed_Control	ATE	ATE_Difference_from_Baseline
Exports, US dollars, exchange rate converted, Billions, Calendar and seasonally adjusted	0,029162458	-0,004524829
Imports, US dollars, exchange rate converted, Billions, Calendar and seasonally adjusted	0,03982015	0,006132862
Financial Market: Real Effective Exchange Rates	0,038420101	0,004732814
Currency Conversions: US Dollar Exchange Rate: Average of Daily Rates: National Currency: USD for Euro Area	0,040556713	0,006869426
Interest Rates: Long-Term Government Bond Yields: 10-Year: Main (Including Benchmark) for Euro Area	0,020378708	-0,01330858

Tablo 3 illustrates the impact of removing control variables in a sequential order during the analysis of treatment effects, as represented by the ATE. The removal of each control variable allows for the assessment of the extent to which the ATE value is affected by the model's outcomes in relation to specific variables. The export variable was removed from the model, resulting in an ATE value of 0.029, which is a decrease of -0.0045 from the baseline ATE. This indicates that export has a relatively minor impact on the model. Upon the elimination of the export, the ATE value increased to 0.0398, exceeding the baseline ATE value by 0.0061. This resulted in a more pronounced impact of the export on the model. Upon the cessation of the real effective exchange rate, the ATE value increased to 0.0384, thereby demonstrating the significant influence exerted by the exchange rate on the model. Following the release of the currency, the ATE increased to 0.0405, representing a 0.0069 unit increase relative to the fundamental ATE. This illustrates the significance of the currency in the model. Upon the introduction of interest rates, the ATE declined to 0.0203, while the fundamental ATE decreased by -0.0133. This illustrates the considerable influence that interest rates exert on the model.

These results highlight the importance of ensuring the accuracy of the model by confirming the validity of the exchange rate and interest rate variables. The removal of these variables results in significant alterations to the ATE value, thereby demonstrating the model's sensitivity to these variables. The analysis reveals that interest rates represent a pivotal variable, a finding that is particularly noteworthy. The observation that the largest change is seen in ATE when interest rates are removed from the model suggests that interest rates exert a significant influence on the relationship between the trade balance and unemployment. This suggests that the treatment effect is directly influenced by macroeconomic conditions (e.g. interest rates) and that the model is more reliant on the inclusion of this variable.

Furthermore, the model demonstrates a moderate degree of sensitivity to imports and exchange rates. A notable elevation in the ATE is evident when these variables are excluded. This finding demonstrates that trade-related factors exert a contributory influence on the explanation of the effect of the trade balance on unemployment. Conversely, a restricted responsiveness is evident with respect to exports and real effective exchange rates. The removal of these variables resulted in negligible alterations to ATE, thereby indicating that the model is comparatively resilient to these variables. This finding indicates that exports and real effective exchange rates exert a constrained influence on the nexus between the trade balance and unemployment.

In general, the model demonstrates resilience to most control variables, exhibiting only minor fluctuations. However, the model demonstrates a notable sensitivity to interest rates, which represents a significant finding. In order to more accurately and definitively estimate the effect of the trade balance on unemployment, it would be beneficial to include interest rates in the model. This also demonstrates that the estimated treatment effect is contingent upon the prevailing macroeconomic conditions, thereby underscoring the pivotal role of macroeconomic variables in ensuring the accuracy of the model.

Treatment 2: Interest Rates and Unemployment

The baseline ATE, as calculated in the interest rate model, is 0.123. This indicates that high interest rates are associated with an increased unemployment rate.

A sensitivity analysis was conducted to ascertain the impact of varying inputs on the model output. The notable alteration in ATE upon the exclusion of trade balance and exchange rate variables indicates that these two factors are pivotal in accurately modelling the relationship between interest rates and unemployment.

Table 4. Interest rates model sensitivity analysis

Removed_Control	ATE	ATE_Difference_from_Baseline
Exports, US dollars, exchange rate converted, Billions, Calendar and seasonally adjusted	0,169725396	0,046697263
Imports, US dollars, exchange rate converted, Billions, Calendar and seasonally adjusted	0,113570831	-0,009457302
Trade balance, US dollars, exchange rate converted, Billions, Calendar and seasonally adjusted	0,021517991	-0,101510141
Financial Market: Real Effective Exchange Rates	0,048083953	-0,074944179
Currency Conversions: US Dollar Exchange Rate: Average of Daily Rates: National Currency: USD for Euro Area	0,525966608	0,402938476

Table 4 illustrates the impact of removing each control variable from the model on the ATE. The removal of the control variables from the model allows for the identification of how the ATE changes, thereby indicating which variables the model is sensitive to. The removal of exports results in an increase in the ATE value to

0.1697, which is 0.0467 units higher than the baseline ATE. This increase indicates that exports exert a significant influence on the model. Upon the removal of imports, the ATE decreases to 0.1136, which is -0.0095 units less than the baseline ATE. This indicates that imports exert a limited effect within the model. Upon the removal of the trade balance, the ATE value decreased to 0.0215, which is -0.1015 units less than the baseline ATE. This substantial alteration implies that the trade balance exerts a considerable influence on the model. The removal of the real effective exchange rate results in a decrease in the ATE to 0.0481, which is -0.0749 units less than the baseline ATE. This indicates that the exchange rate is a significant variable in the model. Upon the removal of the exchange rate, the ATE value increased to 0.5260, representing a 0.4029-unit increase relative to the basic ATE. This considerable increase suggests that the exchange rate is a pivotal variable for maintaining the stability of the model. The results demonstrate that factors such as the trade balance and exchange rate exert a pivotal influence on the model's accuracy, whereas variables such as exports and imports exert a comparatively more constrained effect.

The sensitivity analysis demonstrates that the ATE of the model exhibits considerable variability, particularly regarding the trade balance and exchange rate. The following variables exert a significant influence on the model: The trade balance and exchange rate exert the greatest influence on the ATE in the model; the removal of these two variables from the model results in a notable alteration in the estimated effect. This demonstrates that the relationship between interest rates and unemployment is markedly influenced by these two variables, and that these variables must be incorporated into the model to ensure the reliability of the estimated ATE. The model demonstrates a moderate sensitivity to exports and the real effective exchange rate. The model demonstrates a moderate degree of sensitivity to exports and the real effective exchange rate. These variables contribute to the stabilization of the treatment effect, although their influence is less significant than that of the trade balance and exchange rate. The model demonstrates a certain degree of stability with regard to imports. The treatment effect of the model is the most stable when imports are removed, indicating that this variable has a limited impact on the stability of the ATE of the model.

Consequently, sensitivity analysis demonstrates that the treatment effect of the model (the effect of interest rates on unemployment) is markedly susceptible to fluctuations in the exchange rate and trade balance. It is crucial to incorporate these variables into the model to ensure the reliability of the estimated treatment effect. Conversely, the effect of imports on the treatment estimate is insignificant, indicating that the model is less reliant on this variable to ensure ATE stability.

Treatment 3: Real Effective Exchange Rate and Unemployment

In the real effective exchange rate model, the baseline ATE value was found to be -0.10, indicating that a strong exchange rate tends to reduce the unemployment rate.

A sensitivity analysis was conducted to ascertain the impact of varying the input parameters. Upon removing the exchange rate and interest rates, significant alterations in the ATE were observed, indicating that these variables are crucial for ensuring the precision of the model.

Table 5. Real effective exchange rate model sensitivity analysis

Removed_Control	ATE	ATE_Difference_from_Baseline
Exports, US dollars, exchange rate converted, Billions, Calendar and seasonally adjusted	-0,131365337	-0,02180201
Imports, US dollars, exchange rate converted, Billions, Calendar and seasonally adjusted	-0,098251615	0,011311712
Trade balance, US dollars, exchange rate converted, Billions, Calendar and seasonally adjusted	-0,111955557	-0,00239223
Interest Rates: Long-Term Government Bond Yields: 10-Year: Main (Including Benchmark) for Euro Area	-0,146156516	-0,03659319
Currency Conversions: US Dollar Exchange Rate: Average of Daily Rates: National Currency: USD for Euro Area	-0,042962349	0,066600978

Table 5 illustrates the impact of removing each control variable from the model on the ATE. This sensitivity analysis examines the dependence of the model on different control variables and reveals the changes in the ATE value. The removal of exports resulted in an ATE value of -0.1314, representing a decrease of -0.0218 units from the baseline ATE. This suggests that exports exert a discernible influence on the model.

Upon the removal of imports, the ATE value was calculated to be -0.0983, representing an increase of 0.0113 units from the baseline ATE. This suggests that the impact of imports on the model is relatively limited. The removal of the trade balance resulted in a decrease in the ATE value to -0.1120, representing a reduction of -0.0024 units from the baseline ATE. This minor alteration suggests that the impact of the trade balance on the model is relatively constrained.

The removal of interest rates resulted in an ATE value of -0.1462, representing a decrease of -0.0366 units from the baseline ATE. This suggests that interest rates are a crucial factor in maintaining the stability of the model. Upon the removal of the exchange rate, the ATE is calculated to be -0.0430, which is 0.0666 units greater than the basic ATE. This considerable increase suggests that the exchange rate is a crucial variable for the model to obtain reliable ATE estimates. The results demonstrate that interest rates and exchange rates are pivotal variables in the model, whereas other variables exert a comparatively lesser influence on model stability.

The sensitivity analysis demonstrates that the model's ATE estimate is most susceptible to fluctuations in exchange rates and interest rates. The removal of exchange rates and interest rates as key influences resulted in notable alterations to the ATE, suggesting that these variables exert a considerable influence on the relationship between the real effective exchange rate and unemployment. The removal of these control variables has a significant impact on the estimated effect, and therefore it is essential to include these variables for the model to obtain a reliable ATE. The model demonstrates moderate sensitivity to exports. The model displays moderate sensitivity to exports, with the removal of exports resulting in a discernible but insignificant alteration in the estimated ATE. This indicates that exports contribute to the relationship but are not as pivotal as exchange rates and interest rates. The model displays a certain degree of stability regarding imports and the trade balance. The smallest changes were observed when imports and the trade balance were removed, indicating that the model's treatment effect estimate is relatively stable and robust to these variables.

Consequently, a negative ATE value of -0.10 indicates that higher real effective exchange rates are generally associated with lower unemployment rates. However, sensitivity analysis demonstrates that this relationship is highly contingent on the inclusion of control variables, such as the exchange rate and interest rate, in the model. The exclusion of these variables from the model resulted in a notable bias in the ATE estimate, indicating that the model results are less stable in the absence of these variables. It is therefore essential to include exchange rate and interest rate variables in the model to ensure the robustness and reliability of the treatment effect estimate.

CONCLUSION

This study presents a comprehensive analysis of the causal effects of trade balance, interest rates, and real effective exchange rates on unemployment in the Euro Area. To address the inherent complexity of economic interactions and potential endogeneity, a DML framework is employed. The findings emphasize the intricate and context-specific interrelationship between these macroeconomic variables and unemployment, offering insights that extend beyond the scope of traditional econometric approaches.

The DML model employed in this study demonstrates exceptional accuracy in capturing the causal relationships between macroeconomic variables and unemployment. Model evaluation metrics, including a low MAE of 0.077 and RMSE of 0.13, confirm the reliability of the predictions. Furthermore, the model's R^2 value of 0.993 indicates a high degree of explanatory power, with 99.3% of the variability in unemployment accurately explained. These findings validate the robustness of the DML framework in analyzing complex economic relationships.

The results reveal that a positive trade balance significantly reduces unemployment, emphasizing the role of export-led growth in fostering employment opportunities. However, this relationship is not uniform; it is influenced by the real effective exchange rate. Undervalued currencies amplify the competitiveness of exports, magnifying their impact on job creation. These findings are consistent with earlier studies, such as those by Frenkel and Ros, which underscore the importance of exchange rate management in stabilizing labor markets (Frenkel & Ros, 2012). Furthermore, the study highlights the nuanced effects of interest rates on unemployment. While higher interest rates may constrain economic activity and investment, potentially increasing unemployment, they can also signal macroeconomic stability, which may indirectly foster job creation. These dual effects underline the importance of distinguishing between short-term and long-term impacts of monetary policy (Grodecka-Messi & Hull, 2022).

The observed negative correlation between real effective exchange rates and unemployment indicates the potential benefits of a stronger currency, such as enhanced domestic purchasing power and stimulated internal demand. However, this relationship is highly context-dependent, varying with exchange rate regimes and other macroeconomic factors. In a similar vein, Jeremias (2023) underscored the value of sophisticated machine learning techniques, particularly Random Forest algorithms, in capturing dynamic and non-linear relationships, thereby enhancing unemployment forecasting and exemplifying their utility for real-time economic analysis.

The findings of this study offer not only theoretical insights into macroeconomic interactions but also practical implications for policymaking. For example, maintaining a competitive real effective exchange rate and fostering trade surpluses can be pivotal strategies in reducing unemployment. The results of this research can inform the design of coordinated fiscal, monetary, and trade policies tailored to specific economic contexts within the Euro Area. The implementation of targeted interventions, such as tax incentives or export subsidies, may serve to further enhance the positive effects of trade surpluses on employment levels (Frenkel & Ros, 2012).

Policy and Future Research Recommendations

Building on this work, future research could explore the inclusion of additional variables, such as fiscal policy effects, sectoral employment dynamics, and consumer confidence indices, with a view to providing a deeper understanding of the drivers of unemployment. The application of advanced machine learning techniques, such as hybrid models that integrate time-series data with macroeconomic indicators, could facilitate a deeper understanding of the temporal patterns of unemployment. To illustrate, Güler et al. (2024) have demonstrated that models incorporating diverse economic parameters, including inflation and labor force data, markedly enhance forecast precision in Turkey.

The findings of this study provide a foundation for significant recommendations in the development of policy and the advancement of research. Firstly, it is recommended that policymakers adopt an integrated approach to fiscal, monetary, and trade policies with the objective of increasing employment. In particular, the maintenance of a competitive real effective exchange rate can play a pivotal role in enhancing the employment generation potential of trade surpluses. Furthermore, targeted fiscal measures, such as tax incentives or export subsidies for industries with high employment capacity in export-oriented sectors, can reinforce the favorable impact of trade balances on the labor market (Frenkel & Ros, 2012).

Monetary policies must be carefully calibrated to support economic stability while avoiding adverse effects on unemployment. It is recommended that central banks develop strategies that consider the broad labor market effects of interest rate decisions. These strategies should aim to minimize negative effects while supporting long-term economic growth (Grodecka-Messi & Hull, 2022). Furthermore, future research could concentrate on the employment effects in sectors that are most affected by trade and monetary policies, as well as the effects of demographic variables such as aging populations or migration.

The application of the DML method to a variety of contexts, including regional labor markets and underrepresented economies, could facilitate a more comprehensive understanding of unemployment dynamics. By adopting a granular and innovative approach to data analysis, researchers may be able to increase the accuracy of estimating economic variables by incorporating non-traditional data sources such as Google Trends (Jeremias, 2023).

Subsequent studies may expand the analysis area by incorporating additional inputs, and the current methodology may be applied in different dimensions. To illustrate, the present study, which was conducted in the Euro Area (comprising 20 countries), could be transformed into a series of detailed country-based analyses. This would facilitate a more comprehensive investigation of the distinctive economic dynamics and labor market characteristics of each country. An alternative approach would be to expand the scope of the study to a more global perspective, testing it under different regions and economic conditions. Moreover, causal machine learning techniques may be utilized to analyze the heterogeneous effects. This approach will facilitate the identification of the disparate effects of various sectors, demographic groups, and regional characteristics on unemployment.

Final Reflections

This study demonstrates that robust causal inference methods, such as DML, significantly enhance academic understanding and offer actionable insights for policymakers. By addressing the complexity of macroeconomic interactions, this research provides a foundation for developing strategies that balance economic growth with labor market stability. Future research and policy initiatives should continue to leverage advanced analytical tools to address the challenges of modern economies and promote sustainable, inclusive employment opportunities (Kristiansson, 2023).

REFERENCES

Baldwin, R., & Di Mauro, B. W. (2020). *Economics in the Time of COVID-19*. CEPR Press.

Bartolini, L., Cahill, M., & Wright, M. (2014). The Differential Effects of Trade Policy: Employment Effects in U.S. Manufacturing. *The American Economic Review*, 104(1), 101–122. DOI: 10.1257/aer.104.1.101

Bayoumi, T., Laxton, D., & Pesenti, P. (2004). Benefits and Spillovers of Greater Competition in Europe: A Macroeconomic Assessment. *IMF Working Paper*.

Blanchard, O. (2009). *Macroeconomics* (5th ed.). Pearson.

Blanchard, O., & Katz, L. F. (1992). Regional Evolutions. *Brookings Papers on Economic Activity*, 1992(1), 1–75.

Bussière, M., Fratzscher, M., & Müller, G. J. (2011). Productivity Shocks, Current Accounts, and the Exchange Rate. *Journal of International Money and Finance*, 30(5), 775–795. DOI: 10.1016/j.jimonfin.2010.11.006

Celbiş, M. G. (2023). Unemployment in rural Europe: A machine learning perspective. *Applied Spatial Analysis and Policy*, 16(3), 1071–1095. PMID: 35677346

Chakraborty, T., Chakraborty, A. K., Biswas, M., Banerjee, S., & Bhattacharya, S. (2021). Unemployment rate forecasting: A hybrid approach. *Computational Economics*, 57(1), 183–201.

Chernozhukov, V., Chetverikov, D., Demirer, M., Duflo, E., Hansen, C., Newey, W., & Robins, J. (2018). Double/debiased machine learning for treatment and structural parameters. *The Econometrics Journal*, 21(1), C1–C68.

Claveria, O. (2019). Forecasting the unemployment rate using the degree of agreement in consumer unemployment expectations. *Journal for Labour Market Research*, 53(1), 3.

Davidescu, A. A., Apostu, S. A., & Paul, A. (2021). Comparative analysis of different univariate forecasting methods in modelling and predicting the romanian unemployment rate for the period 2021–2022. *Entropy (Basel, Switzerland)*, 23(3), 325. PMID: 33803384

Egger, P., & Etzel, D. (2012). The impact of trade on employment in China: The case of processing trade. *World Economy*, 35(1), 16–38.

Eichengreen, B. (2019). *Globalizing Capital: A History of the International Monetary System*. Princeton University Press.

Ferrucci, G., Jiménez-Rodriguez, R., & Onorante, L. (2010). Food Price Pass-Through in the Euro Area: Non-Linearities and the Role of the Exchange Rate. *European Central Bank Working Paper*.

Feuerriegel, S., Frauen, D., Melnychuk, V., Schweisthal, J., Hess, K., Curth, A., & van der Schaar, M. (2024). Causal machine learning for predicting treatment outcomes. *Nature Medicine*, 30(4), 958–968. PMID: 38641741

Frenkel, R., & Ros, J. (2012). Unemployment and the Real Exchange Rate in Latin America. *World Development*, 40(5), 919–934. DOI: 10.1016/j.worlddev.2011.11.002

Gostkowski, M., & Rokicki, T. (2021). Forecasting the unemployment rate: Application of selected prediction methods. *European Research Studies*, 24(3), 985–1000.

Grodecka-Messi, A., & Hull, I. (2022). Measuring the Impact of Taxes and Public Services on Property Values: A Double Machine Learning Approach. *Journal of Applied Econometrics*, 37(1), 56–75. DOI: 10.1002/jae.2875

Güler, M., Kabakçı, A., Koç, Ö., Eraslan, E., Derin, K. H., Güler, M., & Namlı, E. (2024). Forecasting of the Unemployment Rate in Turkey: Comparison of the Machine Learning Models. *Sustainability*, 16(15), 6509.

Hünermund, P., Kaminski, J., & Schmitt, C. (2022). Causal machine learning and business decision making. Available at *SSRN* 3867326.

Jeremias, J. (2023). Forecasting Unemployment Rates with Machine Learning Methods: A Case Study in Nonlinear Macroeconomic Relationships. *Applied Economics Letters*, 30(2), 202–216. DOI: 10.1080/13504851.2023.2123445

Katris, C. (2020). Prediction of unemployment rates with time series and machine learning techniques. *Computational Economics*, 55(2), 673–706.

Kreiner, A., & Duca, J. V. (2019). Can Machine Learning Help Forecast the Overall Mortgage Delinquency Rate?

Kristiansson, E. (2023). Advancing Macro-Financial Analysis through Double Machine Learning. *International Journal of Economic Modeling*, 15(4), 345–372. DOI: 10.1016/j.ijem.2023.101346

Krugman, P., & Obstfeld, M. (2003). *International Economics: Theory and Policy*. Addison Wesley.

Krugman, P. R., Obstfeld, M., & Melitz, M. J. (2018). *International Economics: Theory and Policy*. Pearson.

Mankiw, N. G. (2016). *Principles of Economics* (8th ed.). Cengage Learning.

Moraffah, R., Karimi, A. H., Raglin, A., & Liu, H. (2023, August). Socially Responsible Machine Learning: A Causal Perspective. In *Proceedings of the 29th ACM SIGKDD Conference on Knowledge Discovery and Data Mining* (pp. 5819-5820).

Putri, E. S., Hamid, A., & Novitasari, D. C. R. (2022). Prediction of the Tuban Regency Open Unemployment Rate in 2022 with the Backpropagation Method. Numerical: Jurnal Matematika dan Pendidikan Matematika, 25-36.

Rodrik, D. (1997). *Has Globalization Gone Too Far?* Institute for International Economics.

Ryu, P. M. (2018). Predicting the unemployment rate using social media analysis. *Journal of Information Processing Systems*, 14(4), 904–915.

Sachs, J. D., & Warner, A. M. (1995). Economic Reform and the Process of Global Integration. *Brookings Papers on Economic Activity*, 1995(1), 1–118.

Sen, M., Basu, S., Chatterjee, A., Banerjee, A., Pal, S., Mukhopadhyay, P. K., & Tarafdar, A. (2022, December). Prediction of Unemployment using Machine Learning Approach. In *2022 OITS International Conference on Information Technology (OCIT)* (pp. 1-5). IEEE.

Sharma, S., & Singh, S. (2016, January). Unemployment rates forecasting using supervised neural networks. In 2016 6th International Conference-Cloud System and Big Data Engineering (Confluence) (pp. 28-33). IEEE.

Singhania, R., & Kundu, S. (2020). Forecasting the United States unemployment rate by using recurrent neural networks with Google Trends data. International Journal of Trade, Economics and Finance, 11(6).

Stock, J. H., & Watson, M. W. (2019). *Introduction to Econometrics* (4th ed.). Pearson.

Ünlü, R. (2019). An assessment of imbalanced control chart pattern recognition by artificial neural networks. In *Artificial Intelligence and Machine Learning Applications in Civil* (pp. 240–258). Mechanical, and Industrial Engineering. DOI: 10.4018/978-1-7998-0301-0.ch013

Ünlü, R., & Xanthopoulos, P. (2021). A reduced variance unsupervised ensemble learning algorithm based on modern portfolio theory. *Expert Systems with Applications*, 180, 115085.

Vowels, M. J. (2022). Trying to outrun causality with machine learning: Limitations of model explainability techniques for identifying predictive variables. Stat, 1050, 22.

Xu, W., Li, Z., Cheng, C., & Zheng, T. (2013). Data mining for unemployment rate prediction using search engine query data. *Service Oriented Computing and Applications*, 7, 33–42.

Yamacli, D. S., & Yamacli, S. (2023). Estimation of the unemployment rate in Turkey: A comparison of the ARIMA and machine learning models including Covid-19 pandemic periods. *Heliyon*, 9(1). PMID: 36691554

Yuan, J., & Liu, S. (2024). A double machine learning model for measuring the impact of the Made in China 2025 strategy on green economic growth. *Scientific Reports*, 14(1), 12026. PMID: 38797785

Zhao, Y., & Liu, Q. (2023). Causal ML: Python package for causal inference machine learning. *SoftwareX*, 21, 101294.

Compilation of References

A, S., V, M., V, R., & B, U. (2024). COLLEGEBOT: Virtual Assistant System for Enquiry Using Natural Language Processing. *2024 2nd International Conference on Intelligent Data Communication Technologies and Internet of Things (IDCIoT)*, 1407–1414. https://api.semanticscholar.org/CorpusID:268613686

Ab Ghani, N. L., Che Cob, Z., Mohd Drus, S., & Sulaiman, H. (2019). Student enrolment prediction model in higher education institution: a data mining approach. *Proceedings of the 3rd International Symposium of Information and Internet Technology (SYMINTECH 2018)*, 43–52.

Abbass, K., Asif, M., Niazi, A. A. K., Qazi, T. F., Basit, A., & Al-Muwaffaq Ahmed, F. A. (2022). Understanding the interaction among enablers of quality enhancement of higher business education in Pakistan. *PLoS One*, 17(5), e0267919. DOI: 10.1371/journal.pone.0267919 PMID: 35617271

Abbass, K., Basit, A., Niazi, A. A. K., Mufti, R., Zahid, N., & Qazi, T. F. (2023). Evaluating the social outcomes of COVID-19 pandemic: Empirical evidence from Pakistan. *Environmental Science and Pollution Research International*, 30(22), 61466–61478. DOI: 10.1007/s11356-022-19628-7 PMID: 35306646

Abid, S. K., Sulaiman, N., Chan, S. W., Nazir, U., Abid, M., Han, H., & Vega-Muñoz, A. (2021). Toward an integrated disaster management approach: How artificial intelligence can boost disaster management. *Sustainability*, 13(22), 12560.

Agievich, V. (2014). Mathematical model and multi-criteria analysis of designing large-scale enterprise roadmap. PhD thesis – Mathematical modelling, numerical methods and complexes of programs.

Ahmad, A., & Whitworth, B. (2011, December). Access control taxonomy for social networks. In 2011 7th International Conference on Information Assurance and Security (IAS) (pp. 256-261). IEEE.

Ahmad, R., & Pande, S. (2024). Examining the Integration of Artificial Intelligence in Customer Relationship Management. SSRN *Electronic Journal*. https://api.semanticscholar.org/CorpusID:269825841

Ahmad, A., Alzahrani, A. S., Ahmed, N., & Ahsan, T. (2020a). A delegation model for SDN-driven federated cloud. *Alexandria Engineering Journal*, 59(5), 3653–3663.

Ahmad, A., Whitworth, B., Zeshan, F., Bertino, E., & Friedman, R. (2017). Extending social networks with delegation. *Computers & Security*, 70, 546–564.

Ahmad, A., Whitworth, B., Zeshan, F., Janczewski, L., Ali, M., Chaudary, M. H., & Friedman, R. (2019). A relation-aware multiparty access control. *Journal of Intelligent & Fuzzy Systems*, 37(1), 227–239.

Ahmad, A., Zeeshan, F., Marriam, R., Samreen, A., & Ahmed, S. (2021). Does one size fit all? Investigating the effect of group size and gamification on learners' behaviors in higher education. *Journal of Computing in Higher Education*, 33, 296–327.

Ahmad, A., Zeshan, F., Hamid, M., Marriam, R., & Samreen, A. (2022). Application of Gamification in Modern Education. In *Handbook of Research on Promoting Economic and Social Development Through Serious Games* (pp. 60–75). IGI Global.

Ahmad, A., Zeshan, F., Khan, M. S., Marriam, R., Ali, A., & Samreen, A. (2020b). The impact of gamification on learning outcomes of computer science majors. *ACM Transactions on Computing Education*, 20(2), 1–25.

Ahmad, G. (2010). *Domain-Oriented Modeling of Indian Education System Through UML*. IUP.

Ahmed, M., Ahmad, A., Zeshan, F., & Turab, H. (2024). Blockchain Basics: A Deep Dive Into the Blocks, Chains, and Consensus. In Decentralizing the Online Experience With Web3 Technologies (pp. 57-89). IGI Global.

Ahmed, S., Javaid, S., Niazi, M. F., Alam, A., Ahmad, A., Baig, M. A., & Ahmed, T. (2019). A qualitative analysis of context-aware ubiquitous learning environments using Bluetooth beacons. *Technology, Pedagogy and Education*, 28(1), 53–71.

Ahn, M. J., & Chen, Y. C. (2020, June). Artificial intelligence in government: potentials, challenges, and the future. In *Proceedings of the 21st Annual International Conference on Digital Government Research* (pp. 243-252).

AIforEducation. (2024). Generative AI Explainer. https://www.aiforeducation.io/ai-resources/generative-ai-explainer

Akour, I. A., Alshurideh, H. M., Alzoubi, H. M., Alshurideh, M. T., & Antouz, Y. A. (2023). Integrating Artificial Intelligence in Improving Educational System: The Mediating role of Smart Learning. *2023 International Conference on Business Analytics for Technology and Security (ICBATS)*, 1–5. https://api.semanticscholar.org/CorpusID:258728985

Aksoy, M., & Ceylan, T. (2021). An Action Research on Improving Classroom Communication and Interaction in Social Studies Teaching. .DOI: 10.1155/2021/9943194

Alahi, M. E. E., Sukkuea, A., Tina, F. W., Nag, A., Kurdthongmee, W., Suwannarat, K., & Mukhopadhyay, S. C. (2023). Integration of IoT-enabled technologies and artificial intelligence (AI) for smart city scenario: Recent advancements and future trends. *Sensors (Basel)*, 23(11), 5206. PMID: 37299934

Albassam, W. A. (2023). The Power of Artificial Intelligence in Recruitment: An Analytical Review of Current AI-Based Recruitment Strategies. *International Journal of Professional Business Review*. https://api.semanticscholar.org/CorpusID:259639373

Al-Besher, A. & Kumar, K. (2022). Use of artificial intelligence to enhance e-government services. Measurement: Sensors.

Algorabi, O., & Namli, E. (2022). An integrated machine learning-based decision support model for prediction of bank telemarketing success. *Verimlilik Dergisi*, (1), 94–109. DOI: 10.51551/verimlilik.748616S

Al-Hawari, F., & Barham, H. (2021). A machine learning based help desk system for IT service management. *Journal of King Saud University. Computer and Information Sciences*, 33(6), 702–718.

Alhosani, K., & Alhashmi, S. M. (2024). Opportunities, challenges, and benefits of AI innovation in government services: A review. *Discover Artificial Intelligence*, 4(1), 18. DOI: 10.1007/s44163-024-00111-w

Aljneibi, A. A. (2020). Enablers & Barriers to AI Adopting in Public Services (Master's thesis, The British University in Dubai).

Al-Ka'bi, A. H. (2023). Proposed artificial intelligence algorithm and deep learning techniques for development of higher education. *Int. J. Intell. Networks*, 4, 68–73. https://api.semanticscholar.org/CorpusID:257574020

Almahairah, M. S. Z. (2023). Artificial Intelligence Application for Effective Customer Relationship Management. *2023 International Conference on Computer Communication and Informatics (ICCCI)*, 1–7. https://api.semanticscholar.org/CorpusID:258869492

Almaliki, A. H., Derdour, A., & Ali, E. (2023). Air Quality Index (AQI) Prediction in Holy Makkah Based on Machine Learning Methods. *Sustainability*, 15(17), 13168.

AL-Mashaqbeh. (2023). The Relationship Between E-Government and Job Performance.

Alowais, S. A., Alghamdi, S. S., Alsuhebany, N., Alqahtani, T., Alshaya, A. I., Almohareb, S. N., & Albekairy, A. M. (2023). Revolutionizing healthcare: The role of artificial intelligence in clinical practice. *BMC Medical Education*, 23(1), 689. PMID: 37740191

Al-Sai, Z. A., & Abualigah, L. M. (2017, May). Big data and E-government: A review. In *2017 8th international conference on information technology (ICIT)* (pp. 580-587). IEEE.

Aminizadeh, S., Heidari, A., Dehghan, M., Toumaj, S., Rezaei, M., Navimipour, N. J., & Unal, M. (2024). Opportunities and challenges of artificial intelligence and distributed systems to improve the quality of healthcare service. *Artificial Intelligence in Medicine*, 149, 102779. PMID: 38462281

Andersson, C., Hallin, A., & Ivory, C. (2022). Unpacking the digitalisation of public services: Configuring work during automation in local government. Government Information Quarterly.

Ang, K. L. M., Seng, J. K. P., Ngharamike, E., & Ijemaru, G. K. (2022). Emerging technologies for smart cities' transportation: Geo-information, data analytics and machine learning approaches. *ISPRS International Journal of Geo-Information*, 11(2), 85.

Arslan, Y. (2021). Phishing Attacks Awareness Exercise Example. *Duzce Universitesi Bilim Ve Teknoloji Dergisi*, 9(3), 348–358. DOI: 10.29130/dubited.832862

Ateş, E. C. (2021). *Önleyici Kolluk Faaliyetleri Kapsamında Sosyal Medyada Veri Madenciliği: Suçları Önlemek İçin Twitter Analytic'i Kullanma*. Ankara Üniversitesi, Sağlık Bilimleri Enstitüsü.

Athey, S., & Imbens, G. (2016). Recursive partitioning for heterogeneous causal effects. *Proceedings of the National Academy of Sciences of the United States of America*, 113(27), 7353–7360. PMID: 27382149

Atilgan, E., Ertuğrul, H. M., Baycan, O., & Ulucan, H. (2024). Health-led growth hypothesis and health financing systems: An econometric synthesis for OECD countries. *Frontiers in Public Health*, 12. Advance online publication. DOI: 10.3389/fpubh.2024.1437304 PMID: 39114507

Atilgan, K. O., & Yogurtcu, H. (2021). Sentiment Analysis of Twitter Posts of Cargo Company Customers. *Cag Universitesi Sosyal Bilimler Dergisi*, 18(1), 31–39.

Attri, R., Dev, N., & Sharma, V. (2013). Interpretive structural modelling (ISM) approach: an overview. *Research Journal of Management Sciences, 2319*(2), 1171.

Awasthi, I., Gupta, K., Bhogal, P. S., Anand, S. S., & Soni, P. K. (2021). Natural Language Processing (NLP) based Text Summarization—A Survey. *2021 6th International Conference on Inventive Computation Technologies (ICICT)*, 1310-1317. DOI: 10.1109/ICICT50816.2021.9358703

Awoyemi, O. B., & Nwibe, D. A. (2022). A Causal Assessment of Nigeria's Crude Oil Revenue, Health Expenditure, and Economic Growth. *International Journal of Energy Economics and Policy*, 12(5), 420–424.

Azadfallah, M. (2018). *A New Entropy-Based Approach to Determine the Weights of Decision Makers for Each Criterion with Crisp and Interval Data in Group Decision Making Under Multiple Attribute. International Journal of Service Science, Management, Engineering, and Technology (IJSSMET)*. IGI Global. DOI: 10.4018/IJSSMET.2018100103

Bahety, A. (2014). Extension and evaluation of ID3-decision tree algorithm. *Entropy (Basel, Switzerland)*, 2(1), 1–8.

Baldwin, R., & Di Mauro, B. W. (2020). *Economics in the Time of COVID-19*. CEPR Press.

Baltagi, B. H., & Moscone, F. (2010). Health care expenditure and income in the OECD reconsidered: Evidence from panel data. *Economic Modelling*, 27(4), 804–811.

Bandura, A. (1977). *Social learning theory*.

Bankins, S. (2021). The ethical use of artificial intelligence in human resource management: A decision-making framework. *Ethics and Information Technology*.

Banks, F., & Barlex, D. (2021). *Teaching STEM in the Secondary School-Helping Teachers Meet the Challenge* (2nd ed.). Routledge.

Barriento, F., Cheng, W., & Gulledge, T. R. (2003). Customizing CRM for University Implementations. *International Journal of Electronic Business Management*, 1, 63–74. https://api.semanticscholar.org/CorpusID:38148250

Barro, R. J. (1996). Health and Economic Growth. *Journal of Political Economy*, 94(5), S56–S71.

Bartolini, L., Cahill, M., & Wright, M. (2014). The Differential Effects of Trade Policy: Employment Effects in U.S. Manufacturing. *The American Economic Review*, 104(1), 101–122. DOI: 10.1257/aer.104.1.101

Batko, K. & Ślęzak, A. (2022). The use of Big Data Analytics in healthcare. Journal of big Data.

Bayoumi, T., Laxton, D., & Pesenti, P. (2004). Benefits and Spillovers of Greater Competition in Europe: A Macroeconomic Assessment. *IMF Working Paper*.

Begamudra Rangavittal, P. (2024). Transforming Higher Education with Artificial Intelligence - Benefits, Challenges, and Future Directions. *International Journal of Scientific Research*, 13(5), 1635–1642. DOI: 10.21275/sr24525214415

Belenguer, L. (2022). AI bias: exploring discriminatory algorithmic decision-making models and the application of possible machine-centric solutions adapted from the pharmaceutical .... AI and Ethics.

Benedetti, F., Beneventano, D., Bergamaschi, S., & Simonini, G. (2019). Computing Inter-Document Similarity with Context Semantic Analysis. *Information Systems*, 80, 136–147. DOI: 10.1016/j.is.2018.02.009

Berestova, A., Alizade, T., & Umirzakova, Z. (2020). The Role of Social Networks in the Educational Process. *International Journal of Emerging Technologies in Learning*, 15(22).

Berryhill, J., Heang, K. K., Clogher, R., & McBride, K. (2019). Hello, World: Artificial intelligence and its use in the public sector. *OECD Working Papers on Public Governance*, No. 36, OECD Publishing, Paris. DOI: 10.1787/726fd39d-en

Bhumichai, D., Smiliotopoulos, C., Benton, R., Kambourakis, G., & Damopoulos, D. (2024). The convergence of artificial intelligence and blockchain: The state of play and the road ahead. *Information (Basel)*, 15(5), 268.

Bilal, A., Mirza, H. T., Hussain, I., & Ahmad, A. (2024). Investigating Influence of Google-Play Application Titles on Success. *Big Data Research*, 36, 100443.

Bilgin, O., Çetinoğlu, Ö., & Oflazer, K. (2004). Building a Wordnet for Turkish. *Romanian Journal of Information Science and Technology*, 7, 163–172.

Bird, S., Klein, E., & Loper, E. (2009). *Natural Language Processing with Python: Analyzing Text with the Natural Language Toolkit*. O'Reilly Media, Inc.

Bizzdesign. (2022). Digital Transformation. Bizzdesign. https://bizzdesign.com/blog-category/digital-transformation/

Blanchard, O. (2009). *Macroeconomics* (5th ed.). Pearson.

Blanchard, O., & Katz, L. F. (1992). Regional Evolutions. *Brookings Papers on Economic Activity*, 1992(1), 1–75.

Bloom, D. E., & Canning, D. (2000). The Health and Wealth of Nations. *Science*, 287(5456), 1207–1209. PMID: 10712155

Blount, K. (2024). Using artificial intelligence to prevent crime: Implications for due process and criminal justice. *AI & Society*.

Bonaccorso, G. (2018). *Machine Learning Algorithms: Popular algorithms for data science and machine learning*. Packt Publishing Ltd.

Borins, S. (2001). Encouraging innovation in the public sector. *Journal of Intellectual Capital*, 2(3), 310–319. DOI: 10.1108/14691930110400128

Borko, H., & Bernick, M. (1963). Automatic Document Classification. *Journal of the Association for Computing Machinery*, 10(2), 151–162. DOI: 10.1145/321160.321165

Bozkurt, A. (2023). Generative artificial intelligence (AI) powered conversational educational agents: The inevitable paradigm shift. *Asian Journal of Distance Education*, 18(1).

Bracci, E. (n.d.). The loopholes of algorithmic public services: An “intelligent” accountability research agenda. Accounting.

Bragazzi, N. L., Dai, H., Damiani, G., Behzadifar, M., Martini, M., & Wu, J. (2020). How big data and artificial intelligence can help better manage the COVID-19 pandemic. *International Journal of Environmental Research and Public Health*, 17(9), 3176. PMID: 32370204

Brañas, A. (2024). Intelligent Process Automation Costs: Saving with Efficiency. https://qflowbpm.com/intell-auto-costs/

Brause, R. W., Langsdorf, T. S., & Hepp, H. (1999). Neural data mining for credit card fraud detection. *Proceedings 11th International Conference on Tools with Artificial Intelligence*, 103-106.

Brayer, O. (2023). Is Polymath Thinking the Answer to Thriving in the AI Era? Medium. https://medium.com/@opher.brayer/is-polymath-thinking-the-answer-to-thriving-in-the-ai-era-d269000163a3

Breiman, L. (2001). Random forests. *Machine Learning*, 45(1), 5–32. DOI: 10.1023/A:1010933404324

Breiman, L. (2017). *Classification and regression trees*. Routledge.

Bruno, F., & Cocchi, D. (2022). A unified strategy for building simple air quality indices. *Environmetrics*, 13, 243–261.

Bryce, T. (2015). Managing Complexity. Modern Analyst Media LLC. https://www.modernanalyst.com/Resources/Articles/tabid/115/ID/3354/Managing-Complexity.aspx

Buhmann, A. & Fieseler, C. (2021). Towards a deliberative framework for responsible innovation in artificial intelligence. Technology in Society.

Burgess, S. (2016). Human capital and education: The state of the art in the economics of education.

Burke, J. (2022). Group Work in the Classroom: Types of Small Groups. CENTRE FOR TEACHING EXCELLENCE. University of Waterloo. https://uwaterloo.ca/centre-for-teaching-excellence/

Bussière, M., Fratzscher, M., & Müller, G. J. (2011). Productivity Shocks, Current Accounts, and the Exchange Rate. *Journal of International Money and Finance*, 30(5), 775–795. DOI: 10.1016/j.jimonfin.2010.11.006

Busuioc, M. (2021). Accountable artificial intelligence: Holding algorithms to account. Public Administration Review.

Butt, M. J., Malik, A. K., Qamar, N., Yar, S., Malik, A. J., & Rauf, U. (2023). A survey on COVID-19 data analysis using AI, IoT, and social media. Sensors.

Büyükkör, Y., & Doğan, S. (2024). Borsa Endeks Yönünün Ağaç Tabanlı Topluluk Makine Öğrenmesi Yöntemleri ile Tahmini: BİST-100 Örneği. *Bingöl Üniversitesi Sosyal Bilimler Enstitüsü Dergisi*, 27, 324–335.

Cambridge Dictionary. (2023). Academic. https://dictionary.cambridge.org/dictionary/english/academic

Campbell, I. C. G., & Yiming, Y. (2011). *Learning with Support Vector Machines.* Morgan and Claypool., DOI: 10.2200/S00324ED1V01Y201102AIM010

Cao, S.-Y., Wang, W.-H., & Zhang, H.-F. (2011). Research and application on customer satisfaction degree evaluation system in call centers of commercial bank. In *2011 International Conference on Business Management and Electronic Information (BMEI)* (p. 803-807). IEEE.

Carbo-Valverde, S., Cuadros-Solas, P., & Rodríguez-Fernández, F. (2020). A machine learning approach to the digitalization of bank customers: Evidence from random and causal forests. *PLoS One*, 15(10), e0240362. PMID: 33112894

Carol, B.-M. H., Besterfield, G., & Besterfield-Sacre, M. (1998). *Total Quality Management* (Subsequent edition). Prentice Hall.

Cebiroglu, G. (2002). Root reaching method without dictionary (Master's thesis, Istanbul Technical University). Istanbul Technical University, Institute of Science and Technology, Istanbul, Turkey.

Celbiş, M. G. (2023). Unemployment in rural Europe: A machine learning perspective. *Applied Spatial Analysis and Policy*, 16(3), 1071–1095. PMID: 35677346

Ceylan, Z., & Atalan, A. (2020). Estimation of healthcare expenditure per capita of Turkey using artificial intelligence techniques with genetic algorithm-based feature selection.

Chaione. (2022). Digital Transformation-The 4 Types of Digital Transformation. Chaione.com.

Chakraborty, T., Chakraborty, A. K., Biswas, M., Banerjee, S., & Bhattacharya, S. (2021). Unemployment rate forecasting: A hybrid approach. *Computational Economics*, 57(1), 183–201.

Chatterjee, S., Ghosh, S. K., Chaudhuri, R., & Nguyen, B. (2019). Are CRM systems ready for AI integration? *The Bottom Line*. https://api.semanticscholar.org/CorpusID:197781292

Chatterjee, S., Rana, N. P., Khorana, S., Mikalef, P., & Sharma, A. (2021). Assessing Organizational Users' Intentions and Behavior to AI Integrated CRM Systems: A Meta-UTAUT Approach. *Information Systems Frontiers*, 25, 1299–1313. https://api.semanticscholar.org/CorpusID:238650817

Che, C., Hu, H., Zhao, X., Li, S., & Lin, Q. (2023). Advancing Cancer Document Classification with Random Forest. *Academic Journal of Science and Technology, 8*(1), Article 1.

Chen, L., Chen, P., & Lin, Z. (2020). Artificial intelligence in education: A review. *IEEE Access : Practical Innovations, Open Solutions*, 8, 75264–75278.

Chen, T., Gascó-Hernandez, M., & Esteve, M. (2024). The Adoption and Implementation of Artificial Intelligence Chatbots in Public Organizations: Evidence from US State Governments. *American Review of Public Administration*, 54(3), 255–270. DOI: 10.1177/0275074023120052

Chen, T., & Guestrin, C. (2016). Xgboost: A Scalable Tree Boosting System. *Proceedings of the 22nd acm Sigkdd International Conference on Knowledge Discovery and Data Mining*.

Chen, T., & Guestrin, C. (2016). XGBoost: A Scalable Tree Boosting System. *Proceedings of the 22nd ACM SIGKDD International Conference on Knowledge Discovery and Data Mining*.

Cheong, B. C. (2024). Transparency and accountability in AI systems: Safeguarding wellbeing in the age of algorithmic decision-making. Frontiers in Human Dynamics.

Chernozhukov, V., Chetverikov, D., Demirer, M., Duflo, E., Hansen, C., Newey, W., & Robins, J. (2018). Double/debiased machine learning for treatment and structural parameters. *The Econometrics Journal*, 21(1), C1–C68.

Chitra, K., & Subashini, B. (2013). Data mining techniques and its applications in banking sector. *International Journal of Emerging Technology and Advanced Engineering*, 3(8), 219–220.

Chomsky, N. (2002). *Syntactic Structures*. De Gruyter Mouton.

Chowdhary, K. R. (2020). *Fundamentals of Artificial Intelligence*.

Ciner, M. N., Güler, M., Namlı, E., Samastı, M., Ulu, M., Peker, İ. B., & Gülbaz, S. (2024). The Forecast of Streamflow through Göksu Stream Using Machine Learning and Statistical Methods. *Water (Basel)*, 16(8), 1125.

Ciner, M. N., Guler, M., Namli, E., Samasti, M., Ulu, M., Peker, I. B., & Gulbaz, S. (2024). The forecast of streamflow through Goksu Stream using machine learning and statistical methods. *Water (Basel)*, 16(8), 1125. DOI: 10.3390/w16081125

Cingillioglu, I. (2024). What impacts matriculation decisions? Identifying students' university choice factors on a global scale with Artificial Intelligence. *Studies in Higher Education*. https://api.semanticscholar.org/CorpusID:267735802

Cirelli, J., Konkol, A. M., Aqlan, F., & Nwokeji, J. C. (2018). Predictive analytics models for student admission and enrollment. *Proceedings of the International Conference on Industrial Engineering and Operations Management,* 2018(SEP), 1395–1403.

Clancy, L. (2019). Functional programming reaches for stardom in finance. CME Group. https://www.risk.net/risk-management/6395366/functional-programming-reaches-for-stardom-in-finance

Clark, W., Johnson, K., & Turner, C. (2004). Cross-Functional Student Teams as a Teaching Tool for Enhanced Learning. East Tennessee State University, Johnson City.

Clark, M., Fletcher, P., Hanson, J., Irani, R., Waterhouse, M., & Thelin, J. (2013). *Web Services Business Strategies and Architectures*. Apress.

Claveria, O. (2019). Forecasting the unemployment rate using the degree of agreement in consumer unemployment expectations. *Journal for Labour Market Research*, 53(1), 3.

Codd, E. F., Codd, S. B., & Salley, C. T. (1993). *Providing OLAP (On-line Analytical Processing) to User-Analysts: An IT Mandate*. Codd & Date.

Cortés-Cediel, M. E., Segura-Tinoco, A., Cantador, I., & Bolívar, M. P. R. (2023). Trends and challenges of e-government chatbots: Advances in exploring open government data and citizen participation content. *Government Information Quarterly*, 40(4), 101877.

Cosar, N. (2009). *Historical Development of the Banking Sector in Turkey*. Yildiz Technical University, Department of Economics.

Cotellessa, A. (2018). In Pursuit of Polymaths: Understanding Renaissance Persons of the 21st Century. Department Human and Organizational Learning and International Affairs. The Faculty of The Graduate School of Education and Human Development of The George Washington University, USA.

Cress, U., Moskaliuk, J., & Jeong, H. (2016). *Mass Collaboration and Education. Computer-Supported Collaborative Learning Series* (Vol. 16). CULS.

Criado, J. I., & de Zarate-Alcarazo, L. O. (2022). Technological frames, CIOs, and Artificial Intelligence in public administration: A socio-cognitive exploratory study in Spanish local governments. *Government Information Quarterly*, 39(3), 101688. DOI: 10.1016/j.giq.2022.101688

Crittenden, V. (2005). Cross-functional education: The need for case development. February 2005. *Journal of Business Research*, 58(7), 955–959. DOI: 10.1016/j.jbusres.2003.12.004

Crittenden, V., & Wilson, E. (2006). An Exploratory Study of Cross-Functional Education in the Undergraduate Marketing Curriculum. *Journal of Marketing Education*, 28(1), 81–86. DOI: 10.1177/0273475305284643

Crompton, H., & Song, D. (2021). The Potential of Artificial Intelligence in Higher Education. *Revista Virtual Universidad Católica Del Norte*. https://api.semanticscholar.org/CorpusID:234234123

Daellenbach, H., McNickle, D., & Dye, Sh. (2012). *Management Science - Decision-making through systems thinking* (2nd ed.). Palgrave Macmillian.

Dara, S., Dhamercherla, S., Jadav, S. S., Babu, C. M., & Ahsan, M. J. (2022). Machine learning in drug discovery: A review. *Artificial Intelligence Review*, 55(3), 1947–1999. PMID: 34393317

Davidescu, A. A., Apostu, S. A., & Paul, A. (2021). Comparative analysis of different univariate forecasting methods in modelling and predicting the romanian unemployment rate for the period 2021–2022. *Entropy (Basel, Switzerland)*, 23(3), 325. PMID: 33803384

De Sousa, W. G., de Melo, E. R. P., Bermejo, P. H. D. S., Farias, R. A. S., & Gomes, A. O. (2019). How and where is artificial intelligence in the public sector going? A literature review and research agenda. *Government Information Quarterly*, 36(4), 101392. DOI: 10.1016/j.giq.2019.07.004

Della Croce, F., & T'kindt, V. (2002). A Recovering Beam Search algorithm for the one-machine dynamic total completion time scheduling problem. *The Journal of the Operational Research Society*, 53(11), 1275–1280.

Devlin, N., & Hansen, P. (2001). Health care spending and economic output: Granger causality. *Applied Economics Letters*, 8(8), 561–564.

Di Vaio, A., Hassan, R., & Alavoine, C. (2022). Data intelligence and analytics: A bibliometric analysis of human–Artificial intelligence in public sector decision-making effectiveness. *Technological Forecasting and Social Change*, 174, 121201. DOI: 10.1016/j.techfore.2021.121201

Dick, B. (2002). Action research: action and research. Available at https://www.scu.edu.au/schools/gcm/ar/arp/aandr.html

Diener, F., & Špaček, M. (2021). Digital transformation in banking: A managerial perspective on barriers to change. *Sustainability*, 13(4), 2032. DOI: 10.3390/su13042032

Digitaldefynd, (2024). https://digitaldefynd.com/IQ/ai-in-schools-case-studies/

Dimri, S. C., Kumar, B., & Purohit, K. C. (2023). Application of Bayesian theorem for precise analysis of clinical test results. In 2023 6th International Conference on Information Systems and Computer Networks (ISCON) (p. 1-5). IEEE. https://doi.org/DOI: 10.1109/ISCON57294.2023.10112017

Dinçer, H., & Yuksel, S. (2019). Identifying the Causality Relationship between Health Expenditure and Economic Growth: An Application on E7 Countries. DergiPark (Istanbul University). https://dergipark.org.tr/tr/pub/jhesp/issue/39338/413742

Dixit, C., & Kumar, R. (2023). Analyzing Managerial and Technological Barriers to the Adoption of Industry 4.0: An 'ISM' and 'MICMAC' Approach. *IEEE Transactions on Engineering Management*, 71, 3389–3401. DOI: 10.1109/TEM.2023.3343527

Dogan, S. (2006). Turkce dokumanlar icin n-gram tabanli siniflandirma: Yazar, tur ve cinsiyet (A new N-gram based classification for Turkish documents (Ng-ind): Author, type, and gender). (Master's thesis, Yildiz Technical University).

Dogan, S., Çalgici, P., Arditi, D., & Gunaydin, H. (2015). *Critical success factors of partnering in the building design process. METU JFA 2015/2*. Department of Architecture, İzmir Institute of Technology.

Dolgun, M. O., Guzel Ozdemir, T., & Oguz, D. (2009). Veri madenciliginde yapisal olmayan verinin analizi: Metin ve web madenciligi. *Istatistikciler Dergisi*, 2, 48–58.

Dong, W., Liao, S., & Liang, L. (2016). Financial statement fraud detection using text mining: A systemic functional linguistics theory perspective.

Dorhetso, S. N., & Quarshie, B. D. (2023). Ratings of Driving Factors for the Adoption and Implementation of Artificial Intelligence in the Public Sector. *OAlib*, 10(5), 1–20. DOI: 10.4236/oalib.1109982

D'Souza, D., Bement, D., & Cory, K. (2022). Cross-functional integration skills: Are business schools delivering what organizations need? Empirical Research. DOI: 10.1111/dsji.12262

Duke, B., Harper, G., & Johnston, M. (2013). Connectivism as a digital age learning theory. *The International HETL Review*, 2013(Special Issue), 4–13.

Dunham, M. H. (2020). *Data Mining: Introductory and Advanced Topics* (1st ed.). Pearson.

Dunleavy, P. & Margetts, H. (2023). Data science, artificial intelligence and the third wave of digital era governance. Public Policy and Administration.

Du, S., Li, T., Yang, Y., & Horng, S. (2018). Deep Air Quality Forecasting Using Hybrid Deep Learning Framework. *IEEE Transactions on Knowledge and Data Engineering*, 33, 2412–2424.

Easterbrook, S., Singer, J., Storey, M., & Damian, D. (2008). *Guide to Advanced Empirical Software Engineering-Selecting Empirical Methods for Software Engineering Research* (Shull, F., Eds.). Springer.

Edwards, R., Gillies, V., & Gorin, S. (2022). Problem-solving for problem-solving: Data analytics to identify families for service intervention. Critical Social Policy.

Egbemhenghe, A. U., Ojeyemi, T., Iwuozor, K. O., Emenike, E. C., Ogunsanya, T. I., Anidiobi, S. U., & Adeniyi, A. G. (2023). Revolutionizing water treatment, conservation, and management: Harnessing the power of AI-driven ChatGPT solutions. *Environmental Challenges*, 13, 100782.

Egger, P., & Etzel, D. (2012). The impact of trade on employment in China: The case of processing trade. *World Economy*, 35(1), 16–38.

Eggers, A. C., Tuñón, G., & Dafoe, A. (2024). Placebo tests for causal inference. *American Journal of Political Science*, 68(3), 1106–1121.

Eichengreen, B. (2019). *Globalizing Capital: A History of the International Monetary System*. Princeton University Press.

Eira, A. (2022). 72 Vital Digital Transformation Statistics: 2023 Spending, Adoption, Analysis & Data. FinancesOnline. https://financesonline.com/digital-transformation-statistics/

Elek, P., & Bíró, A. (2021). Regional differences in diabetes across Europe – regression and causal forest analyses. *Economics and Human Biology*, 40, 100948. PMID: 33276258

Elezaj, O., Tole, D., & Baci, N. (2018). Big data in e-government environments: Albania as a case study. *Academic Journal of Interdisciplinary Studies*, 7(2), 117–124. DOI: 10.2478/ajis-2018-0052

Enarsson, T., Enqvist, L., & Naarttijärvi, M. (2022). Approaching the human in the loop–legal perspectives on hybrid human/algorithmic decision-making in three contexts. *Information & Communications Technology Law*, 31(1), 123–153.

EURSC. (2022). Organisation of studies. Office of the Secretary-General of the European Schools. https://www.eursc.eu/en/European-Schools/studies/studies-organisation#:~:text=The%20European%20School%20system%20consists,seven%20years%20of%20secondary%20education

Evans, J. R., & Lindsay, W. M. (2019). *Managing for Quality and Performance Excellence* (11th ed.). Cengage Learning.

Faqir, R. S. A. (2023). Digital Criminal Investigations in the Era of Artificial Intelligence: A Comprehensive Overview. International Journal of Cyber Criminology.

Fausett, L. V. (2006). *Fundamentals of neural networks: architectures, algorithms and applications*. Pearson Education India.

Feldman, R., & Sanger, J. (2006). *The text mining handbook: Advanced approaches in analyzing unstructured data.* Cambridge University Press., DOI: 10.1017/CBO9780511546914

Ferrucci, G., Jiménez-Rodriguez, R., & Onorante, L. (2010). Food Price Pass-Through in the Euro Area: Non-Linearities and the Role of the Exchange Rate. *European Central Bank Working Paper.*

Feuerriegel, S., Frauen, D., Melnychuk, V., Schweisthal, J., Hess, K., Curth, A., & van der Schaar, M. (2024). Causal machine learning for predicting treatment outcomes. *Nature Medicine*, 30(4), 958–968. PMID: 38641741

Fitzgerald, J. M. (2005). A case study of a high school's development of teacher collaboration through interdisciplinary curriculum planning (Publication No. 3173664) [Doctoral dissertation, Boston College]. ProQuest Dissertations and Theses Global.

Ford, H. (2008). *My Life And Work.* CruGuru.

Forero-Corba, W., & Bennasar, F. N. (2024). Techniques and applications of Machine Learning and Artificial Intelligence in education: a systematic review. RIED-Revista Iberoamericana de Educación a Distancia, 27(1).

Fox, A., Stoner, J., & Wang, J. (2024). Revolutionizing Student Engagement and Enrollment through Personalized, AI-Driven Dialog Systems in Higher Education. *Proceedings of the 55th ACM Technical Symposium on Computer Science Education V. 2.* https://api.semanticscholar.org/CorpusID:268433080

Frenkel, R., & Ros, J. (2012). Unemployment and the Real Exchange Rate in Latin America. *World Development*, 40(5), 919–934. DOI: 10.1016/j.worlddev.2011.11.002

Gallastegui, L. M. G., & Forradellas, R. R. (2024). Optimization of the Educational Experience in Higher Education Using Predictive Artificial Intelligence Models. *Revista de Gestão Social e Ambiental.* https://api.semanticscholar.org/CorpusID:270006202

Garanhel, M. (2023). What are the top 7 branches of artificial intelligence? AI Accelerator Institute. https://www.aiacceleratorinstitute.com/tag/artificial-intelligence/

Gavade, P. (2024). Enhancing Customer Relationship Management with Artificial Intelligence. *International Journal of Computer Science and Engineering.* https://api.semanticscholar.org/CorpusID:269081575

Giachetti, R. (2012). A Flexible Approach to Realize an Enterprise Architecture. Department of Systems Engineering, Naval Postgraduate School, Monterey, CA USA. Presented: New Challenges in Systems Engineering and Architecting. Conference on Systems Engineering Research (CSER). St. Louis, MO. Elservier.

Gillani, D. Q., Gillani, S. S., Naeem, M. Z., Spulbar, C., Coker-Farrell, E., Ejaz, A., & Birau, R. (2021). The Nexus between Sustainable Economic Development and Government Health Expenditure in Asian Countries Based on Ecological Footprint Consumption. *Sustainability*, 13(12), 6824.

GiniMachine. (2022). *10 Fields that Use Artificial Intelligence and Machine Learning*. GiniMachine.

Gkintoni, E., Dimakos, I., Halkiopoulos, C., & Antonopoulou, H. (2023). Contributions of neuroscience to educational praxis: A systematic review. *Emerging Science Journal*, 7, 146–158.

Gnoh, H. Q., Keoy, K. H., Iqbal, J., Anjum, S. S., Yeo, S. F., Lim, A. F., Lim, W. L., & Chaw, L. Y. (2024). Enhancing Business Sustainability Through Technology-Enabled AI: Forecasting Student Data and Comparing Prediction Models for Higher Education Institutions (HEIs). *PaperAsia*, 40(2b), 48–58. DOI: 10.59953/paperasia.v40i2b.86

Gobillot, N., Lesire, Ch., Doose, D. (2019). A Design and Analysis Methodology for Component-Based Real-Time Architectures of Autonomous Systems.

Golubeva, T. I., Kokhanovskaya, I. I., Fatykhova, A. L., Golovneva, E. V., & Terekhova, N. V. (2020). Social networks and education: the increase in student learning efficiency and the search for means of control. Revista Inclusiones, 7(S3-2), 48-60.

Gostkowski, M., & Rokicki, T. (2021). Forecasting the unemployment rate: Application of selected prediction methods. *European Research Studies*, 24(3), 985–1000.

Granger, E. (2024). Artificial Intelligence-Generative AI and Enterprise Architecture: Modeling the Enterprise. Ardoq. https://www.ardoq.com/blog/ai-enterprise-architecture-modeling

Gripsy, J. V., & Divya, T. (2023). Lung cancer disease prediction and classification based on feature selection method using Bayesian network, logistic regression, J48, random forest, and naïve Bayes algorithms. In 2023 3rd International Conference on Smart Data Intelligence (ICSMDI) (pp. 335-342). IEEE.

Grodecka-Messi, A., & Hull, I. (2022). Measuring the Impact of Taxes and Public Services on Property Values: A Double Machine Learning Approach. *Journal of Applied Econometrics*, 37(1), 56–75. DOI: 10.1002/jae.2875

Güler, M., Kabakçı, A., Koç, Ö., Eraslan, E., Derin, K. H., Güler, M., & Namlı, E. (2024). Forecasting of the Unemployment Rate in Turkey: Comparison of the Machine Learning Models. *Sustainability*, 16(15), 6509.

Guler, M., Kabakci, A., Koc, O., Eraslan, E., Derin, K. H., Guler, M., Unlu, R., Turkan, Y. S., & Namli, E. (2024). Forecasting of the unemployment rate in Turkey: Comparison of the machine learning models. *Sustainability*, 16(15), 6509. DOI: 10.3390/su16156509

Güler, M., & Namlı, E. (2022). Skin Cancer Detection with Deep Learning Methods Using Medical Images. *ROMAYA Journal Researches on Multidisiplinary Approaches*, (3), 1–10.

Güler, M., & Namlı, E. (2024). Brain Tumor Detection with Deep Learning Methods' Classifier Optimization Using Medical Images. *Applied Sciences (Basel, Switzerland)*, 14(2), 642.

Guo, Y. (2024). *Digital Government and Public Interaction: Platforms, Chatbots, and Public Satisfaction: Platforms*. Chatbots, and Public Satisfaction.

Gupta, R., & Gill, N. S. (2012). Financial statement fraud detection using text mining. *International Journal of Advanced Computer Science and Applications*, 3(12).

Gupta, V., & Lehal, G. S. (2009). A survey of text mining techniques and applications. *Journal of Emerging Technologies in Web Intelligence*, 1(1), 60–76. DOI: 10.4304/jetwi.1.1.60-76

Gürsakal, N. (2018). *Makine Öğrenmesi*. Dora Yayıncılık.

Gürsoy, U. T. Ş. (2009). *Veri Madenciliği ve Bilgi Keşfi*. Pegem Akademi Yayıncılık.

Habehh, H., & Gohel, S. (2021). Machine learning in healthcare. *Current Genomics*, 22(4), 291. PMID: 35273459

Hamid, M., Ahmad, A., & Aimeur, E. (2019). Factors contributing in failures of software projects. *International Journal of Computer Science and Network Security*, 19(5), 62–77.

Hamid, M., Zeshan, F., Ahmad, A., Ahmad, F., Hamza, M. A., Khan, Z. A., & Aljuaid, H. (2020). An intelligent recommender and decision support system (IRDSS) for effective management of software projects. *IEEE Access : Practical Innovations, Open Solutions*, 8, 140752–140766.

Hamid, M., Zeshan, F., Ahmad, A., Malik, S., Saleem, M., Tabassum, N., & Qasim, M. (2022). Analysis of software success through structural equation modeling. *Intelligent Automation & Soft Computing*, 31(3), 1689–1701.

Hamid, M., Zeshan, F., Ahmad, A., Munawar, S., Aimeur, E., Ahmed, S., & Yousif, M. (2020). An intelligent decision support system for effective handling of IT projects. *Journal of Intelligent & Fuzzy Systems*, 38(3), 2635–2647.

Han, J., Kamber, M., & Pei, J. (2011). *Data mining: Concepts and techniques* (3rd ed.). British Library. DOI: 10.1016/C2009-0-61819-5

Han, J., Kamber, M., & Pei, J. (2011). *Data Mining: Concepts and Techniques* (3rd ed.). Morgan Kaufmann.

Hannan, E., & Liu, S. (2021). AI: new source of competitiveness in higher education. *Competitiveness Review: An International Business Journal*. https://api.semanticscholar.org/CorpusID:238650032

Han, X., Xiao, S., Sheng, J., & Zhang, G. (2024). Enhancing Efficiency and Decision-Making in Higher Education Through Intelligent Commercial Integration: Leveraging Artificial Intelligence. *Journal of the Knowledge Economy*.

Hasanah, U., & Shimizu, K. (2020). Crucial cognitive skills in science education: A systematic review. Jurnal Penelitian dan Pembelajaran IPA, 6(1), 36-72.

Hayashi, K., Shibata, S., Inoue, E., Adachi, S., & Iba, T. (2022). Online Education Patterns, Part 1: Patterns for Linking Separate Worlds. EuroPLoP'21: 26th European Conference on Pattern Languages of Programs. DOI: 10.1145/3489449.3490003

Hayes, M., & Downie, A. (2024). What is AI transformation? IBM. https://www.ibm.com/think/topics/ai-transformation

He, W. & Chen, M. (2024). Advancing Urban Life: A Systematic Review of Emerging Technologies and Artificial Intelligence in Urban Design and Planning. Buildings.

Heinze, C., Haase, J., & Higgins, H. (2010). An Action Research Report from a Multi–Year Approach to Teaching Artificial Intelligence at the K–6 Level. *Proceedings of the Twenty-Fourth AAAI Conference on Artificial Intelligence (AAAI-10)*. DOI: 10.1609/aaai.v24i3.18830

Henman, P. (2020). Improving public services using artificial intelligence: Possibilities, pitfalls, governance. *Asia Pacific Journal of Public Administration*, 42(4), 209–221. DOI: 10.1080/23276665.2020.1816188

Hermont, R., & Reynoso-Meza, G. (2023). *Predictive Maintenance Strategies in agriculture using Survival Analysis*. Predictive Maintenance Strategies in Agriculture Using Survival Analysis.

Heywood, S., Hillar, R., & Turnbull, D. (2010). *Insights into organization-How do I manage the complexity in my organization? Organization Practice*. McKinsey & Company.

Hine, G. S. C. (2013). The importance of action research in teacher education programs. In *Design, develop, evaluate: The core of the learning. environment. Proceedings of the 22nd Annual Teaching Learning Forum, 7-8 February 2013*. Murdoch University. http://ctl.curtin.edu.au/professional_development/conferences/tlf/tlf2013/refereed/hine.html

Hinkelmann, K. (2016). *Modelling in Enterprise Architecture. University of applied sciences northwest Switzerland*. Business School.

Hoekstra, M., Van Veenstra, A. F., & Chideock, C. (2021). A Typology for Applications of Public Sector AI. In EGOV-CeDEM-ePart-* (pp. 121-128).

Holilah, H., Girsang, A., & Saragih, M. (2019). *Designing IT Blue Print Academic System on Higher Education with Togaf. Journal: Advances in Science*. Technology and Engineering Systems Journal.

Holton, C. (2009). Identifying disgruntled employee systems fraud risk through text mining: A simple solution for a multi-billion dollar problem. *Decision Support Systems*, 46(4), 853–864.

Horowitz, M. C., & Kahn, L. (2021). What influences attitudes about artificial intelligence adoption: Evidence from US local officials. *PLoS One*, 16(10), e0257732. DOI: 10.1371/journal.pone.0257732 PMID: 34669734

Hosiaisluoma. (2022). Holistic Enterprise Development. https://www.hosiaisluoma.fi/blog/archimate-examples

Huang, J., Saleh, S., & Liu, Y. (2021). A review on artificial intelligence in education. Academic Journal of Interdisciplinary Studies, 10(3).

Hünermund, P., Kaminski, J., & Schmitt, C. (2022). Causal machine learning and business decision making. Available at *SSRN* 3867326.

Hu, Q., & Wang, L. (2024). Economic growth effects of public health expenditure in OECD countries: An empirical study using the dynamic panel threshold model. *Heliyon*, 10(4), e25684. DOI: 10.1016/j.heliyon.2024.e25684 PMID: 38370248

Hussain, O., Dillon, T., Chang, E., & Hussain, F. (2010). Transactional risk-based decision making system in e-business interactions. International Journal of ComputSystSci & Eng, 1, 15-28.

Hussain, O., Dillon, Th., Chang, E., & Hussain, F. (2010). Transactional risk-based decision making system in e-business interactions. *International Journal of Computer Systems Science & Engineering*, 2010(1), 15–28.

Hutson, J., & Plate, D. (2023). Enhancing Institutional Assessment and Reporting Through Conversational Technologies: Exploring the Potential of AI-Powered Tools and Natural Language Processing. *DS Journal of Artificial Intelligence and Robotics*. https://api.semanticscholar.org/CorpusID:268580168

Hutson, J., Jeevanjee, T., Vander Graaf, V., Lively, J., Weber, J., Weir, G., Arnone, K., Carnes, G., Vosevich, K., Plate, D., Leary, M., & Edele, S. (2022). Artificial Intelligence and the Disruption of Higher Education: Strategies for Integrations across Disciplines. *Creative Education*. https://api.semanticscholar.org/CorpusID:255298108

IBM. (2014). *Service Oriented Architecture. "Smart Service Oriented Architecture: Helping businesses restructure. Where are you on the Service Oriented Architecture adoption path?* IBM.

IBM. (2024). What is AIOps? IBM. https://www.ibm.com/topics/aiops#:~:text=IBM-,What%20is%20AIOps%3F,service%20management%20and%20operational%20workflows

IBM. (2024a). 10 ways artificial intelligence is transforming operations management. IBM. https://www.ibm.com/blog/ai-in-operations-management/

IBM. (2024b). What is robotic process automation (RPA)? IBM. https://www.ibm.com/topics/rpa

IFR. (2021). Cloud Platform for Robotics Operation and Maintenance and Process Management Based on Industrial Internet. IFR. https://ifr.org/case-studies/cloud-platform-for-robotics-operation

Imran, M., & Ahmad, A. (2023). Enhancing data quality to mine credible patterns. *Journal of Information Science*, 49(2), 544–564.

Indurkhya, N., & Damerau, F. J. (Eds.). (2010). *Handbook of Natural Language Processing* (2nd ed.). Chapman and Hall/CRC.

Ingole, P., Bhoir, S., & Vidhate, A. V. (2018). Hybrid Model for Text Classification. *2018 Second International Conference on Electronics, Communication and Aerospace Technology (ICECA)*, 450-458. DOI: 10.1109/ICECA.2018.8474920

Ishengoma, F. R., Shao, D., Alexopoulos, C., Saxena, S., & Nikiforova, A. (2022). Integration of artificial intelligence of things (AIoT) in the public sector: Drivers, barriers and future research agenda. *Digital Policy. Regulation & Governance*, 24(5), 449–462. DOI: 10.1108/DPRG-06-2022-0067

Ito, K., Bansal, P., & Biljecki, F. (2024). Examining the causal impacts of the built environment on cycling activities using time-series street view imagery. *Transportation Research Part A, Policy and Practice*, 190, 104286.

Ittarat, M., Cheungpasitporn, W., & Chansangpetch, S. (2023). Personalized care in eye health: Exploring opportunities, challenges, and the road ahead for chatbots. *Journal of Personalized Medicine*, 13(12), 1679. PMID: 38138906

Jackins, V., Vimal, S., Kaliappan, M., & Lee, M. Y. (2021). AI-based smart prediction of clinical disease using random forest classifier and Naive Bayes. *The Journal of Supercomputing*, 77(5), 5198–5219.

James, A. & Whelan, A. (2022). 'Ethical' artificial intelligence in the welfare state: Discourse and discrepancy in Australian social services. Critical Social Policy.

Janakova, M. (2023). Artificial Intelligence in CRM Education. *Proceedings of the 17th International Scientific Conference INPROFORUM*. https://api.semanticscholar.org/CorpusID:268696021

Janiesch, C., Zschech, P., & Heinrich, K. (2021). Machine learning and deep learning. *Electronic Markets*, 31(3), 685–695. DOI: 10.1007/s12525-021-00475-2

Järvinen, P. (2007). Action Research is Similar to Design Science. Quality & Quantity. Retrieved August 10, 2018, from https://link.springer.com/article/10.1007/s11135-005-5427-1

Jeremias, J. (2023). Forecasting Unemployment Rates with Machine Learning Methods: A Case Study in Nonlinear Macroeconomic Relationships. *Applied Economics Letters*, 30(2), 202–216. DOI: 10.1080/13504851.2023.2123445

Jiang, Y., Pang, P. C. I., Wong, D., & Kan, H. Y. (2023). Natural Language Processing Adoption in Governments and Future Research Directions: A Systematic Review. Applied Sciences.

Jnr, B. A. (2024). User-centered AI-based voice-assistants for safe mobility of older people in urban context. AI & Society.

Johnson, B. A., Coggburn, J. D., & Llorens, J. J. (2022). Artificial intelligence and public human resource management: Questions for research and practice. *Public Personnel Management*, 51(4), 538–562.

Jonkers, H., Band, I., & Quartel, D. (2012a). *ArchiSurance Case Study*. The Open Group.

Jo, T. (2018). *Text mining: Concepts, implementation, and big data challenge* (1st ed.). Springer International Publishing. DOI: 10.1007/978-3-319-91815-0

Journal, I. (2024). A Study to Know Impact of AI on CRM. *Interantional Journal Of Scientific Research In Engineering And Management*. https://api.semanticscholar.org/CorpusID:267735383

Kamanda, E., Lanpin, Y., & Sesay, B. (2022). Causal nexus between health expenditure, health outcome and economic growth: Empirical evidence from Sub-Saharan Africa countries. *The International Journal of Health Planning and Management*, 37(4), 2284–2302. DOI: 10.1002/hpm.3469 PMID: 35393680

Karliadi, A., & Erawati, D. (2023). The influence of communication and problem handling on customer satisfaction in using call center services: A study on conventional banks in the city of Palangka Raya. Jambura. DOI: 10.37479/jimb.v6i2.19580

Katris, C. (2020). Prediction of unemployment rates with time series and machine learning techniques. *Computational Economics*, 55(2), 673–706.

Keller, P., & Drake, A. (2021). Exclusivity and paternalism in the public governance of explainable AI. *Computer Law & Security Review*, 40, 105490. DOI: 10.1016/j.clsr.2020.105490

Kersten, M. (2021). *Introducing SAFe® 5*. Your Operating System for Business Agility. Scaled Agile Inc.

Kesgin, F. (2007). Topic detection system for Turkish texts (Master's thesis, Istanbul Teknik University).

Khare, K., Stewart, B., & Khare, A. (2018). Artificial Intelligence and the Student Experience: An Institutional Perspective. *IAFOR Journal of Education*. https://api.semanticscholar.org/CorpusID:150179486

Khurana, D., Koli, A., Khatter, K., & Singh, S. (2023). Natural language processing: state of the art, current trends and challenges. Multimedia Tools and Applications.

Kilic, E. K. (2020). Banking crises and history in the world: The banking sector in the world. *International Journal of Financial Economics and Banking Practices*, 1(1), 1–31.

Kim, J., & Lennon, Sh. (2017). *Descriptive Content Analysis on E-Service Research. International Journal of Service Science, Management, Engineering, and Technology (IJSSMET)*. IGI Global., DOI: 10.4018/IJSSMET.2017010102

Kinder, T., Stenvall, J., Koskimies, E., Webb, H., & Janenova, S. (2023). Local public services and the ethical deployment of artificial intelligence. *Government Information Quarterly*, 40(4), 101865.

Kingsly, S. R., & Archana, T. (2025). Understanding AI and Machine Learning Concepts. In AI and Machine Learning Applications in Supply Chains and Marketing (pp. 371-392). IGI Global.

Kohli, P. (2024). AI Transformation: A Three-Step Blueprint For Organizations. Forbes. https://www.forbes.com/councils/forbesbusinesscouncil/2024/02/05/ai-transformation-a-three-step-blueprint-for-organizations/

Koski, E., Scheufele, E. L., Karunakaram, H., Foreman, M. A., Felix, W., & Dankwa-Mullan, I. (2022). Understanding Disparities in Healthcare: Implications for health systems and AI applications. In *Healthcare Information Management Systems: Cases, Strategies, and Solutions* (pp. 375–387). Springer International Publishing.

Kowsari, K., Jafari Meimandi, K., Heidarysafa, M., Mendu, S., Barnes, B., & Brown, D. (2019). Text Classification Algorithms: A Survey. *Information (Basel)*, 10(4), 150. DOI: 10.3390/info10040150

Kreiner, A., & Duca, J. V. (2019). Can Machine Learning Help Forecast the Overall Mortgage Delinquency Rate?

Kretowski, M. (2019). *Evolutionary decision trees in large-scale data mining* (1st ed.). Springer Cham. DOI: 10.1007/978-3-030-21851-5

Krigsman, M. (2008). Business change failures: 9 success tips. Reviewed from https://www.zdnet.com/blog/transformationfailures/business-change-failures-9-success-tips/1080. USA.

Kristiansson, E. (2023). Advancing Macro-Financial Analysis through Double Machine Learning. *International Journal of Economic Modeling*, 15(4), 345–372. DOI: 10.1016/j.ijem.2023.101346

Krugman, P., & Obstfeld, M. (2003). *International Economics: Theory and Policy*. Addison Wesley.

Krysik, A. (2024). All You Need to Know About AI Transformation in 2024. Stratoflow. https://stratoflow.com/ai-transformation/

Kulal, A., Rahiman, H. U., Suvarna, H., Abhishek, N., & Dinesh, S. (2024). Enhancing public service delivery efficiency: Exploring the impact of AI. *Journal of Open Innovation*, 10(3), 100329.

Kuleto, V., Ilić, M., Dumangiu, M., Ranković, M., Martins, O. M., Păun, D., & Mihoreanu, L. (2021). Exploring opportunities and challenges of artificial intelligence and machine learning in higher education institutions. *Sustainability*, 13(18), 10424.

Kumar, A., & Goyal, P. (2011). Forecasting of daily air quality index in Delhi. *The Science of the Total Environment*, 409, 5517–5523. PMID: 21962560

Kumar, B. S., & Ravi, V. (2016). A survey of the applications of text mining in financial domain. *Knowledge-Based Systems*, 114, 128–147.

Kumar, C., Ganguly, A., & Lohan, A. (2022). Understanding the interrelationship of barriers towards business model re-engineering under the evolving privacy laws: An interpretive Structure Modelling approach. *International Review of Law Computers & Technology*, 36(3), 382–403. https://www.tandfonline.com/doi/full/10.1080/13600869.2021.1999302

Kumar, N., & Raubal, M. (2021). Applications of deep learning in congestion detection, prediction and alleviation: A survey. *Transportation Research Part C, Emerging Technologies*, 133, 103432.

Kumar, S., & Sharma, R. (2018). Key barriers in the growth of rural health care: An ISM-MICMAC approach. *Benchmarking*, 25(7), 2169–2183. DOI: 10.1108/BIJ-05-2017-0095

Kumar, V. (2005). *Introduction to Data Mining*. Pearson.

Kuziemski, M., & Misuraca, G. (2020). AI governance in the public sector: Three tales from the frontiers of automated decision-making in democratic settings. *Telecommunications Policy*, 44(6), 101976. DOI: 10.1016/j.telpol.2020.101976 PMID: 32313360

La Mastra, C., Barchitta, M., Maugeri, A., & Agodi, A. (2024). Application of artificial intelligence to study the causality in public health: a systematic review. European Journal of Public Health, 34(Supplement_3)

Lakkaraju, P., Gauch, S., & Speretta, M. (2008). Document similarity based on concept tree distance. *Proceedings of the nineteenth ACM conference on Hypertext and hypermedia*, 127-132. DOI: 10.1145/1379092.1379118

Lalwani, T., Bhalotia, S., Pal, A., Bisen, S., & Rathod, V. S. (2018). *Implementation of a Chat Bot System using AI and NLP*. https://api.semanticscholar.org/CorpusID:69287458

Lankhorst, M. (2009). *Enterprise Architecture at Work Modelling, Communication and Analysis*. Springer.

Lavanya, T. (2011). Customer Relationship Management and Higher Education -A Vision. *Advances in Management, 4*. https://api.semanticscholar.org/CorpusID: 167447950

Lave, J. (1991). *Situated learning: Legitimate peripheral participation*. Cambridge university press.

Lebreton, P. (1957). The Case Study Method and the Establishment of Standards of efficiency. Academy of Management Proceedings.

Ledro, C., Nosella, A., & Vinelli, A. (2022). Artificial intelligence in customer relationship management: literature review and future research directions. *Journal ofBusiness\& IndustrialMarketing*. https://api.semanticscholar.org/CorpusID: 248030053

Lee, M., Lee, G., Lim, K., Moon, H., & Doh, J. (2024). Machine Learning-Based Causality Analysis of human resource practices on firm performance. *Administrative Sciences*, 14(4), 75.

Lee, S., Lee, J., & Jun, C. (2015). Causality Analysis for Public and Private Expenditures on Health Using Panel Granger-Causality Test. *Industrial Engineering & Management Systems*, 14(1), 104–110. DOI: 10.7232/iems.2015.14.1.104

Leitch, R., & Day, Ch. (2000). Action research and reflective practice: towards a holistic view. Taylor & Francis. Queen's University of Belfast, United Kingdom. Retrieved February 10, 2018, from https://www.tandfonline.com/doi/ref/10.1080/09650790000200108?scroll=top

Lewis, C. D. (1982). *Industrial and Business Forecasting Methods*. Butterworths Publishing.

Li, Q. (2023). Textual Data Mining for Financial Fraud Detection: A Deep Learning Approach. arXiv preprint arXiv:2308.03800.

Li, L., Ma, Z., Fan, L., Lee, S., Yu, H., & Hemphill, L. (2024). ChatGPT in education: A discourse analysis of worries and concerns on social media. *Education and Information Technologies*, 29(9), 10729–10762.

Liu, A. (2022). Rumbaugh, Booch and Jacobson Methodologies. Opengenus. https://iq.opengenus.org/rumbaugh-booch-and-jacobson-methodologies/

Liu, H., Li, Q., Yu, D., & Gu, Y. (2019). Air quality index and air pollutant concentration prediction based on machine learning algorithms. *Applied Sciences (Basel, Switzerland)*, 9, 4069.

Liu, Z., Lin, Y., & Sun, M. (2020). *Representation Learning for Natural Language Processing*. Springer.

Li, Y., Zou, C., Berecibar, M., Nanini-Maury, E., Chan, J. C. W., Van den Bossche, P., & Omar, N. (2018). Random forest regression for online capacity estimation of lithium-ion batteries. *Applied Energy*, 232, 197–210.

Lockwood, R. (2018). Introduction The Relational Data Model. Retrieved January 29, 2019, from http://www.jakobsens.dk/Nekrologer.htm

Madan, R., & Ashok, M. (2023). AI adoption and diffusion in public administration: A systematic literature review and future research agenda. *Government Information Quarterly*, 40(1), 101774. DOI: 10.1016/j.giq.2022.101774

Mahor, V., Rawat, R., Kumar, A., Garg, B., & Pachlasiya, K. (2023). IoT and artificial intelligence techniques for public safety and security. In *Smart urban computing applications* (pp. 111–126). River Publishers.

Majeed, A. & Hwang, S. O. (2021). Data-driven analytics leveraging artificial intelligence in the era of COVID-19: an insightful review of recent developments. Symmetry.

Malomo, F., & Sena, V. (2017). Data intelligence for local government? Assessing the benefits and barriers to use of big data in the public sector. *Policy and Internet*, 9(1), 7–27. DOI: 10.1002/poi3.141

Mankiw, N. G. (2016). *Principles of Economics* (8th ed.). Cengage Learning.

Manning, C., & Schutze, H. (1999). *Foundations of Statistical Natural Language Processing*. MIT Press.

Maragno, G., Tangi, L., Gastaldi, L., & Benedetti, M. (2023). Exploring the factors, affordances and constraints outlining the implementation of Artificial Intelligence in public sector organizations. *International Journal of Information Management*, 73, 102686. DOI: 10.1016/j.ijinfomgt.2023.102686

Marchese, M. (2023). Thought Leadership AI Research Qualitative Vs Quantitative Data Research. Tempesta. https://tempestamedia.com/2023/08/30/ai-research-qualitative-vs-quantitative-data-research/

Marginson, S., & Dang, T. K. A. (2017). Vygotsky's sociocultural theory in the context of globalization. *Asia Pacific Journal of Education*, 37(1), 116–129.

Markides, C. (2011, March). Crossing the Chasm: How to Convert Relevant Research Into Managerially Useful Research. *The Journal of Applied Behavioral Science*, 47(1), 121–134.

Marzo, R. R. (2024). Bridging the Digital Divide: AI Solutions for Health Literacy in Underserved Populations. In Modern Management Science Practices in the Age of AI (pp. 151-180). IGI Global.

Massung, S., & Zhai, C. (2016). *Text data management and analysis: A practical introduction to information retrieval and text mining*. Association for Computing Machinery and Morgan & Claypool., DOI: 10.1145/2915031

Mcculloch, W. S., & Pitts, W. (1943). A Logical Calculus of the Ideas Immanent In Nervous Activity. *The Bulletin of Mathematical Biophysics*, 5(4), 115–133.

McDonald, B. D.III, Hall, J. L., O'Flynn, J., & van Thiel, S. (2022). The future of public administration research: An editor's perspective. *Public Administration*, 100(1), 59–71.

Medaglia, R., & Tangi, L. (2022, October). The adoption of Artificial Intelligence in the public sector in Europe: drivers, features, and impacts. In *Proceedings of the 15th International Conference on Theory and Practice of Electronic Governance (ICEGOV)* (pp. 10-18). https://doi.org/DOI: 10.1145/3560107.3560110

Mehr, H. (2017). *Artificial Intelligence for Citizen Services and Government*. Harvard Kennedy School, Ash Center for Democratic Governance and Innovation.

Mellouli, S., Janssen, M., & Ojo, A. (2024). Introduction to the Issue on Artificial Intelligence in the Public Sector: Risks and Benefits of AI for Governments. Digital Government. *Research and Practice*, 5(1), 1–6. DOI: 10.1145/3636550

Mergel, I., Dickinson, H., Stenvall, J., & Gasco, M. (2024). Implementing AI in the public sector. *Public Management Review*, 1–14. DOI: 10.1080/14719037.2023.2231950

Merhi, M. (2023). An evaluation of the critical success factors impacting artificial intelligence implementation. International Journal of Information Management, 69. DOI: 10.1016/j.ijinfomgt.2022.102545

Merugu, M., & Hemachandran, K. (2023). AI in Public Sector. *Artificial Intelligence for Business: An Implementation Guide Containing Practical and Industry-Specific Case Studies*, 336-349. DOI: 10.4324/9781003358411-21

Mhlanga, D. (2020). Industry 4.0 in finance: the impact of artificial intelligence (ai) on digital financial inclusion. International Journal of Financial Studies.

Mhlanga, D. (2023). Open AI in education, the responsible and ethical use of ChatGPT towards lifelong learning. In *FinTech and artificial intelligence for sustainable development: The role of smart technologies in achieving development goals* (pp. 387–409). Springer Nature Switzerland.

Mikhaylov, S. J., Esteve, M., & Campion, A. (2018). Artificial intelligence for the public sector: Opportunities and challenges of cross-sector collaboration. *Philosophical Transactions. Series A, Mathematical, Physical, and Engineering Sciences*, 376(2128), 20170357. DOI: 10.1098/rsta.2017.0357 PMID: 30082303

Millan-Vargas, A. O., Sandoval-Almazan, R., & Valle-Cruz, D. (2024, June). Impact and barriers to AI in the public sector: the case of the State of Mexico. In *Proceedings of the 25th Annual International Conference on Digital Government Research* (pp. 81-89). https://doi.org/DOI: 10.1145/3657054.3657249

Miller, S. (2020). Causal forest estimation of heterogeneous and time-varying environmental policy effects. *Journal of Environmental Economics and Management*, 103, 102337.

Miller, T. W. (2004). *Data and Text Mining: A Business Applications Approach* (1st ed.). Pearson.

Mishra, A. (2019). *Machine learning in the AWS cloud: Add intelligence to applications with Amazon SageMaker and Amazon Rekognition*. Sybex.

Mohri, M., Rostamizadeh, A., & Talwalkar, A. (2018). *Foundations of machine learning* (2nd ed.). The MIT Press.

Moore, J. (2014). Java programming with lambda expressions-A mathematical example demonstrates the power of lambdas in Java 8. Retrieved March 10, 2018, from, https://www.javaworld.com/article/2092260/java-se/java-programming-with-lambda-expressions.html

Moraffah, R., Karimi, A. H., Raglin, A., & Liu, H. (2023, August). Socially Responsible Machine Learning: A Causal Perspective. In *Proceedings of the 29th ACM SIGKDD Conference on Knowledge Discovery and Data Mining* (pp. 5819-5820).

Morawski, R. (2013, November). An application-oriented mathematical meta-model of measurement. Elsevier. *Journal Measurement*, 46(9), 3753–3765. DOI: 10.1016/j.measurement.2013.04.004

Morrison, M. (2016). Critical Success Factors – Analysis made easy, a step by step guide. rapidBI. Accessed and reviewed in April 2019, https://rapidbi.com/criticalsuccessfactors/

Mubarik, M. S., & Khan, S. A. (2024). Disruptive Digital Technologies and Contemporary Supply Chains. In The Theory, Methods and Application of Managing Digital Supply Chains (pp. 15-39). Emerald Publishing Limited.

Muhammad, T., & Ahmad, A. (2021). A joint sharing approach for online privacy preservation. *World Wide Web (Bussum)*, 24(3), 895–924.

Musgrave, P. W. (2017). *The sociology of education*. Routledge.

Mushtaq, S. & Shah, M. (2024). Critical Factors and Practices in Mitigating Cybercrimes within E-Government Services: A Rapid Review on Optimising Public Service Management. Information.

Mutascu, M., & Hegerty, S. W. (2023). Predicting the contribution of artificial intelligence to unemployment rates: An artificial neural network approach. *Journal of Economics and Finance*, 47(2), 400–416.

Mutawa, M. A., & Rashid, H. (2020, August). Comprehensive review on the challenges that impact artificial intelligence applications in the public sector. In *Proceedings of the 5th NA International Conference on Industrial Engineering and Operations Management* (Vol. 10, pp. 2078-2087).

Mutlu, N. M., & Atahanlı, E. B. (2024). Veri Madenciliği ile Hava Kalitesi Tahmini: İstanbul Örneği. *Bilişim Teknolojileri Dergisi*, 17(3), 139–158.

Myers, B., Pane, J., & Ko, A. (2004). Natural programming languages and environments. ACM New York, NY, USA. Accessed and reviewed in April 2019, https://dl.acm.org/citation.cfm?id=1015888

Nadim, K., Ragab, A., & Ouali, M. (2022). Data-driven dynamic causality analysis of industrial systems using interpretable machine learning and process mining. *Journal of Intelligent Manufacturing*, 34(1), 57–83.

Namli, E., Yucel, M., Unlu, R., & Adiguzel Tuylu, A. N. (2022). Smart estimation model for energy performance certificates of residential buildings. Journal of Engineering Research, 1-24. DOI: 10.36909/jer.17597

Naser, M. Z., & Tapeh, A. T. G. (2023). Causality, causal discovery, causal inference and counterfactuals in Civil Engineering: Causal machine learning and case studies for knowledge discovery. *Computers and Concrete*, 31(4), 277–292.

National Academies. (1991). *Artificial Intelligence in Mathematical Modeling. National Academies of Sciences, Engineering, and Medicine. 1991. Research Directions in Computational Mechanics*. The National Academies Press. DOI: 10.17226/1909

Nawaz, N., & Gomes, A. M. (2020). Artificial Intelligence Chatbots are New Recruiters. *Organizational Communication EJournal*. https://api.semanticscholar.org/CorpusID:203646454

Neumann, G. (2002). Programming Languages in Artificial Intelligence. *3rd International Conference on Affective Computing and Intelligent Interaction and Workshops*. IEEE.

Neumann, O., Guirguis, K., & Steiner, R. (2024). Exploring artificial intelligence adoption in public organizations: A comparative case study. *Public Management Review*, 26(1), 114–141. DOI: 10.1080/14719037.2022.2048685

Newhouse, J. P. (1992). Medical Care Costs: How Much Welfare Loss? *The Journal of Economic Perspectives*, 6(3), 3–21. PMID: 10128078

Ngai, E. W., Hu, Y., Wong, Y. H., Chen, Y., & Sun, X. (2011). The application of data mining techniques in financial fraud detection: A classification framework and an academic review of literature. *Decision Support Systems*, 50(3), 559–569.

Ng, D. T. K., & Chu, S. K. W. (2021). Motivating Students to Learn AI Through Social Networking Sites: A Case Study in Hong Kong. *Online Learning : the Official Journal of the Online Learning Consortium*, 25(1), 195–208.

Nguyen, T. N. T., Lai, N. V., & Nguyen, Q. T. (2024). Artificial Intelligence (AI) in Education: A Case Study on ChatGPT's Influence on Student Learning Behaviors. *Educational Process: International Journal*, 13(2), 105–121. DOI: 10.22521/edupij.2024.132.7

Nicolas, C., Kim, J., & Chi, S. (2021). Natural language processing-based characterization of top-down communication in smart cities for enhancing citizen alignment. Sustainable Cities and Society.

Nijboer, F., Morin, F., Carmien, S., Koene, R., Leon, E., & Hoffman, U. (2009). Affective brain-computer interfaces: Psychophysiological markers of emotion in healthy persons and in persons with amyotrophic lateral sclerosis. *3rd International Conference on Affective Computing and Intelligent Interaction and Workshops*. IEEE. DOI: 10.1109/ACII.2009.5349479

Nirala, K. K., Singh, N. K., & Purani, V. S. (2022). A survey on providing customer and public administration based services using AI: chatbot. Multimedia Tools and Applications.

Nordström, M. (2022). AI under great uncertainty: implications and decision strategies for public policy. AI & society.

Novelli, C., Taddeo, M., & Floridi, L. (2024). Accountability in artificial intelligence: what it is and how it works. Ai & Society.

Novillo-Villegas, S., Ayala-Andrade, R., Lopez-Cox, J. P., Salazar-Oyaneder, J., & Acosta-Vargas, P. (2022). A roadmap for innovation capacity in developing countries. *Sustainability*, 14(11), 6686. DOI: 10.3390/su14116686

Ntoutsi, E., Fafalios, P., Gadiraju, U., Iosifidis, V., Nejdl, W., Vidal, M. E., & Staab, S. (2020). Bias in data-driven artificial intelligence systems—An introductory survey. *Wiley Interdisciplinary Reviews. Data Mining and Knowledge Discovery*, 10(3), e1356.

Nurjanah, S., Shalshabilla, V., & Dari, A. (2023). Digital transformation in the banking industry: Challenges and opportunities. International Journal of Accounting. *Management and Economics*, 1(1), 64–71.

Nurski, L. (2023). Artificial intelligence adoption in the public sector: A case study (No. 03/2023). *Bruegel Working Paper*.

Obermeyer, Z., & Emanuel, E. J. (2016). Predicting the Future: Big Data, Machine Learning, and Clinical Medicine. *The New England Journal of Medicine*, 375(13), 1216–1219. PMID: 27682033

OECD. (2019). *Artificial Intelligence in Society*. OECD Publishing., DOI: 10.1787/eedfee77-

OMG. (2022). Decision model and notation (DMN). OMG. https://www.omg.org/dmn/

Orayer, O. (2023). Is Polymath Thinking the Answer to Thriving in the AI Era? Medium. https://medium.com/@opher.brayer/is-polymath-thinking-the-answer-to-thriving-in-the-ai-era-d269000163a3

Osasona, F., Amoo, O. O., Atadoga, A., Abrahams, T. O., Farayola, O. A., & Ayinla, B. S. (2024). Reviewing the ethical implications of AI in decision making processes. *International Journal of Management & Entrepreneurship Research*, 6(2), 322–335.

Ouyang, F., & Jiao, P. (2021). Artificial intelligence in education: The three paradigms. *Computers and Education: Artificial Intelligence*, 2, 100020.

Ozdenizci Kose, B. (2022). Predicting individuals' susceptibility to social engineering attacks using machine learning methods.

Ozyilmaz, A., Bayraktar, Y., Isik, E., Toprak, M., Er, M. B., Besel, F., Aydin, S., Olgun, M. F., & Collins, S. (2022). The Relationship between Health Expenditures and Economic Growth in EU Countries: Empirical Evidence Using Panel Fourier Toda–Yamamoto Causality Test and Regression Models. *International Journal of Environmental Research and Public Health*, 19(22), 15091. PMID: 36429808

Page, L. C., & Gehlbach, H. (2017). How an Artificially Intelligent Virtual Assistant Helps Students Navigate the Road to College. *AERA Open*, 3. https://api.semanticscholar.org/CorpusID:53124313

Page, M., Schagen, S., Fallus, K., Bron, J., De Coninck, Ch., Maes, B., Sleurs, W., & Van Woensel, Ch. (2005). *Cross-curricular themes in secondary education-Report of a CIDREE collaborative project.* Consortium of Institutions for Development and Research in Education in Europe.

Pahlka, J. (2023). Recoding America: why government is failing in the digital age and how we can do better.

Paschalidou, A. K., Karakitsios, S., Kleanthous, S., & Kassomenos, P. A. (2011). Forecasting hourly PM10 concentration in Cyprus through artificial neural networks and multiple regression models: Implications to local environmental management. *Environmental Science and Pollution Research International*, 18, 316–327. PMID: 20652425

Pasquale, F. (2020). *New Laws of Robotics: Defending Human Expertise in the Age of AI.* Belknap Press., DOI: 10.2307/j.ctv3405w6p

Paul, M., Maglaras, L., Ferrag, M. A., & Almomani, I. (2023). Digitization of healthcare sector: A study on privacy and security concerns. ICT Express.

Pearl, J. (2009). *Causality.* Cambridge University Press.

Pejić Bach, M., Krstić, Ž., Seljan, S., & Turulja, L. (2019). Text mining for big data analysis in financial sector: A literature review. *Sustainability*, 11(5), 1277. DOI: 10.3390/su11051277

Pencheva, I., Esteve, M., & Mikhaylov, S. J. (2020). Big Data and AI–A transformational shift for government: So, what next for research? *Public Policy and Administration*, 35(1), 24–44.

Peterson, S. (2011). Why it Worked: Critical Success Factors of a Financial Reform Project in Africa. Faculty Research Working Paper Series. Harvard Kennedy School.

Piccialli, F., Di Cola, V. S., Giampaolo, F., & Cuomo, S. (2021). The role of artificial intelligence in fighting the COVID-19 pandemic. *Information Systems Frontiers*, 23(6), 1467–1497. PMID: 33935585

Pilavcilar, I. F. (2007). *Metin madenciligi ile metin siniflandirma(Text mining and text classification).* Yildiz Technical University, Institute of Science.

Pisonia, G., Gijlersc, H., Ha Nguyend, T., & Chene, H. (2021). Collaboration patterns in students' teams working on business cases. CEUR Workshop Proceedings (CEUR-WS.org).

Plaia, A., & Ruggieri, M. (2011). Air quality indices: A review. *Reviews in Environmental Science and Biotechnology*, 10, 165–179.

Polderman, J., & Willems, J. (1998). *Introduction to Mathematical Systems Theory: A Behavioral Approach. (Texts in Applied Mathematics)* (2nd ed.). Springer Verlag.

Postle, G. (2003). Online Teaching and Learning in Higher Education: A Case Study. Department of Education, Science and Training. University of Southern Queensland, USQ. Canberra. Australia.

Pushpakumara, H., Jayaweera, P., & Manjulan, W. (2021). Using the Open Group Architecture Framework (TOGAF) for Quality Assurance in Higher Education Teaching and Learning. DOI: 10.2139/ssrn.3808691

Putri, E. S., Hamid, A., & Novitasari, D. C. R. (2022). Prediction of the Tuban Regency Open Unemployment Rate in 2022 with the Backpropagation Method. Numerical: Jurnal Matematika dan Pendidikan Matematika, 25-36.

Putri, N., & Yusof, S. M. (2009). Critical success factors for implementing quality engineering tools and techniques in malaysian's and indonesian's automotive industries: An Exploratory Study. *Journal Proceedings of the International Multi-Conference of Engineers and Computer Scientists.*, 2, 18–20.

Rancho Labs. (2021). *6 Major Sub-Fields of Artificial Intelligence*. Rancho Labs. Meduim.

Ravisankar, P., Ravi, V., Raghava Rao, G., & Bose, I. (2011). Detection of financial statement fraud and feature selection using data mining techniques. *Decision Support Systems*, 50(2), 491–500. DOI: 10.1016/j.dss.2010.11.006

RedHat. (2022). Decision Model and Notation (DMN). RedHat. https://access.redhat.com/documentation/en-us/red_hat_process_automation_manager/7.1/html/designing_a_decision_service_using_dmn_models/dmn-elements-example-con

Richards, M. (2024). The Use of AI in Software Architecture. Neueda. https://neueda.com/enterprise-learning/resources/blogs/ai-in-software-architecture/

Riedl, M. (2023). A Very Gentle Introduction to Large Language Models without the Hype. Meduim. https://mark-riedl.medium.com/a-very-gentle-introduction-to-large-language-models-without-the-hype-5f67941fa59e

Riyaz, M., Sawant, P. D., Raju, S., Nijhawan, G., Deepika, N. M., & B, M. L. (2023). Artificial Intelligence for Customer Relationship Management: Personalization and Automation. *2023 10th IEEE Uttar Pradesh Section International Conference on Electrical, Electronics and Computer Engineering (UPCON), 10*, 547–551. https://api.semanticscholar.org/CorpusID:268036115

Rockart, J. (1979). Chief Executives Define Their Own Data Needs. Harvard Business Review. Accessed and reviewed in April 2019, https://hbr.org/1979/03/chief-executives-define-their-own-data-needs

Rodrik, D. (1997). *Has Globalization Gone Too Far?* Institute for International Economics.

Roiger, R. (2002). *Data Mining: A Tutorial Based Primer* (1st ed.). Pearson.

Ronald, D. (1961). Management Information Crisis. Harvard Business Review.

Rose, S. (2018). Robust Machine Learning Variable Importance Analyses of Medical Conditions for Health Care Spending. *Health Services Research*, 53(5), 3836–3854. DOI: 10.1111/1475-6773.12848 PMID: 29527659

Rossen, B., & Faroque, A. (2016). Diagnosing the Causes of Rising Health-Care Expenditure in Canada: Does Baumol's Cost Disease Loom Large? *American Journal of Health Economics*, 2(2), 184–212. DOI: 10.1162/ajhe_a_00041

Roxana, N., & Mos, T. (2022). Machine Learning and Robotic Process Automation Take Higher Education One Step Further. *Romanian Journal of Information Science and Technology, 25*. https://api.semanticscholar.org/CorpusID:264435310

Ryu, P. M. (2018). Predicting the unemployment rate using social media analysis. *Journal of Information Processing Systems*, 14(4), 904–915.

Sachs, J. D., & Warner, A. M. (1995). Economic Reform and the Process of Global Integration. *Brookings Papers on Economic Activity*, 1995(1), 1–118.

Salas-Pilco, S. Z., & Yang, Y. (2022). Artificial intelligence applications in Latin American higher education: A systematic review. *International Journal of Educational Technology in Higher Education*, 19. https://api.semanticscholar.org/CorpusID:248234262

Salem, A. M., Eyupoglu, S. Z., & Ma'aitah, M. K. (2024). The Influence of Machine Learning on Enhancing Rational Decision-Making and Trust Levels in e-Government. Systems.

Salman Khan, M., Ahmad, A., & Humayoun, M. (2022). Building an Effective Automated Assessment System for C/C++ Introductory Programming Courses in ODL Environment. arXiv e-prints, arXiv-2205.

Samreen, A., Ahmad, A., & Zeshan, F. (2020a, February). Searching for truth in the post-truth age. In 2020 3rd international conference on advancements in computational sciences (ICACS) (pp. 1-5). IEEE.

Samreen, A., Ahmad, A., Zeshan, F., Ahmad, F., Ahmed, S., & Khan, Z. A. (2020b). A collaborative method for protecting teens against online predators over social networks: A behavioral analysis. *IEEE Access : Practical Innovations, Open Solutions*, 8, 174375–174393.

Sankaralingam, K., Ferris, M., Nowatzki, T., Estan, C., Wood, D., & Vaish, N. (2013). *Optimization and Mathematical Modeling in Computer Architecture*. Morgan & Claypool Publishers.

Sarfraz, A., Ahmad, A., Zeshan, F., & Mirza, H. T. (2024). Synews: A synergy-based rumor verification system. *Social Network Analysis and Mining*, 14(1), 57.

Sarker, I. H. (2021). Machine learning: Algorithms, real-world applications and research directions. SN computer science.

Sart, G. (2023b). Education and Health Expenditures: Evidence From the New EU Member States. In Advances in healthcare information systems and administration book series (pp. 237–247)

Sartor, G., & Lagioia, F. (2020). The impact of the General Data Protection Regulation (GDPR) on artificial intelligence. *Panel for the Future of Science and Technology*, EPRS | European Parliamentary Research Service. DOI: 10.2861/293

Satish, N., Anmala, J., Varma, M. R. R., & Rajitha, K. (2024). Performance of Machine Learning, Artificial Neural Network (ANN), and Stacked Ensemble Models in Predicting Water Quality Index (WQI) from Surface Water Quality Parameters, Climatic and Land Use Data. *Process Safety and Environmental Protection*.

Satterlee, B. (1996). Continuous Improvement and Quality: Implications for Higher Education. Warner Southern College (FL). USA.

Satterlee, B. (1996). Continuous Improvement and Quality: Implications for Higher Education. Warner Southern College.

Savage, N. (2024). 5 AI Case Studies. VKTR. https://www.vktr.com/ai-disruption/5-ai-case-studies/

Schmelzer, R. (2021). Data science vs. machine learning vs. AI: How they work together. TechTarget. https://searchbusinessanalytics.techtarget.com/feature/Data-science-vs-machine-learning-vs-AI-How-they-work-together?track=NL-

Schmelzer, R. (2021). Data science vs. machine learning vs. AI: How they work together. TechTarget. https://searchbusinessanalytics.techtarget.com/feature/Data-science-vs-machine-learning-vs-AI-How-they-work-together?track=NL-1816&ad=937375&asrc=EM_NLN_144787081&utm_medium=EM&utm_source=NLN&utm_campaign=20210114_An%20open%20source%20database%20comparison

Seckin, K. (2018). Metin madenciliginde kullanilan yontemlerin karsilastirilmasi: Siyasi parti liderlerinin grup genel toplanti konusmalari ile bir uygulama [Sakarya University Institute of Social Sciences].

Seeman, E. D., & O'Hara, M. T. (2006). Customer Relationship Management in Higher Education: Using Information Systems to Improve the Student-School Relationship. *Campus-Wide Information Systems*, 23, 24–34. https://api.semanticscholar.org/CorpusID:62651864

Segovia-García, N. (2024). Optimizing Student Support. A Review of the Use of AI Chatbots in Higher Education. *European Public & Social Innovation Review*. https://api.semanticscholar.org/CorpusID:271026677

Seker, S. E. (2016). Duygu analizi (Sentimental analysis). *YBS Ansiklopedi*, 3(3), 21–36.

Sen, M., Basu, S., Chatterjee, A., Banerjee, A., Pal, S., Mukhopadhyay, P. K., & Tarafdar, A. (2022, December). Prediction of Unemployment using Machine Learning Approach. In *2022 OITS International Conference on Information Technology (OCIT)* (pp. 1-5). IEEE.

Şentürk, C., Sart, G., Şaşmaz, M. Ü., & Bayar, Y. (2023). Health Expenditures, Human Capital, and Sustainable Development: Panel Evidence from the New EU Member Countries. *Sustainability*, 15(19), 14514.

Shahin, M., Chen, F. F., & Hosseinzadeh, A. (2024). Machine-based identification system via optical character recognition. *Flexible Services and Manufacturing Journal*, 36(2), 453–480.

Shahraki, M., & Ghaderi, S. (2019). Investigating the Causal Relationship between Public Health Expenditure and Health Status; Panel Vector Self-Regression Model. *Health Research Journal*, 4(4), 220–226. DOI: 10.29252/hrjbaq.4.4.220

Shao, Z., Zhao, R., Yuan, S., Ding, M., & Wang, Y. (2022). Tracing the evolution of AI in the past decade and forecasting the emerging trends. *Expert Systems with Applications*, 209, 118221.

Sharma, S., & Singh, S. (2016, January). Unemployment rates forecasting using supervised neural networks. In 2016 6th International Conference-Cloud System and Big Data Engineering (Confluence) (pp. 28-33). IEEE.

Sharma, G. D., Yadav, A., & Chopra, R. (2020). Artificial intelligence and effective governance: A review, critique and research agenda. *Sustainable Futures : An Applied Journal of Technology, Environment and Society*, 2, 100004. DOI: 10.1016/j.sftr.2019.100004

Shawon, R. E. R., Rahman, A., Islam, M. R., Debnath, P., Sumon, M. F. I., Khan, M. A., & Miah, M. N. I. (2024). AI-Driven Predictive Modeling of US Economic Trends: Insights and Innovations. Journal of Humanities and Social Sciences Studies, 6(10), 1-15.

Sheng, N., & Tang, U. W. (2016). The first official city ranking by air quality in China—A review and analysis. *Cities (London, England)*, 51, 139–149.

Shilbayeh, S. A., & Abonamah, A. A. (2021). Predicting student enrollments and attrition patterns in higher educational institutions using machine learning. *The International Arab Journal of Information Technology*, 18, 562–567. https://api.semanticscholar.org/CorpusID:235749412

Shobha, G., & Rangaswamy, S. (2018). *Machine learning. Handbook of statistics.* Elsevier., DOI: 10.1016/bs.host.2018.07.004

Shrestha, Y. R., Krishna, V., & von Krogh, G. (2021). Augmenting organizational decision-making with deep learning algorithms: Principles, promises, and challenges. Journal of Business Research.

Shrivastava, R. (2023). Building an enterprise business glossary. Hitachi Vantara. https://community.hitachivantara.com/blogs/rishu-shrivastava/2023/03/23/building-an-enterprise-business-glossary

Siann, G., & Ugwuegbu, D. C. (2024). *Educational psychology in a changing world.* Taylor & Francis.

Sied, M. (2018). Enterprise Architecture: The Great Process Automation Enabler. Ashling Partner. https://www.ashlingpartners.com/enterprise-architecture-the-great-process-automation-enabler-rpa/

Simkovich, S. M., Goodman, D., Roa, C., Crocker, M. E., Gianella, G. E., Kirenga, B. J., Wise, R. A., & Checkley, W. (2019). The health and social implications of household air pollution and respiratory diseases. npj Prim. Care Respir. Med., 29, 12.

Simonin, J., Bertin, E., Traon, Y., Jezequel, J.-M., & Crespi, N. (2010). Business and Information System Alignment: A Formal Solution for Telecom Services. *2010 Fifth International Conference on Software Engineering Advances*. IEEE.

Singhania, R., & Kundu, S. (2020). Forecasting the United States unemployment rate by using recurrent neural networks with Google Trends data. International Journal of Trade, Economics and Finance, 11(6).

Singh, M., Kumar, P., & Rathi, R. (2019). Modelling the barriers of Lean Six Sigma for Indian micro-small medium enterprises: An ISM and MICMAC approach. *The TQM Journal*, 31(5), 673–695. DOI: 10.1108/TQM-12-2018-0205

Smith, A. (1987). Educational Engineering: Heuristics for Improving Learning Effectiveness and Efficiency. Engineering Education.

Song, Y., Tung, P. H., & Jeon, B. (2022, August). Trends in Artificial Emotional Intelligence Technology and Application. In 2022 IEEE/ACIS 7th International Conference on Big Data, Cloud Computing, and Data Science (BCD) (pp. 366-370). IEEE.

Spencer, L. (1955). 10 problems that worry presidents. Harvard Business Review.

Stancin, K., Poscic, P., & Jaksic, D. (2020). Ontologies in education–state of the art. *Education and Information Technologies*, 25(6), 5301–5320.

Steen, R., Haug, O. J., & Patriarca, R. (2024). Business continuity and resilience management: A conceptual framework. *Journal of Contingencies and Crisis Management*, 32(1), e12501.

Stock, J. H., & Watson, M. W. (2019). *Introduction to Econometrics* (4th ed.). Pearson.

Suhud, R., Febriandirza, A., Permatasari, I., & Ramadan, F. (2023). Recognizing Public Satisfaction Toward Kampus Mengajar Program with Naive Bayes. 2023 International Conference on Computer, Control, Informatics and Its Applications (IC3INA), Computer, Control, Informatics and Its Applications (IC3INA), 2023 International Conference On, 125–130. DOI: 10.1109/IC3INA60834.2023.10285769

Syynimaa, N. (2015). Enterprise Architecture Adoption Method for Higher Education Institutions. Doctoral Thesis. Informatics Research Centre Henley Business School University of Reading. UK.

Takeuchia, H., & Yamamotob, Sh. (2019). AI Service System Development Using Enterprise Architecture Modeling. *23rd International Conference on Knowledge-Based and Intelligent Information & Engineering Systems*. Elsevier. DOI: 10.1016/j.procs.2019.09.259

Tanir, D., & Ramazanov, S. (2023). Analysis of factors affecting individuals' e-commerce use in Turkey using data mining methods. *KMU Journal of Social and Economic Research*, 25(44), 46–65.

Tantuğ, A. C. (2016). Metin Sınıflandırma. *Türkiye Bilişim Vakfı Bilgisayar Bilimleri ve Mühendisliği Dergisi, 5*(2), Article 2.

Tao, Y., Xia, Y., Zheng, X., Ding, H., Fang, Y., Tian, C., & Ma, P. (2024). Application of Bayesian Causal Inference in the Study of the Relationship Between Biodiversity and Aboveground Biomass of Subtropical Forest in Eastern China. *Forests*, 15(11), 1841.

Tarisayi, K. S. (2023). Strategic leadership for responsible artificial intelligence adoption in higher education. *CTE Workshop Proceedings*. https://api.semanticscholar.org/CorpusID:261206820

Tasheva, Z., & Karpovich, V. (2024). Transformation of recruitment process through implementation of AI solutions. *Journal of Management and Economics*. https://api.semanticscholar.org/CorpusID:268479962

Taskaya, S., & Demirkiran, M. (2016). The Causality between Healthcare Resources and Health Expenditures in Turkey. A Granger Causality Method. *International Journal of Academic Research in Accounting Finance and Management Sciences*, 6(2). Advance online publication. DOI: 10.6007/ijarafms/v6-i2/2075

Taylor, F. W. (1997). *The Principles of Scientific Management*.

The Open Group. (1999). *Building Blocks*. Introduction to Building Blocks. The Open Group.

The Open Group. (2011a). Architecture Development Method. The Open Group. USA. The link was reviewed and extracted in February 2018, https://pubs.opengroup.org/architecture/togaf9-doc/arch/chap05.html

The Open Group. (2011b). *TOGAF 9.1. The Open Group*. The Open Group.

The Open Group. (2011c). Foundation Architecture: Technical Reference Model. The Open Group. USA. http://www.opengroup.org/public/arch/p3/trm/trm_dtail.htm

The Open Group. (2011d). Architecture Skills Framework. https://pubs.opengroup.org/architecture/togaf8-doc/arch/chap30.html

The Open Group. (2021). TOGAF Model Patterns. The Open Group._https://sparxsystems.com/enterprise_architect_user_guide/15.2/model_domains/togaf_model_patterns.html

Thielmann, A. (2020). Unsupervised Document Classification Integrating Web Scraping, One-Class SVM and LDA Topic Modelling. *Journal of Applied Statistics*, 50(3), 574–591. PMID: 36819086

Thomas, R. N., & Gupta, R. (2020). A Survey on Machine Learning Approaches and its Techniques. DOI: 10.1109/SCEECS48394.2020.190

Thomas, B., Clergue, J., Schaad, A., & Dacier, M. (2004). A comparison of conventional and online fraud. *Proceedings of the 2nd International Conference on Critical Infrastructures (CRIS 2004).*

Thurston, G. D., Kipen, H., Annesi-Maesano, I., Balmes, J., Brook, R. D., Cromar, K., De Matteis, S., Forastiere, F., Forsberg, B., & Frampton, M. W. (2016). A joint ERS/ATS policy statement: What constitutes an adverse health effect of air pollution? An analytical framework. *The European Respiratory Journal*, 49, 1600419. PMID: 28077473

Trad, A. & Kalpić, D. (2022a). Business Transformation Project's Holistic Agile Management (BTPHAM) CBER 2022.

Trad, A. (2021a). The transformation framework-The role security in the global education system. Journal: International Journal of Higher Education Management.

Trad, A. (2021b). The business transformation enterprise architecture framework for innovation: The role of artificial intelligence in the global business education (RAIGBE). Journal: The Business & Management Review.

Trad, A., & Kalpić, D. (2017b). The Business Transformation Framework and Enterprise Architecture Framework for Managers in Business Innovation The role of legacy processes in automated business environments. Journal: The Proceedings of E-Leader.

Trad, A., & Kalpić, D. (2018a). An applied mathematical model for business transformation-The Holistic Critical Success Factors Management System (HCS-FMS). Journal: Encyclopaedia of E-Commerce Development, Implementation, and Management. DOI: 10.4018/978-1-7998-1009-4.ch003

Trad, A., & Kalpić, D. (2022a). Business Transformation *Projects* based on a Holistic Enterprise Architecture Pattern (HEAP)-The Basics. IGI.

Trad, A., & Kalpić, D. (2022b). Business Transformation *Projects* based on a Holistic Enterprise Architecture Pattern (HEAP)-The Implementation. IGI.

Trad, A. (2013). The Selection and Training Framework for Managers in Business Innovation and Transformation Projects-Overview of the development of the empirical model. Recent Advances in Business Administration, Marketing and Economics. *Proceedings of the 2013 International Conference on Business Administration, Marketing and Economics (BAME 2013).*

Trad, A. (2015a). *A Transformation Framework Proposal for Managers in Business Innovation and Business Transformation Projects-Intelligent aBB architecture.* Centeris.

Trad, A. (2015b). *A Transformation Framework Proposal for Managers in Business Innovation and Business Transformation Projects-An ICS's atomic architecture vision.* Centeris.

Trad, A. (2022). *Business Transformation and Enterprise Architecture Projects: Machine Learning Integration for Projects (MLI4P). Book: Unmanned Aerial Vehicles and Multidisciplinary Applications Using AI Techniques.* IGI Global.

Trad, A. (2023a). *Academic and Educational Transformation Projects-The Role Team-Based Learning in Polymathics (RTBLP).* IGI-Global.

Trad, A. (2023b). *Business Transformation Projects: The Role of Psychology-Based Resistance (RPbR). Book: Considerations on Education for Economic, Social, and Environmental Sustainability.* IGI Global.

Trad, A. (2023c). *The Societal and Educational Transformation Projects: The Evolution of the Lebanese Diverse Education (ELDES). Book: Global Perspectives on the Internationalization of Higher Education.* IGI Global.

Trad, A. (2023d). *Organizational and Digital Transformation Projects-A Mathematical Model for Building Blocks based Organizational Unbundling Process.* IGI Global.

Trad, A. (2023d). *The Role Team-Based Learning in Polymathics (RTBLP).* IGI Global.

Trad, A. (2023e). A Relational DataBase based Enterprise Transformation Projects. Journal *International Journal of Mathematics and Computers in Simulation*, 17, 1–11.

Trad, A. (2023g). *The Education Transformation Project: The Role of Information and Communication Systems' Standards on Diversity in Educational Environment. Book: Global Citizenship and Its Impact on Multiculturalism in the Workplace*. IGI Global.

Trad, A. (2024a). *Educational and Public Administration Transformation Projects-The Role of Polymathics Based Artificial Intelligence (RPBAI)*. IGI Global.

Trad, A. (2024b). *Academic and Educational Transformation Projects-The Role Team-Based Learning in Polymathics For University Cycle (RTBLP4UC)*. IGI-Global.

Trad, A. (2024c). *Enterprise Transformation Projects- The use of the Polymathic Rating and Weighting Concept (PRWC)*. IGI-Global.

Trad, A. (2024d). *Academic and Educational Transformation Projects-The Role of Skills in Academic Polymathics Fields (RSAPF)*. IGI Global.

Trad, A. (2024g). *Societal Transformation Projects and the Role and Influence of Human Factors on Natural Resources (RIHFNR). Natural Resource Management Issues in Human-Influenced Landscapes*. IGI-Global.

Trad, A. (2024h). *Educational and Continuous Learning Transformation Projects-The Role of Upskilling and Reconversion (RUR)*. IGI Global.

Trad, A., & Kalpić, D. (2014a). The Selection and Training Framework for Managers in Business Innovation and Transformation Projects-An applied mathematics hyper-heuristics model. *Proceedings of the 2014 International Conference on Mathematical Methods, Mathematical Models and Simulation in Science and Engineering (MMSSE 2014)*.

Trad, A., & Kalpić, D. (2014b). *The Selection, and Training Framework selection and training framework (STF) for Manager's in Business Innovation Transformation Projects–Educational Recommendations*. Journal EDEN.

Trad, A., & Kalpić, D. (2014c, June). The selection and training framework for managers in business innovation and transformation projects: The Profile and Education of a Business Transformation Manager - An enterprise architecture approach. The Business & Management Review.

Trad, A., & Kalpić, D. (2017a). *An Intelligent Neural Networks Micro Artefact Patterns' Based Enterprise Architecture Model*. IGI-Global.

Trad, A., & Kalpić, D. (2017b). *A Neural Networks Portable and Agnostic Implementation Environment for Business Transformation Projects. The Basic Structure*. IEEE.

Trad, A., & Kalpić, D. (2020a). *Using Applied Mathematical Models for Business Transformation. IGI Complete Author Book*. IGI Global.

Trad, A., & Kalpić, D. (2020b). *Business Transformation and Enterprise Architecture: The Holistic Project Asset Management Concept (HPAMC). Book: Handbook of Research on Strategic Fit and Design in Business*. IGI.

Trad, A., & Kalpić, D. (2021a). Business transformation project's architect's profile (BTPAP). *The Business & Management Review.*, 12(2), 137–153.

Trad, A., & Kalpić, D. (2022c). *Business Transformation Project's Holistic Agile Management (BTPHAM)*. CBER.

Trad, A., & Kalpić, D. (2023a). *Educational Transformation Project's Remote Group Work (ETPRGW). Book: Shaping Online Spaces Through Online Humanities Curricula*. IGI Global.

Trad, A., & Trad, C. (2005). Audit, control and monitoring design patterns (ACMDP) for autonomous robust systems (ARS). *International Journal of Advanced Robotic Systems*, 2(1), 4. DOI: 10.5772/5805

Tuononen, T., Hyytinen, H., Kleemola, K., Hailikari, T., Männikkö, I., & Toom, A. (2022). Systematic Review of Learning Generic Skills in Higher Education—Enhancing and Impeding Factors. Frontiers in Education. Systematic Review. DOI: 10.3389/feduc.2022.885917

Turing, A. M. (1950). Computing Machinery and Intelligence. *Mind*, LIX(236), 433–460.

Turkmenoglu, C. (2015). Sentiment analysis in Turkish text (Unpublished master's thesis). Istanbul Technical University, Institute of Science.

Türküz, E., & Akay, E. (2020). Ekonometri ve Makine Öğrenmesi: Tercih Modelleri ve Sınıflandırma Algoritmaları Açısından Değerlendirmeler. *Social Sciences Research Journal*, 9(4), 181–194.

Ullah, S., Jianjun, Z., Hayat, K., Palmucci, D. N., & Durana, P. (2024). Exploring the factors for open innovation in post-COVID-19 conditions by fuzzy Delphi-ISM-MICMAC approach. *European Journal of Innovation Management*, 27(5), 1679–1703. DOI: 10.1108/EJIM-10-2022-0550

Ünlü, R. (2022). An Assessment of imbalanced control chart pattern recognition by artificial neural networks. İçinde *Research Anthology on Artificial Neural Network Applications* (pp. 683-702). IGI Global. https://www.igi-global.com/chapter/an-assessment-of-imbalanced-control-chart-pattern-recognition-by-artificial-neural-networks/288982

Ünlü, R. (2019). An assessment of imbalanced control chart pattern recognition by artificial neural networks. In *Artificial Intelligence and Machine Learning Applications in Civil* (pp. 240–258). Mechanical, and Industrial Engineering. DOI: 10.4018/978-1-7998-0301-0.ch013

Ünlü, R. (2020). An assessment of machine learning models for slump flow and examining redundant features. *Computers and Concrete*, 25(6), 565–574. DOI: 10.12989/CAC.2020.25.6.565

Ünlü, R., & Xanthopoulos, P. (2021). A reduced variance unsupervised ensemble learning algorithm based on modern portfolio theory. *Expert Systems with Applications*, 180, 115085.

Urquhart, L., & Miranda, D. (2022). Policing faces: The present and future of intelligent facial surveillance. *Information & Communications Technology Law*, 31(2), 194–219.

Valle-Cruz, D., Gil-Garcia, J. R., & Sandoval-Almazan, R. (2024). Artificial intelligence algorithms and applications in the public sector: a systematic literature review based on the PRISMA approach. *Research Handbook on Public Management and Artificial Intelligence*, 8-26. DOI: 10.4337/9781802207347.00010

Van Noordt, C., & Misuraca, G. (2020, September). Evaluating the impact of artificial intelligence technologies in public services: towards an assessment framework. In *Proceedings of the 13th international conference on theory and practice of electronic governance* (pp. 8-16). https://doi.org/DOI: 10.1145/3428502.3428504

Van Noordt, C., & Misuraca, G. (2022). Artificial intelligence for the public sector: Results of landscaping the use of AI in government across the European Union. *Government Information Quarterly*, 39(3), 101714. DOI: 10.1016/j.giq.2022.101714

Varian, H. R. (2014). Big Data: New Tricks for Econometrics. *The Journal of Economic Perspectives*, 28(2), 3–28.

Veneberg, R. (2014). *Combining Enterprise Architecture And Operational Data-To Better Support Decision-Making. University of Twente*. School of Management and Governance.

Venkatasubramaniam, A., Mateen, B. A., Shields, B. M., Hattersley, A. T., Jones, A. G., Vollmer, S. J., & Dennis, J. M. (2023). Comparison of causal forest and regression-based approaches to evaluate treatment effect heterogeneity: An application for type 2 diabetes precision medicine. *BMC Medical Informatics and Decision Making*, 23(1), 110. PMID: 37328784

Vieira, A. D., Leite, H., & Volochtchuk, A. V. L. (2022). The impact of voice assistant home devices on people with disabilities: A longitudinal study. *Technological Forecasting and Social Change*, 184, 121961.

Visual Paradigm. (2019). TOGAF ADM Tutorial. Visual Paradigm. Reviewed from https://cdn.visual-paradigm.com/guide/togaf/togaf-adm-tutorial/02-togaf-adm.png

Vogl, T. M., Seidelin, C., Ganesh, B., & Bright, J. (2020). Smart technology and the emergence of algorithmic bureaucracy: Artificial intelligence in UK local authorities. *Public Administration Review*, 80(6), 946–961.

Vowels, M. J. (2022). Trying to outrun causality with machine learning: Limitations of model explainability techniques for identifying predictive variables. Stat, 1050, 22.

Wales, E. (2003). E-commerce counts cost of online card fraud. *Computer Fraud & Security*, 9–11.

Wang, B. (2019). Applying Machine-Learning Methods Based on Causality Analysis to Determine Air Quality in China. *Polish Journal of Environmental Studies*, 28(5), 3877–3885.

Wang, C. W., Hsu, B. Y., & Chen, D. Y. (2024). Chatbot applications in government frontline services: Leveraging artificial intelligence and data governance to reduce problems and increase effectiveness. *Asia Pacific Journal of Public Administration*, 1–24.

Wang, J., Qin, Z., Hsu, J., & Zhou, B. (2024). A fusion of machine learning algorithms and traditional statistical forecasting models for analyzing American healthcare expenditure. *Healthcare Analytics*, 5, 100312.

Warfield, J. N. (1974). Developing interconnection matrices in structural modeling. *IEEE Transactions on Systems, Man, and Cybernetics*, (1), 81–87. DOI: 10.1109/TSMC.1974.5408524

Wasim, A., Hanif, U., & Kanwal, W. (2023). Economic Development and Public Health Expenditures Nexus for South Asian Countries. *Journal of Development and Social Sciences*, 4(IV). Advance online publication. DOI: 10.47205/jdss.2023(4-iv)40

Waters, A., & Miikkulainen, R. (2013). GRADE: Machine Learning Support for Graduate Admissions. *AI Magazine*, 35, 64–75. https://api.semanticscholar.org/CorpusID:212620573

Whitworth, B., & Ahmad, A. (2013a). Polite Computing. In *The Social Design of Technical Systems: Building technologies for communities* (pp. 77–105). The Interaction Design Foundation.

Whitworth, B., & Ahmad, A. (2013b). The evolution of computing. In *The Encyclopedia of human-computer interaction* (2nd ed.). Interaction Design Foundation. Retrieved from https://www.interaction-design.org/literature/book/the-encyclopedia-of-human-computerinteraction-2nd-ed/socio-technical-system-design

Whitworth, B., Ahmad, A., & Soegaard, M. (2006). *Encyclopedia of Human Computer Interaction*. Interaction Design Foundation.

Whitworth, B., Janczewski, L., & Ahmad, A. (2012, July). A Logic of Creation in Online Social Networks. In *2012 World Congress in Computer Science, Computer Engineering and Applied Computing (WORLDCOMP 2012)*.

Wiechetek, Ł., & Pastuszak, Z. (2022). Academic social networks metrics: An effective indicator for university performance? *Scientometrics*, 127(3), 1381–1401.

Willems, J., Schmid, M. J., Vanderelst, D., Vogel, D., & Ebinger, F. (2023). AI-driven public services and the privacy paradox: Do citizens really care about their privacy? *Public Management Review*, 25(11), 2116–2134.

Williamson, B. (2024). The social life of AI in education. *International Journal of Artificial Intelligence in Education*, 34(1), 97–104.

Wirtz, B. W., Langer, P. F., & Fenner, C. (2021). Artificial intelligence in the public sector-a research agenda. *International Journal of Public Administration*, 44(13), 1103–1128. DOI: 10.1080/01900692.2021.1947319

Wirtz, B. W., Weyerer, J. C., & Geyer, C. (2019). Artificial intelligence and the public sector—Applications and challenges. *International Journal of Public Administration*, 42(7), 596–615. DOI: 10.1080/01900692.2018.1498103

Wirtz, B. W., Weyerer, J. C., & Sturm, B. J. (2020). The dark sides of artificial intelligence: An integrated AI governance framework for public administration. *International Journal of Public Administration*, 43(9), 818–829.

Witten, I. H., & Frank, E. (2005). *Data mining: Practical machine learning tools and techniques*. Elsevier.

Witten, I. H., Frank, E., & Hall, M. A. (2011). *Data Mining: Practical Machine Learning Tools and Techniques*. Elsevier.

Woudenberg, M., & Unis, C. J. (2023). Systems Thinking-Skills and Insights to Resolve Wicked Problems. Systems Thinking. https://www.polymathicbeing.com/p/systems-thinking

Xia, L., Semirumi, D. T., & Rezaei, R. (2023). A thorough examination of smart city applications: Exploring challenges and solutions throughout the life cycle with emphasis on safeguarding citizen privacy. *Sustainable Cities and Society*.

Xie, X., Pu, Y. F., & Wang, J. (2023). A fractional gradient descent algorithm robust to the initial weights of multilayer perceptron. *Neural Networks*, 158, 154–170. PMID: 36450188

Xu, W., Li, Z., Cheng, C., & Zheng, T. (2013). Data mining for unemployment rate prediction using search engine query data. *Service Oriented Computing and Applications*, 7, 33–42.

Yadav, A. K. S., & Sora, M. (2021). Fraud detection in financial statements using text mining methods: A review. *IOP Conference Series. Materials Science and Engineering*, 1020(1), 012012.

Yahya, K., Zhang, Y., & Vukovich, J. (2014). Real-time air quality forecasting over the southeastern United States using WRF/Chem-MADRID: Multiple-year assessment and sensitivity studies. *Atmospheric Environment*, 92, 318–338.

Yamacli, D. S., & Yamacli, S. (2023). Estimation of the unemployment rate in Turkey: A comparison of the ARIMA and machine learning models including Covid-19 pandemic periods. *Heliyon*, 9(1). PMID: 36691554

Yendluri, D. K., Ponnala, J., Tatikonda, R., Kempanna, M., Thatikonda, R., & Bhuvanesh, A. (2023, November). Role of RPA & AI in Optimizing Network Field Services. In 2023 7th International Conference on Computation System and Information Technology for Sustainable Solutions (CSITSS) (pp. 1-6). IEEE.

Yigitcanlar, T., Corchado, J. M., Mehmood, R., Li, R. Y. M., Mossberger, K., & Desouza, K. (2021). Responsible urban innovation with local government artificial intelligence (AI): A conceptual framework and research agenda. *Journal of Open Innovation*, 7(1), 71.

Yigitcanlar, T., Kankanamge, N., Regona, M., Ruiz Maldonado, A., Rowan, B., Ryu, A., & Li, R. Y. M. (2020). Artificial intelligence technologies and related urban planning and development concepts: How are they perceived and utilized in Australia? *Journal of Open Innovation*, 6(4), 187.

Yigitcanlar, T., Senadheera, S., Marasinghe, R., Bibri, S. E., Sanchez, T., Cugurullo, F., & Sieber, R. (2024). Artificial intelligence and the local government: A five-decade scientometric analysis on the evolution, state-of-the-art, and emerging trends. *Cities (London, England)*, 152, 105151.

Yıldırım, E., Çetin, F. S., Eryiğit, G., & Temel, T. (2014). The Impact of NLP on Turkish Sentiment Analysis. *Türkiye Bilişim Vakfı Bilgisayar Bilimleri ve Mühendisliği Dergisi, 7*(1), Article 1.

Yuan, J., & Liu, S. (2024). A double machine learning model for measuring the impact of the Made in China 2025 strategy on green economic growth. *Scientific Reports*, 14(1), 12026. PMID: 38797785

Yu, H. Q., & Reiff-Marganiec, S. (2022). Learning Disease Causality Knowledge From the Web of Health Data. *International Journal on Semantic Web and Information Systems*, 18(1), 1–19.

Yu, R., Yang, Y., Yang, L., Han, G., & Move, O. A. (2016). RAQ–A random forest approach for predicting air quality in urban sensing systems. *Sensors (Basel)*, 16, 86. PMID: 26761008

Yusifov, F. (2016, June). Big Data in E-Government: Issues, Opportunities and Prospects. In *Proceedings of 16th European Conference on e-Government (ECEG2016)* (pp. 352-355). ECEG Academic Conferences and Publishing Limited.

Zandia, F., & Tavana, M. (2011). *A fuzzy group multi-criteria enterprise architecture framework selection model. Management Information Systems, Lindback Distinguished Chair of Information Systems, La Salle University, Philadelphia, PA 19141*. Elsevier.

Zeng, X., Lin, S., & Liu, C. (2021). Multi-View Deep Learning Framework for Predicting Patient Expenditure in Healthcare. *IEEE Open Journal of the Computer Society*, 2, 62–71. DOI: 10.1109/ojcs.2021.3052518

Zeshan, F., dar, Z., Ahmad, A., & Malik, T. (2024). A fuzzy ontology-based context-aware encryption approach in IoT through device and information classification. *The Journal of Supercomputing*, 80(16), 23311–23356.

Zeshan, F., Ahmad, A., Abdel-Aty, A. H., Algarni, F., Mahmoud, E. E., & Ahmad, A. (2020). A hybrid semantic knowledge integration and sharing approach for distributed smart environments. *Sensors (Basel)*, 20(20), 5918. PMID: 33092118

Zeshan, F., Mohamad, R., Ahmad, M. N., Othman, M. B., Elhag, A. A. M., Hussain, S. A., & Babar, I. (2019). Context-Aware ontology and web services discovery for distributed embedded real-time systems. *Malaysian Journal of Computer Science*, 32(3), 186–208.

Zhang, Y., & Kimathi, F. A. (2022). Exploring the stages of E-government development from public value perspective. *Technology in Society*.

Zhao, A. P., Li, S., Cao, Z., Hu, P. J. H., Wang, J., Xiang, Y., ... Lu, X. (2024). AI for science: predicting infectious diseases. Journal of Safety Science and Resilience.

Zhao, Y., & Liu, Q. (2023). Causal ML: Python package for causal inference machine learning. *SoftwareX*, 21, 101294.

Zheng, A. (2015). *Evaluating machine learning models*. O'Reilly Media.

Zinger, S. (2006). *Statistical Natural Language Processing: N-Gram Models*. Seminar in Methodology and Statistics.

Zuiderwijk, A., Chen, Y. C., & Salem, F. (2021). Implications of the use of artificial intelligence in public governance: A systematic literature review and a research agenda. Government information quarterly.

Zuiderwijk, A., Chen, Y. C., & Salem, F. (2021). Implications of the use of artificial intelligence in public governance: A systematic literature review and a research agenda. *Government Information Quarterly*, 38(3), 101577. DOI: 10.1016/j.giq.2021.101577

About the Contributors

Gamze Sart completed her undergraduate education at Bogazici University in the Department of Political Science and International Relations. She completed her first master's degree in the Institute of Social Sciences, Department of Psychology in Harvard and Istanbul Commerce University. She completed her second master's degree in the Social Sciences Institute, Department of Educational Sciences in Bogazici University. She received her doctorate from Stanford and Bogazici University, Faculty of Social Sciences, Department of Educational Sciences. Professor Gamze Sart is a faculty member of the Hasan Ali Yucel Education Faculty (HAYEF) and is currently carrying on academic studies at Istanbul University Cerrahpasa (IUC) on the "Innovation and Technology-Oriented Future of Higher Education".

Funda Hatice Sezgin completed her undergraduate education in Faculty of economics in University of Istanbul. She did master of business administration degree (MBA) in Econometrics of University of Istanbul, and doctor of econometrics in Marmara University. Her research interests are time series analysis, panel data analysis and statistical methods. She works in the department of industrial engineering at Istanbul University-Cerrahpasa.

* * *

Vishnu Achutha Menon is an independent journalist, writer, researcher, and an Indian percussionist. He is a recipient of the Junior Scholarship the Ministry of Culture awarded. His research interests are film studies, verbal & nonverbal communication, south Asian performances, Natyasastra, media studies, media analysis techniques, Laban Movement Analysis, and Ethnomusicology.

Akbar, an esteemed academic from Indonesia, is a dedicated scholar and lecturer at the State Islamic Institute of Palopo. Holding a PhD in Education from the

University of Newcastle, his research delves into academic integrity and educational policy, with a focus on the Muslim world. With a Master of Education from the University of Adelaide, he has also contributed to foundational studies in English education, earning recognition for his innovative teaching practices and scholarly contributions. Numerous accolades, including the Australia Awards Scholarship and the LPDP Scholarship, distinguish Dr. Akbar's academic journey. His commitment to excellence was evident when he triumphed in the 3-Minute Thesis Competition at the University of Newcastle, winning Faculty-level and People's Choice awards. His research has earned international acclaim, evidenced by Best Paper awards at global conferences. Beyond academics, Dr. Akbar is an active community leader, serving as President of the Indonesian Students Association in Newcastle and organizing events to foster cultural and educational exchange. He is also a prolific author, publishing in esteemed journals and presenting at international conferences, particularly on challenges surrounding academic integrity in global and Islamic contexts. With a robust background in pedagogy, research methodologies, and interdisciplinary collaborations, Dr. Akbar continues to inspire future generations while addressing critical educational challenges worldwide.

Andi Asrifan, S.Pd, M.Pd, a distinguished figure in the realm of education, particularly in English Language Education, has made significant contributions through his extensive research, teaching, and leadership roles. As the Head of the Institute for Cooperation and International Affairs at Universitas Muhammadiyah Sidenreng Rappang and now a lecturer in Universitas Negeri Makassar (UNM), Dr. Asrifan's academic journey is marked by a rich tapestry of achievements, including a Doctor of Education in English Language Education. His work spans various facets of education, language, and technology, reflecting the diverse topics covered in his publications and research endeavors. These include, but are not limited to, the impact of the COVID-19 pandemic on educational practices, methodologies in English as a Foreign Language (EFL) classrooms, and the integration of technology in teaching and learning processes. Dr. Asrifan's commitment to advancing educational standards and practices is further evidenced by his active participation in international conferences, webinars, and workshops across countries like India, the Philippines, and Pakistan. These events, organized by various institutions and associations, underscore his role as a global educator and thought leader. His dedication to professional development is also highlighted through his involvement in numerous courses and certifications in personal branding, public speaking, and literacy teaching. Moreover, Dr. Asrifan's leadership extends beyond academia into organizational and educational development, where he has served in various capacities, including as an external examiner for Ph.D. dissertations and a reviewer for scientific journals. His accolades, memberships in professional organizations, and roles as an ambassador for international associations speak volumes of his influence and commitment to fostering educational excellence and sustainable development goals globally.

Sinem Buyuksaatci Kiris obtained her Ph.D. in Industrial Engineering from Istanbul University. Her research focuses on areas including Supply Chain Management, Sustainability, Circular Economy, Simulation and Multi-Criteria Decision Making. Her scholarly works have been published in reputable journals such as Annals of Operations Research, IMA Journal of Management Mathematics, and the International Journal of Information Technology & Decision Making. She currently serves as an Assistant Professor in the Department of Industrial Engineering at Istanbul University-Cerrahpasa.

Binnur Akıf Gurul completed her undergraduate education at Istanbul Technical University in the Department of Management Engineering. She received her master's degree in the Institute of Social Sciences, Department of Business Administration in Istanbul Aydin University. She completed her first doctoral degree in the Institute of Social Sciences, Department of Business Administration in Istanbul Gelisim University. She completed her second doctoral degree in the Postgraduate Education Institute, Department of Industrial Engineering in Istanbul University – Cerrahpasa. Her research interests are manufacturing and service systems, multi-criteria decision making, quality management systems, supply chain management, sustainability, management organization, and organizational behavior. Currently, she is Assistant Prof. Dr. in Istanbul Gelisim University, Faculty of Engineering and Architecture, Department of Industrial Engineering.

Robby Hunawa was born in Luwuk and is a dedicated lecturer at the Faculty of Law, Gorontalo University, holding the functional position of Lector with NIDN 0920057903. He completed his primary education at SDN 3 Luwuk, followed by secondary education at Sekolah Teknik Daerah (STD) Luwuk, and graduated from SMK Negeri 3 Gorontalo. He earned his Bachelor's degree in 2008, Master's degree in 2013, and Doctorate in 2020, all from the Muslim University of Indonesia in Makassar. In addition to his academic role, Dr. Amu is a practicing advocate and a member of the Indonesian Advocates Association (Peradi), with membership number 20.10166. He has provided extensive legal assistance to the community in both litigation and non-litigation matters. He is also an active speaker at various academic events, including seminars and legal training, and has served as an expert witness on several occasions. His academic leadership roles include Head of the Law Laboratory at Gorontalo University from 2011 to 2014, Secretary of the Human Rights Study Center since 2014, and Coordinator of the Anti-Corruption Education and Training Division from 2014 to 2019. Currently, he serves as the Head of the Master of Law Program at the Graduate School of Gorontalo University. Dr. Amu teaches and supervises both undergraduate and graduate students in various law courses, including Criminal Law, International Law, and Environmental Law, and has published numerous articles in national and international journals.

Muhammad Nur, born on December 31, 1968, in Radda, is a distinguished academic and public servant in Indonesia. He holds a Bachelor's degree in Office Administration from Universitas Negeri Makassar (1992), a Master's in Development Administration from Universitas Hasanuddin (2003), and a Master's in State Administrative Law from Universitas Bosowa (2011). He completed his Doctorate in Public Administration at Universitas Hasanuddin in 2014. With a robust career in education, Dr. Nur has served as a lecturer at various institutions, including STKIP Cokroaminoto Pinrang (1993-2010), Universitas Indonesia Timur (2011-2018), and currently at Universitas Muhammadiyah Sidenreng Rappang since 2019. He also held the position of Chairman at STIH Cokroaminoto Pinrang from 2008 to 2011. Dr. Nur is an active researcher and has published several works, including an e-book on organization and management, and studies on government policies and smart city frameworks. His contributions to academia and public service reflect his commitment to enhancing educational standards and community development in Indonesia.

Hadi Pajarianto is a distinguished academic in the field of Islamic Education, with a profound focus on research related to religious moderation, tolerance, and local wisdom. Since 2011, he has successfully secured numerous research grants from prestigious institutions such as the Ministry of Education and Culture, LPDP, and Johns Hopkins Bloomberg School of Public Health. His dedication to education is further exemplified by his participation in the Training of Trainers (TOT) for National Values Enhancement organized by LEMHANNAS in 2022. Prof. Pajarianto's professional journey includes roles as a high school teacher and a lecturer since 2004. He has held significant positions such as Head of Quality Assurance Unit and Head of Research and Community Service at AKBIDM Palopo, as well as Vice Director for Student Affairs and Finance. Currently, he serves as Vice Rector II for Resources, Assets, and Business at Universitas Muhammadiyah Palopo. His academic credentials include a Bachelor's degree in Islamic Education from STAIN Palopo (2004), a Master's, and a Doctorate in Education from UIN Alauddin Makassar (2013, 2016). Prof. Pajarianto is renowned for his skills in teaching, research, community service, and higher education management. His motto, “Give One Hundred Percent or Not at All,” reflects his commitment to excellence in all his endeavors.

Index

www.ingramcontent.com/pod-product-compliance
Lightning Source LLC
LaVergne TN
LVHW080344011026
849161LV00009B/2181

* 9 7 9 8 3 3 7 3 2 2 7 2 8 *